The Philosophy of Hebrew Scripture

What if the Hebrew Bible wasn't meant to be read as "revelation"? What if it's not really about miracles or the afterlife, but about how to lead our lives in this world?

The Philosophy of Hebrew Scripture proposes a new framework for reading the Bible. It shows how the biblical authors used narrative and prophetic oratory to advance universal arguments about ethics, political philosophy, and metaphysics.

It offers bold new studies of the biblical narratives and prophetic poetry, transforming forever our understanding of what the stories of Abel, Abraham, Jacob, Joseph, Moses, and David and the speeches of Isaiah and Jeremiah were meant to teach.

The Philosophy of Hebrew Scripture assumes no belief in God or other religious commitment. It assumes no previous background in Bible. It is free of disciplinary jargon.

Open the door to a book you never knew existed. You'll never read the Bible the same way again.

Yoram Hazony is Provost of the Shalem Center in Jerusalem and a Senior Fellow in the Department of Philosophy, Political Theory and Religion (PPR). Hazony's previous books include *The Jewish State: The Struggle for Israel's Soul* and *The Dawn: Political Teachings of the Book of Esther*. His essays and articles have appeared in the *New York Times*, the *New Republic*, *Commentary*, *Azure*, and *Ha'aretz*, among other publications. He is author of a regular blog on philosophy, Judaism, Israel, and higher education called *Jerusalem Letters*. Hazony received a BA in East Asian Studies from Princeton University and a Ph.D. in Political Theory from Rutgers University. He lives in Jerusalem with his wife and children.

The Philosophy of Hebrew Scripture

YORAM HAZONY
Shalem Center, Jerusalem

CAMBRIDGE
UNIVERSITY PRESS

CAMBRIDGE UNIVERSITY PRESS
Cambridge, New York, Melbourne, Madrid, Cape Town,
Singapore, São Paulo, Delhi, Mexico City

Cambridge University Press
32 Avenue of the Americas, New York, NY 10013-2473, USA

www.cambridge.org
Information on this title: www.cambridge.org/9780521176675

First published 2012
Reprinted 2012

Printed in the United States of America

A catalog record for this publication is available from the British Library.

Library of Congress Cataloging in Publication Data
Hazony, Yoram.
  The philosophy of Hebrew scripture / Yoram Hazony.
    p. cm.
  Includes bibliographical references and index.
  ISBN 978-1-107-00317-0 (hardback) – ISBN 978-0-521-17667-5 (pbk.)
  1. Bible. O.T. – Philosophy.   2. Political Science – Philosophy
  3. Jewish philosophy.   I. Title.
  BS1186.3.H39   2012
  221.6–dc23   2011045950

ISBN 978-1-107-00317-0 Hardback
ISBN 978-0-521-17667-5 Paperback

For Yael Rivka

זָכַרְתִּי לָךְ חֶסֶד נְעוּרַיִךְ
אַהֲבַת כְּלוּלֹתָיִךְ
לֶכְתֵּךְ אַחֲרַי בַּמִּדְבָּר
בְּאֶרֶץ לֹא זְרוּעָה:

ירמיה ב, ב

Contents

Acknowledgments

Is there something crucial missing in our understanding of what the Hebrew Bible is all about? This question, along with some preliminary answers to it, can already be found in my doctoral dissertation, "The Political Philosophy of Jeremiah" (Rutgers University, 1993), and in my book *The Dawn: Political Teachings of the Book of Esther*, first published in 1995. This means that I have been trying to develop an answer to this question for twenty years now – the answer that is presented in this book. And during all these years I've been subjecting friends, colleagues, and family members to a steady stream of invited and uninvited lectures on the subject, as well as article drafts and more article drafts. In return, they've offered me encouragement and instruction – a *great* deal of instruction, without which I would never have dared attempt a book of this kind. I wish here to mention in gratitude the names of those who have made it possible for me to bring this project to fruition.

My principal intellectual collaborators during much of my adult life have been scholars at my home institution, the Shalem Center in Jerusalem, especially Joshua Berman, Ofir Haivry, Yael Hazony, R. Joseph Isaac Lifshitz, Ze'ev Maghen, Daniel Polisar, and Joshua Weinstein. So much of what is presented here was originally developed in conversation with one or another of them that I've despaired of being able to offer them proper credit in my notes. This book is a reflection of our more than two decades together discussing these subjects.

My thinking about the Bible has also benefited immensely from give and take with the circle of scholars from different countries that has come together around the Shalem Bible conferences of recent years. Foremost among these are James Diamond, Ethan Dorshav, Steven Grosby, Alan Mittleman, and Jacob Wright, each of whom has invested extraordinary amounts of time and attention to helping me get my head straight on the subject matter of this book, including writing copious comments on successive drafts. I am particularly grateful, as well, for the generous attention this project has received from Kelly Clark, Dru Johnson, and Eleonore Stump – Christian scholars who have commented on the manuscript, gently helping make it a work that would be of greater value to a non-Jewish readership.

Others who have read and commented on parts of the manuscript deserve my thanks as well. Among these are Orit Arfa, Jed Arkin, David Arnovitz, Zvi Biener, Jeremy England, Matt Goldish, Ari Gontownik, Lenn Goodman, Daniel Gordis, William Scott Green, Jeff Helmreich, Jacob Howland, Pini Ifergan, Jonathan Jacobs, Meirav Jones, R. Avi Kannai, Menachem Kellner, Jed Lewinsohn, Diana Lipton, Menachem Lorberbaum, Stewart Moore, Hillel Nadler, Peter Ohlin, Fania Oz-Salzberger, Meir Simchah Panzer, Andrew Pessin, David Portman, Janet Safford, Eric Schliesser, Gordon Schochet, Jonathan Silver, Betty Steinberg, Suzanne Stone, Fred Tauber, and Jonathan Yudelman.

I would like to express my appreciation, too, to Mem Bernstein, Arthur Fried, Roger Hertog, Leon Kass, Bill Kristol, Ronald Lauder, David and Barbara Messer, and Allen Roth for their support and encouragement for my work on Judaism and philosophy during the years this book was reaching maturity. More recently, the philosophical study of the Hebrew Bible has accelerated appreciably under Shalem's auspices with the help of a major grant from the John Templeton Foundation (JTF). Many friends at the JTF have worked to advance and deepen this collaboration, but I wish to thank, especially, Dr. Jack Templeton and Vice President for Philosophy and Theology Michael Murray for their assistance in advancing this project.

A very special thank you to Barry and Lainie Klein for their love and friendship over so many years, going all the way back to the very beginning, as well as for help with this book.

I owe a particular debt to my editor, Lewis Bateman of Cambridge University Press, whose vision simply knows no bounds. Other individuals at Cambridge who have worked hard to bring this project to fruition include, especially, Kerry Cahill, Michael Duncan, Liza Murphy, Melissanne Scheld, Mary Starkey, Nicole Villeneuve, and Helen Wheeler.

Thanks, too, to Suzanne Balaban of BMM Worldwide LLC, whose inspiration has guided and shaped this project since before it was even a proposal. And to Kate Deutsch, Erica Halivni, Rachel Heimowitz, Roni Kovarsky, Igal Liverant, Marina Pilipodi, Marc Sherman, and Taya Sourikov for assistance in preparing the text for publication and for work on the promotion of the book.

To Yael, my best reader, with whom I've raised nine children, this book is dedicated with love.

Note on the Text

I have made every effort to make this book accessible to a general educated readership. I don't think this has required too many compromises. One, however, does bear mentioning: I've given up on trying to discover a system of transliteration that would permit me to render Hebrew words and names in a way that would be both internally consistent and sensible to the average educated reader of the English language. Instead, Hebrew terms are rendered in one of two ways: The most common biblical names follow their standard English-language usage. Thus I write Moses (and not "Mosheh") and Jerusalem (and not "Yerushalaim"). Other Hebrew terms and names, however, appear using a simple system of transliteration whose purpose is to make them as readily pronounceable by English-language readers as possible, with modern Hebrew pronunciation as a benchmark. I realize that the use of this dual system may be a bit annoying to some readers at first. But it has a number of advantages over the alternatives. And you get used to it.

Introduction

Beyond Reason and Revelation

What are we to make of the Bible? It's not easy to say. But a common approach goes like this: There are two kinds of literary works that address themselves to ultimate issues – those that are the product of *reason*; and those that are known by way of *revelation*. Works by philosophers such as Plato or Hobbes are works of "reason," composed to assist individuals and nations looking to discover the true and the good as best they are able in accordance with man's natural abilities. The Bible, on the other hand, is "revelation," a text that reports what God himself thinks about things. The biblical texts bypass man's natural faculties, giving us knowledge of the true and the good by means of a series of miracles. So what the Bible offers is miraculous knowledge, to be accepted in gratitude and believed on faith. On this view, revelation is seen as the opposite of reason in that it requires the suspension of the normal operation of our mental faculties, calling on us to believe things that don't make sense to us – because they are supposed to make sense to God.

The dichotomy between reason and revelation that is the basis for this understanding of the Bible has a great deal of history behind it. The fathers of the Christian Church adopted it as a way of sharpening the differences between the teachings of the New Testament and those of the various sects of philosophers with which they vied for converts in late antiquity. Many centuries later, the philosophers of the Enlightenment embraced this same distinction as an instrument with which to bludgeon the Church, using it to paint Christianity as a purveyor of superstition and irrationality. Fideists and heretics alike have thus had ample reason to insist on this distinction, and many continue to do so even today.[1]

A case can be made that the *reason–revelation* dichotomy does succeed in capturing something of what was unique and compelling about the teaching of Jesus' apostles in the New Testament. But it's much harder to make sense of this distinction in the context of the Hebrew Bible (or "Old Testament" *). After all, the principal texts of Hebrew Scripture were written perhaps *five centuries* before the reason–revelation distinction was applied to them. They were written by individuals who spoke a different language from the Greek in which this dichotomy was framed, and professed a different religion from the Christianity whose virtues it was designed to emphasize. Moreover, nothing in the principal Hebrew texts suggests that the prophets and scholars of ancient Israel were familiar with such an opposition between God's word and the pronouncements of human reason when it is working as it should. In addition, the texts of the Hebrew Bible seem largely uninterested in the subjects that made the concept of revelation so important and useful in explaining Christianity. The hidden secrets of God's previously unrevealed plan for mankind, the salvific power of faith, the availability of eternal life – none of these subjects are even top-forty in the Hebrew Scriptures, a fact so obvious and so jarring that it prompted Kant to argue that the Judaism of ancient Israel was not really a religion![2]

What *is* in the Hebrew Scriptures? Many of the same kinds of things that are found in works of reason: histories of ancient peoples and attempts to draw political lessons from them; explorations of how best to conduct the life of the nation and of the individual; the writings of individuals who struggled with personal persecution and failure and their speculations concerning human nature and the search for the true and the good; attempts to get beyond the sphere of the here and now and to try and reach a more general understanding of the nature of reality, of man's place in it, and of his relationship with that which is beyond his control. God is, of course, a central subject in the Hebrew Bible. But to a remarkable degree, the God of Israel and those who wrote about him seem to have been concerned to address subjects close to the heart of what later tradition calls works of reason.

Which raises the following question: What if the analytic framework that originally assigned the Hebrew Bible to the category of revelation was

---

* The Christian Bible consists of two distinct collections of works, which Christians traditionally call the "Old Testament" and the "New Testament," respectively. The Old Testament found in most Christian Bibles is a translation of a body of originally Hebrew-language works that Jews call the *Tanach* or *Mikra*, which I will refer to as the "Hebrew Bible" or the "Hebrew Scriptures." The books of the Christian Old Testament also appear in a somewhat different order from that of the Hebrew Scriptures. Unless otherwise noted, all references to "the Bible" in this work refer to the Hebrew Bible, which is the Bible that is in use almost universally in Jewish institutions of learning and synagogues around the world.

in fact ill fitted to the older Hebrew texts? What if its effect, historically, has been to force subsequent readers to see the Hebrew Scriptures as the early Christians saw them, eclipsing the concerns of the Jewish prophets and scholars who wrote them? What if the texts of the Hebrew Bible, or many of them, are in fact much closer to being works of reason than anything else – only we don't know it because this fact has been suppressed (and continues to be suppressed) by an alien interpretive framework that prevents us from seeing much of what is in these texts?

It is my contention that something like this is in fact the case: that read into the Hebrew Scriptures, the reason–revelation dichotomy becomes a kind of distorting lens – greatly exaggerating aspects of the old Hebrew texts that their authors would never have chosen to emphasize, even as it renders much that was of significance to them all but invisible. This means that in reading the Hebrew Scriptures as works of "revelation" (as opposed to "reason"), we come pretty close to destroying them. We accidentally delete much of what these texts were written to say – and then, having accomplished this, we find that the texts don't really "speak to us" as modern men and women.

This deletion of much of the content of the Hebrew biblical texts is not just a theoretical problem in hermeneutics or some other esoteric academic discipline. It has a direct impact on the way the Hebrew Scriptures are handled in almost every intellectual, educational, and cultural setting in which the Bible is today considered for an appearance: It affects the standing of the Hebrew Scriptures in the public schools, where they are neglected or banned outright because they are seen as works of revelation, not reason. And it affects their status in the religious schools, too – certainly the Jewish ones, but Christian ones as well – where teachers and administrators confer in bafflement over how to transmit a love of the Bible to the next generation despite the fact that these texts are works of revelation, not reason. It also dictates the way the Hebrew Bible is treated in the universities, where professors of philosophy, political theory, and intellectual history consistently pass over the ideas of the Hebrew Scriptures as a subject worth researching and teaching to their students, since they see their work as the study of works of reason, not revelation. And what is true for the schools and universities is true for the rest of our culture as well. Outside of religious circles, the Bible is often seen as bearing a taint of irrationality, folly, and irrelevance, the direct result of its reputation as a consummate work of unreason. This taint ensures that for most educated people, the Bible remains pretty much a closed book, the views of its authors on most subjects unaccessed and inaccessible.

I am by no means the only person to have felt discomfort over this. The ongoing exclusion of the Hebrew Bible from the universe of texts whose ideas are worth being taken seriously is increasingly a subject of discussion in the universities. And in recent years a number of prominent scholars have actually published studies in which biblical texts are read as though they were works of philosophy – often with fascinating results. But all this is still quite preliminary, and there hasn't yet been a book that takes on the question of the Bible as a work of reason in a systematic fashion. What I hope to provide in this book is the first direct and sustained argument in favor of approaching the Hebrew Scriptures as works of reason. More specifically, I will argue that the Hebrew Scriptures can be read as works of philosophy, with an eye to discovering what they have to say as part of the broader discourse concerning the nature of the world and the just life for man. On the way, I will enumerate the obstacles – both prejudices and genuine problems of method – that stand in the way of reading the Bible in this way, and propose tools for overcoming them. I will then take the reader through a series of studies in which I read the Hebrew texts as works of philosophical significance. By the end, my hope is to have made it clear both *that* the Hebrew Bible can be fruitfully read as a work of reason, and *how* the Hebrew Bible can be read as a work of reason.*

It bears emphasizing that in arguing that the Hebrew Bible can fruitfully be read as a work of reason, I will not be defending any particular thesis concerning its status as revelation. In particular, I am not interested in denying that the Bible is a work of revelation. My point in this book is only this: If we are forced to choose between reading these texts as reason or as revelation, we'll get much farther in understanding them if we choose to read the Hebrew Scriptures as works of reason. But I don't actually think that the reason side of the Christian reason–revelation dichotomy is capable of doing full justice to the teachings of these texts either. As I've said, the reason–revelation distinction is alien to the Hebrew Scriptures, and ultimately this framework is going to have to be thrown out as a basis for interpreting the Hebrew Bible. But getting there won't be easy. In Christian countries,

---

* Some readers will want to know more precisely what I mean by the terms *reason* and *philosophy*. This is a fair question, but answering it requires a detour into issues distant from the present discussion. Rather than go into these matters here, I've positioned an outline of my thinking on the subject in an appendix at the end of Chapter 9. Readers who prefer not to take this detour right now can, I think, get by assuming that I am using these terms loosely, and more or less interchangeably, to refer to man's efforts to attain truths of a general (and therefore not historically conditioned) nature, through the deployment of his natural mental endowment.

the Bible has been read through this distorting lens for many generations. Freeing ourselves from it, I suspect, will not be achieved in a single leap. It will be a two-step process: The first step involves coming to recognize the riches that the biblical texts have to offer as works of reason. The second step involves discarding the reason–revelation distinction completely, and learning to see the world as it appeared to the prophets of Israel – before the reason–revelation distinction was invented.

I have quite a bit to say about this second step, and I'll touch on this subject again in my Conclusion. But the focus of this book has to be that first step: coming closer to the ideas the Hebrew Scriptures were written to advance by learning to read them as works of reason. If we can make headway on that, it will be plenty for this one book. After that, I hope to devote a different work to the question of that second step.

If the reason–revelation dichotomy works so poorly as a lens through which to read the Hebrew Scriptures, as I'm suggesting, what holds this interpretive framework in place? Why do intelligent people keep reading these texts this way, as though they were works of revelation, and have nothing significant to contribute to the advancement of our understanding of the world through reason? There are certainly a number of factors at work here. But only one, I think, has to be considered decisive. This is the way people respond to the fact that these texts are punctuated by phrases such as:

> And the Lord said to Moses ...[3]

Or, in the case of the orations of Isaiah or Jeremiah, by expressions such as:

> Thus says the Lord ...[4]

For many readers today, the presence of these phrases is enough to bring them, more or less immediately, to a number of conclusions about the authors of these texts. First, it is assumed that whenever these phrases appear in the text, the author intended to report that a miracle occurred – a miracle whereby knowledge is revealed to the mind of this or that individual without his having made use of the mental faculties that people normally use to understand things about the world. Second, it is assumed that the author's understanding of the world, in which a God or gods could miraculously impart knowledge to the minds of men, is no more than fantastic nonsense recorded by the weak-minded and gullible; or just plain lies set down in books by unscrupulous manipulators pursuing dreadful ends now forgotten. In either case, the very fact that these texts depict God as acting and speaking is enough to show that the authors of these books, whether

weak-minded or lying, were not the kind of people from whom you'd want
to try to learn anything.

So as lots of people see it, it's the presence in the Hebrew Scriptures of
all those instances of God speaking that makes the Bible a work of revelation, and rules out the possibility that these texts could be taken seriously
as reason.

Now, you can't avoid the fact that the biblical authors very often attribute speech and actions to God. And you wouldn't want to, either, because
such attribution is an essential feature of what the biblical texts have to say.
But the line of argument that's tacked on to this – that these texts are reporting miracles every time God is depicted as saying something; that this way
of looking at the world can have no more to it than rank superstition; that
their promotion of such reports makes the biblical authors weak-minded
or liars, and the texts themselves the product of weak-mindedness or lies;
that this rules the Bible out as a work of reason – all this is something else
entirely. It's basically a propaganda line worked out by French *philosophes*
and German professors in their campaign to discredit the Bible and knock
the Church out of the ring as a force in European public life. Maybe there
were good reasons for them to have adopted this line of argument when
they did. But there's nothing in that to recommend it to us. Like most propaganda lines, it isn't really fair. And when you look at it more closely, you
see that it doesn't make much sense, either.

So let's take the bull by the horns. Is it true that in confronting a text that
depicts God as speaking and acting, we really have no choice but to classify
it as revelation; and, consequently, to rule it out as a work of reason?

The answer that should be given to this question is "No." It is not true
that we have to classify works that have God speaking and acting in them
as revelation, and to rule them out as works of reason. For if that were the
case, then we would long ago have ruled out as works of reason some of
the most famous works of philosophy ever written – works that are today
unchallenged as works of reason, and, indeed, regarded as the basis for the
tradition of Western philosophy.

Consider, for example, the writings of Parmenides (c. 515–440 BCE), an
Eleatic philosopher of the generation before Socrates. Parmenides is no side-
show in the history of philosophy. His examination of the nature of being
had such an impact on subsequent Greek philosophy that Plato has one
of his principal characters call him "father Parmenides."[5] No modern history of philosophy sees him as anything other than crucial. Yet Parmenides,
who lived about 130 years after the Israelite prophet Jeremiah (c. 647–572),
writes philosophy as though it were – revealed to him by a god. Not, as it

seems, a metaphorical god, but one that Parmenides really understood as having taught and inspired him and permitted him to engage in philosophy.[6] Here is a passage from the opening of his only known work:

> The mares that carry me kept conveying me as far as ever my spirit reached, once they had taken me and set me on the goddess' way of much discourse, which carries through every stage straight onwards a man of understanding. On this I was carried, for the sagacious mares were carrying me, straining at the chariot and guided by the maidens along the way. The axle in the naves kept blazing and uttering the pipe's loud note, driven onwards at both ends by its two metalled wheels, whenever the daughters of the sun made haste to convey me....
>
> Whereupon the maidens drove the chariot and mares straight on through the gates along the road. And the goddess received me warmly, and taking my right hand in hers spoke as follows and addressed me: "Welcome, O youth, arriving at our dwelling as consort of immortal charioteers and mares which carry you.... You must be informed of everything."[7]

In this passage, Parmenides carefully describes the experience of climbing into the night sky on a horse-drawn chariot tended by the "daughters of the sun," which ultimately enters the palace of an unnamed goddess who takes his hand and promises to inform him of "everything." And indeed, *everything* we have of Parmenides' philosophy consists of the words of this goddess as she revealed them to him.

What does the goddess's revelation to Parmenides include? Most of the text is lost, but we do know that she tells him of the creation of night and day, the sun and moon, the stars and the ether,[8] and of "the divinity who governs all things," which looks like this:

> For the narrower rings became filled with unmixed fire and those over them with night, in which moves a proportion of flame. Between these is the divinity who governs all things. For everywhere she initiates hateful birth and union, sending female to unite with male, and conversely with female.[9]

Moreover, the goddess tells Parmenides that:

> Being is in a state of perfection from every viewpoint, like the volume of a spherical ball, and equally poised in every direction from its center. For it must not be either at all greater or at all smaller in one regard than in another.[10]

And that:

> First of all the gods she devised love.[11]

The goddess informs Parmenides of these things and of much else. Moreover, she issues commands ("These things I command you to heed"[12]) that are

to govern Parmenides' life going forward. And in all she teaches him, the
goddess insists that only her own "discourse and thought about reality"
is reliable,[13] whereas "human beliefs" are "that on which mortals with no
understanding stray two-headed, for perplexity in their own breasts directs
their mind astray, and they are borne on, deaf and blind alike in bewilder-
ment, people without judgment."[14] But since the goddess has revealed all
these things to Parmenides, he no longer has to rely only on human beliefs,
and so she tells him that "[N]ever shall any mortal outstrip you in practical
judgment."[15]

This dependence of philosophy on revelation is not restricted to
Parmenides. Empedocles (c. 490–430), too, portrays the process of his own
thought and philosophizing as depending on the goddess Calliopeia, who
"sends" him that which is appropriate for men to hear on a chariot from on
high. As he writes:

> And you, maiden muse of the white arms, much remembering,
> I beseech you: what is right for ephemeral creatures to hear,
> Send [to me], driving your well-reined chariot from [the halls of] piety.
> For if, immortal muse, for the sake of any ephemeral creature,
> It has pleased you to let our concerns pass through your thought,
> Answer my prayers now, Calliopeia,
> As I reveal a good discourse about the blessed gods.[16]

Here, Empedocles tells us that the concerns of men may pass through the
thought of the goddess, who answers our prayers by sending down from
heaven those words that are appropriate for human listeners. And indeed, it
is such a revelation that we have recorded in Empedocles' philosophy.

We only have small fragments of the works of Greek philosophers before
the time of Plato, so we can't know for certain how many other significant
philosophers explicitly attributed their thought to the revelation of a god
as Parmenides and Empedocles did. But the snatches we have suggest that
this way of understanding philosophy may well have been characteristic of
others as well. Heraclitus (c. 535–475), for example, says that "The wise is
one alone; it is unwilling and willing to be called by the name of Zeus,"[17] and
that "a god is wise in comparison with a man, as a man is with a child,"[18]
so that he too may well have been inclined to see philosophy as requiring the assistance of a god.[19] And similar suggestions could easily be made
with regard to other pre-Socratic philosophers as well.[20] Even Socrates, the
very archetype of the philosopher guided by reason, is depicted by Plato
(c. 428–348) as receiving revelations and commands and dreams from the
gods that give form and content to his life and work. Here, for example, is

Socrates describing the divine voice he often hears, warning him away from doing "anything I should not":

> You have heard me give the reason for this in many places. I have a divine or spiritual sign.... This began when I was a child. It is a voice, and whenever it speaks turns me away from something I am about to do.... [M]y familiar prophetic power, my spiritual manifestation, frequently opposed me, even in small matters, when I was about to do something wrong.... [I]n other talks it often held me back in the middle of my speaking, but now it has opposed no word or deed of mine.[21]

In this text, Socrates speaks of himself as possessing a "prophetic power" that "frequently" intervenes in his actions and speeches, a "voice" that, "whenever it speaks," warns him to avoid doing or saying certain things. Moreover, the philosophy that Socrates pursues is itself the result of a series of divine commands "enjoined upon me by the god, by means of oracles and dreams and in every other way that a divine manifestation has ever ordered a man to do anything."[22] And while it is true that Socrates does not, like Parmenides, describe his philosophy as itself the speech of a goddess, Plato nonetheless describes him as calling on the Muses and other gods to provide him with answers to the questions that arise in his philosophy, and Socrates does on occasion describe his philosophical speech as being inspired by the intervention of a divine voice.[23] Thus even the Platonic texts can reasonably be said to have presented us with a world in which gods speak to men, guiding them in what they say and how they live.[24]

What these texts suggest is the following: During the two hundred years between Jeremiah and Plato, there flourished a philosophical tradition – the very tradition that gave birth to Western philosophy – in which the ability to conduct philosophical inquiry was frequently seen as partially or wholly dependent on revelation or some other form of assistance from a god. In this tradition human beings were seen as being unable to attain answers to significant questions on the strength of their own native abilities, so revelation or some other form of divine assistance was needed if they were to reach the truth, which was the possession of the gods alone. Where philosophy in this tradition was successful, it was therefore presented as though it were words spoken or sent by a god, or under the direction of a god.

Yet despite the putatively revealed character of such works, they are today read as though they were works of reason, and not revelation – with historians and professors of philosophy writing about them and teaching courses about them as if they were any other philosophical work. Bertrand Russell's *History of Western Philosophy*, for instance, devotes a short chapter each to Parmenides, Empedocles, and Heraclitus without so much as mentioning the role of the gods in producing their philosophies. He does draw attention to the fact that Socrates believed he was guided by a divine voice, oracles, and dreams. But nothing is said to follow from this.[25] And other histories of philosophy aren't much different in this respect. Virtually all of them take the fact that some philosophers presented their works as divine revelation in stride, either ignoring it entirely or mentioning it in passing without drawing any weighty conclusions from it.

Now, what would happen if we were to apply the same rules of interpretation commonly used in reading, say, the prophet Jeremiah, to Parmenides' text about his ascent to heaven in a chariot driven by gods? To his being led by the hand by the goddess and receiving commands from her? To his writing down the words he heard from her mouth, and descriptions of the things she showed him, so mankind could attain truth?

Applying the standards that are often applied today in reading the Bible, we'd have to assume, first, that whenever Parmenides describes the goddess as speaking or acting or showing him things, or when he describes himself riding skyward in the chariot, or the actions of other gods he encounters, he is reporting on the occurrence of a series of miracles to which he was witness – miracles whereby knowledge was revealed to him not due to the operations of his own faculties, but due to the will of the gods who chose to reveal this otherwise hidden knowledge to him. Second, we'd assume that all this is no more than fantastic nonsense, and that Parmenides, in choosing to write these things down, must either have been weak-minded and gullible, or else an unscrupulous liar trying to manipulate his audience for the sake of ends now forgotten. And then, having understood that Parmenides is either a fool or a liar for making such false presentations to us, we'd naturally conclude that his writings aren't works of reason, and that they don't, therefore, have anything significant to contribute to our own effort to understand reality. We'd then dispose of Parmenides the way we've disposed of other ancient texts of unreason.

As it happens, I'm no great enthusiast of Parmenides. My personal assessment is that his attempt to derive metaphysics from something like mathematical logic was a wrong turn in the history of mankind's quest for truth, and that we continue to suffer the consequences down to our own day. But I don't see how it makes sense to dismiss a thinker of Parmenides' stature from serious consideration for no reason other than that his ideas are presented in the form of revelation. As the history of philosophy amply attests, we can't expect the great figures of faraway times and places to see the world as we do on every issue, and not even on every issue we see as crucial.[26] And if the supposition that Parmenides really did experience his philosophy as the revelation of a goddess is just too much for us, it seems to me there are many possible ways of understanding the presence of the goddess in Parmenides' text that don't go quite so far, and yet do not end in a quick and arrogant dismissal of his work: Perhaps we think that in the case of the pre-Socratic philosophers, the invocation of divine revelation was merely a stylistic convention. Or perhaps we believe that the goddess is a metaphor, after all. Or perhaps we believe that in the old days people simply interpreted what we today call the "insight" of the human mind as the speech of a god. Or perhaps we believe that Parmenides was in fact a little crazy, but it doesn't matter because he came up with some good stuff too. Or perhaps we believe that he inherited old traditions concerning the speech of the gods and developed them in such a way as to make the philosophical lines clearer, while retaining the old story line. Any of these would work to permit us at least a first approach to the content of Parmenides' ideas if we find reading revelation difficult to swallow. And I'm sure there are many other ways of approaching his text that leave Parmenides' strength of mind and character intact, and permit us to consider his philosophy with an open mind.

So now the obvious question is this. If it makes little sense to dismiss Parmenides' philosophy from serious consideration just because it is presented as the revelation of a goddess, why should anyone take up this same approach to the text, which would embarrass us in the case of the pre-Socratic philosophers, and apply it shamelessly to the authors of the Hebrew biblical works? Is it not the case that *however* we wish to explain (or explain away) the character of Parmenides' writings as works of revelation, these same explanations, or similar ones, will apply just as well to Jeremiah? If we can forgive the Greeks the strange gods and oracles that speak to them, looking beyond this difficulty and judging them by the content of their teachings, why should not this same standard be applied to the writings of the Jews?

In my opinion, the answer to this question is just this: We don't approach the Greek texts by way of the same interpretive posture as we do the Jewish ones because we look at both through the prism of early Christian doctrine – that is, through the prism of the reason–revelation dichotomy, which teaches us to see Greek wisdom as derived from reason, whereas what the Jews have to say is revelation. This dichotomy is applied a priori, without any need for further investigation or justification. Parmenides' vision is studied as a work of reason because his is Greek wisdom; Jeremiah's writings as revelation for no other reason than that his is Jewish wisdom. And this a priori categorization is self-fulfilling. For once scholars and educated people have been hard at work for generations trying to find what is reasonable and philosophical in Parmenides, they do find it. Meanwhile, the work that is done on Jeremiah's text remains tightly focused on whatever seems to qualify it as revelation.

But this is all wrong. The idea that a given composition can't be a work of reason – indeed, that it can't be philosophy – because it presents itself as revelation is nothing but a bare prejudice. And nothing other than this bare prejudice of ours justifies denying Jeremiah the same consideration as Parmenides. If approached with appropriate respect and common sense, the great Israelite prophet will, I think, be quickly found to have at least as much reasoned discussion and philosophy to offer as many others who have long been studied as philosophers. And the same will be the case with many other texts of the Hebrew Bible, if not all of them.

For much of Western history, the reason–revelation dichotomy was maintained and elaborated primarily through the efforts of the Church.[27] But the cultural terrain has shifted, and over the last two centuries perhaps the most influential purveyor of this distinction has been the modern research university. Before proceeding to describe the outline of this book, I'd like briefly to consider the special role that the universities have played – and continue to play – in holding the reason–revelation dichotomy in place as the basis for our understanding of the Bible.[28]

The Christian reason–revelation dichotomy was intended to impart a conviction that works of revelation were in some important sense superior to works of mere reason, and therefore worthy of especial awe and respect. So it's not the Christian version of the reason–revelation dichotomy that is responsible for the common view that takes Parmenides to have been an epoch-making thinker, while Jeremiah is seen as a half-mad street preacher hearing voices in the air. This view of things owes its force and currency to the philosophers of the end of the eighteenth century, who retained the reason–revelation dichotomy but reworked it to achieve ends entirely alien to those of the Christians who originally popularized it. As is well known, French and German culture during this period was characterized by an extraordinary enthusiasm for Greek philosophy and art. In Germany, especially, it was common to speak of the classical Greeks almost as a kind of super-race, and to hold them up as the sole example of a segment of humanity worthy of serving as an ideal for contemporary Germans. Consider, for example, the following passage from the philosopher Wilhelm von Humboldt, who, as the Prussian minister of education, was the architect of the system of German research universities that eventually became the model for American higher education as well. I will quote at some length so that his message can't be mistaken:

> The study of Greek history is not as it is with the history of other peoples.... [W]e would absolutely misjudge our relationship to them, were we to dare apply the yardstick of the rest of world history to them. Knowledge of the Greeks is not simply pleasing, useful, and necessary to us – it is only in them that we find the ideal which we ourselves would like to be and to bring forth. Although every other period of history enriches us with human wisdom and human experience, we acquire from the contemplation of the Greeks something more than the earthly, something even almost divine....
>
> If we compare our restricted, narrow-hearted situation, oppressed by a thousand shackles of capriciousness and habit, fragmented by countless petty occupations, which never delve deeply into life, with the Greeks' free, pure activity, whose sole goal was the highest in humanity; if we compare our labored works, maturing slowly by repeated efforts, with theirs, which flow forth from the mind and spirit as if from free abundance; if we compare our gloomy brooding in monastic solitude, or mindless intrigues in casual society, with the serene cheerfulness of their community of citizens, who were bound by the holiest bonds; then, one might think the memory of them must make us sad and depressed, just as the prisoner becomes when recalling the unrestrained enjoyment of life; the invalid when remembering his robust health....
>
> But, on the contrary, it is only the transposition to that time of antiquity which, uplifting our heart and widening our spirit, restores us to such a degree to our initial ... human freedom, that we return to our ever so contrary situation with fresh courage and renewed strength, drawing true inspiration at that inexhaustible spring alone. Even a deep awareness of the gap which fate has eternally placed between us and them, urges us to use the ... power born of contemplating them, in order to uplift us to our allotted height. We imitate their models with a consciousness of their unattainability; we fill our imagination with the images of their free, richly endowed life, with the feeling that it is denied us, just as the easy existence of the inhabitants of their Olympus was denied them.[29]

This passage, published two years before the establishment of Humboldt's University of Berlin, captures the sense of the Enlightenment Grecophile frenzy quite well. In it, Humboldt warns that no one should "dare apply the yardstick of the rest of world history" to the Greeks, for it is "only" in the Greeks that "we find the ideal which we ourselves would like to be." Moreover, Humboldt emphasizes that the Greeks are "more than earthly," indeed "almost divine," and says that our relationship to the Greeks is like the Greeks' own relationship to their gods. True health, life, community, freedom, and holiness are all said to have been theirs alone. And he calls upon his fellow Germans to find themselves in "drawing true inspiration at that inexhaustible spring alone."

To find one's ideal only in the Greeks. To draw inspiration from the Greeks alone. These were fighting words in Christian Europe, and one doesn't have to think too hard to figure out whom they were aimed at. The elevation of the Greeks to the *sole* source of learning and knowledge announced a profound reconfiguration of Christian Europe's self-understanding – a reconfiguration in which the old Judeo-Hellenic synthesis was declared to have been, in retrospect, a mistake; and all that was Jewish in the history and thought of Europe would henceforth be deemed as having been, in fact, detrimental and unneeded.

The philosophers of the Enlightenment applied their formidable skills to constructing an understanding of European history that worked in just this way. Associating the texts of the Jews with ignorance and superstition, they argued that no genuine works of reason had arisen among the Jews and that nothing that was originally Hebrew had made a significant contribution to the history of ideas. Kant, for example, wrote that it is safe to bypass the Hebrew Scriptures in a history of the development of Western thought because they were written by an ignorant people, who gained whatever wisdom they may later have obtained from the Greeks. As he writes:

> The Jewish faith was, in its original form, a collection of mere statutory laws upon which was established a political organization; for whatever moral additions were then or later *appended* to it in no way whatever belonged to Judaism as such. Judaism is not really a religion at all but merely a union of a number of people who, since they belonged to a particular stock, formed themselves into a commonwealth under purely political laws.... [Only later was Judaism] interfused, by reason of moral doctrines gradually made public within it, with a religious faith – for this otherwise ignorant people had been able to receive much foreign (Greek) wisdom.[30]

A similar argument is made by Hegel, who argues that philosophy has been the possession of only two peoples, the Greek and the Teutonic.[31] As for the supposition that Christian ideas were in some way indebted to those of Judaism, Hegel explains that this is not the case, and that the content of Christianity arose more or less *ex nihilo,* as if in a "second Creation" of the world:

> In Christianity [the] absolute claims of the intellectual world and of spirit had become the universal consciousness. Christianity proceeded from Judaism, from self-conscious abjectness and depression. This feeling of nothingness has from the beginning characterized the Jews; a sense of desolation, an abjectness where no reason was, has possession of their life and consciousness.... [In Christianity] that nothingness has transformed itself into what is positively reconciled. This is a second Creation which came to pass after the first.[32]

In such passages, the leading thinkers of the German Enlightenment introduced a new twist into the history of the reason–revelation dichotomy, mixing contempt for revelation with an acid anti-Semitism to create a new view of Western history, in which absolutely nothing of worth is to be attributed to the Jews.[33]

The impact of this way of looking at the history of the West was immense. From 1810, the German universities were, under Humboldt's leadership, reorganized, with the new natural sciences rather than Christian philosophy at their center. This revamping of the universities was in many respects an extraordinary success, placing vast new resources in the hands of scholars capable of conducting research in the natural sciences and mathematics. German universities quickly became the world center for academic achievements in a dazzling array of disciplines, including mathematics, physics, biology, and medicine. But the scientific worldview was not supposed to be limited to mathematics and natural science alone. History, too, and the study of religion, were also refashioned as sciences. And what the German universities produced in the name of the scientific study of history was the Enlightenment historical narrative of Kant and Hegel. In this way, the burgeoning prestige of science, so well justified by the achievements of Harvey, Boyle, and Newton, was made to shine as well on a historiographic revolution whose achievements were much more ambiguous, and whose motives were far removed from the simple pursuit of the truth about the history of Western ideas.

In the decades that followed, the German universities became an international engine for the dissemination of the Enlightenment philosophy. Tens of thousands of American and British students flocked to Germany for advanced degrees, and by the 1870s, the German model of the "research university" had been established as the standard for advanced studies as far abroad as America and Japan. Of course, the research university was brought to America mostly because of its success in the sciences and mathematics. But it brought with it the Enlightenment interpretation of the history of Western ideas as well. And it is this interpretation that is studied and taught, almost exclusively, in universities around the world today.

This was much the same view of history that was being taught at Rutgers when I began studying there for a doctorate in political theory in the late 1980s. At Rutgers, as at most leading universities of the time, political theory and the history of political ideas were presented as a tradition that began in pre-Socratic Greece, and proceeded from there to Plato and Aristotle, to the Greek and Roman philosophical schools, and to the political thought of Christianity as found in the New Testament and the writings of the Church

Fathers, especially Augustine. The intellectual storyline then continued through medieval political thinkers such as Thomas Aquinas, and to early modern philosophers such as Machiavelli, Hobbes, Locke, and Rousseau, before finally reaching a rousing grand finale with German thinkers such as Kant, Hegel, Marx, and Nietzsche. This view of the history of Western political thought was what was available in the standard textbooks, of which the most highly regarded was probably that of George Sabine.[34] And it appeared with only minor variations in what were considered the "revisionist" histories proposed by Leo Strauss and Sheldon Wolin.[35] In these works, and in every other competitor I've seen, the contribution of the Hebrew Bible to the political ideas of the West is either passed over in silence, or else dismissed in a handful of (often quite offensive) sentences.[36]

Typical of this trend is Wolin's suggestively titled history, *Politics and Vision*, which devotes all of three sentences to Judaism before going on to a series of chapters describing the contributions to Western thought of Christian political ideas (which he calls "a new and powerful ideal of community which recalled men to a life of meaningful participation"[37]). Here is what he says:

> For the religious experience of the Jews had been strongly colored by political elements.... The terms of the covenant between Jahweh and his chosen people had often been interpreted as promising the triumph of the [Jewish] nation, the establishment of a political kingdom that would allow the Jews to rule the rest of the world. The messiah-figure, in turn, appeared not so much as an agent of redemption as the restorer of the Davidic kingdom.[38]

Thus according to Wolin, a thousand years of Jewish political thought prior to the advent of Christianity can be effectively nutshelled as the belief that the Jews should seek ultimate political power with the aim of establishing their rule over the entire planet.[39]

The situation is even worse in the philosophy departments, in which both the history of philosophy and current constructive philosophy are researched and taught much as though the Bible had never existed. Here, too, you can turn to textbooks to get a feel for the tone of the thing.[40] Bertrand Russell's *History of Western Philosophy* goes out of its way to point out that Greeks of the generation of Thales – usually described as the first Greek philosopher – may actually have met leading Jewish intellectual figures involved in the composition of the Bible. Russell makes this point in order to be able to speculate about what must have happened in these encounters. As he writes:

> The most important [Greek settlement in Egypt] during the period 610–560 BCE was Daphnae. Here Jeremiah and the other Jewish refugees took refuge

from Nebuchadnezzar (Jeremiah 43:5ff.); but while Egypt undoubtedly influenced the Greeks, the Jews did not, nor can we suppose that Jeremiah felt anything but horror towards the skeptical Ionians.[41]

Thus Russell, without a shred of historical evidence to go on, flatly asserts that Jeremiah "did not" have any influence on the Greeks he met, and, indeed, that he must have reacted to them with "horror" – conclusions that are in fact no more than the reason–revelation dichotomy projected back into a historical encounter that may well have taken place, but about which we have no record and in fact know absolutely nothing.[42]

Similarly disappointing is Anthony Kenny's *New History of Western Philosophy*. This work refers to the Hebrew Bible for the first time in a section entitled "Judaism and Christianity," which begins as follows:

> For the long-term development of philosophy the most important development in the first century of the Roman Empire was the career of Jesus of Nazareth.[43]

Kenny then proceeds to discuss the moral teachings of Jesus, nowhere returning to consider what ideas may have entered philosophy from the Hebrew Scriptures.[44] All other histories of philosophy with which I'm familiar proceed in more or less this fashion.

This trend is perhaps at its most blatant in moral philosophy – a field that one intuitively supposes must have been influenced in *some* significant way by the constant exposure of Western thought to the Hebrew Scriptures over more than twenty centuries. Yet this possibility is all but absent from the best overviews of the field of moral philosophy. Gilbert Harman's *The Nature of Morality* and Bernard Williams's *Morality: An Introduction to Ethics* present reasoned discourse on morals as involving a discussion of the ideas of Aristotle, Aquinas, Kant, Hume, and Bentham, among many others. But neither of them makes even a passing reference to the Hebrew Bible.[45] John Deigh's *An Introduction to Ethics* does mention that certain systems of ethics (deontological ones) ultimately have their roots in the Mosaic law. But Deigh doesn't feel the need to pursue this point because in the New Testament Paul says that God's laws are "written on our hearts" and can be studied without recourse to any book. As he explains:

> [Paul] means that we can have knowledge of [God's laws] through reflection on what is in our hearts. For this reason, none of us needs to be familiar with any holy book to have this knowledge. Exercising one's rational and reflective powers is sufficient. *There is, therefore, a distinction to which Paul alludes, between knowing the law through Scripture and knowing it through reason and reflection. The former is knowledge through revelation, and the latter*

is knowledge through reason. Ironically, then, this central tenet of Christian
thought makes recourse to the Bible or any other religious text unnecessary
for having knowledge of right and wrong.[46]

Notice that Deigh does not here rely on Paul's claim that the law is "written
on our hearts" to say we should do away with *all* books and just study ethics
off the top of our heads. Rather, the reason–revelation dichotomy is invoked
to distinguish between those books that we do need for ethics and those
that we do not: It is only "recourse to the Bible or any other religious text"
that is said to be "unnecessary for having knowledge of right and wrong."
Consequently, the Hebrew Bible makes no further appearances in Deigh's
book, whereas thinkers from Plato and Aristotle to Dostoyevsky, Camus,
and Sartre turn out to be sufficiently necessary for the study of ethics to be
brought in time and again.

From what has been said, it would seem that there are quite a few philosophers and historians of ideas who are unable to point, in a professional
way, to a single idea of significance that might have entered the Western
philosophical tradition through the texts of the Hebrew Bible. But I suppose this isn't any more remarkable than the fact that even university *Bible
studies* programs often tend to devote little or no attention to the question of the ideas the Hebrew Scriptures were written to advance.[47] Here,
too, the source of the difficulty can be traced to the academic tradition of
the German research university, which set out to turn the study of religion
into a "science." Perhaps the signal achievement of this effort, in the eyes
of its progenitors, was the development of the "source-critical" method for
studying the Bible, which understood the biblical texts as "corrupt" – the
result of centuries of tampering and abuse by anonymous scribes representing mutually hostile religious sects.[48] This tampering is said to have resulted
in texts that are little better than patchworks of fragments that are at times
less than a single verse in length. The hypothetical authors of these text
fragments – J, E, P, and D – are seen as different "layers" in the biblical text,
with the later layers (P, D) effectively defacing the texts that had been composed earlier on (J, E). For Julius Wellhausen and the founders of the source-
critical method, none of this is innocent either. They saw the later layers
as having been written by the inventors of "Judaism," whereas the earlier
layers had been written by authors whose worldview was much closer to
being Christian – so that in the hands of the scientific Bible scholarship of
Enlightenment Germany, the Jews turn out not to have been the *authors* of
the Old Testament, so much as those who *perverted* and *corrupted* it.[49] The
anti-Semitism of the authors of this theory has been commented upon by
Jewish scholars working in the field of biblical studies time and again.[50] But

here, too, as with Hegel's history of philosophy, it is simply assumed that the truth of the theory is independent of its anti-Semitic provenance.

In light of this picture of a corrupt and fragmented Bible, the idea that the biblical texts could be capable of advancing a consistent view on any subject has come to seem far-fetched in the eyes of many scholars. And indeed, the majority of academic Bible scholars have, for over a century, avoided the investigation of the ideas the biblical texts were written to advance for precisely this reason. The result is that today the field of biblical studies produces a steady stream of works on the philology, compositional history, and literary character of the biblical texts. But the ideas that find expression in the Bible – the metaphysics, epistemology, ethics, and political philosophy of the biblical authors – have all too often eluded the interest of academic scholars of Bible. Moreover, the incapacity to deal with the Hebrew Scriptures as works of reason affects numerous other academic disciplines, including the history and archaeology of the Near East, the history of Judaism, Christianity and Islam, the history and philosophy of law, the history and philosophy of science, the history of Western languages and writing, and more.[51]

The upshot of all this is that there may be no real reason for treating Parmenides as an epoch-making thinker, while Jeremiah's writings continue to languish under the weight of their ill repute as works of unreason. But it makes little difference. At the universities, the reason–revelation dichotomy continues to barrel onward, the many centuries of accumulated momentum carrying it through. Each discipline passes responsibility for inquiring whether there is something wrong to its neighbor. None seem to feel the disgrace and danger that a profoundly flawed understanding of our history may bring in its train.

What was once an unashamedly anti-Semitic revisionism aimed at showing that the Greeks were "almost divine," and that the West – and Germany in particular – was descended from these demi-gods alone, has long since crystalized into an orthodoxy. Of course the anti-Semites are long gone, and the job of promulgating this orthodoxy has been handed down to thousands of well-intentioned professors, many of them brilliant scholars in their own fields, who have never given much thought to the origins of the historiographic framework that determines the bounds of their discipline, the research agenda into which they fit their writings, and the outlines of the survey courses that are the basis for imparting knowledge to their students. None of these scholars has the slightest interest in convincing their students that the Jews contributed nothing of worth to the West. Yet their laudable intentions are contradicted by the academic training they have received and the analytic frameworks they have inherited, which make it difficult, if not impossible, for them to see the Hebrew Scriptures as a potential source for ideas of worth and interest.[52]

The Hebrew Bible is the modern university's blind side.

The way the Hebrew Bible is read in the universities isn't just a problem for scholars. More than any other institution in the modern world, the universities are seen by educated people as the engine for the discovery and dissemination of truth on pretty much every subject of general significance. And if the professors of philosophy, political theory, intellectual history, Bible, and law at the leading universities are, as a collective, propagating the Enlightenment prejudice that the Hebrew Bible is a work of unreason and, as far as important ideas go, an irrelevance, you can be sure that this is ultimately going to be how most educated people see the matter. And in fact, this is more or less where most Western countries have been since the second half of the nineteenth century.

But the last generation has brought important changes in the intellectual climate. We now stand at the far shore after many years of withering attacks on the Enlightenment heritage. And in many places the old prejudices, even if they are still standing, are not what they once were. At the universities, this has found expression in a new openness to different ways of looking at things, which has been especially manifest in everything having to do with the Hebrew Bible. Most striking in this regard has been the emerging understanding that the argument for the corruption of the biblical texts has been given far too much weight in academic discussion of the Bible. A deep impression was made beginning in the 1970s, when scholars of literature such as Robert Alter and Meir Sternberg began using the techniques of literary analysis to show that many of the biblical texts – regardless of their textual prehistory – are in fact polished works of literature with an evident internal unity.[53] This development showed that the Bible scholarship of the universities had radically underestimated the worth of the biblical texts as artistic achievements, and this new respect for the texts has in turn made it legitimate to inquire about the ideas that the craftsmen who composed these texts were concerned to advance in writing them. At the same time, Bible scholars such as Brevard Childs began developing what is now called "canonical criticism" – the academic study of the completed biblical texts, with a particular concern to understand their intended function within the biblical corpus as a whole.[54] By the 1980s, there had been significant pioneering works on the ethics of the Hebrew Scriptures by Bible scholars such as John Barton and Jacob Milgrom, and on the political ideas of these works by political theorists such as Michael Walzer, Aaron Wildavsky, and Daniel Elazar.[55] And since then we've seen book-length academic treatments of the Hebrew Scriptures as works of reason by scholars of widely disparate outlooks such as Joshua Berman, Mary Douglas, Lenn Goodman, Steven Grosby, Leon Kass, Mira Morgenstern, Eleonore Stump, Shmuel Trigano, and Gordon Wenham, among others.[56] The fact that some of the most prestigious academic presses in the world have been at the forefront of this trend suggests that what we are looking at is quite a profound change in attitudes, and not merely a surface phenomenon.

Nevertheless, I don't want to exaggerate what has been achieved. The Hebrew Bible remains a closed book for the overwhelming majority of educated men and women. There are still no books or even encyclopedia articles that can serve as an introduction to the thought of the Bible for professionals and lay persons who want to begin to understand the subject. Undergraduates still cannot sign up for introductory courses in the ideas of the Hebrew Scriptures, and survey courses in philosophy, political theory, intellectual history, and similar subjects still tend to skip the Hebrew Bible as a subject of discussion altogether. Doctoral students in these fields can still study for their general examinations without fear that the ideas of the biblical authors will turn up on the test. And the first book by a prominent philosopher arguing for the need to incorporate the biblical narratives into the discipline of philosophy, Eleonore Stump's *Wandering in Darkness*, has only just recently appeared (2010). So while there has been quite a bit of highly suggestive work showing that it is possible to approach the Hebrew Scriptures as works of reason, this material remains scattered and relatively unknown, its most suggestive findings often familiar only to a small circle of experts. Moreover, these studies for the most part contain little in the way of systematic reflection on reading the biblical texts as works of reason – so that it remains difficult to get a really clear view of the decisive shift in approach that is implicit in the new scholarship.

Given these circumstances, it seems there is a need for an introductory work that can serve as a gateway to the new approach to the investigation of the biblical texts – a gateway that will permit scholars, educators, and interested lay persons to better understand what is happening and what is at stake, and, hopefully, to take part themselves in the enterprise of retrieving the ideas of the biblical authors and bringing them into a more open dialogue with the ideas of the Western philosophical tradition than has been possible until now. This book is intended to serve as such an introduction. More specifically, I've written it with two purposes in mind: First, it is intended to provide a methodological framework that makes clear what I take to be the implicit assumptions of some of the best works on the Bible as a work of reason that have appeared thus far; and to extend these assumptions so as to permit more rapid advance in the direction of a well-articulated under-standing of the philosophical content of the Hebrew Scriptures. Second, it is intended to provide what I hope are some provocative examinations of the philosophical interests of the authors of the Bible. My hope is that this methodological framework and these provocative examinations will together suffice to make the project of investigating the Hebrew Scriptures as works of reason seem more plausible and engaging, both to those who have been skeptical about it, and to those who have been interested in and excited about the prospect of such a project but have felt it to be lacking in clear direction.

The book is divided into two main parts, followed by a conclusion: Part I, consisting of Chapters 1–3, offers an interpretive framework for reading the Hebrew Scriptures as works of reason or philosophy, including a discussion of the Bible's internal structure, the purposes for which it was written, and the ways in which the biblical authors use biblical narrative and prophetic oration to advance arguments of general significance. Together, these chapters provide a proposed roadmap for "how to read the Hebrew Scriptures" as works of reason or philosophy.

Chapter 1, "The Structure of the Hebrew Bible," is devoted to a survey of the internal structure of the Jewish Bible. I suggest that from the point of view of the philosophical reading of Scripture, the most important liter-ary unit of the Hebrew Scriptures is the narrative sequence of nine works extending from the book of Genesis to the book of Kings – the first half of the Jewish Bible – which collectively can be called the *History of Israel*. I then discuss the other principal works of the Jewish Bible in their relation to this History, and make a first approach at answering the question of why the compilers of the Bible brought together such a diversity of viewpoints and genres in a single anthology.

In Chapter 2, "What Is the Purpose of the Hebrew Bible?" I argue that the principal interpretive framework of the New Testament, which sees the Bible as having been written to bear witness or give testimony to the occur-rence of revelations and other miraculous events, is largely absent from the Hebrew Scriptures. I suggest that the History of Israel as we have it was composed with the purpose of preventing the disappearance of the Jews as a people after the destruction of Judah and Jerusalem and their exile from their land. It therefore reissues the law of Moses and calls for its observance. But the narrative in which the law is embedded also strives to provide a broader framework for understanding the significance of this law, offering what I think we should recognize as a philosophical argument for the importance of Israel's covenant with God not only for the Jews but also for "all the nations of the earth." The crux of this argument is that the law of Moses, alone among the laws of the nations, is fitted to man's nature and directed toward his well-being. The History thus holds out the prospect of "life and the good" for all of mankind, and charges the Jews to keep the Mosaic law both for their own well-being and as bearers of this prospect. The narrative tracts of the History of Israel should therefore be seen as intended, among other things, to establish political, moral, and metaphysical truths of a general nature within the context of an effort to explain and understand that which is of particular relevance and concern to the Jewish people after the destruction of their kingdom. I conclude the chapter with a discussion of the other parts of the Hebrew Scriptures, and the way in which they amplify and argue with the standpoint advanced in the History.

The picture that emerges from this discussion is one that sees the biblical authors as concerned to advance arguments of a universal or general significance. But this flies in the face of a series of common prejudices concerning the proper form for the presentation of such arguments. For example, narrative is often said to be a medium that focuses one's attention on the particular, not the universal. Similarly, the metaphors that appear in almost every line of prophetic oratory are considered to be the stuff of poetry, not reasoned argument. In Chapter 3, "How Does the Hebrew Bible Make Arguments of a General Nature?" I therefore look at some of the techniques the biblical narratives and prophetic orations use to advance arguments applicable to the generality of human experience. I conclude the chapter with a look at the way the History and the prophetic orations present their particularistic teachings – concerning the covenant and the Mosaic law – as being based upon, and growing out of, universal characteristics of human nature and of the nature of God's creation more generally.

Having proposed a framework for reading the Hebrew Scriptures as works of reason, I turn, in the next part of the book, to applying this framework to particular studies of the thought of the biblical authors. Part II, Chapters 4–8, thus offers a series of five interrelated studies that examine the metaphysics, epistemology, ethics, and political philosophy of the Hebrew Bible.

I begin, in Chapter 4, "The Ethics of a Shepherd," with an exploration of the ethics of the History of Israel, focusing especially on the book of Genesis. The Bible is often said to advocate an ethics of obedience. But I suggest that this view involves a serious misreading of Hebrew Scripture. Nearly all the principal figures throughout the biblical corpus are esteemed for their dissent and disobedience – a trait the biblical authors associate with the free life of the shepherd, as opposed to the life of pious submission represented by the figure of the farmer. At a certain level this emphasis on disobedience is not too surprising. Since the biblical authors saw most of the human sources of authority with which they were familiar as corrupt, it makes sense that they were advocates of dissent and resistance in dealing with human institutions. The biblical narratives, however, go much farther than this. Abel, Abraham, Jacob, Moses, Aaron, and other biblical figures are at times portrayed as resisting not only man, but *God himself*, with God going so far as to give Jacob the name Israel, "for you have wrestled with God and with man and have prevailed." I suggest that in these stories, the biblical narrative endorses what I call an *outsider's ethics*, which encourages a critique even of things that appear to be decreed by God in the name of what is genuinely beneficial to man. For in the eyes of the biblical authors, what is genuinely beneficial to man is that which will ultimately find favor in God's eyes.

Chapter 5, "The History of Israel, Genesis–Kings: A Political Philosophy," argues that the History of Israel was also composed with an eye to advancing a consistent political philosophy. This part of the Bible issues biting criticism of both the imperial state familiar to the ancient Near East and of its opposite, political anarchy. In place of these, the narrative advocates a new and intermediate form of political association: the unification of all Israel under a limited state, to be ruled by an Israelite whose thoughts "are not lifted above his brothers." This limited state would differ from the imperial states of the ancient Near East in that it would be constrained with respect to its territorial ambitions, the size of its military, and the resources it would expropriate from the people in the form of taxes and forced labor. Such a state has set out on "the good and the just way," and can hope for success and longevity. Thus the freedom of the Israelites is understood to depend not only on maintaining a ban on idolatry, as is often said, but also on adherence to a political theory of a limited government over one nation. The ultimate collapse of the Israelite state is attributed by the biblical narrative to the abandonment of this political theory by the Israelite kings.

The ethics and political philosophy of biblical narratives treated to this point raise pressing questions of epistemology, and in particular the question of how human beings can escape the circle of their own opinions to attain knowledge of that which is enduring and true. In Chapter 6, "Jeremiah and the Problem of Knowing," I suggest that the book of Jeremiah grapples constantly with this question. Indeed, the central theme of the book can be said to be the question of how it is possible for the individual to distinguish truth from falsity and right from wrong in the face of the wildly contradictory views being promoted by prophets, priests, and political leaders. Jeremiah's reflections on how this problem arises and the solutions he offers are shown to constitute an early and substantively interesting attempt to develop a theory of knowledge.

The question of what is meant by *truth* in Hebrew Scripture is pursued in Chapter 7, "Truth and Being in the Hebrew Bible," which seeks a reconstruction of the metaphysical presuppositions of the biblical authors. I begin by observing that in the Hebrew Bible, truth and falsity are not usually qualities of things that are said, but of objects: In Scripture, we find that things such as roads, men, horses, bread, and seeds can be true or false! Examining the way the Hebrew word for truth (*emet*) is used in the Bible, I conclude that an object is considered *true* to the extent that it can be relied upon in the face of hardship and changes in circumstance. But how does this work? It seems to leave the biblical authors without a coherent way of understanding what is meant by *true speech*. Answering this question, I suggest, forces us to look more carefully at the Hebrew term for spoken words (*davar*, pl. *devarim*), which is also the principal term used in biblical Hebrew to refer to objects. I argue that the biblical authors don't subscribe to a metaphysical picture in which word and object are independent from one another because they don't see the world and the mind of the observer as independent from one another. They recognize the *object as understood* as the only reality, and hold that true speech (or true things) is that which can be relied upon in the face of hardship and changing circumstance. In fact, this is what is meant by God's word.

In Chapter 8, "Jerusalem and Carthage: Reason and Faith in Hebrew Scripture," I turn to consider the place of faith in Hebrew Scripture. In contemporary discourse *faith* is often opposed to *reason* (as in the familiar opposition between "Jerusalem" and "Athens"). But I argue that the kind of faith that is usually invoked in establishing this opposition – in the writings of Tertullian or Kierkegaard, for example – cannot be found in the Hebrew Bible *at all*. Indeed, I make the case that the tradition of inquiry found in the Bible is opposed to "faith" in this sense. I then examine the biblical conception of faith, which refers to the belief that God can be relied upon to keep his promises, especially concerning the effectiveness of the Mosaic law in bringing well-being to mankind. Although Moses is depicted as emphasizing the efficacy of the law time and again, the narrative itself limits the extent to which Moses, or indeed any man, can have such knowledge in its portrayal of Moses' attempts to learn God's nature. Thus the narrative is found to both enjoin observance and at the same time to criticize the ideal of a perfect trust in God. I suggest that the absence of a commandment to have faith in God reflects the biblical teaching limiting the desirability of a perfect faith.

I end this book with a Conclusion and Appendix that seek to tie up loose ends and suggest some directions for further thought and discussion. In my brief Part III, Chapter 9, entitled "God's Speech After Reason and Revelation," I return to the question of whether an approach that treats the biblical texts as works of reason can be a sufficient basis for a full under-standing of the teaching of Scripture. A significant difficulty, I suggest, comes from the fact that the medieval understanding of what is meant by *reason* – the one traditionally employed in making the reason–revelation dichotomy work – has been under fire for centuries, and no consensus has yet emerged as to what should replace it. Moreover, the common understanding of what is meant by *revelation*, which depends heavily on Greek metaphysical assumptions, may also begin to totter if something like what I've proposed in Chapters 6–8 concerning biblical conceptions of truth and being turns out to be right. These two considerations lead me to suggest that with our understanding of both reason and revelation in motion, we may find the in-principle differences that made the reason–revelation dichotomy seem plau-sible in the Middle Ages growing more and more difficult to maintain.

Finally, I've attached an appendix entitled "What Is 'Reason'? Some Preliminary Remarks." Throughout this book I use the terms *reason* and *philosophy* without attempting to define them. But philosophers and others who are interested in what I mean by reason are invited to take a look at this appendix, which offers a short sketch of my views on this subject. In it, I point to the fact that the traditional reason–revelation distinction depended on a medieval understanding of reason as a series of deductions proceeding from self-evident premises (or from reports of the senses, which are also evi-dent in themselves). But the success of modern physical science has forced a radical revision of this view. Newton's science was, after all, based on abstracting general laws (or propositions) from experience. Deductions from these general laws were then confirmed or disconfirmed through further experience, and these results were used to confirm or disconfirm his general laws. This shift in the way we conceive of the functioning of human reason is important to the present discussion because it sheds light on why it was so difficult for many medieval thinkers to recognize reason in the Hebrew Scriptures. After all, if what counts as reason is mostly deductions of chains of propositions from other propositions, there really isn't much of this to be found in the Bible. But our view of what reason is has changed, and as a con-sequence the question of whether the kinds of argumentation characteristic of biblical instructional narrative or of prophetic oratory count as good examples of reason should, as it seems, be considered an open one.

In the Appendix, I point to a possible path for updating and developing Newton's conception of reason to incorporate the growing body of scholarship that sees metaphor and analogy as fundamental to the way the human mind reasons about abstract causes or natures. On the view I present, metaphor and analogy appear at a level of conscious human reasoning that is prior to and more basic than the articulation of such reasoning in terms of propositions. Newton's *Principia*, for example, relies heavily on metaphor and analogy in the forging of its basic concepts, which are only subsequently interrelated by means of a superstructure of mathematical propositions from which deductions can be taken. As soon as one recognizes that the operations of the human mind involved in analogical reasoning are basic to human reasoning concerning general causes or natures – and that neither Newtonian science nor any other form of advanced human reason seems to do without it – it becomes much easier to see that many, if not all, of the biblical authors are indeed engaged in reason, and that it is the exercise of reason they hope for in their readers as well.

PART I

READING HEBREW SCRIPTURE

I

The Structure of the Hebrew Bible

In this book, I propose that if we want to understand the ideas the Hebrew Scriptures were written to advance, we should read these texts much as we read the writings of Plato or Hobbes – as works of reason or philosophy, composed to assist individuals and nations looking to discover the true and the good in accordance with man's natural abilities. I don't mean that this is the only way to read these texts. Nor do I believe that the understanding that emerges from such readings has to give us the final picture of the biblical authors' worldview.[1] But for the reasons discussed in the Introduction, I believe that in reading the Hebrew Scriptures as works of reason or philosophy, we come much closer to the teachings the biblical authors meant to place before us than we do if we assume that these works were composed as reports of "revelation" – of knowledge obtained by means of a series of miracles.

The last generation has seen a new openness to reading the Hebrew Scriptures as works of reason or philosophy. Quite a few studies of the ethics and political philosophy of the Bible have already raised the possibility that in composing their texts, the biblical authors sought to investigate subjects similar to those treated in works traditionally recognized as philosophy. But the studies that have appeared so far have been noticeably short on systematic reflection as to what we are doing – and why we are doing it – when we set aside the old interpretive framework and begin reading the Hebrew Scriptures as works of reason. In Part I of this book, comprising Chapters 1–3, my aim will be to clarify and expand what I take to be the interpretive principles implicit in some of the recent works examining the philosophical significance of the biblical texts. The result will be a new interpretive framework for reading the Hebrew Scriptures as works of reason – a framework that I hope will be of assistance to both scholars and lay readers who are interested in investigating the Hebrew Scriptures for their philosophical content; and that can serve as a guide to instructors, both at the university level and more generally, who are interested in bringing the study of the ideas of the Bible into the classroom.

This part of the book is divided into three chapters, which are intended to address what I see as the principal challenges facing contemporary readers in trying to retrieve the philosophical substance of the biblical texts: These are (i) a lack of familiarity with the structure of the Hebrew Bible, and a consequent discomfort with what seems to be the endless profusion of genres and different kinds of texts included in the corpus; (ii) confusion about the purpose for which the texts of the Hebrew Scriptures were originally composed; and (iii) uncertainty as to how to get at the ideas of the biblical authors given that much of the Bible looks much more like literature, or law, than philosophy. I don't believe these chapters can remove these difficulties entirely. In the end, it is only studying Hebrew Scripture – and not any framework I might propose – that can substantiate the claim that these texts are more easily read as works of reason than as anything else. But the obstacles that stand in the way of such a reading are real and not to be underestimated. In clearing them away, at least in part, I believe we can make the work of reading the Hebrew Bible that much easier.

I. THE HEBREW SCRIPTURES: A BRIEF OVERVIEW

Opening the Hebrew Bible can be an intimidating business. Readers have often heard the Bible referred to as the "Book of Books," or as the "Good Book." Even the word *Bible* comes from the Greek *biblion*, which means simply *book*. All of which might lead one to think the Hebrew Bible is a book. And yet the Hebrew Bible is not, in any conventional sense, a book. It is rather a collection or anthology of works of different lengths and genres – some of which (such as Isaiah or Job) are large and self-sufficient enough to be considered books in their own right; some of which (such as Genesis or Judges) are so dependent on what comes before or after them that they more closely resemble chapters in a larger literary work; and some of which (such as Esther or Ecclesiastes) are so small that one might consider them simply to be poems or short stories.[2] Yet for all these differences, many English-language editions of the Bible present these works as an undifferentiated string of thirty-nine different "books," without providing any indication as to which of them were meant to be parts of larger literary formations within the corpus, or what the character or purpose of these larger formations might have been. As a result, the biblical text can easily appear to be a vast, rambling pastiche that, in terms of its form, is experienced by uninitiated readers as a work possessing neither order nor reason.

This is perhaps not such a terrible thing if you don't expect the Bible to be a work of reason anyway. But if our aim is to read the Hebrew Scriptures as works of reason, the first thing we need to know is whether there is not, after all, some kind of rational order that may be discerned in this profusion of biblical materials – an order that will permit us to understand what the different literary units are of which it is composed, and to begin laying out a strategy for examining the ideas these different parts of the Bible were intended to advance. Fortunately, there is no reason to think that the authors of the respective biblical texts, or the editors who assembled them into the Hebrew Bible as we now have it, intended them to be read as one giant pastiche. The Hebrew Scriptures do possess what is, in my view, a clear internal structure that can be discerned without too much difficulty. And while I am sure not everyone will see this matter as being as straightforward as I do, my approach should at any rate be good enough to get a philosophical reading of the Hebrew Scriptures off the ground. And perhaps it will prove useful for other purposes as well.

The Hebrew Bible consists of three massive literary units, each of which includes a number of subsidiary compositions.* Of these, the first is (i) a unified and largely narrative work, comprising one-half of the biblical corpus, which in effect tells a single story extending from the creation of the world in Genesis to the destruction of the kingdom of Judah at the end of Kings. I will refer to this work as *The History of Israel.*** This History is then followed by two compilations of different works, each of which

---

* The version of the biblical text I will be describing is what scholars call the Masoretic text (from the Hebrew *masoret*, meaning "tradition") – the version of the Bible accepted as canonical by nearly all Jews around the world. This choice comes naturally to me. I'm an Orthodox Jew. This is the version of the Bible I've been reading my entire life. But I also think the Jewish Bible has advantages for a philosophical reading of Scripture over the versions of the "Old Testament" found in most Christian Bibles. For a brief discussion of some of the issues here, see note 43 to this chapter.

** It is an indication of the awkwardness with which the Western tradition has approached this great historical narrative that it does not, as far as I can tell, even have a name. The Bible scholar David Noel Freedman has proposed calling it the "Primary History." See David Noel Freedman, *The Unity of the Bible* (Ann Arbor: Michigan University Press, 1993), pp. 5–6. But to me it seems terribly misleading to refer to this work using a name that is relative to (and derived from) its place in the larger corpus of the Bible. We have no reason to think that the Bible existed when the History was composed; and the author or editor of this history did not, so far as we know, write with the rest of the biblical corpus in mind. Like other great literary works that have come down to us from antiquity, this work deserves to be referred to by a name that at least in some degree reflects its own content and spirit. On the use of the term "history" with reference to biblical works, see Baruch Halpern, *The First Historians: The Hebrew Bible and History* (University Park: Pennsylvania State University Press, 1984), pp. xvii–xxxvi, 1–35; R. N. Whybray, *The Making of the Pentateuch* (Sheffield: Journal for the Study of the Old Testament Press, 1987), pp. 225–235.

appears to be a kind of commentary – or rather, a cluster of commentaries –
on the great History that they follow. I'll refer to these two compilations as
(ii) *The Orations of the Prophets* and (iii) *The Writings*.[3]

The structure of the Hebrew Bible as a whole is presented in Figure 1.
From this figure it is possible to see that the two latter compilations that
follow the History – the Orations and the Writings – are quite similar to
one another in terms of their own internal structure. Each of them consists
of three principal works, followed by a group of brief works that serve as
"retainers" for the larger works. From this similarity in structure, it seems
reasonable to assume that the Orations and the Writings were intended by
the editors of the biblical anthology to be parallel collections, each of them
providing support and elaboration to what was the principal biblical work,
which is the great narrative of the History of Israel.[4]

The image that came to my mind when I first saw this structure was that
of Moses standing above the battle at Refidim with his arms outstretched,
one arm being supported by Aaron and the other by Hur.[5] I don't mean
to suggest that this specific image was before the eyes of the editors of the
Bible when they constructed their anthology.[6] But I do believe they would
have seen the principal work of the Bible, the History, as being "supported"
in much this way by the two additional parts of the biblical structure, just
as the three major works in the Orations and the three major works in the
Writings are themselves "supported" by the formation of minor works that
follow.

Thus the Hebrew biblical corpus should be seen as built in the form of
a hierarchy, with (i) the History of Israel forming the top tier; (ii) a second
tier consisting of six principal works divided into two groups of three; and
(iii) the rest of the biblical corpus as a third tier consisting of two assemblies
of minor supporting works.

Let's take a look at each of these three principal literary formations in
turn.

1. *The History of Israel*. The first half of the Hebrew Bible is a single,
largely unbroken narrative, which begins with the creation of the world but
whose focus is the emergence of the Israelites as a people and the rise and fall
of the independent state established by this people. The completed narrative
embraces nine works: Genesis, Exodus, Leviticus, Numbers, Deuteronomy,
Joshua, Judges, Samuel, and Kings.* And while these works contain codes

* The division of Samuel and Kings into smaller works, as in many editions of the Bible, is a
  late innovation that was still unknown in the period of the Talmud, several centuries after
  these works were written.

The History of Israel

| Genesis-Numbers | Deuteronomy | Joshua-Kings |

Orations of the Prophets

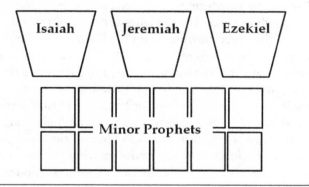

Isaiah   Jeremiah   Ezekiel

Minor Prophets

Writings

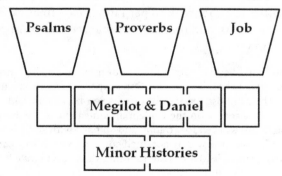

Psalms   Proverbs   Job

Megilot & Daniel

Minor Histories

FIGURE I.

of law, poems, and other types of material, these materials are presented to us not as something separate from the third-person historical narrative, but rather as being embedded within it. For example, the Mosaic law is recounted, in part, when Moses goes into the darkness on Mount Sinai and God teaches him the law; and other collections of laws are similarly woven into the narrative at relevant points.[7] The History thus possesses a strong internal integrity, with the non-narrative materials being worked into the storyline of the narrative in such a way as to impart to them their context and significance. In many respects, the centerpiece of the sequence is the middle book of the nine, Deuteronomy, which consists largely of a first-person speech in which Moses offers the Israelites his own final understanding, on the eve of their invasion of Canaan, of the rise of Israel, of the law, and of what is to come as they struggle to establish their kingdom.[8]

Who composed this History of Israel and when? Many suggestions have been made on this score, and I will certainly not resolve the issue here. But I'll say a few words on the subject, since it has some bearing on other issues I'll be discussing. At least from the time of the Talmud (compiled c. 500 CE), it has been obvious that the History was composed from multiple sources written at different times. The Talmud suggests that parts of the History were written by Moses, Joshua, and Samuel – with Jeremiah writing the last portions of it.[9] Modern scholarship has made many alternative proposals as to who wrote the different texts that were brought together when the History of Israel was put into its final form, the form in which we have it today.[10] But it seems to me that these proposals have not brought us much closer to really knowing what the original sources were from which the History was constructed, who wrote them, when, or why. This is not for want of good arguments. There are plenty of good arguments. Rather, the problem is that in the end, the internal evidence from the texts is often just too weak to permit scholars to advance beyond the level of hypotheses. As one prominent Bible scholar, Meir Sternberg, describes the situation:

> [We have now seen] over two hundred years of frenzied digging into the Bible's genesis.... Rarely has there been such a futile expense of spirit in a noble cause; rarely have such grandiose theories of origination been built and revised and pitted against one another on the evidential equivalent of the head of a pin; rarely have so many worked for so long and so hard with so little to show for their trouble. Not even the widely accepted constructs of [historical criticism], like the Deuteronomist, lead an existence other than speculative.[11]

Or, as another Bible scholar, Roger Whybray, puts it:

> It is difficult to avoid the conclusion that the likelihood of modern scholars succeeding in discovering – except, perhaps, in very general terms – how the Pentateuch was compiled is small indeed. This does not necessarily mean that it is not worthwhile to make the attempt. But the self-assurance with which many scholars, especially in the last hundred years, have propounded their views on the subject should be regarded with suspicion.... It will be found that often conjecture has been piled upon conjecture.[12]

I suspect that these scholars are right. The question of what the original sources were from which the History of Israel was composed is one I do not believe can be answered based on the internal evidence available in the Bible itself. Given this reality, I don't think that readers whose main interest is to understand the ideas the History of Israel was written to advance will gain a great deal by delving deeply into the question of the "prehistory" of the text as we now have it.[13]

We're in a somewhat different situation, however, if we are trying to understand the circumstances surrounding the composition of the History of Israel as a *completed* literary work. With respect to the History as a whole, I think we at least have the option of adopting a simple and straight-forward reading as to when it was written, who wrote it, and why. What we have before us, after all, is the story of the rise of the people of Israel, the establishment of their kingdom (by Saul and Samuel, putatively in 1047 BCE), its subsequent division into the two kingdoms of Israel and Judah, and the decline and destruction of these two kingdoms – the northern kingdom of Israel meeting its end in 722 BCE, and the southern kingdom of Judah falling in 586 BCE. The History ends with the imprisonment and murder of the last kings of Judah at the hands of the Egyptians and the Babylonians, and with the exile of Judah's leading political and spiritual figures, either to Babylonia (where Ezekiel lived and wrote) or to Egypt (where Jeremiah apparently completed his writings).[14]

These are facts I don't think anyone would dispute. And as I say, they give us at least the option of a simple and straightforward reading regarding the question of who composed this History, when, and why. Since the text ends with the exile of Judah's leading political and spiritual figures, the most straightforward reading is that this history is the product of the exile from the land and its aftermath.[15] Moreover, although we know that the Jews did in fact begin to return to their land in the time of Zerubavel some fifty years after the destruction and exile described at the end of the History (that is, around 538 BCE), the History of Israel knows nothing of such a return. The History, then, is written – as the rabbis of the Talmud suggested – as though its final author, who put it in the form in which we now have it, were Jeremiah or some other great intellectual figure among the Jews during the first decades of the exile.[16]*

---

* I've gone back and forth as to whether to use *author* or *editor* to describe the individual (or individuals) who were responsible for composing the final edition of the History. Neither term really does what I'd want it to. The word *editor* seems to me to be insufficient, since the final author of the History, especially if he were an individual of Jeremiah's stature, could

I've said that the evidence in the biblical texts gives us the *option* of such a straightforward reading. It is of course possible that the History was actually composed a century later than this, once the return to the land and its rebuilding were already under way. For many reasons, I doubt this. My strong sense is that it was composed by someone who saw the destruction of the kingdom and the Temple with his own eyes, and did not live to see the beginning of the return, as the simplest reading of the text suggests. In other words, I do think that this narrative was assembled by Jeremiah, or under the hand of one of his students. But I could be wrong, and for our purposes here I don't think it makes much difference. Let it be a century later, then, or even two. It doesn't matter. It is the experience of the Jews in their degradation and exile, and the attempt to survive it, that gave rise to the text we have before us. And this experience continued for long years even after some Jews began to return, in small numbers, to Jerusalem.

The History of Israel is a work of 150,000 words in Hebrew, which in the King James edition came to a text about a third longer than Hobbes's *Leviathan*. As I've said, it encompasses almost exactly half the material in the Hebrew Scriptures. But this statistic doesn't quite capture its importance. The positioning of the History as the first half of the Bible, with all other texts of the Hebrew Scriptures arranged around it, suggests that this text is presented as the kernel of and basis for everything that follows it in the Scriptures. I don't mean by this that the composition of the History predates everything in the second half of the Bible. This is exceedingly doubtful. But I do mean that the editors of the Bible wanted us to see the History as the basis for the biblical teaching – and I do believe this is the way they saw the matter themselves. It is with the appearance of the completed History of Israel and its circulation among the exiles in Babylonia and Egypt that Jewish ideas gained a power of expression and a reach unprecedented not only in the history of Israel and Judah, but also among the surrounding nations.[17] It was this national Scripture that then became, I believe, the benchmark against which further additions to the

---

easily have been responsible for writing parts of the text more or less as a modern author would, thereby taking full responsibility for the shape of the ideas that would be presented in the History as a unified work. But I've found that if I refer to "the author of the History" I leave the misimpression that I am talking about an author who "wrote the whole thing himself" – in the sense of writing every word from scratch – which is hardly conceivable. I do prefer the term *author*, but only to the extent that it is possible to bear in mind that much of the History must consist of texts that the final author inherited and incorporated into the finished narrative.

national corpus were measured. Indeed, the Hebrew Bible that we have today appears to have been constructed in order to elaborate, comment upon, argue with, and deepen the impact of the History, which is the central and principal biblical text.

2. *The Orations of the Prophets.*[18] The third quarter of the Hebrew Scriptures is devoted almost entirely to a collection of speeches by the prophets of Israel. This collection is focused on three major works, the books of Isaiah, Jeremiah, and Ezekiel, largely consisting of speeches presented as the words of these prophets. These are then followed by an anthology of twelve minor prophetic works (Hoshea, Joel, Amos, Ovadia, Jonah, Micha, Nahum, Havakuk, Tzefania, Hagai, Zecharia, and Malachi), which are for the most part – Jonah being an exception – much shorter collections of prophetic orations. Although the Hebrew word for prophet (*navi*) is used in the Hebrew Scriptures in various ways (for example, Abraham is called a *prophet* in Genesis[19]), its normative meaning is with reference to a tradition of orators in Israel and Judah who made use of public speeches to challenge abuses of power and misguided policies on the part of the kings of Israel, the priesthood, and other officials of the state, and to argue for the improvement of morals and religious practices among the people.[20] Prophecy, in this sense, is described as having a kind of constitutional standing in Moses' description of Israelite monarchy in Deuteronomy,[21] and the History of Israel introduces us to prophets of this type as early as the period of the Judges, when the prophetess Deborah speaks publicly against those tribes that did not join with their brothers in the public defense.[22] But the first substantial written records of the poetic orations of the prophets of Israel seem to be those of Amos (c. 750 BCE). Thereafter, we have records of the oratory of Israelite prophets all the way down to the Babylonian exile and on into the Persian period, including the speeches of prophets who were involved in the first attempts of the exiles to return to Jerusalem. The last of the biblical prophetic texts that can be dated with reasonable accuracy are from the 510s BCE, a generation before the composition of the prophetic poems of Parmenides and Empedocles.

Perhaps the most striking aspect of the tradition of prophetic literature captured in the Hebrew Bible is its relationship to the destruction of the kingdoms of Israel and Judah. The first of the major prophetic authors, Isaiah, witnessed the downfall of the kingdom of Israel and the forced deportation of its inhabitants at the hands of the Assyrian empire in 722 BCE – a deportation that ultimately resulted in the assimilation of the people of the northern kingdom into the populations among whom they were dispersed, and their disappearance from history. While there had been a tradition of prophetic writings prior to this event, it is the shock and horror surrounding the disappearance of the northern kingdom that appear to have been responsible for the extraordinary flowering of speculative, moral, and political thought in Judah as its people struggled to develop appropriate tools for understanding what had happened – and for attempting to prevent a similar fate from befalling their own kingdom. In this tradition, the book of Isaiah is the first great masterwork,[23] presenting the first extended attempts by the prophets to develop an understanding of the mechanisms by which evil befalls nations, and to advance a systematic critique of Israelite political and religious practices in light of the lessons of the downfall of Israel. The books of Jeremiah and Ezekiel, on the other hand, represent the thought of prophets who saw the end of the kingdom of Judah in 586 BCE, and can be seen as developing, in very different ways, ideas that made their first systematic appearance in Isaiah's writings more than a century earlier.

3. *The Writings*. The last one-fourth of the Hebrew Scriptures is a diverse collection of works traditionally known as the *Writings* (Hebrew, *ketuvim*; Greek, *hagiographa*). As discussed above, the internal structure of the Writings is patterned on the structure of the Orations, with three principal works being placed at the front, and an assembly of brief works following. But unlike the Orations, the Writings is not a collection that is meant to reflect a single genre of Israelite thought.[24] Of the three principal books included in the Writings, Psalms is a compilation of 150 works of poetry; Proverbs is a composition principally concerned with moral philosophy; and Job is a narrative largely devoted to theological inquiry. This diversity of genres and subject matters is continued in the minor works, which include five short poetic and narrative compositions known as the *Megilot*, or "Scrolls" (Song of Songs, Ruth, Lamentations, Kohelet [Ecclesiastes], and Esther); and the book of Daniel, half in Aramaic, which includes symbolic visions of future history all the way down to the Greek period. These are followed by two minor historical works – Ezra and Nehemiah, in Jewish tradition read as a single work that serves as a supplement to the History of Israel, describing the reconstruction of Jerusalem by returning exiles perhaps a century after Zerubavel;[25] and Chronicles, which provides an alternative account of Israel's history.*

---

* A number of the works included in the Writings, including Proverbs and Kohelet (Ecclesiastes) are often described as "wisdom literature." This reflects a scheme of categorization of the biblical works common among scholars of the ancient Near East, but which I will not adopt in this book. For a brief discussion of the issues involved, see note 26.

II. THE DIVERSITY OF BIBLICAL THOUGHT

The Hebrew Scriptures encompass a large number of works of various kinds. In the Orations, we have before us what are presented as the works of no fewer than fifteen different prophets, whose writings appeared over a period of nearly 250 years. The Writings consist of eleven different works, apparently by different authors.[27] Thus even according to traditional accounts, these two supplementary compilations give voice to at least two dozen different authors writing over a number of centuries.

And as one might suspect, these biblical authors disagree among themselves time and again, even over what might seem to be issues of the greatest importance. For example, one would have a hard time reconciling the political understanding of the book of Daniel, in which faith in God is virtually all one needs to gain political salvation, with that of Esther, which comes closer to the view that in politics God tends to help those who help themselves. Nor can one harmonize Isaiah's claim that in the time of the king to come all the earth will have one God with the prophet Micha's vision, in which each nation will walk with its own god, and Israel will walk with theirs.[28] Similarly, Isaiah sees mankind beating their swords into plowshares and coming to be judged at Jerusalem. But the vision of Joel is different, and he writes that when the nations come to Jerusalem to be judged, they will beat their plowshares into swords – for judgment will come on the battlefield.[29] And countless other examples could be adduced.

To understand the Hebrew Bible, then, is first to recognize it as an artful compendium, whose purpose is not – and never was – to present a single viewpoint.[30] I do not mean by this that there is no center or heart to the tradition of thought encompassed by the Hebrew Scriptures. There is indeed such a center, such a heart.[31] But this center of the biblical teaching is not something handed to us. It must be *sought*, and the Bible points to it not by way of one brief and sharply delineated understanding, but by way of a family or a school of viewpoints, each of which brings us to this center from a different place. It is of the essence of what we mean when we speak of something as being biblical in character that it presents a certain core of truths, but by means of a diversity of views.

In part, this insistence on approaching truth through a plurality of perspectives is the result of the fundamentally political character of the biblical corpus. Having been assembled to embrace and heal a broken people after the loss of its land and freedom, the Hebrew Bible could not afford the parochialism of a narrow religious sect, because it was consciously assembled to serve as the basis for the thought of an entire nation. But the Bible's accommodation of the plurality of points of view goes deeper than this. The compilers of the Bible also had to be skeptical about attempts at imposing a single point of view regarding issues of importance due to the Bible's oft-repeated observation that ultimate knowledge of God's thoughts is beyond the powers of man, which are by nature weak and fallible. This is not just a latter-day view to be found in medieval mysticism or in Maimonides' negative theology, but a characteristic that is manifest in the biblical texts themselves, in which encounters with God are depicted, time and again, as elusive and fraught with lack of clarity and uncertainty.[32] This recognition of the chronic difficulty involved in attaining truth on subjects of ultimate importance is apparently also reflected in the broad plurality of points of view that found admission into the finished biblical corpus. (I will return to this subject in Chapters 6–8, which deal with the biblical authors' understanding of reason, knowledge, and the nature of truth.)

This having been said, I also think it would be a mistake to think of the Bible as a kind of literary democracy, in which everything is seen as being worth the same as everything else. As I've said, the Hebrew Scriptures appear to be constructed with the History of Israel as the central and principal text. The narrative from Genesis to Kings is not only by far the largest literary structure in the Bible. It is pre-eminent in its position, being granted the *first* half of the biblical corpus. And as I've said, the structure of the corpus, as depicted in Figure 1, seems intended to give the impression that the subsequent works are a kind of commentary to it – an impression that is, I think, borne out by the content of these works. The Orations, especially, are written with reference to persons and events that later generations would have known little or nothing about had they not been able to refer to the History (and to the competing history presented in Chronicles) for the basic storyline; and with reference to laws that are known, after a certain point, only by consulting the Mosaic law as it is presented in the History.[33] This is true to a lesser extent of the Writings, many of which can be read as self-contained works. Nonetheless, one is hard-pressed to find any of them – the Song of Songs being a possible exception – that do not, once placed within the orbit of the History, speak directly to issues that are central to the teachings of the great historical narrative.

I should emphasize that when I speak of the second half of the biblical corpus as presenting us with what appear to be "commentaries" on the History, I mean *critical* commentaries. For many of the texts in the Orations and Writings do take up positions that are at odds with the views presented in the History, as when Ezekiel challenges the History's understanding that the mistakes of each generation inevitably spill punishment on those that follow;[34] or when Daniel challenges the supposition that Joseph had to adopt Egyptian norms of behavior to be successful in Pharoah's court;[35] or when Chronicles argues with the History over David's virtues as a ruler.[36] But even where these works register criticism of the History, these criticisms take on such significance due to their appearance in a text that is presented to us as contrasting with ideas already familiar from the History of Israel.[37]

All of this suggests that while there may be many points of vantage in the Hebrew Bible, the first to be reckoned with is that of the History. Regardless of what may have been the compositional history of the various works in the Bible, it is the History in its present form that is the defining statement of ancient Israelite thought. All roads lead to it, and from it. And so it must be for us the point of departure in all that concerns biblical thought, or the philosophy of Hebrew Scripture.

It may reasonably be asked whether I am not placing too much emphasis on the History at the expense of the what Jews often refer to as "the Tora" (or, in Greek, the Pentateuch) – the sequence of works from Genesis to Deuteronomy, which rabbinic tradition awards a unique status within the biblical corpus due to its presumptive authorship by Moses, the greatest of the prophets. Isn't it important to keep this sequence of works, which constitute the first half of the History of Israel, distinct from the rest of Scripture? In my view, this distinctiveness is important, and the rabbis were right to insist on it. But this distinctiveness derives the greater part of its force from the fact that the books of Moses present us with almost the only legal codices within the Hebrew Scriptures:[38] Jewish jurisprudence necessarily flows from these works, which consequently take on a kind of constitutional status within Jewish law. I don't know that the special standing of these texts in discussions of the Jewish law should automatically be seen as extending into the realm of philosophical investigation as well. The *halacha* (law) has its basis in the books of Moses, but the *agada* (philosophical teaching) that accompanies it should, I think, be seen as following the contours of the complete narrative all the way to the end of the book of Kings.[39] Indeed, even if this special concern for the elaboration of the Jewish law, and the consequent focus on the five books of Moses, is completely reasonable on its own terms, it may still be the case that with the passage of time this has led to an undue neglect of the teachings of the History of Israel as the unified agadic work it was intended to be.

This point is perhaps an unfamiliar one, so it is worth sharpening it a bit. The issue here is this: I am not at all certain that the books of Moses can be fully understood in isolation from the rest of the History in which they were embedded. Consider, for example, the following parallels between the opening of the History of Israel in Genesis and Exodus, and its close in Judges, Samuel, and Kings:[40]

1. At the beginning of the narrative, Adam and Eve are exiled from Eden; at its end, the Jews are exiled from their homeland.

2. At the beginning of the narrative, we are told of the destruction of the Tower of Babylon, whose purpose was to reach the heavens; at its end, we are told of the destruction of the Temple in Jerusalem, whose purpose was to win the favor of heaven, by the Babylonians.

3. At the beginning of the narrative, Abraham flees the urban centers of Babylonia[41] to begin life anew as a shepherd in the wilds of Canaan; in the end, his descendants are returned to the urban centers of Babylonia in chains.

4. In Genesis, we are told of how Abraham is called upon to sacrifice his only child as a burnt offering to God, but does not do so; in Judges, we are told of how Yiftah sacrifices his only child as a burnt offering to God, although he is not called upon to do so.

5. In Genesis, we are told of how Jacob's sons Shimon and Levi go out and slaughter all of the inhabitants of the northern city of Shechem in an act of righteous zealotry; in Kings, we are told of how Elisha's men Yehu ben-Yehoshafat and Yehonadav ben-Rachav go and slaughter all their opponents in the northern capital of Samaria in an act of righteous zealotry.

6. In Genesis, we are told of how Joseph is sold into slavery in Egypt by Judah and the rest of his brothers; in Kings, we are told of the deportation of the house of Joseph (the northern kingdom) into exile, while the house of Judah (the southern kingdom) remains on its throne.

7. In Exodus, we are told that Moses, having found God while driving his flock in the wilderness, returned to face Pharoah's chariots with a shepherd's staff; in Samuel, we are told that the young David walked onto the battlefield at Gat with a shepherd's staff, having spurned the armor that was offered to him.

8. In Exodus, we are told of how the Israelites despoiled Egypt of its gold as they left for the desert; in Kings, we are told of how the Babylonians grew jealous of Jerusalem's wealth and waged war on it until they despoiled the Israelites of their gold.

9. In Exodus, we are told of how Aaron fashioned a calf of gold to shore up the tottering confidence of the Israelites in the wilderness; in Kings, we are told of how Yarovam, king of Israel, fashioned two calves of gold to shore up the tottering confidence of the Israelites at Samaria.

10. In Exodus, we are told of how Moses climbed Horev in search of God's ways, but God went by him, showing him only his back; in Kings, we are told of how Elijah climbed Horev in search of God's justice, but God went by him, leaving him only a still small voice.[42]

All these examples – and one could bring many others – reflect what seems to me to be a very important fact: The biblical History of Israel is a work with a strong internal coherence. And to the extent that we are concerned to understand the ideas of this History, we should refrain from studying certain parts of it in isolation from the rest of the text unless we have good reason to do so. This does not mean only that the later passages in the History should be read as referring back to the earlier ones – that the story of David purposely refers back to Moses, for example. It also means that in reading the earlier stories in the History, we run the risk of missing their meaning if we do not understand them as foreshadowing subsequent events. It is very uncertain, for instance, that we can really understand the story of Cain, a farmer, murdering his brother Abel, who is a shepherd, if we do not recognize that this first act of violence between farmers and shepherds is a premonition of the violence between farmers and shepherds that appears in the later story of Abraham, and then again in the story of Moses, and yet again in the story of David. Or that we can understand Abraham's flight from Babylonia without recognizing that it is precisely the reverse of this flight that the History sees taking place with the destruction of Jerusalem. Or that we can understand the story of Joseph and Judah without reference to the later history of the house of Joseph and its relationship to the house of Judah. Our only hope of being able fully to understand what these various events in the narrative were meant to teach us therefore comes of reflecting on the text of the History as a unified whole.[43]

This discussion should be enough to allow us at least an approach to the question of the plurality of viewpoints presented in the Bible. As I've suggested, the Hebrew Scriptures purposely provide us with multiple perspectives on a great many issues. But the History of Israel remains the central work, and the standpoint it advances dominates Hebrew Scripture, as it seems the editors of the Bible intended. Indeed, without the point of view presented in the History, it is unlikely that there would *be* a Hebrew Bible – for without it, there would be little to hold the rest of the disparate pieces together. This is not something that can be said of any other text in the corpus.

A reader wishing to investigate the philosophy of the Hebrew Scriptures for the first time, or an instructor thinking about how to construct an overview course on the subject, may therefore want to consider the project as one that can be broken down into stages in accordance with the internal structure of the corpus itself: On this view, the first order of business will be to gain an understanding of the ideas presented in the History of Israel. Thereafter, the work of retrieving the ideas of the Scriptures continues with the investigation of the major works included in the Orations and Writings – Isaiah, Jeremiah, and Ezekiel; Psalms, Proverbs, and Job – because it is in these works that we find the most developed elaborations of, and arguments with, the standpoint familiar to us from the History. After this we can turn to the minor works, which complete the assembly of perspectives that together present the biblical view of the world.

What Is the Purpose of the Hebrew Bible?

Perhaps the greatest obstacle to reading the Hebrew Scriptures is a widespread confusion over the purposes for which these texts were written. That these purposes are so poorly understood is largely a consequence of the fact that the Hebrew Scriptures have for so long been read in light of the writings of Jesus' apostles in the New Testament. Today, many readers automatically read the aims of the Gospels and of Paul's letters back into the Hebrew biblical texts. And this is the case even if they have not themselves read much New Testament. The apostles' conception of what "Scripture" is all about is simply part of the cultural background in most Western countries, and it's hard to avoid picking it up. This means that if we want to identify the purposes that stood before the eyes of the Israelite prophets and scholars who wrote the Hebrew Bible, these will have to be carefully disentangled from the concerns of the New Testament texts, which were written centuries later and, by and large, with very different aims in view.

In this chapter, my goal will be to do exactly that. I'll begin by trying to get a picture of what it is the principal works of the New Testament were written to achieve. I'll then distinguish these purposes from the ones that can be seen as having motivated the composition of the primary Hebrew biblical work, the History of Israel. Finally, I will consider the purposes of the editors who assembled the corpus of the Hebrew Scriptures as a whole.

I. THE NEW TESTAMENT AS "WITNESS"

For an understanding of the *meaning* of a text, nothing is more important than a view to the author's *purpose* in composing it. It is the intended purpose of the text that imparts a pattern to the whole, from which each of the particular parts of the text, often down to the level of the individual words, derive their specific meanings.[1] Change what you suppose to be the purpose of a given text to any significant degree, and you immediately find you've altered the meanings of the words as well. By contrast, we can often make quite radical changes in what we take to be the identity of a text's author, the date of its composition, and the circumstances under which it was composed, and yet have only a marginal effect on the meaning of the text – except, of course, to the extent that these facts affect the way we understand the purpose for which it was written.

A homely example will suffice to make the point. Suppose we have before us a brief text listing foodstuffs of different kinds and in different quantities, as well as instructions for things to be done with them. If we believe that this text was intended as a recipe for preparing a pot pie, we will be quite certain we've understood the meaning of what is written on the page once we see that we can follow its instructions and, in doing so, prepare a meal that at least some would be pleased to eat. Changes of authorship, dating, or the circumstances under which it was composed will have only the most marginal effect on the meaning of the text: We may suspect that this text was composed in the year 2000 CE or in the year 1000 CE; and that its author was a poor commoner or the Queen of England – yet the meaning of the words on the page will remain more or less stable. But the same can't be said regarding the purpose of the document. One need only suggest that this same document was intended to assist in the preparation of a sacrifice in a religious ceremony, or that it is a parable with moral significance, or the encrypted message of a spy reporting on the deployment of an enemy army, and suddenly every aspect of its meaning will be up for grabs. And this is true, even if the author who composed the document and the date of its composition are certain and fixed.

More than anything else, the purpose of a text is what determines its meaning. But as I've said, great confusion obtains with respect to the purpose for which the Hebrew Scriptures were written. It is by now commonly recognized that in reading the Hebrew Bible as a prelude to the New Testament, the fathers of the Christian Church took up an interpretive posture that was not especially conducive to appreciating the original sense of the Hebrew Scriptures.[2] Indeed, as the theologian Paul Ricoeur has candidly written, the result of the imposition of the Christian story on these texts was the introduction of a "mutation" into the meaning of the old Hebrew sources:

> Let us understand this situation well. Originally ... there was one Scripture [i.e., the Old Testament] and one event [i.e., Jesus' coming].... [T]here is a hermeneutic problem because this novelty [i.e., Jesus' coming] is not purely and simply substituted for the ancient letter; rather, it remains ambiguously related to it. The novelty abolishes Scripture and fulfills it. It changes the letter into spirit like water into wine. Hence the Christian fact is itself understood by

effecting a mutation of meaning inside the ancient Scripture. The first Christian hermeneutics is this mutation itself.[3]

Passages such as this one, in which it is admitted that the New Testament "abolishes" the Hebrew Scriptures in their original sense, transforming them into an entirely different substance as Jesus is said to have turned water into wine, are not uncommon these days.[4] But so far as I am aware, there has been little recognition of the fact that this "mutation" of the Hebrew Scriptures into something entirely new and different was achieved *by depriving the old Hebrew texts of the purpose for which they were originally written*. Yet this is precisely what happened. The New Testament texts were composed for a very particular purpose: They were intended, first and foremost, to bear *witness* to certain events that, in the absence of such *testimony*, would be disputed or dismissed. This is a purpose that the texts of the Hebrew Scriptures do not share, and in reading them this way, Christians, and the Enlightenment philosophers who followed their lead, transformed the Israelite texts into something very different from what their authors intended them to be.

Let's take a closer look at the way in which Jesus' followers present their reasons for writing the works collected in the New Testament. Of course, the books of the New Testament are not simple works. The author of any given literary work usually has multiple purposes in mind in composing his text. But some of the author's purposes are more important to him than others, and it is these that have the greatest impact on what it is we find in the text. In the case of the New Testament, the authors of the principal texts of the New Testament were quite explicit about the main reasons for which these works were composed: They tell us that they are intended to bear witness or to serve as testimony to certain events in the life of Jesus of Nazareth. For example, the Gospel of John opens with a declaration that John the Baptist's purpose is to "bear witness" to the coming of God's son into the world, so that others might come to believe that this event took place. As we are told:

> There appeared a man named John.... He came as a witness to testify to the light, that all might become believers through him. He was not himself the light. He came to bear witness to the light.[5]

In the same way the Gospel closes by confirming that it was written by John the Apostle, who was an eyewitness to the events described, and that it is therefore to be taken as reliable testimony concerning the facts it describes:

> Peter looked around and saw the disciple whom Jesus loved following [him]....
> It is this same disciple who attests what has here been written. It is in fact he who wrote it, and we know that his testimony is true.[6]

Likewise, the Gospel of Luke describes Jesus, having risen from the dead, as appearing before his disciples and instructing them that they must go out and tell of what they have seen, as "witnesses to it all":

> [T]here he was, standing among them. Startled and terrified, they thought they were seeing a ghost.... "This," he said, "is what is written: that the Messiah is to suffer death and to rise from the dead on the third day, and that in his name repentance bringing forgiveness of sins is to be proclaimed to all nations. Begin from Jerusalem; it is you who are the witnesses to it all."[7]

And in the book of the Acts of the Apostles, Jesus is reported to have told the disciples that their mission is to "witness for me ... to the ends of the earth":

> [Y]ou will receive power when the holy spirit comes upon you; and you will bear witness for me in Jerusalem, and all over Judaea and Samaria, and away to the ends of the earth.[8]

It is in Paul's letters that this mission of "witnessing for Jesus" is given its definitive form. In the First Letter to the Corinthians, for example, Paul writes that all who are involved in spreading the Christian reports of Jesus' miracles act as "witnesses for God" – witnesses whose principal responsibility, as he understands it, is to relate "the facts" about the life and resurrection of Jesus as they are known to have happened:

> [M]y brothers, I must remind you of the gospel that I preached to you.... First and foremost, I handed on to you the facts which had been imparted to me: that Christ died for our sins ... ; that he was buried; that he was raised to life on the third day ...; and that he appeared to Cephas, and afterwards to the Twelve. Then he appeared to over five hundred of our brothers at once, most of whom are still alive, though some have died. Then he appeared to James, and afterwards to all the apostles. In the end he appeared even to me.

Paul continues and decrees utter doom for anyone who has misreported the facts, for then he becomes a *lying witness*, in which case all is "utterly lost":

> [T]his is what we proclaim, that Christ was raised from the dead.... [A]nd if Christ was not raised, then our gospel is null and void, and so is your faith; and we turn out to be lying witnesses for God, because we bore witness that he raised Christ to life, whereas ... he did not raise him.... [In that case], your faith has nothing in it and you are ... utterly lost.[9]

In these and many similar passages, we encounter a framework for thinking about the events recounted in the New Testament that appears time and again: First, Jesus made claims about being the "Son of God," and about having come into the world to bring men eternal life; and these claims are confirmed by miraculous events, especially his resurrection from the dead after being crucified. Second, witnesses who have heard Jesus speak and have seen these miracles come forward to testify in support of these claims, so that those who are within earshot of the testimony "might become believers." It is these "witnesses" who are understood as being the authors of the New Testament texts themselves. Third, these texts, having been written by those who witnessed the miraculous events in question, serve as testimony so that one may judge the claims being made by Jesus and on his behalf. If the testimony is credible, the claims are supported, and one can and must believe and so gain salvation through Jesus. If one can show that the witnesses are unreliable – that their testimony is inaccurate or internally contradictory – then these claims are no longer supported, and one has no grounds for belief.[10]

Notice that this framework for understanding the New Testament is essentially *juridic* in character – that is, it relies on metaphors drawn from a court of law. Listen to these cadences: *He came as a witness. He attests what has here been written. We know that his testimony is true. You will bear witness for me. I handed on to you the facts. We turn out to be lying witnesses.* The juridic metaphor is central, indeed paradigmatic, to the self-presentation of the Christian texts.[11] It begins with Jesus himself, who speaks time and again in its terms;[12] and continues in the systematic efforts of the Gospels to establish the reliability of witnesses who are thought able to substantiate Jesus' claims. Even the very names given the Christian scriptures come from this same metaphor: The term *testament* derives from the Latin *testari*, which means "to serve as a witness"; and which scholars have associated with the Latin *tres*, three, and *stare*, to stand – that is, from the witness standing as a third party in litigation. Indeed, we may loosely translate the terms "Old Testament" and "New Testament," as the *Old Witnessing* and the *New Witnessing.*[13]

Why were the early Christians so concerned to bear witness to the events surrounding Jesus' life and death? Why establish an entire volume of scripture around such a juridic discourse? The answer is that in the Christianity of the New Testament, everything is made to depend on the question of whether certain events did in fact take place as reported. As Paul emphasizes in the passage above, *"[I]f Christ was not raised, then our gospel is null and void, and so is your faith; and we turn out to be lying witnesses for God, because we bore witness that he raised Christ to life, whereas ...*

he did not raise him." Paul's Christianity thus insisted on an extraordinarily stark dichotomy regarding the facticity of Jesus' resurrection and the other miracles described in the Gospels and in the letters of his apostles. It is all or nothing. Either these miracles happened, precisely as described by the witnesses, or they are liars, and there is nothing to be learned from them. This means that the purpose of the New Testament texts is, fundamentally, to establish that certain events did in fact take place.

The interpretive framework that is established when we read the biblical text as witness or testimony shares a great deal with journalism, which is likewise concerned to establish that certain facts took place on the basis of reliable witnesses. It is for just this reason that the Gospels have so often been called the "Good News" (Greek, *evangelion*), for they are, in a sense, works of reportage. But this framework shares almost nothing – one might even say *nothing at all* – with philosophy. When, after all, do we recall a philosopher seeking to establish that this or that event took place?[14] Socrates speaks constantly of specific instances of cities, of persons, of objects, of events that he has encountered in experience. But for him, all these particulars are only examples. His aim is to use these particular events and particular things to gain insight into general truths. Indeed, for Plato, it is this escape from the particular to the general, to the realm of ideas, that is man's highest end. If we ask what tools philosophy can bring to bear to assist us with settling questions of contingent fact – *Was a given document written by the Queen of England or not? Did Jesus rise from the dead on the third day or not?* – the answer is that philosophy, whose purpose is to attain knowledge of that which holds good in general, can contribute relatively little to answering such questions. A philosopher can tell us what he has learned, on the basis of past experience, regarding the natures of things. But this is only knowledge of what happens in general. To know what happened in fact, one will have to turn to the witnesses – to those who were there and saw it themselves.

I've purposely drawn the opposition between philosophical texts, which are concerned with what happens *in general*, and texts of testimony, which are concerned with what happened *in fact*, a bit too sharply. Plato's dialogues, for example, are entirely narrative in form. That is, they report an endless cascade of contingent facts: *Socrates went to the games. There he met Polemarchus. They spoke of the ideal city.* And so forth. It is possible to read these texts as works of testimony, whose purpose is to tell us the facts about what happened on one occasion or another. In choosing to write dialogues about actual historical figures, Plato does to an extent invite such a reading. And indeed, for some purposes (as when we are attempting to write a biography of Socrates), this is precisely how we do read these texts. Still, we say that these are works of philosophy and not testimony because we suspect that they were written to teach us about the generality of things, and not in order to establish that precisely this and not something else took place. In the dialogues, the events of Socrates' life and death are made to become a lesson in philosophy – and from them we are meant to learn, among many other things, what it is to pursue truth relentlessly in the face of danger and fear, to defend this pursuit nobly, to die for the sake of that for which we have lived.

So a text can serve to witness certain events, and at the same time strive, by its presentation of these events, to teach truths of a general nature – in which case we can call it philosophy despite its narrative form. But notice, especially, the following fact: While Plato's teaching does unquestionably gain in power and poignancy due to its association with the actual life of Socrates, nowhere do we find Plato saying something like *"if Socrates was not executed, then our teaching is null and void ...."* On the contrary, precisely because Plato's works were composed to investigate and provide instruction into matters of a general nature, the facticity of his account is, in many respects, secondary. Much of what Plato has to teach would still be as significant if it were to turn out that the historical Socrates was very little like the one we know from the dialogues. Indeed, we would still have reason to read Plato *as philosophy*, even if it were to turn out that the story of Socrates were all a great fiction.

Why should this not be true of the Gospels as well? Why should Paul insist that *"if Christ was not raised, then our gospel is null and void"*? Could he really have meant that, deprived of their facticity, the Gospels have little or nothing to offer mankind? How could this be?

The answer, it seems, lies in the character of the knowledge that has been given to man by means of the Christian revelation. The knowledge that Jesus was God's only son; that he lived on earth for a time in the form of a man; that he died to atone for man's sins; that he was resurrected; and so forth – all these things are presented in the New Testament as absolutely singular events, things entirely without precedent, and which have had no parallel since. As such, they really do stand beyond the reach of philosophy, which knows nothing but those natures whose character can be gleaned from experience and relied upon to hold in general. The Christian revelation, having no precedent in man's historical experience, and being a singularity without reference to any known nature, is thus, from the perspective of human beings, something that was kept as God's "hidden secret" throughout all generations until suddenly, in a flash, it was "revealed." Precisely this message appears time and again in Paul's writings and those of other New Testament authors:

> [S]urely you have heard how God has assigned the gift of his grace to me for your benefit. It was by a revelation that his secret was known to me.... [Y]ou may perceive that I understand the secret of Christ. In former generations, this was not disclosed to the human race; but now it has been revealed.... [T]o me ... he has granted of his grace the privilege of proclaiming to the Gentiles the good news of the unfathomable riches of Christ, and of bringing to light how this hidden purpose was to be put into effect. It was hidden for long ages in God, the creator of the universe.[15]

> [I bring] not a wisdom belonging to this passing age, nor to any of its governing powers.... I speak God's hidden wisdom, his secret purpose framed from the very beginning.... The powers that rule the world have never known it.... [T]hese it is that God has revealed to us through the Spirit.[16]

In these and similar passages, we are told that the newly revealed teaching of Christ is something that no man could have known before. As the text says explicitly: *In former generations, this was not disclosed to the human race. It was hidden for long ages in God. I speak God's hidden wisdom.* No one, by his knowledge of the workings of the world, could have gained the slightest knowledge of these things. What God chose to keep secret, no human mind could have known even in the most remote fashion.[17]

All of which takes us back to the reason–revelation dichotomy, with which I began my Introduction. In the New Testament, revelation is unapproachable to reason because that which is revealed appears in the world in the form of bare contingent facts – facts that stand alone, without relation to anything that has come before in human experience. Such a revelation is, by definition, opposed to human reason, and can be accepted only as a "secret" and a "mystery."[18]

Paul is right. One cannot disbelieve the facts reported by the New Testament witnesses without losing the crux of the Gospel. This is not because disbelieving these facts would make John or Paul a liar, and we can't learn anything significant from liars. It is because these facts *are* the crux of what the Gospel wanted to tell us. Unlike Plato's dialogues, which strive to impart truths of a general nature, and can thus be studied as philosophy even if the historicity of the events they report is cast into doubt, the New Testament authors went far out of their way to deny the existence of general truths drawn from experience from which the Christian Gospel could in some measure have been inferred; or to which it could be supposed to have much to contribute.

None of this is to say that the New Testament authors did not have additional concerns and aims in composing their texts. The New Testament writings certainly include passages that strive to address the generality of human experience, and so to take positions on questions of philosophical interest. But on the whole, the principal works of the New Testament direct the best part of their energies elsewhere, in keeping with a self-understanding that is essentially juridic in character. The main purpose of the New Testament really is bearing witness to certain events whose occurrence might otherwise be disputed or dismissed. And this purpose would seem to be quite far removed from the study of truths of a general nature – which is to say, from the study of philosophy.

II. THE PURPOSE OF THE BIBLICAL "HISTORY"

The Hebrew Scriptures are often read as though their main purpose, like that of the New Testament, is to bear witness to certain miraculous events. Although it is perhaps becoming less common to hear the "Old Testament" described as bearing witness to the coming of Jesus, there are nonetheless many who continue to suppose that the works of the Hebrew Bible were written to testify to the occurrence of miracles performed by God, including revelation of knowledge miraculously obtained, so that its audience might, through crediting these events, come to believe in the Jewish dispensation. In this way, the Hebrew Scriptures are transformed into a kind of low-octane version of the New Testament, with some body of Jewish religious doctrine – God's existence? His creation of the world *ex nihilo*? His having given the law at Sinai? The coming of the messianic age? – awkwardly substituted for the Gospel of Christ as the hidden "secrets" that God has revealed, confirmed through his miracles, and established for men by way of the testimony of the prophets.[19]

As will already be evident from my discussion in Chapter 1, such a reading of the Hebrew Bible does not seem to me to make much sense.[20] The central text of the Hebrew Bible is the History of Israel, and this work does not present itself as the testimony of a credible eyewitness to miraculous events the Jewish exiles might have been inclined to disbelieve; nor as a work purporting to reveal hidden secrets that God has hitherto withheld from mankind. In fact, quite the opposite is the case. Instead of a witness such as Paul or Peter who gives us his name, tells us who he is, and informs us that he himself saw certain events, the History of Israel presents itself as the composition of an anonymous author (how can an anonymous individual be credited as a reliable witness?) who has gathered together from various sources an account of the history of the Jews.[21] This account is clearly intended to assist in understanding and explaining the horrific events of the recent past: the horrible destruction of the kingdoms of Israel and Judah, of the Temple, and the rape and pillage of the people and their land by the Babylonians. But the author of the History makes no explicit claim to having personally witnessed any of this. Nor is there any particular reason why he should. For the events with which the History is principally concerned – the destruction of the kingdoms – are not miracles, not hidden secrets now revealed. The events with which the History struggles so painfully were known to all.

The same must be said regarding the events of the more distant past that are described in the History of Israel. The final author of the History certainly did have works by earlier Israelite writers, prophets, and scholars whose accounts he incorporated into his own.[22] In preparing his text, he obviously had to distinguish those materials he thought were more reliable from those that were less so. Yet as a rule, he does not name his sources, or emphasize that they were themselves eyewitnesses to the events described, or in any other way try to establish that their testimony is particularly to be trusted.[23] He didn't need to: Most of what he wrote was adapted or copied from books or traditions with which educated Jews were at least broadly familiar. Like all texts from the distant past, these various works were considered reliable by some, less reliable by others. But no one would have felt a need to ask the author of the History to produce more credible witnesses to back his account of events. His History was a sharpened and elaborated retelling of a story that they had, in many respects if not in most, already heard before and accepted.

This makes it sound as though the History of Israel was not a revolutionary work when it first appeared. But this is obviously wrong. The History was a revolutionary work, one that reframed the way Jews and others thought about the history of Israel and, indeed, the purpose of Israel in the world, forever. No book has approached its impact on the history of mankind, before or since. But the revolution brought about by the History was not attained – as was the influence of the New Testament – by bringing its readers the good news about miracles they'd never heard of before; or about God's secrets, long hidden and now finally revealed. Its impact was attained in providing a broken people with a comprehensive understanding *of what the history of the world was all about, of the role of the Jews in this story, and of why they should resist the decree of history and continue their work so that a blessing might come to them and to all nations.* Moreover, it provided them with instructions as to *how* to continue their role in this story, if they so chose. None of this depended on bringing witnesses or testimony, because what was at issue in the History was not principally the facts of what had happened. What was at issue was rather *how to understand what had happened, and how to live in light of what had happened.* And for this enterprise, witnesses just aren't all that helpful.

Let's try to get a clearer view of the purposes that stood behind this effort of understanding the historical events leading up to the destruction of Jerusalem, and the prescription of a certain way of life in response to them.

The History of Israel is a text of extraordinary breadth, treating many different subjects. Yet the great number of its interests does not prevent the History from having certain central issues that seem to be kept firmly in view over the course of the narrative as a whole. I'll discuss a number of these in the coming chapters. But right now I would like to focus on just one of them – the one that I suspect is the key to understanding what brought the author of the final version of the History to compose the work we have before us today. This is the question of whether the Jews who had been exiled into Babylonia and Egypt would survive as a historical people, or whether they would take up the ways of the surrounding peoples and quickly disappear.[24] He had good reason to think that this is exactly what might happen. The great empires of Mesopotamia had made a specialty of erasing peoples from the face of the earth. The Assyrians, who had destroyed the kingdom of Israel in 722, had made a policy of forcibly assimilating the people they conquered, scattering them throughout their empire in an attempt to make of them a single, undifferentiated people.[25] And this policy had been as successful when applied to Israel as it was with others. In the course of a mere century and a half, the people of the northern kingdom had been absorbed so completely into the surrounding peoples among whom they were exiled that they were already well on their way to disappearing into legend – the legend of the "lost tribes" of Israel.

That such could easily be the fate of the exiles from Judah is a fear that is palpable in the biblical texts. The book of Jeremiah, for example, records a debate between the prophet and the Jewish exiles in Patros in upper Egypt, in which they argue that the worship of foreign gods could have protected Jerusalem from destruction – and inform Jeremiah that now that they have been sent into exile, they will certainly pursue the worship of foreign gods.[26] It seems that many Jews were making arguments of this kind, amounting to a one-way ticket to disintegration and disappearance. Jeremiah, Ezekiel, and the other great leaders of the exiles could see what was coming, and the text of the History is throughout concerned to make the case for a rejection of foreign customs and a return to Jewish ways as holding the key to the ultimate restoration of Jerusalem and Judah.[27]

The History of Israel was thus a work conceived in an effort to staunch the hemorrhaging of the community of exiles as they sought solace in foreign ways. In this sense the purpose of the History is to build a nation in the midst of exile.[28] But this formulation is too simple. I said earlier that a sophisticated text can be composed with a number of different purposes in view, and this is certainly true of the History, which can be seen as pursuing its project on different levels. At one level, the text obviously aims to be a single repository of memory, to which men and women could turn to remember what had been and what had been lost. In reading and rereading the story of their forefathers, unrivaled in the sagas of the surrounding nations, the Jews could discover a source for national pride, and thus a reason to hold fast to their national identity.[29] Yet the History is not merely an account of past glories. It is also an account of repeated successful returns from past exiles and other tragedies, whose aim is to prepare the Jews for their ultimate return to their land.[30] The emphasis on the Jews' return to Israel after the hardships of exile in Egypt and Babylonia is emphasized time and again: first in the time of Abraham, then in the time of Jacob, then in the time of Joshua – each time reinforcing the belief that return is possible.[31] In this story, Moses himself is portrayed as the archetypal exilic figure, and the very model of right behavior for a Jew in Egypt or Babylonia. Standing at the threshold of Canaan, he will not himself enter the land. But he is responsible for teaching Israel their history and their law, and for preparing the way for the next generation to go back and found the kingdom anew.[32]

In a way, it is easy to read the History as a political work. And in a certain sense, at least at first glance, the History's theological concerns can be seen as no more than an extension of its political aims. In the ancient Near East, there were plenty of national or tribal gods who helped particular peoples fight their battles, and who were understood to have turned their backs on the nation in anger when defeat and tragedy struck. A nation or tribe that had been spurned in this way sought to placate its god, and in so doing, return him to their side. In this context, the biblical History's call for the Jews to return to the ways commanded by the God of Israel, and thereby regain something of their own lost glory, looks much like the kind of interpretation of political events that any idolater belonging to the surrounding nations might have proposed.[33]

But while such a reading is not in all respects mistaken, I do think it misses what is perhaps the central point around which the teaching of the History turns. It is only when one realizes that the History of Israel understands the God of Israel not only as the benefactor of this or that nation, but as creator of the entire earth, whose concern is for the good of all his creatures, that certain extraordinary qualities of what this text was written to achieve begin to come into view. For if the God of Israel is indeed the god and benefactor of all the earth, then his actions, commands, and pronouncements, unlike those of the other tribal or national gods known to the ancient world, must in some way be a reflection of that which is good, not only for this or that nation, but for all mankind.[34] The attempt to gain insight into the will of the God of Israel ceases, in other words, to be an attempt to gain insight into what will be good for the Jews alone, and becomes an investigation into the nature of the moral and political order in general – an investigation of the kind the Greeks gave the name of *philosophia*.[35]

Let's look a bit more closely at the relationship between the political purpose of the History and its broader theoretical project of attempting to understand the nature of the moral and political order in general. As I've said, the political problem that stands constantly before the eyes of the final author of the History is the threat that the Jewish exiles in Babylonia and Egypt will simply disappear as a people. And the question posed by this looming catastrophe is whether there is, really, any *reason* for the Jews to resist the decree of history, reject the local customs of the lands in which they now live, and work for the restoration of their city and their nation. Put a little less delicately, the question is this: In a world filled with nations, many of them much older and more powerful than the Jews, what possible reason could there be to strive for the collective survival of these refugees, whom Moses pointedly calls "the smallest of peoples,"[36] and for the restoration of their small kingdom in the land of Israel?[37]

The answer that the History of Israel proposes for this question is breathtaking in its audacity: The History suggests that *the Israelite cause is worthy because it is, in fact, the cause of all mankind.* A précis of this view appears near the beginning of Genesis in the first sentences with which the books of Moses introduce Abraham, the first Jew. As God tells Abraham:

> Get you out of your country, from the place you were born, and from the house of your father, to the land I will show you. And I will make of you a great nation, and I will bless you and make your name great, and *you will be a blessing.... [I]n you will all the families of the earth be blessed.*[38]

Thus the father of the Jewish people is introduced to us as a man who will somehow be a "blessing" to all the peoples on the earth, with the implication that Abraham's people will somehow bear this blessing with them for all nations. This message appears again a few pages later in the crucial story in which Abraham presumes to challenge God's justice in his treatment of Sodom. There, we have God saying:

> And Abraham will surely become a great and mighty nation, *and in him all the nations of the world will be blessed.* For I know him, that he will command his children and his household after him, that they might keep the way of the Lord, doing righteousness and justice.[39]

In this passage, as well, it is suggested that the Jews will bring a blessing to all nations, but here this suggestion is linked to the fact that Abraham is a man who understands the nature of righteousness and justice; that he will know how to pass these things on to future generations; and, in the subsequent story, that he possesses the uncanny willingness to challenge even God's own judgments.

I will not here go into the question of how, precisely, Abraham's descendants are supposed to bring about the change for the better in the fortunes of mankind that is alluded to in these passages.[40] Showing how this is possible is the theoretical project undertaken by the History as a whole, and I will treat aspects of it when I look at the moral and political philosophy of the History in Chapters 4–5. What is important for present purposes is that the question of why the Jews should see themselves (and should be seen by others) as bringing a blessing to the nations of the world is not a matter of passing interest in the biblical narrative. It is the subject of focused attention no later than the fourth chapter of Genesis,[41] with the division of mankind into two theoretical types: that of the farmer, Cain, who represents tradition-bound and idolatrous societies such as Egypt and Babylonia, whose highest value is obedience; and that of the shepherd, Abel, who stands for the spirit of freedom in search of that which is the true good. Abel is not a Jew, of course. What the image of the shepherd represents in the History is a *general* type – a type of individual, and a type of society, that is willing to forsake the might and riches of the great civilizations for the sake of personal freedom and the hope of something higher.[42] In Abraham, the first Jew, this shepherd ideal is merged with an extraordinary political ambition: to extend the moral order represented by the shepherding ideal to the life of an entire nation. Should this prove to be possible, it will be the Jews' gift to the whole world.

It is this theoretical posture, which sets forth a political program founded on a general conception of what constitutes the best life for individuals and for nations, that is the basis for the History's argument that the Jews as a people have reason to resist the decree of history and try to restore their kingdom.

I've said that the New Testament presents itself as the "revelation" of secrets long kept hidden by God. As should be evident on the basis of what I've said so far, the biblical History takes up a posture that is almost diametrically opposed to this. The story it tells suggests time and again that Israel stands for a certain way of life, and a certain way of looking at the world, that are *no secret at all* – indeed, that have been available since the moment man set foot on the harsh soil outside Eden. Abel, after all, needed no revelation of any secrets in order to gain God's favor.[43] Neither did Noah, who was able to become a "just man, innocent in his generations" without any instructions from God.[44] Nor did Abraham receive instructions from God as to how to live, yet God loved him because he believed Abraham would "command his children and his household after him, that they might keep the way of the Lord, doing righteousness and justice."[45] And the History provides us with many additional examples throughout, including the emergence of laws that are from God and known to the nations even before the time of Abraham.[46]

The law that Moses brings down from Sinai is not, therefore, the revelation of a secret that has been withheld from man. Quite the opposite, in fact. When God is depicted as speaking to Moses, what he is saying is an articulation of what has been known, at least in part, all along. Far from claiming to have privileged insight into inscrutable secrets, Moses presents his law as being precisely what the other nations of the world should readily be able to recognize as "wisdom," "understanding," and "justice":

> This is your wisdom and your understanding in the eyes of the peoples, who will hear all these laws and will say, "What a wise and understanding people is this great nation!" ... [For] what nation is so great that it has laws and ordinances so just as all that is in this teaching [*tora*] that I have given before you this day?[47]

Similarly, the non-Israelite prophet Bilam, who represents the view of a gentile "whose eyes are open,"[48] is depicted as looking upon Israel living in the desert in accordance with Moses' law, and immediately recognizing that their ways represent goodness and the life of the just:

> How can I curse whom God has not cursed? ... From the mountaintops I see him [i.e., Israel], and from the hills behold him.... Let me die the death of the just, and let my end be like his! ... [God] has blessed, and I cannot reverse it. He has beheld no iniquity in Jacob, and has seen no perversity in Israel.... How goodly are your tents, O Jacob, your dwelling places, Israel! Like winding brooks, like gardens by the river's side. Like aloes that the Lord has planted, and cedar trees beside the waters.[49]

Bilam's exclamation – *"Let me die the death of the just, and let my end be like his!"* – permits us to see how the biblical authors think the Mosaic teaching would be regarded by anyone, Israelite or not, if only he were able to set aside custom and prejudice and evaluate the matter on its merits.[50]

The early rabbinic commentators were quite radical on the question of whether God's law is, in principle at least, accessible to all men, suggesting that in fact Abraham, Isaac, and Jacob could have observed the law of Moses even without having been present at Sinai;[51] and that the law of Moses was not unique to the Jews, but had actually been offered to many nations before Sinai, but that only the Jews had chosen to accept it.[52] But this hyperbole is designed to make a point not very far removed from what is already there in the text of Genesis or Numbers or Deuteronomy: the point that the Mosaic teaching, despite being God's word, is not supposed to be something too wondrous for human minds to understand, and which could never have been known but for God's special grace. Rather, the Mosaic teaching is supposed to capture that which the human mind, if it is thinking straight, *should* be able to understand.[53] It is this view of the law that finds expression in Moses' own description of his teaching in Deuteronomy:

> That which is hidden belongs to the Lord, our God, and that which is manifest is for us and for our children forever, to do all that is in this teaching [*tora*]....
> *For this command that I command you today is not a wonder to you, and it is not distant....* For the thing is very near to you, in your mouth, and in your mind, to do it. See, I have given before you this day, that which is life and the good, and that which is death and evil.[54]

In this passage, Moses himself is reported as insisting that his teaching is *not* of the "hidden things," and that it is *not* "a wonder to you," but something that is, on the contrary, manifest and very near, presenting that way which brings "life and the good."

It bears emphasizing that in speaking of his teaching as capturing that which holds the key to "life and the good," Moses makes no reference whatsoever to an afterlife, or to an eternal soul, or to some realm or world other than this one. He speaks only of those things that constitute good and evil for men *in this world*. That is, his teaching is explicitly presented as a teaching concerning that which brings about "life and the good," and that which brings about "death and evil," in our own lives. No wonder, then, that the nations, upon examining the Mosaic law, are supposed, of their own abilities, to be able to judge the law correctly. This derives directly from the fact that the subject of the Mosaic teaching is that which brings life and the good in this world – precisely that concerning which human reason should, if it is working right, be able to make some progress.

My conclusions concerning the purpose for which the History of Israel was written, then, are as follows. The History was written in a specific time and place, in the hope of achieving a desperate political purpose – namely, preventing the disappearance of the Jewish exiles as a people, and preparing them for the long struggle to return to their land and restore their city and their kingdom. At the simplest level, then, the History is a work whose aim is to bring the Jews of the exile to reject foreign gods and return to the God of Israel and his law, so that they may have a hope of returning to their land. But this immediate purpose is only the beginning, providing the impetus and literary framework for a much broader theoretical investigation leading to a general account of the nature of the moral and political order. The History's larger purpose is this investigation of the moral and political order; and the provision of a general account of why "life and the good" have escaped the nations, and of how mankind may attain them nonetheless. In the History, this general account and the cause of the Jews of the exile are intertwined to create a single, breathtaking whole – with the general account of mankind's moral and political predicament permitting the broader significance of the Jews' immediate political cause to come into view. It is this dual purpose, constantly in view as the History unfolds, that permits this work to transcend the concerns of the Jews of Babylonia and Egypt who were its immediate audience, speaking in a remarkably lucid voice to Jews in all times and places, and to individuals and nations to the ends of the earth.

III. THE HEBREW SCRIPTURES AS A TRADITION OF INQUIRY

In the last section, I considered the purposes that appear to have guided the composition of the History of Israel in its current form. I would like now to look at what stood behind the assembly of the broader anthology of works that is the Hebrew Bible as a whole. As discussed in the last chapter, the second half of the Bible provides us with two compilations of works, fifteen works assembled in the Orations of the Prophets and another eleven in the Writings. Their diversity of form and content suggests that no specific purpose will be found that is common to all of these works. But I think it is possible to say something about the general purpose that stands behind them as a collection.

In some respects, the speeches preserved in the Orations are even broader in their interests than the History, venturing deep into questions of psychology and epistemology arising from the problem of why it is so difficult for men to recognize the true and the good.[55] Nevertheless, it is also the case that the Orations stand in a very intimate relationship with the History of Israel.

The History, after all, is written, in no small part, to honor the memory of
the minority of Israel's prophets, who saw that the destruction of the kingdom could really come, and were willing to warn king and people at great
risk to themselves – and even at the price of their lives.[56] And it is written as
though the teachings of this minority among the prophets are the basis for
its own understanding of the world, even if the views of particular prophets
are at times quite at odds with those of the History. The Writings are a looser
compilation, wandering much further afield in terms of subject matter. And
yet even here the commonality of subject matter with the History remains
visible: Proverbs is in many respects a work on ethics, presenting arguments
concerning the manner in which moral precepts relate to life and the good; Job
investigates the reasons good individuals (and, by implication, good nations)
should suffer catastrophe; Esther seeks an account of how God's will works in
political circumstances in which one sees nothing but the decisions and deeds
of human actors; and so forth. Thus there is hardly a work in the Orations and
Writings that does not relate in more or less direct ways to questions raised by
the History's effort to provide an account of the moral and political order.

In addition to this broad unity of themes, one can also discern a pattern
in what is *not* included in the Hebrew Scriptures. For the most part, the
works of the Orations and Writings continue the History's lack of interest
in issues of afterlife, eternal salvation, and, more generally, the revelation of
God's secrets. That is, the biblical works are in general distinctly uninterested in speculation concerning some "other" world, or some "other" life,
retaining a tight focus almost throughout on trying to attain knowledge and
wisdom about the ways of the present world.[57] One may wish to say that
an exception is the prophets' interest in describing the future state of the
world, once humanity has been delivered from its moral and political barbarism, since this takes readers into a sphere in which reason is irrelevant, and
what is revealed has to be accepted on faith, just as in the case of promises
concerning the afterlife or eternal salvation. But I don't think this is entirely
right. The fact that the prophetic visions about the future condition of the
world contradict one another so sharply, and that the compilation purposely
juxtaposes these conflicting visions with one another (as the compilers of
the Talmud would later do in their own treatment of the subject), strongly
suggests that at least the editors of the Bible, and perhaps even many of the
prophets themselves, did not view this aspect of their oratory as issuing in
unequivocal statements of what necessarily had to happen. Instead, these
texts appear in our Bible as alternative visions of the ideals toward which
the world of men is moving, and of the catastrophes that our failures may
yet bring upon us along the way.

Precisely this multiplicity of perspectives among the authors of the Hebrew Bible is the subject of Paul's famous charge that God spoke to the prophets of Israel only "in fragmentary and varied fashion," whereas in the New Testament he has finally spoken clearly and univocally.[58] But it seems the editors of the Hebrew Scriptures were not troubled by the fragmentary and varied fashion of our understanding of God's word. The fact is that man's mind is limited, and his understanding only partial. The biblical narrative makes this point unequivocally with respect to Moses, in reporting that he could not see God's face, but only his back.[59] And it was no less true of the other prophets of Israel, who saw things in different ways because each of them was limited in his understanding, and to his own point of vantage.[60] On this understanding, an unequivocal revelation such as Paul apparently believed he had experienced would have been considered unlikely indeed.

These observations point to a very specific purpose for the Hebrew Bible as an anthology of works. If the understanding of each of the biblical authors is understood to be only partial, then the reader's approach to the truth will, of necessity, have to be by way of a number of different viewpoints. If this is right, then the purpose of the biblical editors, in gathering together such diverse and often sharply conflicting texts, was not to construct a unitary work with an unequivocal message. It was rather to assemble a work capable of capturing and reflecting a given *tradition of inquiry* so readers could strive to understand the various perspectives embraced by this tradition, and in so doing build up an understanding of their own. In this tradition, the History of Israel is given pride of place. But the other texts gathered around it are each given their own chance to extend, elaborate, and provide an alternative vision. What is created is a space in which a certain discourse arises, and a search for truth that is, in effect, unending.[61] The reader who takes up the Hebrew Bible is thus invited and challenged to take up a place within this tradition of inquiry, and to continue its elaboration out of his or her own resources.

3

How Does the Bible Make Arguments of a General Nature?

In the Introduction, I suggested that most or all of the works in the Hebrew Scriptures are more readily understood if read as works of reason rather than works of revelation. This is a view that will strike many as counterintuitive, if only because when we think of "works of reason," we think of works written to advance theses concerning the way the world is *in general*, beyond the experiences of any given individual or nation. And most of the biblical texts just seem to be of the wrong genre for making such arguments: More than two-thirds of the Bible consists of narrative prose recounting histories or stories. And narratives seem, by their very nature, to deal with the contingent and the particular. Similarly, the orations in the books of the prophets report to us about particular things that God or individual prophets said or did in response to specific historical events that took place in Jerusalem or Babylon. The specificity of these texts seems to rule out any real possibility that they were intended to engage a tradition of discussion about subjects of a general nature.

In this chapter, I will argue that the suspicion that the biblical texts are unable to advance theories or arguments of a general nature derives from a lack of familiarity with the way in which the biblical authors present such arguments. In fact, the biblical authors did develop methods for overcoming the limitations of narrative and oratory so as to be able to express themselves on general questions, just as the early Greek philosophers adapted the forms of poetry and stage dramas to the needs of their philosophical investigations. In what follows, I will describe some of the techniques employed in the Bible for this purpose, looking first at (i) the biblical mode of argument as it finds expression in the narratives, and then at (ii) the prophetic orations. I'll close with a discussion of (iii) the way in which the legal material included in the History of Israel – the law of Moses – fits into the larger pattern of argumentation in the History and in prophetic oratory.

I. INSTRUCTIONAL NARRATIVE

The great majority of the Hebrew Bible consists of narrative works, including the History of Israel, parts of Jeremiah, Jonah, Job, Ruth, Esther, Daniel, Ezra and Nehemia, and Chronicles. Two considerations, both commonly voiced, make it seem unlikely that the biblical narratives are concerned to advance clear theoretical positions that could be compared to those one finds in the writings of the Greek philosophers. On the one hand, it is argued that the ambiguity inherent in all but the crudest forms of narrative make the biblical histories and stories a hopelessly imprecise instrument for conveying ideas.[1] For example, the Bible scholar John Barton, who pioneered the academic study of the ethical thought of prophetic oratory, throws up his hands when it comes to understanding the ethical standpoint of the biblical narratives. His reason is that the narrative form of works such as Genesis and Judges makes it impossible to know what the author of such a work thought about the events depicted in the text. As he writes:

> Clearly some very complex problems are involved in using [biblical] stories as a source for ethical material.... [T]he fact that the ethical material is embedded in literary *narrative* is itself a severe handicap.... [W]here a writer as reticent as the "Yahwist" is concerned, one can hardly say with assurance how he viewed the actions of his characters – whether with approval, disapproval, or benign indifference.[2]

On this view, one simply cannot know what the biblical author thought about a story such as, for example, Jacob's stealing his older brother Esau's blessing from his father Isaac, now blind and on the verge of death. The author of this story may well have approved of Jacob's doings, thinking it morally justified given Esau's brutish character and apparently amoral behavior. Or he may have been appalled, and included the story in the narrative as an example of immoral behavior. Or perhaps he neither approved nor disapproved of Jacob's trickery, considering it simply an exploit by a "larger-than-life figure" in whom the reader "is to see the great past of the nation, when the divine purposes were achieved by men and women who did things which would hardly be permissible or possible in the reader's own day."[3] There's just no way to tell, because narrative literature is, by its nature, too imprecise to give clear expression to the ideas of its authors.[4]

A competing view, on the other hand, suggests that narrative is actually *superior* to abstract theoretical discourse in conveying ideas, for the simple reason that it deals in the fine-grained, complex, and infinitely variable situations that we encounter in real life. The philosopher Martha Nussbaum, for example, quotes approvingly from Henry James, whom she sees as proposing that narrative works are better equipped than philosophical treatises to conveying the truths that emerge under particular and concrete circumstances. As she puts it:

> [C]ertain truths about human life can only be fittingly and accurately stated in the language and forms characteristic of the narrative artist. With respect to certain elements of human life, the terms of the novelist's art are ... perceiving where the blunt terms of ordinary speech, or of abstract theoretical discourse, are blind ... [,] drawn from the concrete and deeply felt experience of life in this world and dedicated to a fine rendering of that life's particularity and complexity. His [i.e., James's] claim is that only language this dense, this concrete, this subtle – only the language (and the structures) of the narrative artist, can adequately tell the reader what James believes to be true.[5]

This is, in a sense, almost the precise opposite of the view expressed by Barton above. On this view, the actual circumstances of life are complicated, and the devil is in the details. Clean theoretical constructions are inept at reaching the truths that are relevant to real-life situations precisely because they abstract from the details that alone can lead us to the answers we're looking for. But narrative, because it is tailored to the representation of the relevant detail, is capable of both preserving the ambiguity inherent in all real-life situations and of taking a standpoint with respect to them.

Notice that both of these positions – both that which sees narrative as too ambiguous to convey a clear point of view and that which sees narrative as being exquisitely capable of defining a standpoint with respect to the fine-grained, the concrete, and the particular – militate against the view that the narrative form can be well suited to the handling of abstract conceptual schemes such as those familiar from philosophy. Consequently, both leave us suspecting that the biblical authors could not have seen it as an important part of their business to present arguments of a general nature, since these have to be conveyed using concepts abstracted from the details of time and place. And both, I believe, are mistaken on this score.[6] The biblical authors do possess techniques for using narrative to propose conceptual schemes just as abstract as those that appear in Aristotelian-style treatises with paragraphs that begin, *Now there are three kinds of X.* Let's look at a few of these techniques.

One of the principal means by which the biblical narratives propose schemes of general concepts is by setting up contrasts between two or more biblical figures that come to represent opposed principles or complexes of principles. Such *type contrasts* (also called *typologies*[7]) are initially between particular characters in the narrative, evoked vividly in the details of a contest or conflict between them, and then developed over the course of subsequent generations of characters. These later versions of the conflict often vary considerably in detail. The relevant principles will be presented in different degrees and proportions, as befits a realistic narrative describing new persons and new circumstances. But it is just this variation that permits the contrast between abstract concepts to be liberated from the particularity of the characters with which they are originally associated, sharpened, and made useful for the advancement of a standpoint that transcends the details of time and place.

I've already mentioned one of the most important such type contrasts in the Bible: that which is initially framed by the conflict between Cain and Abel, the first two sons born to Adam and Eve. The narrative in Genesis depicts God as having sent man from Eden to live the life of a farmer, "a servant of the soil" who slaves to bring food from the ground "by the sweat of your brow." And Adam's firstborn son, Cain, does precisely this. He becomes a farmer like his father, and invents the idea of sacrificing to God in thanksgiving for what he has.[8] In this, Cain embodies the virtues associated with the agrarian societies of the ancient Near East: Cain obeys God's instructions; he perpetuates the order inherited from his father; and he exhibits piety to the gods who have created this order. His brother Abel, however, resists the fate that God has decreed for him. He ignores God's decree and becomes a shepherd – a man whose station is elevated in that he lives a life of relative ease, leaving the job of extracting nourishment from the ground to his sheep and goats. Abel thus embodies virtues that are associated with the nomadic societies that were the bane of ancient Near Eastern civilization: He is disobedient, preoccupied with improving his own lot and that of his dependents, and willing to overturn the inherited order to achieve this end. He too sacrifices to God, but in this he follows Cain.[9]

The History of Israel is extraordinarily diligent in developing this initial type contrast between Cain and Abel. God, of course, is depicted as preferring Abel to Cain – a thesis that becomes the basis for the biblical authors' theorizing not only about different human personality types, but also about competing systems of morality, political order, and approaches to God's will. The most important heroes in the History – Abraham, Jacob, Moses, and David – are all shepherds. And although each of these figures is very different from the others, they do in different ways share the same characteristics that we see in Abel. Abraham, for example, leaves his parents' home in Mesopotamia to take up shepherding, stands his ground against the kings who rule about him, and challenges God (in the case of Sodom) over the nature of justice.[10] Moses, too, leaves the Egyptian palace where he was raised to become a shepherd, and is willing to contend not only with kings but also with God himself.[11] On the night of the first Passover, the Israelite slaves are all required to slaughter a sheep and smear its blood on their doorposts to prove that they, too, have gone over to the side of the "shepherds."[12]

There is much more to be said about the type contrast between Cain and Abel. In this book, Chapters 4–5 will examine some of the ethical and political implications of the initial version of this contrast in Genesis and its subsequent development in the History of Israel. Chapter 8 will develop further some of the ways in which this contrast unfolds in the area of man's relationship with God. But for our purposes here, it suffices to say this: The first telling of the story of Cain and Abel is exceedingly spare, and one is hard-pressed to see it as bearing a great deal of content if it is read on its own, detached from the rest of the narrative. However, when it is recognized for what is – the establishment of a type contrast, which then serves as the basis for repeated rounds of further elaboration as the History progresses – it can be seen to present the initial basis for a sophisticated critique of the systems of thought officially endorsed in Egypt and Babylonia, and for the presentation of an alternative set of positions that the History wishes to associate with Israel.

I would like to devote a bit more attention to a second example of such a type contrast, one that I don't discuss in detail in the rest of this book (much as such attention would be warranted). This is the type contrast that is established in Genesis by the contest for leadership that develops among five of Jacob's twelve sons: the four oldest sons of Jacob's first wife, Leah – Reuven, Shimon, Levi, and Judah; and the oldest son of Jacob's second wife, Rachel – Joseph. The struggle for predominance among the five young shepherds extends, in its initial telling, over one-third of Genesis,[13] with each son representing a complex of characteristics and values associated with a politics of a certain type: Reuven, the protectiveness, sentimentality, and foolishness of the first born; Shimon, the tendency to assert leadership through violence; Levi, the relentless insistence on justice and purity in all things; Judah, the capacity to correct one's course and reestablish moral principle despite personal weakness and error; and Joseph, the unmatched capacity to manipulate power in the service of some end.[14]

I have said that each of these characters represents a complex of characteristics, and the thumbnail sketches I've just now presented don't do justice to these figures except as a very first approach. For example, Joseph's character is disfigured by arrogance. His shockingly self-important dreams disturb his family, and the way he plays on his father's love for him is troubling as well.[15] Yet Joseph's relationship with his father is not merely a scheme to gain power within his family. His desire to be of service to Jacob is genuine and intense, and he has the abilities to make good on this desire as well. Both of these qualities set him apart from his brothers, all of whom are portrayed as stumbling badly on matters of loyalty to their father.[16] On the other hand, Joseph's burning desire to excel in the service of his superiors is not directed only at Jacob. He excels equally in his service of Potifar, the Egyptian captain who buys him as a slave; then of the master of the Egyptian prison into which he has been cast; and finally of Pharaoh.[17] Joseph's capacity to adapt himself to the needs of his master, which is unmistakably depicted as a great virtue, is thus shown to be a two-edged sword. For it is Joseph's seemingly boundless ability to advance Pharaoh's interests that is blamed, in no small part, for the fact that the Israelites, whom Joseph brings down to Egypt to save them from famine, never leave Egypt again. Joseph is indeed unmatched in his capacity to manipulate political power in the service of some end. But too often it seems as though for him the end in question is dictated by considerations of political expedience, and not something higher than this.[18]

All five of the contending brothers are complicated characters in just this way. But this complexity doesn't prevent the History from making them the basis for a type contrast that can be used in advancing abstract arguments. Here, too, the five contrasting characters serve as the basis for round after round of development later in the History. For example, the brothers Shimon and Levi seem, at first, to be Joseph's opposites. When their sister Dina is raped, they push their father Jacob aside as the decision maker, and massacre the locals whom they see as having been accessories – an act of excessive zealousness undertaken against Jacob's will. In this story, as in the subsequent selling of Joseph into Egypt, their fanaticism in the service of what they perceive to be justice is shown as cutting against the loyalty to their father's concerns that Joseph represents.[19] But once Pharaoh is Joseph's master, the picture changes considerably. Joseph, we learn, goes as far as he can to accommodate himself to Egyptian norms of behavior, whereas when his brothers arrive in Egypt they insist on their identity as shepherds, deploying their accustomed intransigence to defending the honor and integrity of their family's way of life.[20] Just as Joseph's tendency to look for a beneficial accommodation seems misdirected when harnessed in the service of the king of Egypt, the impulse to purism and confrontation that Shimon and Levi represent now becomes a significant asset. Indeed, as the narrative emphasizes, Moses' father and mother are both Levites, and it is this Levite inheritance that finds expression in Moses' willingness to kill one of Pharaoh's servants in what he sees as a just cause – at one stroke throwing away his position in Pharaoh's court and placing his own life in jeopardy.[21] Similarly, it is the Levites who, at the golden calf, take up the sword and massacre three thousand of their idol-worshiping brothers at Moses' behest.[22] And when the Israelites take up public fornication with Moabite women sent to turn Israel to idolatry, Pinhas ben-Hofni, from the Levite leadership, impales the head of the tribe of Shimon, Zimri ben-Salu, with a spear through the belly, together with his new girlfriend.

It is at this point in the narrative that the Levites are finally recognized as being too radical in their idealism to be able to rule men wisely: God awards them the priesthood in perpetuity,[23] but they are to be awarded no tribal territory in Israel, being scattered throughout the land.[24] In the end, the History sides with the view that Levitical extremism is a virtue without which Israel would never have left Egypt. But it is nonetheless best to leave such extremism without control over territories, populations, and armies.

And what of Shimon? Even in the famous curse Jacob calls down upon their heads on his deathbed, Shimon's fate is still indistinguishable from that of Levi. "Instruments of cruelty are their swords," says Jacob of the two of them. "Let not my soul come into their councils, and to their assemblies let not my soul be united.... I will divide them in Jacob, and scatter them in Israel."[25] And the tribe of Shimon, like that of Levi, is indeed scattered. The portion of the land of Israel that is given to his tribe is said to lie within the boundaries of the tribe of Judah, so that Shimon, too, is effectively deprived of being able to rule over any part of Israel.[26] Here, however, the similarity in the fate of the two tribes ends. For with the killing of the tribal chief of Shimon, Zimri ben-Salu, by the Levite leader Pinhas, the narrative teaches us that there was always a crucial, if as yet invisible, difference between the two: Levi, as we learn, resorted to extremism and violence out of a yearning for purity and justice; whereas the extremism of Shimon, so closely allied as to be at times indistinguishable, had always been motivated by a lack of moral concern and personal self-control whose emblem is the wild sin of Zimri at Shitim. It is this difficult difference, the History teaches, that distinguishes a well-intentioned zealot whose excesses can be fittingly channeled into the priesthood, from one who is ill fitted for any leadership role and best left out of the public life of the nation entirely.

Other figures in this type contrast are also extensively developed, and in fact they are used to advance a number of the History's most interesting theses with respect to the political order. Ultimately, it is the qualities associated with Judah that are vindicated by the narrative as being most suited for ruling over men, and this despite the fact that Joseph's political abilities (including his abilities in foreign relations, administration, finance, and perhaps warfare as well[27]) are recognized to be superior. Why should this be? In the view advanced by the History, Judah's capacity to make public admission of his own errors, as first evidenced in the story of his illicit liaison with his son's widow Tamar[28] – and then repeated in his willingness to sacrifice himself for his brother Benjamin's sake, in order to not repeat his earlier betrayal of Joseph[29] – is held in the highest regard as a trait to be valued in a ruler. This is not a matter of simple moralizing over the fact that Judah could easily have had Tamar killed to cover up his misdeeds, but chose public humiliation instead so as not to do an injustice. Rather, the ability of the ruler to humble himself and change his ways is seen as the only hope of correcting the direction of the state when it is off course. A ruler who is capable of such correction is thus needed as a matter of political prudence – prudence on which the fate of the kingdom depends. It is leadership of this type that is reflected in the History's portrayal of a number of the kings, but especially in the character of David, and of Hezekiah, who restores the strength of Judah after the fall of the northern kingdom.

David's son Solomon, on the other hand, may be greatly esteemed by the History for his breathtaking gifts in foreign relations, administration, finance, and the physical construction of the kingdom. Indeed, during his reign, Israel is depicted as achieving the utmost that any nation can hope for on this earth.[30] Yet it is precisely Solomon's political genius that is depicted as leading him to embrace alien aims, just as was the case with Joseph: Solomon's marriage to Pharaoh's daughter reminds us of Joseph's marriage to the daughter of a prominent Egyptian priest; Solomon's forced conscription of the population of the land in building projects reminds us of Joseph's enslavement of Egypt; and so on.[31] In the end, Solomon is lacking in the ability of David (and Judah) to see his own errors, and he loses his way just as Joseph did.[32] A similar case is that of Yarovam ben-Nevat, who begins as Solomon's energetic overseer of enforced labor from the house of Joseph.[33] Yarovam's gifts make it possible for him to tear the northern tribes away from Judah and establish an independent kingdom of Israel under the leadership of the house of Joseph. But once he is master of this new kingdom, these very political skills are depicted as his undoing. Yarovam correctly reasons that if he permits the northern tribes to keep sacrificing at the Temple of Solomon in Jerusalem, they may soon be moved to demand reunification with Judah. He therefore sets up golden calves for the northern tribes to worship at two shrines in the northern kingdom. This use of idolatry to manipulate the population's political sentiments works beautifully, ensuring that the split between the two Israelite kingdoms is permanent.[34]

The History thus proposes that leaders of Joseph's type, who swim so strongly in the fetid waters of political power in an idolatrous world, cannot but fall prey to idolatry in the end. It is the usefulness of idolatry, and of reaching an amicable and beneficial accommodation with the surrounding world, that is, for men of Joseph's type, the source of its allure. Political prudence dictates accommodation. So if it is not accommodation that is one's ultimate aim, there must be some degree of imprudence introduced into the equation – imprudence that can be supplied only by men such as Judah or Levi. Nevertheless, the History does not call for the exclusion of leaders such as Joseph from rule, for their abilities are much needed.[35] Rather, the thesis that the History seeks to advance is that for Israel to succeed and prosper, one must have figures of the type of Judah and Joseph working as allies. This alliance is represented by the joint work of Joshua (Joseph) and Caleb (Judah) who together are responsible for the successful conquest of the land, when Israel fought and served God almost as with one heart. It is the successive reigns of David (Judah) and Solomon (Joseph) that were together able to bring Israel to the greatest heights it was ever able to achieve. What might have happened, we are moved to ask, had David had a man of the type of Joseph as his second in command, instead of an individual of wanton violence such as Yoav ben-Tzruia (who plays the part of Shimon in the David narrative)?[36] Or if Solomon had had a man of the type of Judah by his side, rather than Yarovam ben-Nevat? Everything might have turned out differently.[37]

I've tried in this brief discussion to give some sense of the way in which the History of Israel uses the type contrast among Judah, Joseph, Levi, Shimon, and Reuven to establish a scheme of abstract concepts which are then deployed in advancing general arguments. In doing so, I have, of necessity, slighted the literary quality of the narrative, which certainly does not remain satisfied with depicting biblical figures only in terms of their place in such a scheme of abstract types. In fact, the biblical texts are able to do what I cannot do here – they present us with finely drawn characters, each one of which is a unique original with all the lavish particularity that narrative characterization can provide; and, at the same time, show us how these unique figures nonetheless stand as instances of certain human types that appear time and again, thus permitting general arguments concerning the desired moral, political, and religious order to emerge.

The construction of schemes of concepts based on contrasting character types is one of the techniques the biblical narrative uses to establish concepts of a general nature. But there are others as well. A related technique involves the repetition, not of character types, but of certain events across widely scattered intervals in the narrative. These doublings and triplings of events are the subject of a well-known principle of rabbinic biblical exegesis: "The deeds of the fathers are a sign for the sons"[38] – meaning that in the Bible, what has happened will happen again. The biblical stories are understood as being purposely told in such a way as to draw our attention to the fact that events taking place generations apart, and differing from one another in certain crucial details, are nevertheless in some fundamental sense the same. What results from the construction of these *sets of events* from far-flung instances is a generalized account of a certain kind of circumstance – often including both the motives of the individuals involved and the consequences of their actions – which can easily be seen as referring to a thesis of a general nature.

Consider the following example. When Moses disappears up Mount Sinai after the giving of the commandments, the Israelites demand a god and Moses' brother Aaron calls upon the Israelites to give him their gold earrings, which he melts down to make them a golden calf. Similarly, the warrior-judge Gideon, in refusing Israel's demand that he become king over them, also calls upon the Israelites to give him their gold earrings, which he melts down to make a golden fetish to be worshiped in his home town of Ofra. Once we've noticed the biblical author's use of the gathering of the gold earrings to signal that the two events should be read, at least in part, in parallel, we can look further to understand why they should be seen in this way.

Here's my view of it. The sin of the golden calf takes place immediately after the giving of the law at Sinai in Exodus, itself occurring less than two months after the Israelite slaves' escape from Egypt. When the people hear God's voice amid the flames and the blast of the ram's horn on the mountain, they beg Moses to intercede and bring them God's word instead. Moses agrees to this and goes up the mountain alone to hear the rest of God's teaching. But once he's gone, the people seem to lose their minds, telling Aaron: "Rise and make us a god that will walk before us. For as for this man Moses, who brought us up out of the land of Egypt, we know not what has become of him."[39] Aaron collects their gold earrings and makes them a calf of gold, and they go about telling one another, "These are your gods, O Israel, which brought you up out of the land of Egypt"[40] – this despite the fact that no calf (and nothing resembling a calf) has been involved in the story at any point; and despite the fact that the true God has himself just spoken to them and told them not to make a graven image!

This story is so implausible – the ingratitude, ignorance, stupidity, and contempt displayed by the Israelites are all so extraordinary – that one might

be moved to think of it as a one-time deviation from normal human psychology induced either by the ravages of long servitude in Egypt or by the
terror of God's appearance on the mountain. Yet in the story of Gideon in
Judges, we find much the same pattern repeated. The Israelites, now on their
land, have been conquered and forcibly starved by Midian for seven years
before being liberated by Gideon with the help of a series of interventions
on God's part.[41] With the war at an end, the people ask Gideon to be their
king, and for his descendents to rule them thereafter. He refuses, reminding
them that it was not his might that won the war, and that their rightful ruler
is only God. As he says, "I will not rule over you, nor will my son rule over
you. But God will rule over you."[42] This is a noble and rightly famous sentiment. But in the next breath, Gideon asks the people to give over the gold
earrings and other spoils captured in the war against Midian, and uses them
to fashion a gold fetish, "and all Israel whored after it there, and it became
a snare for Gideon for his house."[43]

The repetition of the story, then, permits us to escape the supposition
that the sin of the golden calf was an event unique in human history, and
to recognize that a more general thesis is being offered concerning human
nature, and how it operates under certain kinds of circumstances. Coming
out of a terrifying bondage, a people may believe that what it wants above
all else is freedom. But this is illusion. True freedom – in which a man stands
on his own feet, responsible for his own actions, with nothing but the open
sky between himself and God – *is* in such cases experienced as something
terrifying and even dreadful. What a newly liberated people want more than
anything else, the narrative suggests, *is to have someone above them again*,
someone who can bear responsibility for them so that they do not have to
shoulder this terror and dread themselves. And when this man, this Moses
or Gideon, proves unwilling to play a role so similar to that played by their
recent oppressors, this people will seek something that is more solid than
man, something enduring that will not abandon them in need – the calf, the
fetish.[44] Even leaders such as Aaron or Gideon, who have been the agents
of God's will and know the folly of mistaking anything else for God, are
not less in danger than the people themselves, since their ear is given to
the people's needs and they are moved to give the people what they want,
ostensibly so that they will not do yet worse things. On this view, the act
of liberation carries within itself the seeds of its own destruction, tending
immediately to tear open a void in the lives of those who have been freed
that is most easily filled by idolatry, whether of one form or another.[45]

Similarly, consider the scene in Genesis in which the people of Sodom
pound on the door the Lot's house, demanding that he turn out the strangers

he has put up for the night so they may rape them. Much the same scene appears again at the end of Judges, when the men of the Benjaminite town of Giva pound on the door of a house in which a Levite traveler is staying, demanding that his host turn him out so they may rape him. In the first story, Lot offers his daughters to the mob, but this never takes place; whereas in the second, the Levite does give his concubine over to the mob, letting the men of Giva rape her until she dies. But in both cases, the History uses this scene to suggest that when the maltreatment of strangers, sexual impropriety, and abuse of women in a given place have reached a certain pitch, the society in question can be recognized to be on the verge of actual dissolution.[46]

Or consider Lavan's innocuous-seeming effort to get his sister Rebecca to tarry in Aram for "a few days, at least ten," rather than going immediately to Canaan to marry Isaac.[47] Lavan's attempt to detain Rebecca is repeated years later, in his invitation to his nephew Jacob to stay with him a while in Aram,[48] which ends in the young shepherd's enslavement for long decades; in Pharaoh's not dissimilar displays of generosity to Jacob and his sons, which turn into a lifetime of imprisonment in Egypt;[49] in the prelude to the story of the rape in Giva, just discussed;[50] and yet again in a story of the rival of King Solomon who was raised up in Pharaoh's court.[51] In this set of scenes, the History urges the counterintuitive view that hospitality and protection are in fact a form of rule over others, and that in accepting an offer of hospitality, one takes the first step toward forfeiting one's freedom.[52]

In all these and many other cases, the narrative's construction of sets of events permits the biblical authors to argue for the lawfulness of the world, and to present to us the nature of things as they understand it. Of course, these sets of events are built up out of cases that are never perfectly identical. And often enough the biblical authors do use a nearly identical scene to refer to its predecessor in such a way as to draw a contrast between them, or to register criticism of what took place in the preceding text. For example, it is significant that in the story of the concubine in Giva, it is the leadership of the tribes of Israel that decides to destroy the city, and not God, as was the case in Sodom. This difference is significant in the context of the book of Judges, where the annihilation of virtually the entire tribe of Benjamin in response to what took place in Giva is presented as a wild overreach and an atrocity in itself.[53] But the fact that the stories of Sodom and Giva can be contrasted in this way does not in any way diminish the power of the narrative's general teaching, which is emphasized by the similarity in the way the two cases are described.

I would like to consider one final technique used in biblical narrative for the advancement of substantive arguments of a general nature. The technique I have in mind is the repetition of a certain phrase or word-combination to create a kind of technical language for the expression of precise generalized concepts. A well-known example is the expression "Here am I" (*hineni*), which is used to indicate devotion and readiness to act in response to God's call – often in the face of extraordinary hardship. For example, Moses says *hineni* in response to God's call at the burning bush, immediately before he learns that he is to be sent down to Egypt to confront Pharaoh. But this term does not stand in isolation at this point in the narrative. When the reader comes upon it, he is supposed to remember Abraham saying *hineni* in response to God's call on the day he is told to sacrifice his son; and Jacob saying *hineni* on the day God tells him he must go down to Egypt and into slavery; and the prophet Samuel, as a child, saying *hineni* on the day God tells him that the house of Eli is to be overthrown.[54] But once this term is seen as taking on such precise connotations, it can also be deployed in slightly different ways to bring these connotations to bear on related contexts. Thus when Abraham walks with his son Isaac toward Mount Moria, where God has told Abraham he is to offer him up as a sacrifice, Isaac says to him: "My father," and Abraham responds, "Here am I, my son" (*hineni beni*).[55] It is only because the word *hineni* is used time after time to signify utter devotion to God that we are able to recognize its use in this passage to indicate Abraham's utter devotion to his son. Moreover, in the story of Abraham's binding of his son upon the altar, this term appears three times: Abraham responds to God's first call to him (before the command to sacrifice his son) with *hineni*. Then, during their journey to Moria, Abraham responds to his son's question with *hineni beni*. Finally, as he raises his hand as if to slaughter the boy, Abraham responds to the angel's call with *hineni* before hearing that he should not lay his hand upon the youth.[56] In this way, the expression "Here am I," which is so often used to signify a simple submission and devotion to God, becomes a window into Abraham's mind, permitting us to see that he is in fact being torn apart by conflicting ultimate loyalties that have been pitted against one another.[57]

In the same way, other biblical expressions come through repetition to bear specific connotations that can be deployed as a technical language. Thus the expression "he lifted up his eyes" (*vayisa et einav*) suggests a shift in the character's understanding such that something that was hidden from him is revealed;[58] "he rose early in the morning" (*vayashkem baboker*) designates actions undertaken with focused and even aggressive intent;[59] "wood and stone"(*etz va'even*) refers to taking the concrete and common for a god;[60] "what was just in his eyes"(*hayashar be'einav*) indicates that which appears right by a certain standard;[61] "each under his vine and under his fig tree" (*ish tahat gafno vetahat te'enato*) refers to times of abundance and personal well-being for the nation as individuals;[62] "what does not profit" (*lo mo'il*) refers to those things that are wrong because they do not contribute to man's well-being;[63] and so forth. I suspect that there are hundreds of such phrases, which together permit the biblical authors to describe what appear to be one-time occurrences in the narrative in terms that are both general in nature and extremely precise.

I have described three techniques used by the authors of the biblical narratives for overcoming the putative limitations of the narrative form and adapting their narratives and orations to the needs of discourse concerning subjects of a general nature. In doing so, their stories become what might be called *instructional narrative* – narrative that seeks to investigate and advance ideas concerning the general natures of things, and to teach us, in Leon Kass's phrase, *not what happened, but what always happens.*[64] In this discussion, I have not attempted to be exhaustive. I've only tried to give a sense of the extent to which the claim that biblical texts can't be engaged in careful theoretical discourse due to limitations of literary form derives from simple unfamiliarity with the way the genre of biblical instructional narrative works. In fact, the authors of the Hebrew Scriptures had plenty of tools at their disposal for making their narratives address questions of a general nature. By means of techniques such as those I've described, they are able to make their positions understood in a fashion that is clearly and distinctly spelled out to readers who know what to look for in their texts. They had the tools, and the question is only to determine what it is they did with them.

This view flies in the face of much modern Bible interpretation, which has tended to emphasize the inscrutability and reticence of the biblical authors, and the difficulty of knowing what, if anything, they intended to say about the things that appear in the texts they wrote. If I am right in my appraisal of the abilities, intentions, and achievements of the biblical authors, what accounts for the frequent invocation of biblical inscrutability? One difficulty, I think, has been an unspoken, or even unconscious, assumption that the biblical authors' point of view on subjects of interest to them must necessarily be a primitive one, and that we can't expect to find complexity or sophistication in their works.[65] If it is the ethics of a given text that are under discussion, for example, it is often simply assumed that the author's view of what is taking place in a given passage must be locatable on a map of simplistic categories such as: (i) approves, (ii) disapproves, or (iii) is amused and intrigued but passes no moral judgment.[66] Of course we know that in real life, ethical judgment is in fact much more complicated. People constantly entertain multiple motives, weighing competing concerns against one another and acting in consideration of all of them at a given moment, only to find that the passage of time has forced a shift in their understanding as to the relative weight of the different considerations when another decision point is reached later on. Any good contemporary novelist takes this kind of moral complexity into account. Yet the events depicted in the biblical narratives are assumed to be incapable of reflecting such complexity. Instead, they are supposed to be like the stories of Aesop – little fables that go on for a few lines and then pop out an unequivocal "moral of the story" at the end, before moving on to the next fable.

But the biblical stories are not little fables that go on for a few lines before ending in an unequivocal "moral of the story." In fact, just the opposite is the case. Many of the best-known biblical stories are fraught with moral ambiguity, carefully balancing multiple reasons for approving of what has been done against a no less impressive arsenal of reasons for reaching the opposite conclusion.[67] No amount of poring over the story itself will yield up the standpoint of the narrative towards the characters or their actions, because this standpoint isn't expressed within the confines of the story itself. It is only later – sometimes *much* later – that the standpoint of the author about a given character or event comes to light, as the consequences of the events depicted unfold. For example, one can scour the story of Jacob stealing the blessing from his older brother Esau to one's heart's content, but one will never begin to discern the standpoint of the text concerning this act of deceit until one recognizes that it is recapitulated seven or eight years later when Lavan gives Jacob his daughter Leah for a wife in place of Rachel.[68] This later deception rehearses the earlier one almost exactly, except that the second time it is Jacob, blinded by the darkness of his marital bed, who is the victim of a deception aimed at enforcing the right of the firstborn, rather than the beneficiary of a deception aimed at undermining it. It is only here, when the tables are turned on Jacob, that the actual standpoint of the biblical narrative concerning the earlier deception begins to emerge. By the time his sons deceive him (using animal blood) just as he had deceived his own father (using animal skins) in order to get their own brother out of the way and get their father's favor for themselves, we know this beyond all shadow of a doubt.[69]

Similarly, the story of Shimon and Levi massacring the Shechemites after the rape of their sister Dina will not, when read alone, yield up any unequivocal view as to whether the author understands the bloodshed as having been justified. It is only later, when the violence and the willingness to manipulate their father that appears in this story is repeated in the brothers' plot to murder Joseph, that the author's standpoint with respect to what they did in Shechem starts to become evident.[70] Even the story of Yiftah's sacrifice of his daughter on an altar is not accompanied by authorial censure within the confines of the specific verses that describe it. It is only later, when the butchering of Yiftah's daughter is repeated in the story of the concubine in Giva, that the depravity of Yiftah's deed, and the general collapse of moral norms to which it so lavishly contributed, can be seen in full light.[71]

In the face of these and many other such examples, I think we need to draw a few conclusions. First, it would seem that the inability of contemporary readers to find the biblical teaching in the stories often derives, in significant part, from their attempt to extract a "message" from a brief passage on the assumption that the story was intended to be read as a stand-alone fable or folk tale, rather than as a small piece in a carefully integrated text that must be read as a whole. This is a point emphasized in the talmudic dictum that "The words of the Tora are impoverished in their own place, but rich when read elsewhere."[72] Cut a biblical story out of the context of the events that preceded and followed it, and you immediately lose any ability to understand what it's all about. Second, the fact that there *is* a clear authorial standpoint with regard to what happens in these stories, but that this standpoint emerges only in the context of later events, should tell us something about the way the biblical authors (or some of them) approach the entire issue of moral judgment. It is the consequences, these stories tell us, that ultimately determine the moral quality of a given action. But human beings are exceedingly limited in their ability to foretell consequences. If we are to improve in moral judgment, we will have to learn to look forward to consequences that remain buried in the future, and to withhold judgment as much as possible so long as these have not become known. (I will have more to say on the unfolding of consequences in time in my discussion of the biblical authors' conception of *truth* in Chapters 6–7.)

Third, the fact that a *clear* authorial standpoint can be seen as emerging with respect to the different characters and events does not necessarily mean that a *simplistic* authorial standpoint is what emerges. The initial moral ambiguity that is present with respect to a certain biblical figure or event is rarely, if ever, just a smokescreen that the author, as artist, imposes in order to delay the onset of an otherwise quite black-and-white view to be delivered later. Across a large number of significant questions, the biblical narrative continues carefully to keep the ambiguity of the moral circumstances it is treating fully in view, even after the reader has a pretty good idea of where the text's commitments are. I don't think, for example, that there is much question that the narrative portrays Jacob's having deceived Isaac as a significant moral failing. In a sense, Jacob's entire life is described as being lived in the shadow of this one terrible mistake he made as a young man. And yet the narrative is equally insistent that Jacob was right to resist Isaac's wish that Esau, the firstborn, be his heir. The very name "Israel," which God gives Jacob, is said to mean "you have contended with God and with men and have prevailed" – reflecting the pleasure that God takes, not in Jacob's execrable deception, but in the fact that Jacob has resisted the fate his birth as the second twin had decreed for him.[73] This means that as the story unfolds, Jacob is punished for the way he treated his father and brother, even as the narrative reconfirms that his motives were the right ones, and even shows respect for his willingness to act on these motives. Similarly, the terrible wrong that Shimon and Levi commit in Shechem is condemned and punished.[74] Yet the narrative maintains that the brothers were right both in their desire to punish the rapist and in their rejection of their father's excessive fear of what the people of the land might do to them if they were to take action.[75]

In these and similar cases, the biblical narrative provides us with a clear judgment of particular characters and their actions, but not an unequivocal one. And the same pattern – a clear view, but not an unequivocal one – appears with respect to the more general concepts that the biblical authors deploy, and the arguments they make with them. Thus while the biblical author sees in Abel and in the line of shepherds that follow him the better path for humanity, Cain is depicted as superior to his brother in honoring his father's ways and in piety: It is Cain, after all, who obeys God's decree that man is to work the soil, and who comes up with the idea of offering God a sacrifice of thanksgiving. And indeed, the agrarian societies that Cain represents are seen as honoring the ways of their forefathers, and as careful in their concern to honor the gods as well. Similarly, while Judah, who is able to admit his mistakes and change course, is to be preferred over Joseph as a ruler of men, Joseph is depicted as superior to Judah not only in politics and finance, but also in loyalty to his father and control over his sexual appetites.[76] It is not until Joseph proves incapable of extracting his family from Egypt that we realize that his political and financial skills, great as they are, do not extend to rebellion against his master – even when his master is Pharaoh.[77] For rebellion you need Judah, or even, in truly dire circumstances, the extremism of Levi.

The care with which the biblical narratives draw these contrasting alternatives, distributing virtues and vices among different types and pitting them against one another, may seem to some more literary than philosophical. But

I think this view should be rejected. A great philosopher such as Plato is able, in discussing a scheme of personality types, or regime types, to admit that these different types possess both characteristic virtues and vices. The insistence that all virtue is on one side of a given clash of principles, and all vice on the other, rarely follows from the successful framing of an issue in terms of general concepts, and abstract discourse embarrasses itself when it strikes such poses. That the instructional narratives of the Bible are usually very far from such didacticism is no sign of the inscrutability of their authors, or of their reticence, but of their competence as theoreticians.

II. PROPHETIC ORATION

After instructional narrative, the largest and most significant block of biblical writing is in the form of collections of prophetic orations, amounting to nearly one-fourth of the corpus of the Hebrew Scriptures. In this section, I will touch on some of the characteristic ways in which prophetic oratory presents arguments of a general nature; and some of the obstacles that stand in the way of our reading the speeches of the prophets as works of reason.

From a literary point of view, prophetic oration is a fascinating form, at once both poetry and argument. The orations of the prophets of Israel are written in a style that is charged with evocative imagery and bone-rattling turns of phrase. Part of what has made them literary classics is the rhetorical heights they attain. But at the same time, it is important to remember that the orations of the Israelite prophets are also intended to make an *argument*, a case for a certain view of things or a certain course of action, and that these arguments frequently lead them into an investigation of subjects of general concern. (In fact, the Talmud suggests that those writings of the prophets of Israel that were preserved in the Bible are precisely those that rose to a level of enduring, and not merely local, significance.[78]) This means that despite their interest in making their point, the prophets are also concerned to stake out clear and consistent positions on the subjects they treat – positions that are developed in their public disputations with those who later came to be known as the "false prophets" (who play a role in the Hebrew Scriptures not dissimilar to that played by "the Sophists" in Plato's works), as well as in disagreements among themselves.

In reading the Orations of the Prophets as works of reason, our aim is to bring these positions to light, and this means, first and foremost, making sense of the way in which the prophets use *metaphor*. Metaphor is the mainstay of the Hebrew oratorical style. It is often impossible to advance a line in the Orations without colliding with a metaphoric figure, in which the subject under discussion is analyzed or critiqued by describing it in terms borrowed from what seems to be an entirely different sphere of life. In fact, much of what the prophets have to say is said using such devices, so that the philosophical investigation of the prophetic orations is, to a very large extent, the investigation of arguments delivered by way of such techniques. In principle, this should not pose too much of a problem, as most contemporary readers are familiar with metaphor from the study of literature in school, and their grasp of the way it works is usually intuitive and immediately helpful as they begin examining a prophet's message. But here, too, certain assumptions or prejudices tend to get in the way.

One such prejudice is the supposition that the prophetic use of metaphor and analogy is intended, not as a vehicle for communicating ideas clearly, but rather for obscuring them. In this, the literary tradition of the prophets suffers from being lumped together with later esotericism of the kind one finds in Daniel,[79] and from the influence of the New Testament, which repeatedly presents Jesus as speaking in parables whose meaning is hidden so as to be inaccessible to many or most of those who hear them. For example, the Gospel of Mark tells this story about Jesus invoking the metaphor of a farmer planting seeds while teaching before a large crowd:

> As he taught, he said: "Listen! A sower went out to sow. And it happened that as he sowed, some seed fell along the footpath; and the birds came and ate it up. Some of the seed fell on rocky ground, where it had little soil.... And some of the seed fell into good soil, where it came up and bore fruit; and the yield was thirtyfold, sixtyfold, even a hundredfold." He added, "If you have ears to hear, then hear."

Afterward, Jesus' disciples inquire concerning this use of a metaphor that many in the crowd might not understand, and receive an answer as follows:

> When he was alone, the Twelve and others who were round him questioned him about the parables. He replied, "To you the secret of the kingdom of God has been given; but to those who are outside everything comes by way of parables, so that (as Scripture says) they may look and look, but see nothing; they may hear and hear, but understand nothing; otherwise they might turn to God and be forgiven."[80]

In this and similar passages, Jesus is reported to have informed his students that the purpose of the metaphors he employs is to *obscure* a teaching that is intended only for certain members of the audience – "concealing their intention in such a way that the minds of the impious are either converted to piety or excluded from the mysteries of the faith," as Augustine writes.[81] That some will understand, while many others are left "outside" or "excluded," is thus something to be desired, in keeping with the more general view of God's word as the revelation of secrets long hidden – secrets that, were it not for God's grace, would in any case be known to no one.[82]

As I say, the association of biblical metaphors with parables and riddles provides a part of the explanation for why the prophetic orations of the Hebrew Scriptures seem, to many readers, to be something quite different from reasoned discourse. But here, too, what is involved is the importation into the older Hebrew texts of purposes that are quite alien to them. As far as I can tell, the use of metaphor to obscure God's teaching from certain segments of the population occurs rarely, if at all, in the orations of the prophets of Israel.[83] Indeed, the constant reliance on metaphor in the Israelite prophetic orations seems to have precisely the opposite purpose: Its aim is to make difficult subjects *easier to understand* for the broad audiences to whom prophetic oratory was, in the first instance, intended to appeal.[84] This tendency to look for metaphors that will be readily accessible is evident in just about any prophetic metaphor one may come across, including the way in which the prophets use the metaphor of the farmer planting seeds. Here, for example, is one appearance of the metaphor of the farmer sowing his crop in Isaiah:

> [T]hough you plant pleasant plants …. Though in the day of your planting you can make it grow, and in the morning of your sowing you make it flourish, yet the harvest will disappear in the day of grief and desperate pain.[85]

In this passage, Isaiah uses the experience of a harvest that had flourished initially, and yet which ultimately has come to nothing, to teach one of the most important principles of the biblical ethics: the distinction between an action that *appears initially* to produce good results and one that produces good results *in the end*.[86] Notice, however, that the metaphor isn't intended to obscure something that might otherwise have been clear, but precisely the opposite. An abstract ethical distinction is made accessible to a broad audience by means of an analogy with something with which nearly everyone in Isaiah's day would have been painfully familiar.

Here is another example from Isaiah, who argues that the evildoing of individuals and collectives[87] is to be compared to a fire burning out of control in the forest:

> For wickedness burns like fire: It devours the briars and thorns, and kindles the thickets of the forest, raising up billows of smoke. Through the wrath of the Lord of Hosts is the land darkened, and the people are as fuel to the fire.[88]

Here, too, the metaphor of the fire in the forest is used to advance a substantive thesis concerning the moral realm: Isaiah insists, as he does in numerous other passages, that the reason one should not perform evil deeds is that they cause immediate harm not only to one's victims, *but to oneself and to one's entire nation*. In the metaphor of the fire in the forest, this counterintuitive argument is advanced by means of an analogy that everyone in Isaiah's audience can understand, in that a fire set among dry brambles in the woods cannot damage only a particular victim, but must devastate everything around it, the damage being immediate, inevitable, and automatic, and deriving from the nature of fire itself. Similarly, Isaiah claims that the harm that comes of evildoing is immediate, inevitable, and automatic, deriving from the nature of wrongdoing itself.

I won't now enter into the fascinating questions these passages raise concerning Isaiah's ethics: How does he believe one can distinguish between that which appears to be flourishing and that which flourishes in the end? How does evildoing come to harm oneself and one's nation? For now my point is simply this: In the tradition of prophetic oration, metaphor is not intended to obscure but rather to clarify. It is used to stake out substantive general positions concerning morals and other abstract subjects, positions that are rendered more readily understandable to the audience due to the fact that they are delivered by way of analogies to things they understand well rather than by means of abstract theoretical discourse. By returning to the same metaphor in different ways and from different directions, and by backing up one metaphor or analogy with a second and then a third, the prophetic orator corrects and sharpens his position, ultimately reaching a standpoint that is not necessarily any less precise than what can be said on the same subjects by speaking in non-metaphorical generalizations.

The fact that prophetic oratory consistently aims to advance positions of a general nature by way of arguments framed in terms of analogy and metaphor is something that seems easy enough to verify. Yet modern readers are, as it seems, at a double disadvantage in approaching the arguments in these orations: First, they are not used to thinking of works of reason or philosophy as being poetic in form; and second, as a consequence, they easily fall into the mistake of reading the arguments that the prophets were at such pains to advance to their audience as though they are principally concerned with the revelation of secrets – for example, revealing the hidden content of the future. Now, I do not mean to deny that the prophetic orations offer predictions and interpretations of future events. This, too, is an important aspect of Israelite prophecy. I mean only that the hunt for revelations of future events in the prophetic texts has systematically obscured the fact that most of what the prophets have to say has nothing to do with such predictions.

Let's take, as an example, the passage from Isaiah to which the New Testament accounts of the parable of the sower refer, with the Gospel of Matthew explicitly saying that in speaking in parables, Jesus is fulfilling the events prophesied by Isaiah centuries earlier. As Jesus says:

> That is why I speak to them in parables; for they look without seeing, and listen without hearing or understanding. There is a prophecy of Isaiah that is being fulfilled in them.[89]

But if we look at the original passage with an eye to understanding the argument Isaiah is making, we see that he isn't making a prediction of future events at all – and is in fact saying something quite different. Here is the original text from Isaiah:

> Also I heard the voice of the Lord, saying, "Whom shall I send, and who will go for us?" Then said I, "Here am I. Send me." And he said: "Go and tell this people: Hear indeed, but understand not, and see indeed, but perceive not. Make fat the mind of this people, make heavy their ears, and smear over their eyes, lest they see with their eyes, and hear with their ears, and understand with their mind, and return, and be healed." Then said I, "Lord, how long?" And he answered, "Until the cities be wasted without inhabitant ... and the Lord removed men far away."[90]

This oration describes the first moment in which Isaiah hears God's call, and steps forward to volunteer himself as a messenger to the people Israel and to the nations. What God is depicted as telling Isaiah at this moment is in fact a kind of summary of Isaiah's entire mission, folding together a thesis about the psychology of Jerusalem's inhabitants, along with a bitter assessment of where this will lead. The psychological thesis is itself an important argument about human nature: Isaiah advances the claim that what the senses report, and what the mind understands, are not necessarily what is real. If the people could see and understand what was real, then they would know that their path is leading them to ruin, and would repent and change course. But they cannot see and they cannot understand because the human mind cannot simply see and understand the reality before it. The metaphor that Isaiah uses – that of a mind that is fattened and senses that are glued shut so that they are useless – is aimed at making this difficult point clear to his audience: There is a reality, but it is obscured by the very mental organs that the people think are reporting it. Moreover, the consequence of this incapacity to see reality for what it is will be the destruction of the land and the exile of the people. So there is also a causal thesis here that will be elaborated in Isaiah's works, which is that this incapacity of the people to understand reality is what is ultimately responsible for the destruction of their nation. (This thesis, as extended later by Jeremiah, will be one of the central subjects of Chapter 6.)

Is this passage the revelation of the secret future course of Israel's history? Is it the presentation of inevitable future events that have been hidden from human reason, and which must come true so that the prophecy be fulfilled? One reads the text this way at the cost of missing Isaiah's evident purpose in writing it. Isaiah does not step forward to be God's messenger, devoting decades of his life to speaking before people and kings at great danger to himself, only in order to inform the nation that he has foreseen its inevitable destruction. What possible purpose could there be for engaging in such a cruel, debilitating, and ultimately futile mission? But of course, Isaiah does not believe that this is what he is doing at all. He knows quite well that the God of Israel is capable of changing his mind, and that that which is prophesied does not in every case come true. (The History of Israel is quite pointed about this, describing various cases in which prophecies do not come true, including at least one prophecy of Isaiah himself.[91]) And so he depicts God as speaking in anger, and as giving vent to a bitter sarcasm, saying: *Hear indeed, but understand not, and see indeed, but perceive not. Make fat the mind of this people, make heavy their ears, and smear over their eyes, lest they see and hear and understand.* Yet this is not the prediction of some future series of events that Isaiah is revealing, some secret of the future that he is telling. What he is describing is rather a view of present reality, and of the direction in which things are headed, *which he believes should be obvious to everyone.* Far from revealing an inscrutable secret, this oration before the people of Jerusalem is intended, precisely by means of the shocking words that it brings in the name of the God of Israel, to open the eyes and minds of the people, to pave the way for insight and self-understanding, so that they may be able to change the way they look at things and understand things.

Much of what tends to be read as the revelation of secrets in the prophets' orations is of this nature: an inquiry into the nature of present reality, presented in terms of what will happen if no change takes place in the mind of the nation and its leaders. In this the prophets of Israel depart somewhat from the writings of the Greek philosophers, in that their concern is not only to understand what is, but to understand what is so as to be able to influence what is to be. This concern to develop better conceptual tools that can be of service in predicting events is in fact one of the most important characteristics of the writings of the prophets, and in Deuteronomy we find

Moses explicitly stipulating that the truth of a prophet's words cannot be judged on the basis of miraculous signs, but only on the basis of whether the things he says come true.[92] Modern readers, who tend to think of prophecy as a kind of magic, often miss what is at stake here. The prophetic authors, in constantly probing the realm of psychology, morals, and political behavior in search of principles for understanding what is happening, are trying to impose an order on these realms that will permit men to attain some degree of certainty as to what will happen if they choose one course over another. What they are searching for is, in fact, *lawfulness* in moral order – those laws that are God's will, in the sense that they lead, naturally and reliably, to life and the good.

It is in this light, too, that I think we should view those parts of the prophetic orations that are, in fact, devoted to speculation about the future course of events – most notably those passages that are frequently (and mistakenly) taken to be descriptions of the "end of days." These are passages that break with the often harsh analysis of man's current condition that characterizes the prophetic orations, and offer consolation by way of a description of what will happen to Israel and the nations in times to come. I say that these passages are mistakenly understood to refer to the "end of days" – to some kind of end of the world, resulting in an entirely different order of reality – because there is little evidence that the biblical prophets thought in these terms. The Hebrew expression *miketz yamim*, which has often been translated "in the end of days,"[93] actually means something like *in the course of time* (as, for example, in the story of Cain and Abel, in which this expression is used in the sentence, "And it came to pass *in the course time* that Cain brought an offering to the Lord of the fruit of the ground"[94]). This means that when the prophets offer their understanding of the good days that lie somewhere beyond the trouble and turmoil of the current times, they are not usually speaking of the end of the world, but rather of a closer time when God's goodness will be manifest in the world. This is a distinction that is of some significance, since the "end of days" reading tends to skew every prophetic utterance in the direction of things that are mysterious, miraculous, and make little sense to human reason. It is such readings of the prophets that give us visions of wolves literally lying down with lambs, mountains being laid low, and so on.[95]

To be sure, there is plenty of idealism in these prophetic theories of a coming age of well-being and peace. The fact that the God of Israel is understood to be the creator of all nations, and to desire the well-being of all nations, is what permits the prophetic corpus to open human speculation, perhaps for the first time, to such subjects – and the different answers the prophets of Israel give the question of what history has in store for Israel and for humanity certainly include some with which not all readers will be comfortable. Nevertheless, what is important and valuable in these descriptions of the future world has often been overlooked, because readers fail to bear in mind that the most basic tool of prophetic argument, in all subjects, is analogy and metaphor. When Isaiah speak of wolves lying down with lambs, and lions with calves,[96] he merely recapitulates, in the style of poetic argument that I've already described, his vision of a world in which ravenous empires such as Assyria and Babylonia will no longer hunt Israel, but will befriend it. A perhaps less familiar passage makes exactly the same point, but it does so without the metaphorical presentation:

> In that day there will be [a] highway from Egypt leading to Assyria, and Assyria will come to Egypt, and Egypt to Assyria, and Egypt will worship with Assyria. In that day will Israel be a third with Egypt and Assyria, a blessing in the world. Which the Lord of Hosts will bless, saying, "Blessed is my people, Egypt, and the work of my hands, Assyria, and my inheritance, Israel."[97]

The proposal that in our world, Israel may some day live in friendship and peace with the larger and more powerful nations all around it is, I think, sufficiently radical in its implications so that we can marvel at how Isaiah dared to see this far and to speak of what he saw. There is no need to encumber his extraordinary argument as to what the good of the world would be like with misread metaphors that transform an important moment in the history of mankind's reasoning on political matters into a fantasy of little interest.

III. LAW, COVENANT, AND TORA IN HEBREW SCRIPTURE

Most of the biblical corpus consists of narrative works and prophetic oratory. The only biblical works that do not, on the whole, fit into these categories are two major works, Psalms and Proverbs; and the minor works Song of Songs, Lamentations, and Kohelet (Ecclesiastes). Of these, Proverbs and Kohelet have often been considered works of reason by contemporary scholars.[98] But as discussed in the Introduction, my concern here is not to establish that certain works in the Hebrew Scriptures can and should be read as works of reason. Rather, I'd like to show that the biblical corpus as a whole can for the most part be read in this light. Given this aim, a discussion of these works would take me too far afield, and I will forgo it for the time being, staying focused on the narratives and orations that make up most of the collection of texts in question.

Before leaving the subject of the techniques employed in the biblical narratives and orations to advance arguments of general nature, I would like to say a few words about the place of the Bible's *legal* texts within the overall approach I am proposing for reading the Scriptures. In terms of quantity, the actual law of Moses constitutes only a small fraction of the biblical corpus. Nevertheless, the Mosaic law is in many respects the heart of the Hebrew Bible. This is certainly so for Jews, who strive to live according to it every day. But I think that even without reference to Jewish tradition, the centrality of the law in the biblical corpus would be quite evident. The History of Israel in which it is embedded, the Orations of the Prophets, Psalms, Proverbs, and other works refer to the law constantly. And the biblical corpus itself is structured so as to make the central place of the Mosaic law unmistakable: The Bible is built around the History of Israel, and the History in turn pivots around Deuteronomy – both structurally, in that Deuteronomy is the centerpiece of the nine parts of this work, and stylistically, since Deuteronomy is the only portion of the History that presents itself as Moses addressing Israel in his own voice. Thus while the biblical corpus investigates a great many subjects far beyond the law, there is an important sense, given graphic representation in Figure 1 (see p. 35), in which Deuteronomy is the jewel in the crown of the entire biblical corpus. And more than any other biblical work, the subject matter of Deuteronomy is the Mosaic law. The structure of the Hebrew Bible is such as to place the law of Moses at its very center, and to make it the touchstone for the entire enterprise.

This having been said, it is also the case that only a very small portion of the Hebrew Scriptures is devoted to actually elaborating the Mosaic law. The fact that there are some, both Jews and Christians, who tend to speak of the *tora* (the Jewish teaching) as though this term were little more than a synonym for the *halacha* (the Jewish law) does not make this right.[99] Neither the biblical History nor the editors of the Hebrew Bible would have accepted the reduction of the tradition of inquiry encompassed in the Hebrew Scriptures to a wholly, or even primarily, legal endeavor.[100] Nor were the editors of the Talmud willing to accept this reduction, so they interspersed their legal discussions with philosophical stories whose purpose is to provide the broader theoretical framework for the law. The Mosaic law is one part of a much larger intellectual enterprise – a decisive part, and yet only a part. Had the final author of the History thought otherwise, he could simply have circulated his edition of the law of Moses with a suitable commentary among the exiles of Babylonia and Egypt. But such a definitive edition of the Mosaic law alone would not have had the effect that the History had on the Jews, and the course of human history would have been very different indeed.

How, then, are we to think of the relationship between the law of Moses and the rest of the material in the Bible? How does Scripture present this relationship?

As I suggested in the last chapter, the juridic metaphor of the New Testament, with its language of *secrets* and *revelations*, *claims* and *witnesses*, is largely absent from the Hebrew Scriptures. But the authors of the Hebrew Scriptures do use metaphors to assist in defining the enterprise in which they are engaged – it's just that the metaphors they use are different ones. Here I will discuss three of the most important metaphorical frameworks employed to describe the biblical enterprise in the Hebrew Bible itself (and then carried forward into the Talmud), namely, the metaphors of *law*, *covenant*, and *teaching*. These are not the only metaphors that are used in Hebrew Scripture to establish the purpose of these texts, and to position the reader with reference to them.[101] But so far as I know, they are the most frequently invoked. My purpose, then, will be to show how these different metaphors work together to place the Mosaic law within the context of the broader theoretical standpoint of the History and the prophetic orations.

I suggested earlier that the thought of the biblical authors strives constantly to identify that way of thinking, and those actions, that can be relied upon to bring "life and the good" to those that embrace them. This means that their inquiry is one that is centrally concerned to identify *lawfulness* in the moral world – in effect, a causal relationship between one's actions and what then takes place in the world. This concern is expressed in the Hebrew Scriptures in different ways. But its most prominent expression is obviously the metaphor of our lives as being governed by *laws* that are given by God, who will reward those who obey and punish those who do not.

Perhaps one may wonder at my describing the application of the term *law* to the laws of Moses as a metaphor. We are so accustomed to thinking of the Mosaic teaching as *laws* (Hebrew, *hukim*) or as *commandments* (Hebrew, *mitzvot*) that we tend to forget that this way of understanding what God wants from us is itself based on a metaphor, which draws on our experience of a human king governing a political state in an effort better to understand the broader moral and natural order. The metaphor works as follows. A human king is responsible for the well-being of the political state of which he is the ruler. He issues laws and commands to his people, whose purpose is to create orderly patterns of behavior among his subjects, so that they are all in effect working together to bring about a common good. What is expected of the king's subjects is, on this view, only that they obey his laws, and thereby do their part in attaining the overall well-being of the nation. If they do not, the king will punish their disobedience so that good may come to all.

According to a view advanced time and again in the Hebrew Bible, our experience of a human king, if we consider it well, is seen to provide a useful analogy to our experience of God's action in the world. On this analogy, God is concerned to govern the world as a human king is concerned to govern a political state, and God does this by providing laws and commandments to all things, whose purpose is to create an orderly behavior that is to the good of all. In prophetic oratory and in Psalms, these laws and commandments are seen as governing *everything*: The sea has its own laws; the sun, moon, and stars, their own laws; the animals and the plants have laws of their own.[102] And the well-being of the good world that we see is the result of this obedience. There are laws for human beings, too, whose purpose is to bring order and well-being into the realm of nations and individuals – a law whose greatest articulation is the laws of Moses. But human beings will not so quickly obey, as the sea and the stars and the animals do, and so God, like a king of flesh and blood, punishes the violation of his laws to try to retain order and direct the world toward life and the good.

Notice that to the extent that the biblical texts are understood by way of the metaphor of law – to the extent, that is, that we think in terms of the *law of Moses*, rather than the *teaching of Moses* – the reader places himself, by analogy, in the position of a subject or a soldier seeking to obey the directives of his king. He therefore reads the text in the way that he would read the law book of his king, or a letter of instruction from an officer of the state or one of its military commanders, so that he may know what to do. And here, as in the state or armed service of a human king, what is expected is principally obedience, which is the key to order and well-being.

How different is the metaphor of Scripture as *law*, which places the reader in the position of a subject or soldier; from that of Scripture as *testimony*, which places the reader in the position of a judge!

But as I have said, the metaphor of the law is not the only one defining the relationship of the reader to the Hebrew Scriptures. A second, crucial, metaphor is that of the *covenant* or *alliance* (Hebrew, *brit*), which likewise appears throughout Scripture. This too is a metaphor that is drawn, in the first instance, from the political realm. And here, too, God is understood by analogy to our experience of a human king. But the experience that gives rise to the metaphor of the covenant or alliance with a king is quite different from that which gives rise to the metaphor of obeying a king's law. For while obedience before the king's law is something that is expected of, and usually proffered by, even subjects who have never laid eyes on the king, a covenant or alliance is something that can only take place where there is a personal relationship and a personal history with the ruler in question.[103] More specifically, the king grants a covenant *to someone whom he respects, and whose services and assistance he needs and may not be able to obtain without his agreement.* Unlike a royal law or decree, which is nothing but an order, a covenant or alliance thus involves a relationship in which the king, even if he is vastly more powerful than his ally, nonetheless concedes that he is not powerful enough to enforce his will all by himself, and that he is in need of assistance and collaboration if he is to attain the order he seeks. In other words, the covenant is a relationship that recognizes the weaker party's *voluntary contribution* to the king's order – and the king's *need* of such help.[104]

It is precisely this understanding of God as wanting and needing man's help that pervades biblical covenant-talk, and sets it apart from law-talk with its connotations of coerced obedience. The biblical covenant – the covenant that God makes with Abraham, for example – is a new metaphor for understanding man's relationship with God, which arises precisely from the fact that man, who is free to choose, is not in God's pocket, as the ocean and the stars and the animals are. Man is, on this view, an independent player who makes decisions for himself as to how to dispose of his strength and abilities; and this means that God, powerful though he may be, *is not all-powerful.* Quite to the contrary, God is found to be vulnerable before man's rebelliousness and depravity. If God's will is to be done, he will be in need of allies, of assistance. And those who turn to him of their own, placing themselves in his service, are described as attaining something that mere obedience could never have obtained – God's *love.*[105]

In the oratory of the prophets, this concept of a covenant between man and God becomes the basis for what is surely one of the most extraordinary metaphors in all of Scripture, that which portrays God as Israel's husband and the people of Israel as his young wife who rebels and turns to the affections of other men. Here, the metaphor of the covenant shifts somewhat. It is no longer the covenant between a king and his weaker ally, but a marriage covenant.[106] Yet the underlying structure of the covenant remains much the same, even as the emotions involved burn all the more brightly: The marriage covenant is still the alliance of a (usually) more powerful husband and a weaker wife. And yet despite being stronger, the husband can never really control his wife. In the end, he can control neither her love nor her actions. If she chooses, she is loyal; if she chooses, she is not. And the same is true, the prophets suggest, of the God of Israel and his people, who swore allegiance to him in their youth. God is more powerful, to be sure. But he can coerce neither their love nor their actions. If they choose, they are loyal; if they choose, they are not. God, too, like the husband who has been betrayed, is shown to us in unspeakable pain, as he recalls the ardor and devotion that were once his when his wife was young, and which are now long lost.[107]

The stunning vulnerability of the God of Israel as he watches Israel in her disloyalty releases emotions of astonishing power, which serve the prophets well in calling for the Jews to keep faith with their people, their law, and their God. Here, the rules of engagement are shockingly reversed, and the Jews are called to return to God, not because he is an all-powerful ruler who must be obeyed; but precisely because he is vulnerable, and needs our help – because he is in need of the help our forefathers once promised him, but which we have not been willing to render him.

Notice that to the extent that the biblical texts are understood by way of the metaphor of covenant, the reader places himself, by analogy, in the position of a less powerful ally to a great king, or of the young wife of a great man, who wishes above all to know what the demands of loyalty require.[108] Here, the motive of obedience, so important when Scripture is read as law, evaporates. What is at stake is rather the love that God once felt for those who would join him in his cause – and the question of whether the old alliance can be honored now, or whether it has in fact been lost for good.

Let's consider one last metaphor used by the biblical authors to describe the enterprise in which they are engaged, the metaphor that sees the Hebrew Scriptures as *instruction* or *teaching* (Hebrew, *tora*).* The Hebrew term *tora* is a cognate of both *parent* (Hebrew, *horeh*); and *teacher* (Hebrew, *moreh*). But since most children in ancient Israel received little, if any, instruction from teachers, the term *tora* should be seen as invoking, first and foremost, the relationship between a child and his or her parents, who are the ones most concerned to see to it that the child gains wisdom, and consequently the best life possible. We can see the word *tora* used in just this way, for example, in the following passage from Proverbs:

> My son, heed the instruction [*musar*] of your father, and forsake not the teaching [*tora*] of your mother.[109]

---

* Note that that Jews often use the term *tora* in two different ways. At times, *tora* is used as a shortened form of *torat mosheh* – "the teaching of Moses" – which is another name for the five books of Moses (i.e., the Pentateuch). But *tora* can as easily be used to refer to the entire body of classical Jewish texts, including the Hebrew Bible, the Talmud, and subsequent rabbinic sources. It is this latter usage, in which the Bible and later sources are all approached by way of the metaphor of "teaching" or "instruction," that is of interest in the present discussion.

The metaphor that approaches Scripture as instruction or teaching, then, is drawn from a very different range of experiences than that which informs the metaphors of law and covenant. Here, for the first time, we find the God of Israel being understood, not by way of analogy to a king, but to a father. A father, of course, is concerned for order and for obedience within the family, and he frequently looks to his children for their assistance as well. But none of this is central. What is central is the compassion a father feels for his children, his desire that things go well for us, and the pain he feels over our failures. He wishes to instruct us for no other reason than for our own well-being. And this means that he wants us to be wise, to gain understanding so we will be able to stand by ourselves, and conduct ourselves rightly when he is gone.[110] Thus when God is depicted by means of an analogy to a father, the ground shifts and we are asked to see reality, not in terms of our responsibilities to uphold his law and so contribute to some general order, but rather in terms of the understanding and knowledge of the world that God wants us to have so that we can attain the good for ourselves.[111]

And so in the metaphor that sees Scripture as *tora*, the relationship of the reader to the Bible shifts as well, and we now read the old texts – as is explicitly the case in Proverbs – as though they were written by our father, who wishes to assist us in gaining wisdom and understanding, so that we may know how to think about things and what to do about them. In this metaphor, we study Scripture so that we may act, not out of obedience or loyalty, but out of the power of our own understanding and insight to recognize that which is true and right. Thus the metaphor of Scripture as instruction or teaching places a premium on our own understanding, and on the good that comes of it.

What is the relationship among these three very different metaphors? One can, perhaps, read the Hebrew Scriptures as though these metaphors exist side by side – so that one of them dominates the reading of the text at a given moment, and then gives way to another. But I think this is too simple an approach, especially given that these three metaphors do not exist in isolation from one another, but are constantly run together in the biblical texts. A better approach, I think, is to consider them as ordered in a hierarchy, with the covenant providing the basis for the law, and the reading of Scripture as *tora* – as instruction or teaching – in turn providing the basis for the covenant. Let's see how this works.

The Hebrew Scriptures often depict the prophets of Israel as calling for the observance of God's laws and commands, and a crude reading can easily lead to the conclusion that an unthinking obedience is all the biblical authors are interested in. Indeed, the very fact that man can be urged to obey, as the sea or the stars or the birds obey the laws that have been prescribed for them, strongly reinforces the view that the demand being made is one of simple, unthinking obedience. But this reading of Scripture is too simplistic, leaving too many obvious questions unanswered – and, indeed, unanswerable. Unthinking obedience, after all, would require suspending the operation of man's natural faculties and his transformation into an automaton; and it would require that God should desire this. It is exceedingly doubtful, however, that the authors of the History of Israel and the other biblical works believed that man should become an automaton, or that God would want something like this. In Eden, God makes man "in our image, after our likeness,"[112] and he delights in the freedom he has given man to give names to things in speech:

> [T]he Lord God formed every beast of the field, and every bird of the air, and brought them to the man to see what he would call him, and whatever the man called every living creature, that was its name.[113]

And the same freedom that is given to man in the realm of speech and thought is given to him in the realm of action as well. God places man in Eden "to till it and keep it,"[114] and commands him to "fill the earth and subdue it,"[115] and gives him rule over all the beasts and birds and fish,[116] and commands him concerning what he may eat, and concerning the tree from which he may not eat.[117] In all this, man's freedom to choose appears to be a delight to God. And even once this freedom leads man to evil, God does not repent having given man this freedom. On the contrary, it is man's freedom to act against mankind's evildoing, and even against God, that is presented in the narrative as man's greatest glory, with those whom God loves best – Abel, Abraham, Jacob, Moses – being those who presume to challenge God, to wrestle with him, and even to defeat him for the sake of what is good.[118] No, there is no hint that the biblical authors would have found virtue in a man denuded of his freedom, an automaton.[119]

Moreover, there is this problem as well: A code of law and exhortations to obey it, even if these are accompanied by ample threats of punishment, do not constitute an explanation as to *why* one should obey the law. One can always say that disobedience is preferable, even if the cost is high. To decide to obey, then, requires reasons that cannot be supplied by the law itself. And so the law is found, when examined with care, to be incomplete. It is in need of something other than itself, which will explain why a man or a woman gifted with freedom should nonetheless obey it.

These considerations make it clear that one cannot just read the Hebrew Scriptures as law and emerge with a coherent understanding of what they are about. Pressing on the structure provided by this legal metaphor, one finds that a more sophisticated framework is needed. And this more sophisticated structure is provided by the view of God's relationship with the Jews offered by the metaphor of the covenant. The covenantal framework sacrifices the claim of God's perfection to make room for the fact that the world of God's creation is in terrible need of man's active assistance.[120] In doing so, it opens up a space in which it is possible to understand God as having loved Abraham as a man willing to stand by him and pursue his works; and as loving Israel for the sake of Abraham's alliance with him, and for those Jews who have been loyal to this alliance. This love is then understood to be the basis for the promise God has made to preserve Israel, and to make the Jews a great nation. Within this context, the question of obedience to the law takes on a completely different aspect. On the one hand, the law itself is seen as an expression of God's promise to preserve the Israelites and make them a great nation. On the other, they are given a battery of reasons to keep the law, which are quite independent of the logic of command and punishment: We should obey the law out of loyalty to an old alliance and an old love that has held firm for so long. We should obey the law out of a desire to keep the promise made by our forefathers, and renewed time and again by Jews throughout history. We should obey the law out of gratitude for having been preserved alive in exile, and for all the good that has come to us through so many ages. We should obey the law as a way to repair a world that is as yet only partially formed, and which we can help God bring into being.[121]

For most Jews, in most times and places, these answers as to why one should observe and keep the law have been sufficient. But it seems that the authors of the Bible were not comfortable letting the matter rest there. And this, I suspect, is because the metaphor of the covenant is not without its difficulties either. As mentioned earlier, the relationship between the Jews and the God of Israel was not entirely unique. Every people of the ancient Near East had a god of its own, and these gods were sometimes depicted as speaking and acting in ways that remind us of the God of Israel in the Bible: These gods, too, made promises and demands, and claimed their peoples' loyalty as only fitting given the services they had rendered them in the past.[122] And when disaster befell the people, these gods, too, were said to have been angry over the people's disloyalty and contempt. I don't mean to say that the covenant between Israel and its God was in every respect replicated in other nations. It wasn't. But the similarities were great enough to raise the question of *why* the covenant with the God of Israel should be taken any more seriously than the arrangements that had characterized the relationships between other peoples and their gods. As mentioned in the last chapter, the argument that other gods can protect the Jews just as well as, if not better than, the God of Israel is one that is quoted explicitly in the Bible. As the exiles in Egypt tell Jeremiah:

> And they answered Jeremiah, all the people who knew that their wives burned incense to other gods and all the women standing in a great crowd, and all the people living in the land of Egypt in Patros, saying: "The word that you have spoken in the name of the Lord we will not hear from you. For we will surely do everything that we have vowed to do, to burn incense to the Queen of Heaven and pour libations to her, as we did, we and our fathers and our kings and our princes, in the cities of Judah and the streets of Jerusalem, when we were sated with bread and were well, and saw no evil. And from the time we stopped burning incense to the Queen of Heaven and pouring libations to her, we have lacked in everything and ended with the sword and famine."[123]

In this report, the exiles of Judah living in Egypt argue explicitly that the beneficence of the Canaanite gods is superior to that of the God of Israel. And we can only suppose that in exile, this argument was applied to the Babylonian and Egyptian gods as well. In the absence of a compelling reason to prefer Abraham's covenant to the bargains that might be struck with other gods that seemed more powerful or more loyal, one could always say the old alliance with the God of Israel had failed, and that the time had come to try something else.

This challenge of the exiles makes it clear that one cannot just read the Hebrew Scriptures as a covenant and emerge with a complete understanding of what they are about. Pressing on the structure provided by the metaphor of the covenant, one finds that a more sophisticated framework is needed. And this more sophisticated structure is provided by the view of God's relationship with the Jews offered by the metaphor of the Hebrew Scriptures as *tora*, or instruction. It is this metaphor that brings us into contact for the first time with a view of God, not as our king, but as our father, whose compassion brings him, time and again, to attempt to teach us, so that we may be able to gain understanding and find a life of well-being and good. It is this, the broadest level on which Scripture operates, that explains the presence in the biblical texts of such vast quantities of material that appear to be related neither to the law nor to the covenant. It is this, for example, that explains why the *tora* should begin with creation, and not with the establishment of the covenant with Abraham;[124] or why it should take an interest in the law given to Noah after the flood, rather than focusing exclusively on the giving of the Mosaic law at Sinai.[125] It is this material that seeks to provide the reader with an understanding of what God expects of the world of his creation, and of the nations that populate it; why God should need an alliance with a man, or with men; what the reasons are for preferring a life in tents to the splendor of Mesopotamian civilization; what kinds of men, and what kinds of deeds, can gain God's love; what may be done to secure blessings for oneself and for the nations; and so on. Covenant-talk is particular in nature – it describes the relationship of a particular individual or a certain people to its god. But the teaching offered by the Hebrew Scriptures goes beyond covenant-talk and seeks to instruct us as to the underlying reasons for the covenant. And in so doing it has recourse to concepts of a general nature, introduced by means of techniques such as those I've described over the course of this chapter. Because of their generality, such concepts require no prior commitment to the historic Jewish alliance with the God of Israel to be understood. Thus while they were written for the instruction of the Jews, there is no reason why the standpoint and argument they make should not be heard and debated among all nations.

PART II

THE PHILOSOPHY OF HEBREW SCRIPTURE

Five Studies

4

The Ethics of a Shepherd

It has often been said that there is little more to the ethics of the Hebrew Scriptures than doing whatever God commands you to do: If you have instruction directly from God himself or from a prophet, you should obey it. If you have God's law, obey that. There isn't supposed to be much more to biblical ethics than this principle of unfailing *obedience*.[1]

But this view rests on an overly simplistic, even careless, reading of the biblical texts. In fact, the God of Hebrew Scripture holds individuals and nations morally responsible for their actions even where they appear to have received no laws or commands from him of any kind. Thus, for example, Cain is punished for murdering his brother despite the fact that neither he nor anyone else has heard anything from God on the subject.[2] And Noah's generation is destroyed for their violence, and Sodom is annihilated for its perversity – despite the fact that they, too, have received no commands from God on these subjects.[3] Similarly, the reader is expected to know, as the persons depicted in the narrative are expected to know, that Adam errs in trying to pin the blame on God for his having eaten the forbidden fruit (because God gave him Eve); that Noah sins in his drunkenness; and that his son Ham sins in looking upon his drunken father's nakedness and telling his brothers all about it – although God has commanded nothing on these subjects.[4] And we are supposed to know, as the persons in the narrative are supposed to know, that there is something wrong with getting your father drunk and having sex with him, as the daughters of Lot do; or with raping your neighbor, even if you love her, as Shechem does; or with entrapping and enslaving your kinsman, as Lavan does; or with enslaving another nation, as Pharaoh does – although God has commanded nothing on these subjects either.[5] And one could easily fill pages with additional such examples. Moreover, Abraham's famous challenge to God over the justice of destroying Sodom ("Will the judge of all the earth not do justice?"[6]) is but the first of a series of texts in which biblical figures seem to hold God's actions to a moral standard that does not derive from these actions themselves.

The sheer quantity of such examples has led to the suggestion that the biblical authors in fact see God's commands as either supplementary to, or themselves expressions of, a fundamental moral law that derives from the nature of things; and that the biblical authors believe that human beings should be able to discern this law, at least in its contours, even without explicit instructions from God. On this view, the ethics of the Bible is based, in the first instance, on a form of *natural law*.[7]

But even if this is right, much remains uncertain: What precisely is the content of the natural law ethics that emerges from the History of Israel? How is this ethics related to the content of the Mosaic law embedded in this History? And how does it relate to the instructions God is depicted as giving individuals on particular occasions regarding specific actions they are to undertake? All three of these questions will have to be given satisfactory answers if we are to attain a clear view of the ethics of the History. And such a view will be needed, I suspect, if we wish to gain a full picture of the ethics of the prophetic orations and other biblical works as well.

In this chapter, I will address the first of these questions, examining central aspects of the natural law ethics of the History of Israel, drawing largely from the stories in Genesis, which I see as setting the stage for everything that follows. I will suggest that the ethics of the History cannot be understood without recognizing the central role played in the narrative by the metaphor of the shepherd.[8] In the History, the shepherd and the farmer are taken as representing contrasting ways of life, and two different kinds of ethics, which come into sharp conflict time and again – especially in the stories of Abraham, Joseph, Moses, and David. But the History sees the question of the shepherd's ethics as dating all the way back to the time of Cain and Abel. God's preference for the ethics of the shepherd is therefore portrayed as being prior to almost all of the laws or commands God gives to human beings.[9] Any interpretation of God's subsequent covenants with biblical figures such as Abraham, Moses, and David must therefore be understood in the context of a prior ethical stance upon which the force of these covenants is based.

I will conclude the chapter with some preliminary remarks concerning the relationship between the natural law ethics of the History and the laws of Moses and other instances of God's commands that appear in the narrative.

I. THE MURDER OF ABEL: FARMERS AND SHEPHERDS

Ancient narratives are usually about heroes of royal or noble birth. But the biblical History of Israel is something quite different. It is a story about shepherds. Abraham, Isaac, Jacob, Joseph and his brothers, Moses, and even David, are all shepherds. And the History, which is to a great extent the story of these individuals, overflows with shepherding imagery: Mankind's life after Eden begins with the murder of Abel, a shepherd, by his brother Cain, who was a farmer; and this because God accepted the shepherd's sacrifice but rejected that of the farmer. Abraham, the first Jew, is born in the urban metropolis of Ur, but we are told that he leaves it to take up the nomadic life of a shepherd because God himself wished him to do this. At the climax of the story of Abraham, we are told that God commands him to offer up his son Isaac as a burnt offering, but that God then forgoes the sacrifice of the child and accepts instead the sacrifice of a sheep. Jacob raises his children as shepherds, but his beloved Joseph is different. Joseph's dreams are of harvesting grain – that is, of farming; and after hearing of it, his brothers sell him into Egypt, a powerful and grain-rich nation where shepherds are detested as an "abomination." It is in Pharaoh's palace that Moses, the greatest leader of the Hebrews, is raised as a child. But instead of accepting Egyptian ways, he flees to the desert and becomes a shepherd like his fathers. It is while herding his flock that Moses is called by God. And when he returns to Egypt to confront Pharaoh and rain plagues down upon the land, he does so with a shepherd's staff in his hand. Moses frees the Hebrew slaves, but only those among them who slaughter a sheep and smear its blood on their doorposts. Having taken the Hebrew slaves out of Egypt, Moses brings them to Sinai to hear the voice of God, which appears to them in the midst of the sound of the *shofar* – the ram's horn, which is also a symbol of Joshua's conquest of Canaan.[10] Even the land into which Moses is to bring the people is repeatedly said to be "a land flowing with milk and honey," an evocative pastoral image sharply at odds with the fleshpots and bread that the Israelites remember as the emblem of their slavery in Egypt.[11] But the former slaves fear to enter the land of God's promise, and as punishment they are forced – the entire people – to take up shepherding in the wilderness for forty years as their forefathers had done, until they are ready to conquer the land.[12] Later, after the misery of the period of the judges, David makes his first appearance on the field of battle without armor, but with a shepherd's staff in his hand, and kills Goliath with stones drawn from his shepherd's pouch. And when he is crowned king of Israel, all the tribes of Israel come and tell him, "the Lord has said to you: You will shepherd my people Israel."[13]

What is all this about? It can hardly just be a reflection of the fact that the first Jews happened to have been shepherds. The biblical History emphasizes the shepherd character of the Israelites' story in ways that go far beyond the needs of mere reporting: We are told that the Egyptians would not break bread with shepherds, and that Joseph's brothers emphasize that they are shepherds in speaking to Pharaoh;[14] or that David comes to battle from grazing his sheep in the wilderness, that he puts stones for his sling in his "shepherd's pouch," and that he stashes the defeated Goliath's armor in the tent he had used in tending his flock.[15] None of these facts are of the slightest intrinsic interest to us as readers, and they take on meaning only within the context of a much larger story – one in which being a shepherd, and thinking and acting like a shepherd, have some special significance that is worth dwelling upon.[16]

What, then, is the shepherding imagery of the History about?

The natural place to begin examining this question is at the beginning of Genesis, with the story of the murder of Abel. Other than the two brothers' births, Cain's killing of Abel is the first thing the biblical narrator feels the need to tell us about after man is expelled from Eden. This dominant place in the narrative turns the murder of Abel into a kind of introduction to everything that happens in the rest of the History – to everything that happens, that is, after the conditions of plenitude and ease described in the garden disappear, and human beings find themselves cast into a world in which they live constantly on the verge of starvation. Now in this story there is already an assumption as to how man is to contend with these terrifying conditions: Starvation is avoided by working the land, which yields up grain so that man may eat bread only by way of the greatest hardship and suffering. This is in fact portrayed as a decree of God himself, who has condemned man to farm the land as part of his punishment for eating of the forbidden fruit. Here is how the text in Genesis describes the life that God has decreed for man after Eden:

> And to the man [God] said ... "Cursed is the ground due to you, and in sorrow shall you eat of it all the days of your life. Thorns and thistles shall it give forth for you, but you will eat the grasses of the field. By the sweat of your brow will you eat bread, until you return to the ground from which your were taken ...." And the Lord sent him out from the garden of Eden to work the ground from which he was taken.[17]

A tone of utmost bitterness pervades this passage. And it is the bitterness over mankind's being condemned to live the life of a farmer. The soil, we are told, has been "cursed,"[18] so that man can barely scratch out his bread from it. It opposes him and forces him to engage, constantly, in hard labor.

It is also, in a sense, his master, which dictates to him the course of his life every day from morning until night, always in the shadow of the fact that it will eventually reclaim him for itself. This bitterness of the farming life, as the biblical text sees it, is captured in a particularly poignant way by the Hebrew expression *la'avod et ha'adama*, which I have translated as "to work the ground." The word *la'avod*, to work, also means "to serve," so that God has in fact punished man by sending him "to serve the ground" – to become the servant and slave of the earth itself.[19]

It is immediately after these extraordinary verses that the biblical narrative turns to the story of Cain and Abel. Eve, we are told, bore two children, Cain and Abel. "And Abel became a keeper of sheep, and Cain was a worker of the ground [*oved adama*]."[20] In time, Cain brings a sacrifice to God from the "fruits of the ground," and Abel follows his lead by sacrificing from the firstborn of his flock. God accepts Abel's offering, but he rejects that of his brother. In shame and rage, Cain rises up and murders his brother, burying him in the ground.[21] God curses Cain, who flees before him, and goes on to the east, where he founds a city called Hanoch, the first city.

On the face of it, this story makes no sense. Why should God reject Cain's sacrifice, and not Abel's? The text emphasizes that the idea of making a sacrifice to God is Cain's. It is Cain who inclines to piety, and thinks to take some of his meager supply of food, which he has scraped from the soil, and sacrifice it to God in gratitude. Abel only follows his lead. Even more disturbing is the fact that God rejects what seems in context to be an act of submission on Cain's part. God has cursed the land and sent man to farm it, telling Cain's father, Adam, "By the sweat of your brow will you eat bread." Then "the Lord sent him ... to work the ground from which he was taken," which is exactly what Cain does: He works the ground just as God had told his father to do.[22] He submits to God's will, and even, amid the curse and the hardship, finds it in his heart to be grateful to God for what he has. Why should God not accept the sacrifice of a man of piety, who does what God has sent him to do, as his father did before him?[23]

On the other hand, God has said not a word about shepherding. And when Abel takes it up, he's doing something that God had *not* sent man to do.[24] Abel sees that the ground has been cursed, and that man can only eat bread if he serves the ground. But sheep can feed themselves without human toil, and so if a man will keep sheep, he can free himself from serving the accursed ground. Abel has, in other words, found a way to escape the curse upon the soil.[25] And the fact that this is about what Abel wants, first and foremost, rather than about what God wants, is emphasized by the text itself, which tells us that Abel "also" offers a sacrifice after Cain. Yet despite this, God accepts Abel's sacrifice. How can this be?

The contest between Cain and Abel is carefully constructed to present the reader with two archetypes, which appear time and again over the course of the biblical History, and on into the subsequent biblical works as well. Each archetype represents a way of life and an approach to living as a human being, to ethics. The text presents the reader with a rather stark choice and presses the reader to recognize that God's choice, the *right* choice, is not necessarily the one we would have chosen. These archetypes are:

The life of the farmer. Cain has piously accepted the curse on the soil, and God's having sent Adam to work the soil, as unchallengeable. His response is to *submit*, as his father did before him. And within the framework of this submission, he initiates ways of giving up of what little he has as an offer of thanksgiving. In the eyes of the biblical author, Cain represents the life of the farmer, a life of pious submission, obeying in gratitude the custom that has been handed down, which alone provides bread so that man may live.

The life of the shepherd. Abel takes the curse on the soil as a fact, but not as one that possesses any intrinsic merit, so that it should command his allegiance. The fact that God has decreed it, and that his father has submitted to it, does not make it good. His response is the opposite of submission: He *resists* with ingenuity and daring, risking the anger of man and God to secure improvement for himself and for his children. Abel represents the life of the shepherd, which is a life of dissent and initiative, whose aim is to find the good life for man, which is presumed to be God's true will.[26]

As the biblical story is told, it's evident that shepherding is not what God had in mind when he sent man forth from Eden. But as it turns out, it's something that God wants anyway: an improvement in man's station, a greater goodness which comes of man's own unsolicited efforts.[27] Although God has not spoken on this subject previously, once the sacrifices have been offered and Cain's sacrifice has been refused, God delivers precisely this message in explaining why Cain has been rebuffed:

> "Why are you angry, and why is your face fallen? If you improve [*teitiv*], will you not be lifted up?"[28]

God accepts the offering of a man who seeks to improve things, to make them good of himself and his own initiative. This is what God finds in Abel, and the reason he accepts his sacrifice.[29]

Perhaps this is not so difficult to understand. But what is rather shocking here is the fact that God does not accept *both* sacrifices: the fact that despite

Cain's evident virtues, God rejects his way outright. Why should this be? Why should God not accept Cain's innovation and initiative, which is the very fact of bringing a sacrifice to God in thanksgiving? Here, as elsewhere in Scripture, it transpires that God is not particularly impressed with piety, with sacrifices, with doing what you are told to do and what your fathers did before you. He is not even that impressed with doing what you believe has been decreed by God. *All* these things, which Cain has on his side of the ledger, can be a part of a beast-life, or even of a life of evil. They are worth nothing if they are not placed in the service of a life that is directed toward the active pursuit of man's true good.

The story of Cain and Abel and the curse on the soil raises fascinating theological questions, but I'll leave these for another time. My subject here is the biblical ethics, and in this regard, a postscript to this story is of some importance. As mentioned above, in the wake of Abel's murder and its aftermath, we learn that "Cain went out from before the Lord ... and he built a city."[30] So it is a farmer who becomes the first murderer, the murderer of the first shepherd – and this very farmer is also the builder of the first city. To the modern ear, this may perhaps seem a meaningless concatenation of facts. We tend to think of town and country as opposites, and of rural provincialism as a world apart from the unrooted cosmopolitanism of urban life. But in the Bible, the association of Cain with the rise of the city is not arbitrary at all. In fact, it is of great significance. For the ultimate fruit of the way of the farmer, in the eyes of the biblical narrative, is the city that grows out of it. It is the city, with its extraordinary accumulation of wealth and power, that is the logical consequence of the farming life associated with Cain. I'd like to consider this for a moment.

For more than a thousand years before the time of Abraham, the might of the Nile and Euphrates had been harnessed for massive irrigation projects that had given rise to agriculture on an a vast scale, creating the wealth that made possible the Babylonian[31] states in Mesopotamia and Egypt of the Pharaohs. In both Mesopotamia and Egypt, the imperial state engaged in public works on an unprecedented scale to increase the land available for farming, creating ever greater wealth and power. To achieve this, they employed their populations as slaves for periods of weeks or months when important projects were under way. This enforced management of hundreds of thousands of people was considered a form of taxation, which necessitated the creation of a large military apparatus capable of enforcing the impressment of multitudes into service, and defending the public works against nomadic peoples who coveted the wealth and power being accumulated in the river valleys. It also led to the spectacular enrichment of the king and his court, as represented by physical structures such as the pyramids in Egypt or the ziggurats of Babylonia; and to the view that the king was a descendant of the gods, their principal servant and chief priest, wherever he was not himself a deity.[32]

All these characteristics appear in a concentrated form in the story of the tower of Babylon, in which the rulers of Babylon, the most important city in the basin of the Euphrates, decide that all of humanity is to be mustered in a single city with a single language and a single monomaniacal aim: the conquest of heaven.[33] The life of the city and of the state, then, is for the biblical narrative the natural extension of the way of the farmer. All the virtues that we find in Cain – submission to the decrees of the gods, pious sacrifice and self-sacrifice, honoring the customs of past generations – are brought to perfection in the great cities and their empires.

And all the virtues we find in Abel – his dissent from the supposedly unalterable decrees of the gods, his hesitation to accept that which is customary as authoritative, and his keen interest in innovation in order to improve things – are by the same token anathema in the world of the god-kings who rule the cities and their empires, and seen as an "abomination."[34] The nomad views civilization from the outside, looking down from the hills at the doings of society and state as he charts his own independent course through the wilderness. The splendor and lies of urban life are of little worth to him, and even less the beast-life of the farmers in the fields, living out their days in toil that these lies may be fed. The nomads have what is more precious to them than all else – independence: Political independence in that they live as nomads, ungoverned, their labor and their property and their actions unregulated and untaxed by anyone other than themselves; ethical independence in that their vantage point and the freedom and dignity of their work allow them to focus on what truly matters – the proximity of all men to danger, error, and death, and the consequent responsibility they must take for discovering the true course for themselves and acting on it.[35]

Thus from the perspective of the biblical authors, *shepherd* and *farmer* are contrary categories, characterizing two possible fundamental ethical orientations that have struggled with one another since the founding of the world.[36]

II. ABRAHAM'S ETHICS: OUT OF UR

In Genesis we learn of a man named Abraham who leaves the metropolis of Ur in Babylonia, the very heart of the civilized world, to begin life anew at the age of seventy-five as a herder of sheep and goats in the unsown hill country of Canaan. This idea of leaving Ur did not originate with Abraham.

It had been the dream of his father Terah, who had himself set out for Canaan but had made it only as far as Haran,[37] a city in the land of Aram, which is roughly present-day Syria. We know, too, that God sees this journey as his own project,[38] and that when Terah proves unable to execute it, he intervenes and calls upon Abraham to take it up again. When God speaks to Abraham of resuming this journey, we get our first glimpse of what is at stake. As we are told:

> And the Lord said to Avram,[39] "Get yourself out of your land, and out of the place you were born, and out of your father's house, to that land that I will show you. And I will make of you a great nation, and I will bless you and make your name great, and you will be a blessing.... [I]n you will all the families of the earth be blessed."[40]

Why does Abraham leave Mesopotamia? God's words in this passage give us some insight into what is at stake. To be sure, God offers Abraham some things that any man might want, whether he is good or evil – to attain fame in history, to be the father of a great nation. But in addition to these, God speaks to Abraham about two moral dimensions that are to attend this project of exchanging the great metropolis for life in a shepherd's tent in Canaan:[41] Abraham is told that he will be *blessed*; and he is told that he will be a *blessing to all the families of the earth*. And in fact, the biblical History is insistent on both of these dimensions, returning repeatedly to the suggestion that in the subsequent history of Abraham's children "all the nations of the earth will be blessed";[42] and telling us explicitly, at the end of Abraham's life, that "the Lord had blessed Abraham in all things."[43]

This is no small achievement – pulling off a life that has attained the good "in all things," while at the same time passing something of this goodness on to all the rest of humanity. And while it seems unlikely that any one character in the History of Israel was intended as a definitive model for the life well lived, the fact is that these pronouncements on the part of God himself nevertheless suggest that Abraham's life is to be seen as something of a paradigm for future generations to learn what it is that God would want from a human being. It is therefore worth attending to the content of this life, as the biblical narrative presents it, with an eye to asking what makes of Abraham's life one that can be said to be blessed, and to confer blessings on subsequent generations.

As has been noted many times, Genesis is far from depicting Abraham as morally perfect. We see him make some terrible mistakes, and we see him punished.[44] But despite these failings, God has confidence in Abraham and in his ability to "command his children and his house after him, and they will keep the way of the Lord, to do justice and right."[45] And indeed, the stories told of Abraham are written in such a way as to present him as possessing a number of virtues that do set him apart from most of the other biblical figures, whether Jews or gentiles. By my count, there are five virtues that the reader is supposed to associate with Abraham:

1. He can be extraordinarily generous, whether to kinsmen or to strangers.[46]
2. He is troubled and angered by injustice and is quick to take action, even at the risk of his life, to protect the innocent.[47]
3. He insists on taking only what is his and paying for everything he takes from others.[48]
4. He is pious, initiating sacrifices, sanctifying places, and calling out to God.[49]
5. He is exceedingly concerned to safeguard his own interests and those of his family.[50]

Of these characteristics, the first three are not just moral virtues that Abraham happens to possess, but qualities that we are to understand as having been horribly lacking in the world around him. For instance, Abraham's remarkable generosity to the three strangers who appear at the entrance to his tent is in dramatic contrast with the barbaric welcome these same strangers receive at the hands of the people of Sodom, young and old together, who come to rape them.[51] Doubtless there are other sins being committed in Sodom. Nevertheless, the juxtaposition of the two scenes teaches us something important: Abraham's generosity is something that, when absent, has the power to lead to the annihilation of entire cities.

The same can be said of the third virtue on my list, Abraham's scrupulous insistence on defining property boundaries between himself and others. This is the subject of no fewer than three different stories: Abraham's refusal to accept the king of Sodom's execrable offer that he take for himself the recaptured property that the four kings had stolen from the people of the city;[52] Abraham's voluntary payment to the Philistine king of Gerar in purchase of a well that Abraham had himself dug;[53] and his refusal of the Hittites' offer to give him the cave of Machpela in Hebron without payment that he might bury his wife.[54] Here, too, the contrast is significant: We see that in Sodom, Philestia, and Hebron, kings and others disrespect property systematically – giving away what is not theirs to give, not troubling themselves to know when their men are stealing, and giving "gifts" that they will surely reclaim later. This moral failing is one of the central subjects of the History of Israel, and the text later suggests that the houses of Eli the priest, of Samuel the prophet, and Ahav, king of Israel, were all removed by God from positions of power and authority over Israel in response to their inability to establish and respect property boundaries.[55] Freeing oneself from it is evidently seen as one of the central ethical imperatives of the biblical History.

This being the case, it is remarkable that the biblical narrative so systematically insists on Abraham's sharply developed sense of, and ability to assert, his own interests. This concern for his self-interest finds expression in Abraham's relationship with God, of whom he dares ask guarantees;[56] in his preoccupation with alliances and treaties with the people of the land;[57] and in his willingness to make unpleasant demands and to fight where his interests have been impinged upon.[58] No doubt this constant pursuit of his own interest is the cause of his most obvious moral failings – his decision to take his wife's servant to bed in a misguided effort to secure for himself and Sarah an heir being the most striking example, and one for which they are both punished terribly. His willingness, in the early parts of the story, to expose his wife to the predations of others in order to save his own skin is in the same category (and in this case Abraham's concern for his self-interest leads him into a sin – that of throwing the women supposedly under one's protection to the dogs to save oneself – later associated with two of the most reviled societies the Bible knows: Sodom in his own day, and Giva in the period of the judges).[59]

But Abraham's pronounced sense of his own interest does not only lead him to moral errors. It is also the source of the very virtues for which we are supposed to admire him – all of which are tinged with this same concern for his own interest and that of the members of his family. This is the case with respect to Abraham's insistence on maintaining clear property boundaries, a trait which is hardly derived from a selfless disinterest. For it is by means of these boundaries that he can hope to evade the inevitable hatred and strife that erupts time and again in the narrative where such boundaries are unclear.[60] But it is also in evidence with respect to Abraham's readiness to risk his life to save others, as seen in his battle with the raiding party of the four kings. This is a military mission that apparently results in the freeing of numerous persons who had been taken captive, and the text could have presented it as such. But instead we are told that Abraham's principal motive is the rescue of his nephew Lot. Similarly, Abraham's great disputation with God over the justice of destroying the just men of Sodom together with the wicked is plainly conducted against the background of his interest in protecting Lot and his family, who are, as Abraham well knows, among the only just men in Sodom.[61] Even Abraham's extraordinarily gracious welcome to the three strangers who appear at his tent is presented so as to reflect the fact that Abraham himself must have been wondering whether God has sent them. And much the same may be said for virtually everything that Abraham does.

The biblical narrative has no difficulty with showing us what an entirely selfless welcome to a travel-weary stranger looks like when the occasion calls for it – as is the case where Rebecca welcomes Abraham's servant Eliezer and his caravan in Padan-Aram.[62] Nor is there any difficulty in showing us what it looks like where the motive is principally the desire for personal advantage, as when Rebecca's brother Lavan extends his courtesies to Eliezer after having spied the gold bracelets the traveler had given his sister.[63] But in almost everything Abraham does, the text chooses to take a middle path, placing remarkably virtuous actions in precisely such a light as to tell the reader that these deeds derive their force at least in part from concerns for self and family. He is the very model of the man whose virtues are those that stem from, and coincide with, his interests.

I realize that for readers accustomed to Kantian ethical principles, which urge us to seek perfect disinterest in all of our actions, this may not seem like much of a basis for an ethics. Yet Abraham, as it turns out, possesses precisely the kind of virtue that we glimpsed ever so briefly in the story of Abel's turn to shepherding: Just as Abel was able to improve his own lot, and that of others, by means of a risky initiative that he well knew might even provoke God – so too with Abraham. And if you think about it, this makes sense. For in Abraham, God is looking for a man whose name can become great, and of whom a great nation can arise. God's concern here is not merely to find a just man, but to raise up an individual who can lay the foundations for a just society with the ability to survive in a sea of injustice. He must be the kind of man whose virtues come of strength and success. Evidently, the God of Abraham is one who believes that "all the nations of the world" can be blessed as a result of this kind of virtue – and quite possibly *only* as a result of this kind of virtue.

Yet central though all this is to Abraham's personality, and to the example he sets for future generations, there is another side to him. He shares with Cain one virtue: For all his ambition and success, he is also a man capable of piety. And thus we see time and again that Abraham, at his own initiative, erects altars, sacrifices, and calls out in God's name. This capacity to give thanks for what he has, to acknowledge that nothing we have is ultimately the result of our own efforts, serves as a crucial counterweight to Abraham's constant concern for his own advancement.

Until now, I have discussed virtues that the biblical texts directly attribute to Abraham, and that do not require much interpretation to recognize. I would like to look at another virtue that is not presented in so straightforward a manner as the others I've discussed, but which I think is there in the text nonetheless. This is Abraham's horror over the shedding of innocent blood. This is a virtue that we can discern in various places, but it is perhaps most evident in his argument with God over the fate of the just men of Sodom. Abraham's willingness to challenge God's actions in no uncertain terms ("Has the just man become like the evildoer to you, heaven forbid? Will not the judge of the entire world do right?"[64]) is an outrageous impudence and runs the risk of sacrilege. We can see that Abraham knows just how far he is going from the fact that he apologizes repeatedly for what he is doing. But he does it anyway, courting God's wrath because he believes that the danger to the lives of the innocent of Sodom merits such a risk on his part.[65] In this, Abraham is something very different from the peoples of Canaan and its immediate environment, who sacrifice even their own children to their god.[66] And he is different, too, from the Egyptians, Philistines, and Babylonians, who routinely sacrifice human lives in their building projects and their needless wars; and whom Abraham sees as ready to murder an innocent man for their advantage.[67] Indeed, Abraham is in this different even from Saul and from David, who are both depicted by the biblical History as acting, at times, without sufficient respect for human life.[68] In this context, Abraham's sense of the need to protect innocent human life, even if this involves a risk to oneself, stands out as something unusual and as a virtue that God is concerned to see handed down to future generations.

Unfortunately, this crucial fact tends to be overlooked because Abraham's apparent willingness to sacrifice his son Isaac at God's command has made him seem to be an exceedingly doubtful exemplar of the concern for human life. Indeed, the story of Abraham and Isaac on Mount Moria has come to be associated with the willingness to act in horrifying, absurd, and morally repugnant ways in God's name. It is now a commonplace to hear this story called the "sacrifice of Isaac," and for Abraham's frame of mind to be described as his "willingness to sacrifice his long-awaited son at God's command."[69] These are tropes that fit well with Christian readings of the Bible, which see the so-called "sacrifice of Isaac" as foreshadowing the New Testament God's sacrifice of Jesus, understood as his only son, on the cross; and with certain Christian views of faith in God as involving the acceptance of the absurd. And of course, such an understanding of this text makes it the cornerstone of any interpretation of the biblical ethics as boiling down to an unconditional obedience to God's commands.[70]

But none of these interpretations of Abraham on Mount Moria can or should be accepted. Common though such conclusions may be, one reaches them by reading the story out of the context of the larger narrative in which the biblical author has placed it; and by ignoring those verses that indicate that Abraham never was "willing" to sacrifice Isaac. Because this passage has so often been pressed into service in support of distorted and tendentious accounts of the ethical teaching of the History, it is worth looking at it again with some care.

Consider first the ethical context in which the story of Abraham on Mount Moria is situated. As I have suggested, we are being told the story of Abraham, a man whom God takes out of Babylonia to pursue a life freed from the depravities of the societies around him. The narrative assumes a moral order that is intrinsic to the world, and sees nations and individuals as being judged by God in accordance with this moral order – an assumption that appears in the Abraham narrative repeatedly.[71] Within this context, the point of the story of Abraham at Moria is first and foremost *to establish a moral distinction between the God of Abraham and the gods of the surrounding nations*.[72] The most pressing lesson that the reader is to take away from this story is that while the other nations may expect a contempt for innocent human life from their gods (a contempt whose epitome is the Canaanite custom of child sacrifice), Abraham's God is one who values innocent human life above the piety of giving honor and thanksgiving to the gods. Given the choice between the sacrifice of Abraham's most prized possession – his only son – and the sacrifice of a ram that Abraham did not even own, the God of Israel prefers the ram. Indeed, it is the *sacrifice of a ram* that is the symbol of the God of Abraham, who is a god of shepherds; and it pleases this God to accept such a sacrifice "in place of his son,"[73] which is to say, in place of human sacrifice. In other words, what this story is about is precisely the opposite of the virtue of blind obedience, come what may. It is told in a context of child sacrifice, and emphasizes that the universe is ruled by a God who has no interest in seeing human beings make the ultimate sacrifice for his sake, because innocent human life is more precious to him than such honor as can be bestowed by misguided men.

The second aspect of the narrative context requiring our attention is the unfolding drama of Abraham's tendency to pursue his own self-interest. I have said that this quality of Abraham's is the source of his greatest virtues, and of his ability to be the progenitor of a great nation. Yet it also leads him to terrible mistakes – most notably, in this context, his willingness earlier in his life to sacrifice his wife Sarah in order to protect himself from perceived threats to his life. Although Abraham grows as the story progresses, the fact that he is so extraordinarily good at finding ways to align virtuous behavior with his own interests presents a dilemma that must somehow be brought to resolution. Even someone as adept at this as Abraham cannot always align his interest with virtue, and the question on the table is whether Abraham is in fact capable of making great sacrifices with respect to his own interests when necessary. It is in order to determine whether Abraham is capable of acting against his own interests to follow God – and perhaps to bring him to the point at which he is capable of such self-sacrifice – that God "tests Abraham," as we are told.[74] Abraham has already had a foretaste of such testing in the command to circumcise himself and his newborn son; and there, too, Abraham is told to put the knife to his son in a way that threatens the future.[75] But if this was supposed to have had the effect of tempering Abraham's concern for self-interest, it does not succeed.[76] Having failed this first time, God resorts to the much more extreme test of telling Abraham to journey three days to Moria, and there to sacrifice his son.[77]

Now, there is no question as to God's intentions concerning Isaac's life. In the History, as in the rest of Scripture, we are told time and again that the God of Israel deplores the shedding of innocent blood. Indeed, the sacrifice of children is particularly invoked as that which God hates, and as the reason for the destruction of the peoples of Canaan who engage in this practice.[78] God's intervention at the last moment to make sure that Abraham does indeed spare the boy is, as I've said, the whole point of the story, and there is no trace of an indication that God at any point intended anything else. Indeed, if it were the sacrifice of the boy that God had wanted, he could have instructed Abraham to do the dirty deed without undertaking a three-day journey to do it. No, God did not intend for Abraham to sacrifice his son.[79]

But what about Abraham? Does Abraham in fact stumble, intending to murder his son, because of a command he believes he has from God, during the course of the three days God has appointed as the period of his trial?[80] What does he say and do during these days, when both Isaac and the two young servants traveling with them can plainly see that they are on their way to make a sacrifice without an animal to place on the altar? Here is what we are told about what took place on this journey:

> [H]e split wood for the sacrifice and he arose and went to the place to which God had directed him. On the third day, Abraham lifted up his eyes and saw the place from afar. And Abraham said to his young men, "Stay here with the ass, and the lad and I will go there and prostrate ourselves and return to you." And Abraham took the wood for the offering and he placed it on Isaac, his son, and he took in his hand the fire and the knife, and the two of them walked together.
>
> And Isaac spoke to Abraham, his father, and said, "My father."
>
> And he said, "I am here, my son" [*hineni beni*].

> And he said, "Here is the fire and the wood, but where is the sheep for an offering?"
>
> And Abraham said, "God will see to the sheep for an offering himself, my son." And the two of them walked together.[81]

This passage gives us plenty of information, if we are interested, about Abraham's state of mind during this journey, both with respect to the command he has received from God and with respect to his feelings regarding his son. Twice we are told that "the two of them walked together," suggesting a personal closeness, but also a singleness of purpose.[82] Abraham's devotion to his son is likewise emphasized by the dramatic use of the word *hineni*, "I am here," in responding to Isaac, a word that Abraham uses on other occasions, but only in speaking to God – again signaling that Abraham's loyalty to his son during this journey has not flagged, and is in fact akin to his loyalty to God himself. Finally, Abraham says twice, quite explicitly, *that there will be no sacrifice of Isaac*: First, he tells the youths that "the lad and I will go there and prostrate ourselves and return to you," the Hebrew verb for "return" (*nashuv*) being conjugated, unmistakably, in the plural. And then again, when Isaac asks Abraham what they will do for a sheep since they have not brought one, Abraham tells the boy precisely what is going to happen: "God will see to the sheep for an offering himself, my son."

It is not my intention to suggest that Abraham faces this trial with equanimity. The days of the journey, which are days of trial, are days filled with anguish, horror, and doubt. Nevertheless, the text is free of ambiguity as to where he ends up. Abraham at every point keeps firmly in view what is to him a fact – that whatever God may have said to him, he will not require him to murder his son. God himself will provide a ram for the sacrifice. The *two* of them, Abraham and Isaac, will return to the youths and the ass together. Readings that see Abraham as lying to the youths, and then to Isaac, in order to cover up the fact that he is planning to murder his son, miss the entire point of this passage, which is that the two of them continue to walk together, with one heart, for Abraham remains fully loyal to his son, believing as he does in a just God who does not require the spilling of innocent blood.

This understanding of what takes place on Abraham's journey to Moria is confirmed by an oft-neglected verse that tells us how Abraham understood the entire ordeal in its aftermath. Here is the passage that immediately follows God's intervention, in which he tells Abraham not to harm Isaac:

> And Abraham raised up his eyes, and looked, and saw that there was a ram behind him, caught in the brambles by its horns. And Abraham went and took

the ram, and offered it up as an offering in place of his son. And Abraham
called the name of that place "The Lord Will See" [*adonai yireh*].[83]

As it turns out, Abraham does not leave the terrible scene at Moria without comment. He gives the place a name, and in so doing, tells us precisely
what he believes is significant about what happened there. The name he
gives the place is "The Lord Will See [*adonai yireh*]," this being a reference
to his own words, reported a few lines earlier, when he tells Isaac that "God
will see [*elohim yireh*] to the sheep for an offering himself." The meaning
here is unmistakable. For Abraham, there is one and only one thing that is
worthy of remembering here and passing on to future generations: This is
the fact that he had held fast to the conviction that God would provide the
ram so that there would be no human sacrifice – and that God had indeed
come through for him, providing a ram in place of his son, as Abraham had
believed he would.[84]

This reading, which emerges once one takes into account the verses that
describe Abraham's speech and actions before and after the immediate
scene of the binding of Isaac, permits us to recognize that at no point does
Abraham intend to murder Isaac. In fact, the whole point is that Abraham is
able to maintain his moral bearings – holding fast to his own understanding
of what is right, and to his faith in an ultimately just God, despite having his
understanding that God had decreed an unspeakable wrong.

But if this is right, and God never intends for Abraham to murder Isaac,
then what is the meaning of that verse that is so often quoted out of context,
and at the expense of all other verses in this text – God's words upon calling on Abraham not to harm his son: "Lay not your hand on the boy, and
do nothing to him, for now I know that you fear God, in that you have not
spared your son, your only son, from me"?[85] If God has not now discovered that Abraham is willing to murder his son at his behest, then what is it
Abraham has done so that God can now see that he is truly god-fearing? And
what does it mean to say that Abraham "has not spared" Isaac from God?

I know that many readers are committed to the idea that Abraham really
planned to kill his son to please his God. But the text itself does provide a
different answer to the question of what it was that Abraham did during the
three-day journey to Moria to prove that he feared God. This answer is to
be found in a number of indications, well known in rabbinic tradition, that
Isaac does not emerge from God's test unharmed.[86]

Among these is, first, the fact that after Abraham sacrifices the ram on
Moria, he is no longer described as walking with his son, "the two of them ...
together," as before. Indeed, we are told just the opposite: that "Abraham

returned to his young men" – that is, that Abraham *alone* returned to his young men, and not father and son walking together as Abraham had predicted a few lines earlier.[87] Second, the story of Isaac, when he appears again in the narrative, continues with the phrase, "And Isaac ... dwelled in the land of the Negev,"[88] suggesting, rather starkly, that he no longer lives with Abraham. Indeed, Isaac is not mentioned again in Abraham's company until the day he comes to bury his father.[89] Third, the narrative goes to some trouble to suggest that after the ordeal at Moria, Isaac turns toward his banished brother Ishmael. Not only do Isaac and Ishmael come to bury their father together, but the narrative emphasizes twice that after Moria, Isaac goes to live "near" Be'er Lahai Ro'i, where Ishmael nearly met his death after Abraham had sent him away.[90] In associating Isaac with Ishmael in this way, the text opens a window into the soul of a son who believes that his father was really prepared to sacrifice him on the altar, or at least that he may have been. It matters not that Abraham knows the truth to be otherwise. No words of Abraham's can mend this. The damage is done, and the wounds do not heal.

Thus while Abraham never intends to slaughter his son and to burn him on the altar, he does sacrifice something exceedingly precious to him on that journey of three days to Moria, which he undertook on God's behest: the trust and love of his only son, which it seems he never regains. Both Abraham and Isaac bear this the rest of their lives.

This reading also explains the meaning of the term *hasachta* in the verse "now I know that you fear God, in that you have not spared [*hasachta*] your son, your only son, from me." The verb *hasachta* is often translated "withheld" – as though God is praising Abraham for his willingness to let his son leave him and go to God.[91] But as far as I can tell, the word *hasachta* is never used in this way in the Bible, and the impression left by this translation is just wrong. The word *hasachta* is actually used to refer to circumstances in which someone (or something) has been spared or saved by being withheld from danger.[92] Here, however, the verb is employed in the negative, meaning that Isaac is *not* spared or saved as a result of Abraham's holding him back from danger. The Hebrew, then, means this: Abraham has *not* spared or saved his son from danger. By the time God intervenes, it is already too late. Isaac will live, but he has not been spared or saved.[93]

III. JOSEPH: THE HUNGER FOR GRAIN

The accounts of the lives of Abel and Abraham tell us much about the ethical standpoint of the History of Israel and other biblical works. But before proceeding to a more general discussion of the ethics of the History, I think it's worth considering a third story, which is constructed almost as a mirror image of Abraham's life: that of his great-grandson Joseph. In Genesis, the narrative of the Israelites begins with Abraham leaving the urban and agricultural centers of Mesopotamia to start life anew as a shepherd living in tents in Canaan; and it ends with Joseph, born a shepherd living in tents in Canaan, leading the Israelites back to the urban and agricultural centers of Egypt. There they are effectively prisoners for the rest of their lives, and their own children become slaves to Pharaoh. Together with the story of Moses, who reverses both Joseph's achievements and his mistakes and brings the Israelites out of Egypt again, the Joseph narrative is at its heart a story about the ethics of farmers and that of shepherds – and serves to highlight many of the same moral themes that we have already encountered in the Abraham narrative, albeit from a very different direction.

How is that the Israelites, who have been brought by God himself out of Babylonia to lead a purer, truer life, end up being enslaved to Egypt? The pressure to give up the shepherding life is principally economic: There was threat of starvation in Canaan in every generation from Abraham's arrival until the Jews finally resettled in Egypt, and when trouble came, it was to the wealth and technology of Egypt that he and his followers turned to survive. Here is what we are told, shortly after Abraham arrives in Canaan:

> And there was famine in the land, and Avram went down to Egypt to sojourn there, for the famine was heavy in the land.[94]

When Abraham returns from Egypt, his men fight with Lot's men over scarce grazing space for their animals.[95] Isaac, too, goes down to the land of the Philistines because of hunger,[96] and his son Jacob is reduced to despair by the lack of grain, speaking to his family of their deaths, as follows:

> And Jacob saw that there was grain in Egypt, and Jacob said to his sons, "Why are you looking at one another?" And he said, "Behold, I have heard there is grain in Egypt. Go down there, and provision us from there, and we will live, and not die."[97]

There is a bitter lesson to be learned here. The shepherd's life is perhaps to be desired, but it cannot provide reliable sustenance. It is best, but it ultimately depends on that which is not best – indeed, on what is hated. When drought comes, the sheep and goats cannot sustain themselves off the land,[98] and only the agricultural might of Egypt can then save them.

This inevitable incursion of the state into the idyll of the Hebrew shepherds in Canaan is the subject of the Joseph tale in Genesis. The patriarch

Jacob has twelve sons, with no fewer than five of the brothers aspiring to inherit the leadership of the clan: Reuven, Shimon, Levi, Judah, and Joseph. Of these, Joseph is the youngest, yet by the time he is seventeen, it becomes apparent that he possesses very special traits. He has a particular talent for using the ways of worldly power – appearance, favor, influence. The narrative speaks of how Joseph "shepherds his brothers," how he serves as his father's agent in his efforts to control them, and wins his father's favor so that he gives him special gifts.[99] Moreover, Joseph reports being visited by dreams in which he and his brothers are binding sheaves of grain, their sheaves prostrating themselves before his own grain; and in which the stars and the heavenly bodies prostrate themselves before him. To these the brothers retort in hatred: "Would you indeed reign over us? Would you rule over us?"[100]

Joseph's dreams reflect what the brothers might otherwise have guessed: that Joseph sees them not as shepherds, as nomadic and independent agents and therefore fundamentally as equals; but as farmers, members of a vast structure of earthly power in which their lives depend on the protection of rulers who provide sustenance and arms. There is, in fact, no small measure of realism in Joseph's view.[101] But unlike Jacob, the brothers are incapable of seeing this. To them, their younger brother, with his manipulations and his dreams of rule, is everything that their fathers rejected. He is like a Babylonian, an Egyptian. Even the interpreting of dreams itself is not an Israelite custom but a science of Bablyonia and Egypt.[102] It is therefore with no small pleasure that they take the first opportunity to sell him to a caravan of traders and send him where they believe he rightly belongs: Egypt.

In Egypt, Joseph thrives, rising rapidly in the household of Potifar, the Egyptian official who has purchased him. At first it seems as though all he must do to succeed is apply his formidable talents, and all will be well. But it soon turns out that there is a contradiction between the ways of power and the ideals on which Joseph was raised. This difficulty makes its first appearance in a scene in which Joseph is subjected to the advances of Potifar's wife. When it turns out that she cannot be deterred, Joseph must make a decision. Everything he has achieved stands to be destroyed if he refuses her, and yet to accept her is to sacrifice the most elementary teachings of his father's house.[103] At this moment, Joseph evidences the exceptional strength that is in him and succeeds in resisting.[104] If the price of power is adultery, we believe him to be saying, this price is too high. And his career comes to a wretched close in an Egyptian dungeon. For long years he rots in the pit, his life ruined.

Since Joseph does succeed in remaining a member of the house of Israel to the end of his days – and one whose children themselves become leaders of their people – the rabbinic commentators recognized this first spiritual victory as being symbolic of his far greater achievement of wielding power in Egypt, and yet using it in the service of his people. It is thus the refusal of Potifar's wife that, according to R. Meir, earned Joseph the right to see himself as a shepherd.[105]

Yet this sanguine assessment of Joseph's life was not accepted by the rabbis unanimously. Among the great commentators were those who claimed that Joseph's behavior in Egypt was flawed, criticizing his adoption of Egyptian customs;[106] his willingness to permit his service to Egypt to bring dishonor to his father;[107] and the arrogance of rule that disfigured his character even as an adult.[108] And these unflattering statements come on top of the criticism leveled against Joseph by the books of Esther, Daniel, and Ezra and Nehemia, all of which considered his performance in Egypt to be in one way or another troubling.[109]

The reason for this ambiguity in the tradition is that, despite Joseph's survival in Egypt as a Hebrew, it is far from obvious what lessons he actually draws from the years lost in Pharaoh's prison. For the truth is that the story of Potifar's wife, in which Joseph sacrifices all he has gained of earthly power in order to triumph as an Israelite, does not repeat itself. If anything, the opposite seems to be the case: Never again does Joseph refuse the order of a superior, and nothing he does for the rest of his life works against his own accumulation of power, or against his efforts to increase the might of the god-king he serves. It is almost as though his encounter with Potifar's wife is also Joseph's *last* stand as a shepherd, and the lesson he draws from the dungeon is that to be an idealist in Egypt is untenable. To be sure, Joseph's work in the service of Pharaoh prepares Egypt to survive seven years of famine – apparently saving the Jews and all of Egypt from starvation. But from the viewpoint of the shepherd, there is a horrible sense in which everything is lost here. For Joseph's life's work becomes the construction of the Egyptian house of bondage, an idol such as Abraham had sacrificed everything to reject. Dying in political triumph, ruler of the world as he had dreamed as a boy, the narrative nevertheless posthumously hands Joseph his punishment for having collaborated with idolatry: It is two centuries and more before his final, Jewish wish is granted and his bones are brought out of Egypt to be buried in Shechem in the land of his fathers. In the meantime, the idol he has himself assisted in building goes about flaying the flesh from the backs of his children and their descendants – until Moses, raised amid the idolatry of the Egyptian court, follows in the steps of his forefather Abraham, becoming a shepherd, returning to the God of Israel, and destroying the work of Joseph's hands with a stick.

The bitter ironies of this tale reflect the conflict that is at the heart of the biblical ethics: Yes, mankind might have perished were it not for the successes of the Egyptian state; and a young Israelite can save his people and the world by building up the might of the greatest empire of them all. But what kind of salvation is it to return to the house of bondage, to serve it, to build it that others may serve it and so increase the suffering and idolatry in the world? Is this not evil itself?

In the History's account of Joseph in Egypt, this dilemma returns time and again in different forms: When to obey and fit in? When to resist and reject? As a Hebrew shepherd arriving in Egypt, Joseph is, as I have said, considered an "abomination." A slaughterer of the Egyptian god by trade, he is the very incarnation of the idol-smasher: arrogant, self-absorbed, unassimilable. With remarkable skill he leaves all this behind, the narrative detailing a seemingly endless series of acquired traits and skills that render him ever more palatable to Egyptian tastes: He shaves, he interprets dreams, he adopts an Egyptian name, he wears Egyptian clothes, he adorns himself in gold and silver, he rides a chariot, he has men bow before him, he swears by Pharaoh, he marries the daughter of the Egyptian high priest, he has his father embalmed, he is himself embalmed.[110] He even names his firstborn son Menasheh, meaning "for God has made me forget ... all my father's house."[111] And, indeed, he inexplicably declines to inform his grieving father that he is still alive. At virtually every turn, Joseph renders himself pleasing to his superiors so that he may find favor in their eyes, while his relationship with his own people is permitted to languish.

But this surface conformity to Egypt calls our attention to something deeper. For Joseph is forever acting to please his lord, zealously harnessing his will to his father's interest, then to Potifar's interest, then to that of the keeper of Pharaoh's jails, and finally to that of Pharaoh himself. No wonder Joseph's economic proposals "were good in the eyes of Pharaoh, and in the eyes of all his servants"[112] – for Joseph never proposes anything that he doesn't see as being in the best interest of his master.[113]

In a certain sense, Joseph's preoccupation with worldly interests reminds us of Abraham. But where Abraham is portrayed as always seeking that which is in his own interest and that of his household, Joseph is always concerned with the interests of his current master. And in this tireless pursuit of his master's interest, Joseph is forever persuading himself that he is doing what is best for his people at the same time. Thus even as the minister responsible for the grain of Egypt, Joseph always speaks to his brothers of the salvation from famine that it was his role to bring the Israelites. Here is what he says when he first reveals to them that he is their brother:

> I am Joseph, your brother, whom you sold into Egypt. And now, do not be grieved nor angry with yourselves because you sold me here, for God did send me here before you to preserve life. For these two years has the famine been on the land, and there will be five more years in which there will be neither plowing nor harvest. God did send me here before you to preserve you upon the earth, and to save your lives through a great deliverance. So it was not you who sent me here, but God.[114]

As Joseph explains it, he has spent these years accumulating power in Egypt so that he might be able to save the lives of the Jews, and he will now do so by taking them under his protective wing and nourishing them through the coming years of privation:

> Come down to me, do not delay. And you will live in the land of Goshen, and you will be close to me, you and your children and your children's children, and your flocks and your herds and all you have. And I will nourish you there, for there are still five years of famine to come, lest you and your house and all that is yours fall into poverty.[115]

All this seems very generous at the time. But seventeen years later, with the great famine long past, the brothers are still living in Egypt, and Joseph is still repeating these same claims:

> You thought badly of me, but God meant it all for good, that I might this day preserve such a multitude of people alive. And now, have no fear, I will nourish you and your little ones.[116]

That these statements are repeated yet again so long after the original threat has passed is no credit to Joseph. Of course, everything he says in these passages is literally true. With successful management of the empire, he can truly pride himself on providing life-sustaining nourishment to his people and many others year after year. The trouble with Joseph's theory is that it equates the will of God with the accumulation of economic and political power by the state. That is, so long as Joseph is operating the food production of Egypt, he is saving lives. And so long as the Jews depend on his providence, he is saving their lives as well – famine or no famine. Indeed, all this had been the official government philosophy of Egypt long before Joseph's arrival, as is evident from the records the Pharaohs left of their activities. As one of them wrote of his rule:

> I was the one who produced barley and loved the grain god. The Nile [the source of water] respected me at every defile. None hungered in my years or thirsted in them. Men dwelt in peace through that which I wrought.[117]

Pharaoh's very status as god and idol was based on precisely the capacity that Joseph keeps claiming for himself: "I preserve such a multitude of people alive. I will nourish you and your little ones, as well."

Joseph's equation of the accumulation of power with the mission of the Jews in the world is problematic in other ways as well. First, since Joseph did not know that his success in the Egyptian hierarchy would result in saving the lives of the Jews until he had already been in Pharaoh's service for nine years (and in Egypt for twenty-two), there is in his statement a retroactive justification of the accumulation of all power at all times – as though it is *always* the will of God that one pursue power. By the same token, Joseph has to make sacrifices in terms of his connection to his people and their ways to be able to gain this power, and this too he seems to justify as being part of God's work, since without it he would not have been able to "save your lives through a great deliverance," and could not now continue indefinitely "nourishing you and your little ones." In other words, if saving life is the highest value, and all accumulation of power is understood to be saving life, does not God then condone any and every action taken in the service of building up political and economic power – in this case the political and economic power of the Egyptian house of bondage?

Only once in his life is Joseph depicted as doing something that can be construed as being contrary to the political and economic interests of his master. The event in question concerns the burial of Jacob, who calls Joseph to his deathbed after seventeen years in Egypt and makes him swear he will see to burying him in the land of his fathers: "He called Joseph, his son, and said to him: '... Do not bury me, I pray you, in Egypt. But I will lie with my fathers, and you will carry me out of Egypt, and bury me in their burying place,' and he said: 'I will do as you say.' And he said: 'Swear to me,' and he swore to him."[118]

Jacob suspects his son, the servant of Pharaoh. And not without reason. Pharaoh and his ministers are depicted as being enthusiastic about only two ideas during the eighty years that Joseph rules in Egypt: Joseph's proposal for meeting the emergency of the famine; and Joseph's invitation to his father and brothers to come and weather the last five years of famine under his protection in Egypt. Upon hearing this last idea, Pharaoh reissues the invitation to Joseph's brothers, although in slightly stronger terms: "Now you are commanded: Do this...."[119] And they *obey* this command, bringing Jacob and his household to be resettled in Egypt. Moreover, Pharaoh orders them to leave their possessions behind, promising to replace them. But Jacob, already suspicious, ignores him and brings their possessions down to Egypt anyway.[120] The motive behind Pharaoh's interest in Jacob and his clan is plain: He fears that his great adviser may decide to return to his home in Canaan, and perhaps even stir up trouble on the border, and he moves to neutralize the threat by transplanting the Hebrews to within easy reach. And these political calculations are apparently sufficient to justify what otherwise might have been a rather unseemly decision to import a tribe of shepherds into the land.

For twelve years after the famine abates, Pharaoh succeeds in keeping the Hebrews in Egypt. The silence of the text suggests that no one dared to raise the subject of returning to Canaan, since Pharaoh was in any case not about to let anyone leave. The issue finally comes to a head as Jacob lies dying, the old patriarch using his last breath to challenge the will of Pharaoh by making Joseph – the only son with the influence to press Pharaoh to do anything[121] – swear to bury him in Hebron with his fathers. For the first time in his life, Joseph finds himself bound to act against the king's interest: Jacob has demanded that the brothers be allowed to return to Canaan, albeit only for a burial. But what if they make use of the opportunity to refuse to return? Indeed, might not Joseph himself, seeing his brothers go, succumb to the temptation and defect himself?

Trapped in a commitment to his father that he cannot break, the reaction of Joseph, ruler in Egypt, is astonishing. He goes to Pharaoh's *ministers* and begs for their help in getting Pharaoh to let him go to Canaan to bury his father:

> When the days of mourning were past, Joseph spoke to the house of Egypt, saying: "If now I have found favor in your eyes, speak, I pray you, in the ears of Pharaoh, saying: My father made me swear, saying, Behold I die, and in my grave which you have dug for me in the land of Canaan will you bury me. Let me go up and bury my father, I pray you, and I will come back."[122]

Pharaoh does allow Joseph and his brothers to go up to Canaan – with a military escort, while their children and herds are held hostage in Goshen.[123] But what kind of behavior is this on Joseph's part, going to Pharaoh's servants and begging them to try to influence him, and this only if he has managed to "find favor in your eyes"?[124] And why does he blame it all on Jacob, who "made me swear," as though he, Joseph, would never have dreamed of such a thing? Is Joseph, after twenty-six years of rule over Egypt, after having saved the nation from starvation, after having concentrated all of its wealth and might in Pharaoh's hands – is he *afraid* to go in and ask the king for leave to go and bury his father?

The answer is that he is. For mighty though Joseph may be, he is not free. No longer a shepherd like his fathers, he is instead a servant to Pharaoh in the house of bondage. There is no question, of course, but that this house of bondage remains one of the great political and economic powers on earth, with the ability to give life and take it away. And there is likewise no question but that a man such as Joseph necessarily feels himself free as he gives out orders to others morning and night, and disposes of their lives, loved ones, and property as he deems fit. But compelling as this experience may be, it is an illusion. The first among slaves may be powerful, but a slave he remains, subject to annihilation by his master at a moment's notice, in Pharaoh's house no less than in that of Potifar. And when once Joseph realizes that he must act contrary to the will of Pharaoh, when once he is faced with the prospect of Pharaoh's wrath and a possible *loss* of favor, Joseph is struck with the selfsame terror of the Hebrew slaves facing that other Pharaoh generations later. Before this terror Joseph gives in, dooming his family to a life of servitude at the hands of a Pharaoh that he – unlike his father Jacob – could not bring himself to challenge.[125]

In the end, it seems that Joseph, too, knew that he had been defeated. For as he lay near death, looking back at the results of his life's efforts, he felt compelled to say to his brothers: "I am dying, but God will surely remember you and bring you up out of this land ... and you will carry my bones out from here."[126] Joseph had succeeded in fulfilling his dreams, but he had ultimately delivered no one, not even himself. The closing words of Genesis are among the most haunting in all of Scripture:

> And Joseph died at the age of one hundred and ten years, and they embalmed him, and placed him in a box in Egypt.[127]

Where is the power of Joseph now? – we ask ourselves. And what is to become of his people, now that he and all his great wisdom and abilities are gone? The answer is delivered in the lines that follow, at the beginning of Exodus:

> And there arose a new king over Egypt who knew not Joseph.... And he said to his people, "Let us deal shrewdly with them ...." And Egypt ruthlessly enslaved the children of Israel. And they made their lives bitter with hard labor, in mortar and in brick, and in all manner of labor in the field. And in all the labors that they imposed on them, they imposed ruthlessly.... And Pharaoh charged all his people, saying, "Every son that is born [to Israel], you will cast into the Nile, and every daughter you will keep alive."[128]

The slavery begins, and soon thereafter the murder of the Israelite children at Pharaoh's hands. But the work of redeeming Israel's children, which Joseph had seen as his own, is left to someone else, who would succeed where he had failed.

The message could hardly be more pointed. There is a road that beckons to a good man who believes he can harness the power of an empire for the good of his people and of mankind. On this view, one will serve the king in building up his state, and will exchange this favor for material well-being and physical protection, attaining these things while remaining loyal to those moral principles that are most essential. But this road is illusory. It is the retention of one's shepherd freedom, the ability to act *against* the interest of worldly power in the service of something higher, that is the source of man's capacity to act justly. And this is something that no man, if he is in the service of the state idols erected on their empires of grain, can in fact achieve. To serve them is to become like them, and thereby, to lose everything.

IV. OUTSIDER ETHICS

I want now to draw some more general conclusions concerning the ethics of the History of Israel based on what we've seen in the stories of Abel, Abraham, and Joseph.

The farmer whose labor was the foundation of the great cities of ancient Egypt and Babylonia worked within the framework of a very particular kind of ethics. He obeyed the instructions he received from his father, the laws of the king, and the rituals prescribed by the priests; and he did this because he understood that grain, obedience, and piety were that which holds the state together. The grain he produced provided not only sustenance for himself, but also the wealth the king needed to pay his officers and officials, who alone could protect the population from the ravages of foreign invasion and from the crimes of ill-meaning individuals; and to maintain the official priesthood, which interceded with the gods and protected the people in this way as well. In obeying the laws, he upheld the state, which afforded him and the rest of mankind protection. And in obeying the gods, he bought goodwill for himself and for others, both for this world and for the next. Thus in the ethics of the ancient Near East, all action was ultimately directed toward the maintenance of the state since all goodness was seen as flowing from it. Indeed, whatever served to maintain the closed circle of farmer, tax collector, king, soldier, and priest was on its face for the good, since it kept the clockwork of the state in motion for another day and another generation, maintaining the mass of people alive and protected.

It is useful to compare this type of ethics to that of Athenian philosophy, which, for all the distance it placed between itself and the state religions of antiquity, nevertheless continued to find it difficult to think of the ethical life of man as having reference to anything outside the common life of members of the political community constituted by the state.[129] In this respect, the thought of Plato and Aristotle is still much like that of the great empires of the ancient Near East, accepting it as a given that if we are to make sense of the moral order, we must begin with the individual *as part of the state that governs him.*

Consider, for instance, Plato's account of the death of Socrates in the *Crito.* Socrates has been condemned to death by the Athenian state for his contempt for the city's gods, and for his baleful influence on the young men he taught. As punishment, the Athenian law requires that he commit suicide by drinking hemlock. Crito, a friend and student of Socrates, has arranged for him to escape the prison house and flee to safety in Thessaly. But Socrates rejects the idea, calling upon his friends to think of the harm he would do to the laws and to the state if he were to disobey the law. In the following passage, Socrates puts in the mouth of the laws and the Athenian state the accusation that in disobeying them, he would in effect be destroying them:

> If, as we were planning on running away from here, the laws and the state came and confronted us and asked: "Tell me, Socrates, what are you intending to do? Do you not by this action you are attempting intend to destroy us, the laws, and indeed the whole city, as far as you are concerned? Or do you think it possible for a city not to be destroyed if the verdicts of its courts have no force but are nullified and set at naught by private individuals? ... Come now, what accusation do you bring against us and the city, that you should try to destroy us? Did we not, first, bring you to birth, and was it not through us that your father married your mother and begat you? ... [And did we not] instruct your father to educate you in the arts and in physical culture? ... [A]nd after you were born and nurtured and educated, could you, in the first place, deny that you are our offspring and servant, both you and your forefathers?"

Socrates here gives eloquent affirmation to the very same view I have ascribed to the imperial states of Near Eastern antiquity – namely, the claim that it is the state and its laws that give man his life and education. Even if a child may naively think that his life and education were given to him by his parents, this view is mistaken, for the laws and the state protect his parents, giving *them* life, and provide the laws of marriage and education without which the individual would have no family and education. This being the case, it only makes sense that the individual should see himself as the "offspring and servant" of the state, repaying his debt to the state by way of pious obedience:

> Do you think you have [a] right of retaliation against your country and its laws? That if we [i.e., the laws] undertake to destroy you and think it right to do so,

you can undertake to destroy us, as far as you can, in return? ... Is your wisdom such as not to realize that your country is to be honored more than your mother, your father, and all your ancestors, that it is more to be revered and more sacred, and that it counts for more among the gods and sensible men, that you must worship it, yield to it and placate its anger more than your father's? You must either persuade it or obey its orders, and endure in silence whatever it instructs you to endure, whether blows or bonds, and if it leads you into war to be wounded or killed, you must obey. To do so is right, and one must not give way or retreat or leave one's post, but both in war and in courts and everywhere else, one must obey the commands of one's city and country, or persuade it as to the nature of justice. It is impious to bring violence to bear against your mother or father; it is much more so to use it against your country.[130]

The state, then, is to be held sacred, and more revered than one's parents. One serves it at its pleasure, and one does not leave the post one has been assigned – whether in wartime or at any other time, or even if the state should command one to die an unjust death.

In the writings of Aristotle, this point of view is systematized and made to serve as the basis for the science of ethics. Thus Aristotle begins the *Nichomachean Ethics* by asserting that if one wishes to recognize the highest good, the discipline that will reveal this good is the study of politics, the art of governing the state. As he writes:

If, then, there is some end ... which we desire for its own sake ..., clearly this must be the good and the chief good.... If so, we must try ... to determine what it is, and of which sciences or capacities it is the object. It would seem to belong to the most authoritative art and that which is truly the master art. And politics appears to be of this nature; for it is this that ordains which of the sciences should be studied in the state, and which each class of citizens should learn and up to what point they should learn them.... [N]ow, since politics ... legislates as to what we are to do and what we are to abstain from, the end of this science ... must be the good for man. For even if the end is the same for a single man and for a state, that of the state seems at all events something greater and more complete both to attain and to preserve; for though it is worthwhile to attain the end merely for one man, it is finer and more godlike to attain it for a nation or for city-states.[131]

In this passage, we are told that politics is the "master art," and that knowledge of how to govern the state is the source of our knowledge in all other matters having to do with man's good. And since it is from a knowledge of man's good that we learn how to act, an understanding of ethics must be seen as deriving, in the first instance, from an understanding of how to govern the state. Indeed, Aristotle does not seem to think that the end of man – the highest purposes for the sake of which the individual acts and lives his life – can even be usefully distinguished from the end of the state.

Thus while Athenian philosophy was in many respects quite distant from the political cosmologies that characterized the great Near Eastern empires, it continued to develop their view of man as being essentially a creature of the state that governs him, and of ethics as a discipline that aims to understanding how the virtuous individual goes about contributing to the good of this state.

It is against just this understanding of what defines the good for man that the ethical standpoint of the History is directed. The very first instruction that the God of Israel issues to Abraham *is the command to leave the country of his birth and to sever his ties with it* – just that which Socrates presented as being unthinkable. Even more striking in this regard is the story of Moses. If ever there was a child who owed his ruler gratitude, it was this child, who was saved from death by an Egyptian princess and raised in the royal palace of Egypt. And yet Moses kills an Egyptian, violating the laws of the Egyptian state; and then, with the threat of execution over his head, does *precisely* that which Socrates declares to be the epitome of injustice: Faced with the accusation of a crime that he has really committed, Moses will submit to neither trial nor punishment, rejecting outright the state's jurisdiction over him. And much the same can be said of the other heroic figures of the Hebrew Scriptures, virtually all of whom are portrayed as being in a condition of acute conflict with the rulers of the nations in which they live, and as disobeying their laws and commands almost as a matter of course.[132] Indeed, it often seems is as if the authors of the biblical narratives believe that the laws of states, and the commands of the kings who rule them, are no better than empty words, bearing no normative force whatsoever.

Now we know that this is not really true. As we will see in Chapter 5, the powerful anarchic impulse in Hebrew Scripture is ultimately rejected. The History of Israel presents the united Israelite monarchy, and especially the early years of Solomon's reign, as the pinnacle of what man can achieve; and Solomon's invocation at the dedication of the Temple of Jerusalem is one of the finest expressions of that to which mankind aspires that appears anywhere in Hebrew Scripture.[133] Moreover, not only the History, but also prophetic authors such as Isaiah, Jeremiah, and Ezekiel, and the author of the Chronicles of Israel as well, all wished to see the kingdom restored, and wrote and taught so as to bring this about. These biblical texts are no less concerned with the preservation and flourishing of the state than are the Athenian texts just discussed. But they are willing to contemplate precisely those things that Greek thought cannot: the violation of the laws, the abandonment of one's post, and even the destruction of the state. All of these things are constantly on the mind of the biblical authors, and the heroes of these texts contemplate these things and do them. And in doing them, they are portrayed time and again as winning God's love and his assistance.

How are we to make sense of this?

The answer lies in recognizing that the biblical ethics proposes to evaluate human action from a completely different point of vantage than that of Greek ethics – a point of vantage associated with the life of the nomad, who observes and evaluates all that goes on in human life from a perspective that is *outside* the political state and free of any prior commitment to it.[134] From this shepherd's perspective, ethics cannot begin with the state because human beings can leave the state and lead a worthy life outside of it just as Abraham did. Ethics must therefore begin with a view of the human being – or, to be more precise, with the human family – as being independent of the state. Ethics thus begins with the adult individual responsible for the fate of his family and proceeds from there.[135] If the state can play a role in assisting the individual to fulfill his responsibilities and obligations, which are prior to the state and entirely independent of it, then the machinery of the state and its laws can be seen as having a purpose and a reason to exist. But when the state cannot or does not serve this end, the state and its laws cease to have a claim on the individual. So far as he is concerned, they no longer have any reason to exist at all.[136]

What all of this means is that in the History of Israel and other biblical works, obedience to the laws of the state – and even the existence of the state itself – are to be justified, if at all, on ethical grounds alone. The History thus rejects the Egyptian and Babylonian claim, which appears again in Athenian philosophy, that one can derive an ethics from politics. On the contrary, it is one's politics that must be built up out of one's ethics. And so if Abraham, Moses, and Elijah, for example, do not stand by the rulers of the state into which they were born and their laws and commands, it is because the state in question and the laws in question cannot be justified in terms of their responsibilities and obligations as individuals. A state that does not serve the right kind of ethical purpose is for them no state, just as a god that does not serve this purpose is for them no god.

What, then, is the content of the shepherd's ethics, which in the Hebrew Bible presumes to judge kings and their laws? This is evident from the stories in Genesis, which are largely devoted to answering this question. As suggested above, in my discussion of Cain and Abel, the ethics of a shepherd begins by asking what an individual must do *for his own well-being and for that of the members of his household who depend on him*. It is persistence in trying to answer this question that the God of Israel prefers over the piety of a man such as Cain, who does just what his father did and just what his god instructs him to do, and is ready to sacrifice from his own meager possessions in gratitude for what this obedience has brought him. God's rejection of Cain is not a rejection of piety and obedience as virtues, of course, when these appear in proper measure and in the right place and time. But it is a rejection of these as the foundations of an ethical life. The proper foundations for the moral life, from which all else must flow, are the concern for the well-being of oneself and one's household. And only once this foundation is established, as we see it being established in the lives of Abraham, Isaac, and Jacob, does the shepherd's ethics move on to invoke other crucial aspects of a moral life as elaborated in the stories of the patriarchs and of Israel in Egypt: generosity and bravery in assisting those in distress; avoidance of needlessly harming others; insistence on establishing and observing property boundaries and marital boundaries; piety; loyalty; a willingness to admit errors in judgment; and so on.

It is against this backdrop that the significance of the contrasting stories of Abraham and Joseph comes to the fore. Abraham pursues a shepherd's ethics, abandoning the state and choosing to live in tents in the hill country beyond the control of corrupt men. Joseph, on the other hand, challenges this way of life, presenting us with the picture of a man who chooses to live in the heart of the state. Like most of us, Joseph does not join the state in which he lives of his own free will. But once there, he does choose to remain a part of it, serving it and trying achieve good within it, instead of abandoning it as Abraham and Moses did. It is important to notice that at the most basic level, what Abraham and Joseph want is not so different: Both wish to protect themselves and their families – from hunger, from enslavement, from rape and theft and murder – and both are concerned to accumulate wealth and power to this end. Both want to achieve these ends while being just, and both are concerned to live in light of God's will. But a chasm separates Joseph from his fathers in terms of the means to be used in pursuing these ends, for Joseph represents the belief that the apparatus of empire can be harnessed to serve Abraham's ends. And while it does seem for a time as though Joseph may have been right,[137] we know that in the end, his efforts bring his people centuries of bitter oppression. The Joseph narrative thus confirms and clarifies the moral standpoint so boldly asserted in the story of Abraham, suggesting that whatever may appear to be the case at any given moment, accommodation with the evil and idolatry of the imperial state is ultimately impossible. We strive for such accommodation at the expense of our children and their children, who will surely pay the price.

But the accord between the stories of Abraham and Joseph runs much deeper than this. For both are premised on the belief that the indispensable root of right action is the maintenance of independent moral judgment and action in the face of the quite formidable forces that are perpetually arrayed against it. In the account of Abraham's life, this independence of moral judgment before men is dramatically represented by his repeated confrontations with the kings that encircle Canaan on every side. In the Joseph narrative, this issue is brought to the fore twice: first, when Joseph refuses the advances of Potifar's wife, accepting personal downfall and ruin as the price of doing what he knows to be right. And then a second time in the story of Joseph's fear of asking Pharaoh to let his family go up out of Egypt even just to bury his father – a story that alerts us to the fear of Pharaoh's might that operated on the Jews in Egypt, to the point that they could no longer do what they knew to be right. The narrative emphasizes that Joseph remained aware that Israel had to leave Egypt, but his fear was such as to prevent him from taking action. It is this fear itself, rather than any action of Pharaoh or his ministers, that is to be seen as the cause of Israel's enslavement and countless innocent deaths. Indeed, the physical enslavement in works of mortar and brick is really nothing more than the concrete expression of an inner enslavement that has visibly taken hold from the moment the famine ends and the Israelites, whether for want of understanding or for want of will, find themselves unable to come out of Egypt again.

Independence of judgment and action, then, depends on an ability to resist the creeping advance of justified fears and unjustified commitments to human beings and their institutions – which together work to deprive the individual of his freedom to discern what is right and to act in its name. A vigilant maintenance of one's ability to resist these justified fears and unjustified commitments is thus basic to the ethics of a shepherd, the ethics of the History of Israel.

To this one may wish to respond that although the Hebrew Bible does not begin with an ethic of obedience to human institutions or human beings, it does insist on obedience to God's commands. But even this is not so straightforward. I have already mentioned that the biblical History portrays Abel as disobeying God's will – not a *direct* command, perhaps, but God's explicit intentions nonetheless – in taking up shepherding after God had sent man to farm the soil from which he was taken. Abraham, who had challenged God's intentions once with respect to the destruction of Sodom, also refuses, as we've seen, to accept what appears to be God's will with respect to the slaughter of his son, and even names the site of the binding so as to emphasize this refusal. And subsequent stories hew to this pattern as well: Moses is

repeatedly depicted as arguing with God and preventing him from destroying Israel in his anger. Indeed, in the course of these arguments, we get to see
Moses refuse God's direct command, given twice, to break camp and proceed to Canaan.[138] Aaron the high priest, Moses' brother, likewise refuses
to obey God's commands concerning the proper conduct of the sacrifices
on the day that two of his sons are killed. "Would this have been good in
the Lord's eyes?" Aaron asks, and we are told that Moses approved of his
actions.[139] Pinhas, too, disobeys God's instructions and kills the head of the
tribe of Shimon in his tent as he is engaging in relations with a Midianite
princess, but earns God's explicit praise, and is awarded the priesthood,
as a result.[140] And the daughters of Tzelofhad challenge the plain sense of
God's law granting the right of inheritance only to sons, arguing that as their
father has no sons, it is they who should inherit. Here, too, the challenge is
received by God as just, and God tells Moses that the law is to be revised in
light of their plea.[141]

When taken together, these passages and others like them raise significant
questions concerning the supposition that in the Bible, man is always to
obey what he takes to be God's will at any given moment. At the same time,
they draw our attention to what, on such a supposition, must be regarded
as one of the most baffling passages in Scripture: the scene in which Jacob
is given the name *Israel*, which we are told means that he has "wrestled
with God and with men and ha[s] prevailed." The passage in question is
positioned just as Jacob has escaped from bondage to his kinsman Lavan in
Aram, and on the night before he confronts what he fears will be the murderous rage of his brother Esau on his way back into Canaan:

> And Jacob was left alone, and there wrestled a man with him until the break-
> ing of the dawn. And when he saw that he did not prevail against him, he
> touched the hollow of his thigh, and the hollow of Jacob's thigh was put out
> of joint as he wrestled with him.
>
> And he said, "Let me go, for the day breaks."
>
> And he said, "I will not let you go unless you bless me."
>
> And he said to him, "What is your name?"
>
> And he said, "Jacob."
>
> And he said, "No longer will your name be Jacob, but Israel, because you have
> struggled with God and with men and have prevailed." ... And he blessed him
> there.[142]

Why does God here give Jacob the name "Israel" – meaning, as we are
told, *because you have struggled with God and with men and have prevailed*? That Jacob has struggled with men and has prevailed is evident,

or at least will be on the morrow: Lavan had kept Jacob a bondsman in Mesopotamia for more than twenty years, cheating and abusing him. But Jacob has succeeded in fleeing Lavan with his family and great wealth thanks to his strength of will, cunning, and, in the end, God's help. Now, these same skills are about to permit Jacob to defeat Esau, the brother whom he had wronged, who wished to murder him, who approaches with a force of four hundred men, and whom Jacob fears to the depths of his soul. By the next evening, this great opponent, too, will have been overcome. Yes, Jacob has struggled *with men* and has prevailed.

But what about God? Isn't he supposed to be on Jacob's side? What could it possibly mean to say that Jacob has struggled *with God* and has prevailed?

Consider again the man with whom Jacob wrestles through the long night. It is not Esau against whom Jacob contends in his dream – if it is a dream – but God himself. And if we think about it, we can see that Jacob's lifelong struggle with his brother Esau is indeed a struggle to resist the decrees of God himself: After all, is it not God who put Jacob in the womb with another, and who gave Esau the strength to best him so that Jacob was second-born? Is it not God who gave Esau the character and skill he needed to win his father's favor, so that his position as heir should come to be, in Isaac's eyes, a settled matter? To be sure, God promised Rebecca that Jacob would defeat his brother when they were yet in the womb, but from that moment on, it was as if he had abandoned him.[143] In Hebrew Scripture there is no fate, but only decisions made by men and the decrees of the God of Israel. So these things are, in Jacob's eyes, as in the eyes of the narrative, the decrees of God. It is with God that Jacob has been wrestling his entire life.[144]

Once we recognize this, we can understand the metaphor of the struggle with the man all through the night – a struggle in which Jacob is crippled, and yet even after this will not let go. As he tells God as he contends with him: *I will not let you go until you bless me.* Jacob contends with God, and though God punishes him, he will not desist until he has wrung from God that blessing which was his aim all along. And Jacob is indeed blessed, as he never would have been had he accepted his fate and become the servant of his older, favored, violent brother: He returns home now a free man, with eleven sons, with great wealth, having married the love of his life and brought her back to Canaan with him. By the next day, he has disposed of the last human obstacle to his taking up his great inheritance, the land of his fathers. Jacob has won every blessing, and all this despite what appeared to be God's irreversible decree. Yes, Jacob has struggled with God and has prevailed.[145]

The account of Jacob's wrestling with God at the ford of the Yabok thus reprises crucial themes that first appeared in the story of Cain and Abel. Jacob, like Abel, is a man who refuses the hand he has been dealt, and is willing to take enormous risks to try to improve things for himself and his posterity – even if these risks involve dissenting from what appears to be God's manifest will. And like Abel, he finds that God admires and cherishes those who defy the decree of history, and who dare to better things for themselves and their families in ways that conflict with the order that has been created for them by king and state, by their fathers, by God himself. Indeed, we are to understand that it is just such individuals who gain God's blessing.

Moreover, Jacob is not just an individual, as Abel was. Jacob appears in the History of Israel as the founder of a people that will bear the name *Israel*. Israel is, in the understanding of the History, the founder of an entire nation of shepherds: an entire nation that will not accept the command of a king, or the command of a god, unless it can be shown to conform to the demands of a shepherd's ethics. Time and again the biblical History and the writings of the prophets return to precisely this point, to the insistence on examining one's allegiances and obligations each time anew, each time from the vantage point of an outsider, a "stranger and sojourner" (as Abraham calls himself after sixty-two years living in Canaan[146]) who owes nothing and has committed to nothing that cannot be reconsidered in light of one's independent judgment as to what is really right.[147]

What in other cultures would have been sacrilege – the claim to have struggled with God himself and prevailed – is thus elevated into a national symbol and the crux of biblical belief: the refusal of the shepherd to accept the order of the universe as it has been decreed, and the demand to know why it cannot be made to conform to the demands of his own outsider ethics.

There is much to say about the theological implications of the biblical narrative's standpoint with respect to God's will. But my focus here is the ethics of the Hebrew Scriptures, so I will defer careful discussion of the theology underpinning these passages for another time. Suffice it to say that the God of Israel loves those who disobey for the sake of what is right, and is capable of being pleased when a man has used his freedom to wrestle with him and to prevail, so long as the path on behalf of which he struggles ultimately proves to be the right one in God's eyes.

How, it may be asked, can such an ethical teaching coexist in the same work as the commands that God issues to individuals in the expectation that they be obeyed? And how can it coexist with the law of Moses, which is given by God in order that it be obeyed? These are crucial questions, which I will take up again at the end of Chapter 8. For now, I will say only a few words to provide a sense of the direction in which the answers lie. Both in the History of Israel and in other biblical works, the calls to keep the Mosaic law are many and unequivocal; while the considerations the narrative brings to bear in support of possible disobedience before what appears to God's will are few in number, even if they are striking in character. Moreover, even in the biblical narratives, there is a keen awareness of the virtues – obedience, piety, stability, productivity – that belong principally to the farmer rather than the shepherd, and which are ascribed to figures such as Cain, Noah, Isaac, and Joseph. Thus while the line of shepherds represented by Abel, Abraham, Jacob, and Moses receives by far the greater emphasis and praise, the History also recognizes the central role that individuals of the contrasting type must inevitably play in building up any human society, including that which is to be established by Israel.[148] By means of this careful balance, Scripture is able to impart a view of the ethical realm that takes into account two moments: On the one hand, the Mosaic law is indeed held to be the key to a just and prosperous life, and this because it is so much in conformity with the natural law that even from the perspective of the shepherd, who examines its strictures from the outside, it can be accepted and obeyed. On the other hand, the History does not present the law of Moses as superseding or abrogating the natural law that came before it. The natural order and the natural law are still there, in the History as in the orations of the prophets. And these permit us to look beyond obedience and that which appears to be required in a given moment, to seek what God truly loves, and what the Mosaic law is truly intended to achieve. It is the biblical stories of dissent and disobedience, then, that give us the courage to wrestle with man and with God where we must.[149] Such a posture is the only guarantee that the Mosaic law itself, whose interpretation is in the hands of men, will continue to serve as an expression of justice and of God's will.

5

The History of Israel, Genesis–Kings

A Political Philosophy

As discussed in Chapters 1–2, the History of Israel is a single, largely unbroken narrative extending from creation of the world in Genesis to the destruction of Judah at the end of the book of Kings.[1] The History is focused on the emergence of Israel as a people, and on the rise and fall of the kingdom established by this people. One of its central concerns is evidently to offer an account of the causes of the rise and decline of the Israelite kingdom, a question that would have been of more than scholarly interest to the Jewish exiles in Babylonia and Egypt. At least some of them blamed the catastrophe on the weakness or irrelevance of Israel's God, and argued for the embrace of foreign gods instead.[2] The History of Israel was evidently composed in opposition to this view, and its account of the rise and decline of the Israelite kingdom suggests that the calamity was entirely the result of decisions the Israelites themselves had made. Better choices by human beings, the History suggests, could have saved the Israelite kingdom, had they been made early enough.[3] Moreover, the option of making right choices was open to the exiles even now, and might yet bring about the restoration of Judah and Jerusalem, and the establishment of a more enduring kingdom than the one that was lost.

What kind of an account does the History of Israel provide of the rise and collapse of the kingdoms of Israel and Judah? What kinds of causes does it see as having brought about the collapse of the kingdom?

The History is often read as though what it has to say on the subject is that the Israelite kingdom fell because the Jews abrogated the terms of the covenant they had made with God, and because they had violated his laws and commands. And these messages are plainly there in the text. Indeed, it is precisely the presentation of the argument of the History in these terms – that is, in terms of covenant and law – that has earned it a reputation of being a text that is concerned with the *particular* relationship of the Jews with their God, as opposed to one that is concerned to present arguments of a *general* nature that could have a relevance beyond the given time and place for which they were written.

But while there is no question that the History presents its argument in such particularistic terms, it does not present its argument *only* in these terms. In the History, the rise and fall of the Israelite kingdom is set in the context of a broader argument that is general in nature, and out of which its particularistic argument concerning Israel's covenant with God emerges.[4] That is, the History presents the covenant of Abraham, and later on the Mosaic law, as a response to the nature of political states and their rulers *in general*. It presents the establishment of the kingdom of Saul as a reaction to the nature of anarchic political order *in general*. And it presents the ultimate failure of Solomon's kingdom as a result of natural political laws that govern states *in general*. En route, it grapples with many of the central issues in political thought, ultimately offering a coherent argument of a general nature on questions such as the relationship of the individual to the state, the virtues and dangers of anarchy, the reasons for the establishment of government, the dangers of government, the best form of political order, the responsibilities of rulers, and the causes of the decline of the state. The systematic nature of the argument, as well as the impact of aspects of the biblical political teaching on this history of subsequent political thought, should suffice to make the History of Israel one of the masterpieces in the history of political philosophy.

In the present chapter, I will suggest an initial approach to the political philosophy of the History of Israel, with a particular focus on its account of the causes of the rise and fall of the Israelite kingdom. Since the History is a work of instructional narrative, a discussion of its political thought has to proceed from the overall arc of the narrative itself. Here, I will place an emphasis on four events in the narrative that are particularly important in the History's account of the rise and decline of the Israelite kingdom, and on the political philosophy that emerges from the way in which these events are presented. These are: (i) the exodus from Egypt; (ii) the rape of the concubine in Giva, which concludes the biblical account of the anarchic period of the judges; (iii) the founding of the Israelite state in the time of Samuel; and (iv) the division of the kingdom of Solomon.

I. EXODUS AND REVOLUTION

As the great medieval commentator Isaac Abravanel emphasized, the Hebrew Bible is fundamentally suspicious of worldly power, and particularly of the state.[5] There are intimations of this even at the very beginning of the biblical narrative, as when the establishment of the first city is attributed to Cain, who is also the first murderer.[6] But the biblical aversion to the state is presented in a much more direct fashion in the story of the tower of Babylon:

> The whole earth was of one language and of one speech.... And they said to one another, "Come, let us make bricks and fire them thoroughly...." And they said, "Come, let us build us a city and a tower, whose top may reach to heaven. And let make us a name, lest we be scattered abroad the face of the whole earth." And the Lord came down to see the city and the tower, which mankind were building. And the Lord said, Behold, they are one people and they all have one speech, and this they begin to do. Now nothing that they scheme to do will be withheld from them. Come, let us go down and confound their language, that man may not understand the language of his neighbor. And the Lord scattered them from there across the face of the earth, and they stopped building the city.[7]

In these verses we get to see the biblical suspicion of the state in its distilled form. The tower of Babylon is the very image of the imperial states of the Bible, and the biblical teaching concerning these states could hardly be more direct: When men come to see themselves as a single people and live together in a single state, their ambition knows no bounds.[8] By virtue of ruling the earth they come to believe that they can rule heaven; by virtue of making themselves a great name they come to believe they can be eternal. They come to think, in other words, that they are themselves God.[9] And indeed, it is in this way that the great emperors of the Bible are portrayed: The Pharaohs, Sanherib, Nebuchadnezzar, and Ahashverosh (apparently Xerxes) are all men whose self-worship is such that there is no limit to the evil they may be moved to do.[10] Nor is this impression limited to emperors. Petty kings, too, are depicted as being of this same kind: "Seventy kings, having had their thumbs and their big toes cut off, gathered food at my table," boasts the Canaanite king Adonibezek.[11] Even lesser kings, it seems, would extend their rule over all the earth and heaven as well, if only they could. The evil they do is limited only by the strength of their arms.[12]

It is in opposition to this picture of the nature of kingly power that the History of Israel introduces us to the Hebrews. Indeed, from the first moment they are presented to us in the narrative, the Hebrews appear as rebels against the hubris and self-worship of kings and their states. God takes Abraham out of the great metropolitan centers of Babylonia[13] and leads him into a veritable wilderness, Canaan, where he lives his life as a nomad, making his home in a herdsman's tent. The point of this departure from civilization is evidently to be free from the rule of men, so that one may properly turn one's heart to God. There is, in other words, a palpably anarchic tendency at work here.[14]

The Hebrew Bible, however, is no utopia, and the idyll of the herdsman's life is spoiled time and again by the kings that keep appearing in it, and by the terrible deeds they do: trying to purloin one's wife, kidnapping one's kinsman, stealing one's wells, raping one's daughter.[15] Moreover, it's not the violence that puts an end to this experiment in living beyond the state. It's the economics of the thing that makes the life Abraham builds for himself and his family so questionable. Canaan is on the verge of famine in every generation from the time Abraham arrives there, and this threat of starvation forces the Hebrews to turn to the Egyptian state for help time after time.[16] And each time, Egypt does indeed save them. Like any crime family, it offers protection – but at the price of one's freedom.[17]

As we have seen, the God of Israel doesn't much like the state. When he cares for someone, as he does for Abraham, his inclination is to tell him to get out. But in the case of Israel in Egypt, we have an entire people enslaved. They can't just walk away. What then?

To this, the biblical answer is breathtakingly bold, and in line, once again, with its tendency towards anarchism: The answer, we are told, is resistance and revolution.[18] Indeed, to make sure that we get the point, the book of Exodus, which tells the story of the departure of the Israelites from Egypt, opens with no fewer than *three* consecutive scenes of resistance against the state. In the first, Pharaoh instructs the Hebrew midwives to murder all the male children born to the slaves; but the midwives refuse the order of the king.[19] In the second, a Hebrew woman hides her infant son from Pharaoh's men, and Pharaoh's own daughter conspires with her to save the boy, again in direct contravention of the order of the king.[20] In the third, this child of disobedience, Moses, is introduced to us as a grown man. Here is what we are told about him:

> And the child grew ... and he became her son. And she called his name Moses.... And it came to pass that when Moses was grown, he went out to his brothers and saw their suffering; and he saw an Egyptian beating a Hebrew man, one of his brothers. He looked this way and that, and when he saw that there was no man, he slew the Egyptian and buried him in the sand.[21]

In this scene, as in the others, there is no pretence of anyone's being under some kind of obligation to obey Pharaoh, his law, or the agents of his state. There is not even some kind of divine intervention to justify rebellion against the state. On the contrary, in all three scenes, women and men violate the law of the state simply because they think it is the right thing to do. And the Bible evidently considers it the right thing to do, as well. For as a direct result of these acts of disobedience, the Hebrews are given Moses, the man who will deliver them out of Egypt. Not until Moses has slain an Egyptian, fled from Egypt, and taken up the life of a shepherd that was the life of his ancestors – and all of this at his own initiative, without any word from God – does the God of Israel reveal himself to him.[22]

The message here is unequivocal: God loves those who resist the injustice of the state. It is to those that he reveals himself, and those whom he is willing to help. True, the Hebrew slaves who are brought up out of Egypt are depicted as being largely passive, and it is God who delivers them "with a mighty hand and an outstretched arm."[23] But the story of the exodus does not reach its climax until each Hebrew family has obeyed God's command to slaughter and eat a lamb, smearing the blood on their doorposts. God asks them, in other words, to attest publicly to having killed and consumed the god of the Egyptians.[24] An act of public disobedience and contempt towards Egypt is, as it were, the minimum price one had to pay to be delivered from the "house of bondage" and to freedom in the promised land.[25]

II. JUDGES AND THE EXPERIENCE OF ANARCHY

To this point, the choice between anarchy and the state is rather straightforward. Although marred by violence and hunger, there can be no doubt that the biblical narrative regards enslavement in Egypt as far worse than anything experienced by the patriarchs in Canaan. For this reason, it is to a condition of anarchic liberty – and not to subjugation under the heel of a king – that the Israelites hope to return in Canaan. This is a hope that is famously expressed by Gideon after the people press him to be their king in the wake of his victory over Midian in the book of Judges:

> And the men of Israel said to Gideon, "Rule over us, you and your son and your grandson also, for you have saved us from the hand of Midian. And Gideon said to them, "I will not rule over you, nor will my son rule over you. But God will rule over you."[26]

Similar sentiments are given powerful expression by Yotam, Gideon's son, after the death of his father;[27] and by the prophet Samuel, the greatest of the judges of Israel, who repeatedly inveighs against the establishment of a permanent state, arguing that the establishment of a king will bring Israel back to that state of oppression from which Abraham had originally fled. As he tells them:

> And [Samuel] said, "This will be the custom of the king who will reign over you. He will take your sons and post them for himself on his chariots, and to

be his horsemen, and to run before his chariot. And he will appoint himself captains over thousands and captains over fifties, and will set them to plow his ground and reap his harvest, and to make his instruments of war, and the instruments of his chariots. And he will take your daughters for perfumers, and for cooks and bakers. And he will take your fields and your vineyards and your best oliveyards and give them to his servants. And he will take a tenth of your seed and of your vineyards to give to his officers and to his servants. And he will take your manservants and your maidservants, and your best young men and your asses, and put them to his work. He will take a tenth of your sheep, and you will become his servants [*avadim*]. And you will cry out on that day from before the king that you have chosen for yourselves, and the Lord will not answer you on that day."[28]

Notice that the picture Samuel paints here is not intended to describe a king who is *especially* evil: There is no mention of the murder and mutilations and rape commonly associated with the rulers of nations in the Bible. Rather, Samuel focuses on the taking of the people's sons and daughters and servants, their lands and their livestock, which are nothing other than the impressments and taxation understood to be necessary for any king who had to maintain standing armies and bureaucracies. Yet from the perspective of the biblical authors, whose eye is to the freedom of the shepherd living in tents, this picture is one of very real suffering and bondage. And indeed, when Samuel tells the people that if they establish a king, they will all of them become his *avadim*, he necessarily uses the very same word that the biblical narrative uses in referring to the Hebrews as the slaves of Pharaoh in Egypt.[29] In the eyes of the prophet Samuel, the establishment of a political state and a king is akin to returning to Egypt.[30]

But much as the narrative evidences sympathy for the dream of an anarchic political order, its verdict is not for anarchy. It is for a state. And the reason is simple: Anarchy just doesn't work out as one might have hoped. Indeed, the entire book of Judges is one long indictment of anarchy, making it the pivot on which the political teaching of the Hebrew Bible turns.

The book of Judges describes the aftermath of the Israelite invasion of Canaan under Joshua. The conquest under Joshua is depicted as being – in one sense, anyway – a kind of ideal, in which the Israelites act virtually as one man, almost with one heart, in their common effort to conquer the land and cleanse it of the abominable practices of its inhabitants.[31] But men, it seems, cannot maintain such unity of purpose indefinitely, "and there arose another generation after them, which knew not the Lord, nor what he had done for Israel."[32] What follows is a series of eight episodes or stories, arranged in such a way as to describe the gradual disintegration of everything that the Israelites' invasion of the land was supposed to have achieved.[33]

The first three stories, which are devoted to the judges Otniel, Ehud, and Deborah, continue to reflect some of the cohesion and moral strength that characterized the period of Joshua. In these tales, the leadership belongs to the most significant tribes – Judah, Efraim, and Benjamin – and the judges themselves are, so far as we can tell, individuals of exceptional character. Each of these results in a dramatic and complete victory over the enemies of Israel, and we are told that "the land was quiet for forty years."[34]

By the third episode, however, the tribal alliance begins to show signs of cracking.[35] The song of the prophetess and judge Deborah explicitly names four tribes – Reuven, Gad, Dan, and Asher – that refuse her summons to go to war against Yavin, king of Canaan. "Why did you sit among the sheep-folds," she cries, "to hear the bleating of flocks?"[36]

In the fourth episode, Gideon, himself from a minor tribe,[37] is followed only by four of the lesser tribes. He does not really exercise leadership over any of the greater tribes, and indeed, he nearly comes to blows with the leaders of Efraim.[38] Moreover, the tribe of Gad has such contempt for him that they will not even give his men bread in the midst of battle.[39] Later, Gideon returns and kills the men of Gad in revenge, marking him as the first judge of Israel to turn his sword against his own people.[40] As if this is not enough, it transpires that Gideon has a weakness for idols. He fashions himself a fetish that he displays in Ofra, and we are told that "all Israel went astray after it, and it became a snare to Gideon and to his house."[41] When Gideon dies, his son Avimelech massacres the rest of Gideon's sons and declares himself king, only to die himself in a bloody altercation after a falling out with his followers.[42]

In the fifth episode,[43] Yiftah is depicted as leading only the Giladites, which is to say, at most the two-and-a-half tribes of Transjordan alone. The son of a prostitute, we are told that he has gathered about him a band of *anashim reikim* – "worthless men"[44] – and that he speaks of Kemosh, the god of the Moabites, as though he were a living being and comparable to the God of Israel.[45] In order to defeat the Ammonites, he swears an oath that results, after his victory, in his sacrificing his own daughter as a burnt offering to the God of Israel.[46] And he does not bring peace to the land:[47] Indeed, Yiftah deepens the rift with Efraim to the point of open civil war between that tribe and the men of the east bank of the Jordan, in which he massacres tens of thousands.[48]

In the sixth, Samson is even more deeply immersed in the ways of the idolaters than his predecessors. He is depicted as associating with Philistine men, marrying a Philistine woman, sleeping with Philistine prostitutes. And these betray him time and again until his eyes are put out and he is put on display, a freak-show in Gaza.[49] He delivers no one, not even himself. He dies a suicide in the land of the enemy.

In the seventh episode, there appears to be no judge in Israel at all, and we are told that "every man did that which was right in his own eyes."[50] The Danites, unable to defeat the enemy that God has judged deserving of destruction,[51] find a weaker, innocent people on the northern border of Israel, fall upon them, and destroy them instead.[52] Their priest is a feckless man, a Levite who ministers to a statue fashioned from silver that becomes the idol of the tribe of Dan.[53] The name of this purveyor of idolatry before a desperate tribe, we are told, is Yehonathan, son of Gershon – the grandson of Moses.[54]

One might think that Israel could sink no lower. But they can, and they do. In the last episode, we meet a Levite returning with his concubine to his home in Efraim. Along the way, he stops in the Benjaminite town of Giva for the night. There, the traveler is discovered by an old man who begs him to not to spend the night in the street, as he had intended. It turns out that the old man has good reason for his concern. As we are told:

> They turned aside there to go in and to lodge in Giva.... And behold, there came an old man out of his field at evening, who was also of Mount Efraim, and he sojourned in Giva.... And he lifted up his eyes, and saw a traveler in the open place of the city....
>
> And the old man said, "Peace be with you. Only let all your wants lie upon me, but lodge not here in the street." So he brought them into his house, and gave fodder to the asses, and they washed their feet, and they did eat and drink.
>
> Now, as they were gladdening themselves, behold, the men of the city, worthless men, beset the house round about, and beat at the door, and spoke to the master of the house, the old man, saying, "Bring out the man that came into your house, that we may know him."[55]
>
> And the man, the master of the house, said to them, "No, my brothers, no, I pray you, do not so wickedly. Seeing that this man is come into my house, do not carry out this vileness. Behold, here is my daughter, a virgin, and his concubine. I will bring them out now. Ravish them, and do to them what is good in your eyes. Only to this man do not such a vile thing."
>
> But the men would not hearken to him, so the man seized his concubine and brought her out to them. And they had their desire of her and abused her all the night until morning. And when the day began to break, they let her go. Then came the woman in the dawning of the day, and fell down at the door of the man's house where her lord was until it was light. And her lord rose up in the morning, and opened the doors of the house, and her hands were upon the threshold.
>
> And he said to her, "Up, and let us go."
>
> But there was no answer.[56]

Having pushed his concubine out into the street and received her back a brutalized corpse, the Levite carries her body back to Efraim with him. There he
takes a knife and cuts her into twelve pieces, and sends one to the elders of
each of the twelve tribes. Outraged, the tribes muster and demand that the
Benjaminites hand over the men responsible. The Benjaminites refuse, evidently seeing no real need for punishment here. A civil war ensues involving
virtually all of Israel, with horrendous casualties on both sides. But Israel
has the upper hand, and in the end they manage to destroy nearly every
man, woman, and child in Benjamin. Only at the verge of the annihilation of
the entire tribe do they pull back, sparing six hundred young men.[57]

Now, this episode, with which the book of Judges closes, carries a very
powerful, and very specific, message. For the story of the concubine in Giva
is a reenactment of another scene much earlier in the biblical narrative. It
is a reenactment of the destruction of Sodom, which is told in Genesis as
follows:

> There came two angels to Sodom that evening, and Lot sat in the gate of
> Sodom. And Lot, seeing them, rose up to meet them.
>
> And he bowed himself with his face to the ground and said, "Behold, now, my
> lords. Turn in, I pray you, into your servant's house ...."
>
> And they said, "No, but we will abide in the street all night."
>
> And he pressed upon them greatly, and they turned in to him, and entered into
> his house. And he made them a feast, and baked unleavened bread, and they
> did eat.
>
> But before they lay down, the men of the city, the men of Sodom, compassed
> the house around, both old and young, all the people from every quarter. And
> they called to Lot, and said to him, "Where are the men who came in to you
> this night? Bring them out to us, that we may know them."
>
> And Lot went out at the door to them, and shut the door after him, and said,
> "I pray you, brothers, do not so wickedly. Behold now, I have two daughters
> who have not known man. Let me, I pray you, bring them out to you, and do
> to them as is good in your eyes. Only to these men do nothing, seeing that they
> have come under the shadow of my roof."
>
> And they said, "Stand back." And they said again, "This fellow came in to
> sojourn, and he needs be a judge ...." And they strongly urged the man, Lot,
> and came near to break down the door.
>
> But the men put out their hand ... and they smote the men that were at the
> door of the house with blindness.... And the men said to Lot, "Have you
> any here besides? ... Bring them out of this place, for we will destroy this
> place."[58]

It is immediately evident from a comparison of the two texts that the story
of the concubine in Giva is the story of Sodom.[59] It was composed in such

a way that the parallel could not be missed. But coming as the capstone of the slide into barbarism described in the rest of Judges – in which each generation, as we are told, "became more corrupt than their fathers"[60] – it is intended to teach a very particular lesson. This lesson is that while enslavement to the Egyptian state was an evil of unfathomable proportions, so too is an anarchy in which "every man did that which was right in his own eyes." For what happened in Benjamin could as easily happen anywhere – or everywhere: Without a state to maintain order, nothing stands in the way of a descent into ever greater depravity, until finally the people find themselves reenacting the corruptions of Sodom. And Sodom, of course, was judged so perverse that it was destroyed from the face of the earth.[61]

III. SAMUEL AND THE ESTABLISHMENT OF THE KINGDOM

On four occasions, the narrative refers to the period of rising barbarism depicted in Judges as one in which "there was no king in Israel." Twice we are told explicitly that "there was no king in Israel, and every man did that which was right in his own eyes."[62] Indeed, it is the revulsion against every man doing "that which was right in his own eyes" that is the central theme of the Bible's account of the period of the judges of Israel. In the end, it becomes clear that anarchy is unlivable.[63] The only alternative to anarchy is the establishment of a standing political and military power that will be strong enough to maintain order internally and protect the people from the predations of foreigners – that is, the establishment of a political state, or kingdom.[64]

The establishment of the Israelite state is described in 1 Samuel 8, in a scene that is apparently one of the sources of the Early Modern conception of the state as having been founded on the basis of a social contract that brings to an end the terror of a preceding "state of nature." The Israelites turn to Samuel, the judge in their day, and demand a king – that is, a permanent and united sovereignty that will be able properly to defend the people in war and to judge them in peace:

> And the elders of Israel gathered and came to Samuel in Rama. And they said to him, "You have grown old and your sons have not followed in your ways. Now establish for us a king to judge us as in all the nations."[65]

Samuel is appalled,[66] but God, whose wisdom is greater, acquiesces:

> And the Lord said to Samuel, "Listen to the voice of the people, in everything that they say to you. For it is not you they have rejected, but me, whom they have rejected from being king over them."[67]

The Jews are to have their state.

Significantly, the man chosen to be the first king of Israel is Saul of Giva, a youth from the very town in which the infamous atrocity occurred, and apparently one of the six hundred young men spared death in the war against Benjamin.[68] The fact that Israel is able to accept a king from among the Benjaminites is perhaps the ultimate sign of the tribes' contrition over what they had done. Saul's very election, then, must be seen as a symbol of the new era of brotherhood and internal integrity that the kingdom was to bring about. And indeed, the narrative in Samuel portrays the election of the Israelite king as repairing the chaos and civil strife that had characterized the life of the tribes in Judges.[69] When the Ammonites threaten to enslave Yavesh Gilead and put out the eyes of its inhabitants – the very same Gadites who had been in open rebellion against Israel under the judges – Saul raises an army from all Israel to save them:

> And Saul said, "What troubles the people that they weep?" And they told him of the message of the men of Yavesh. And the spirit of God came upon Saul when he heard these things, and his anger burned greatly. And he took a yoke of oxen and cut them up in pieces, and sent them throughout the land of Israel by the hands of messengers, saying, "Whoever does not come forth after Saul and Samuel, so shall be done to his oxen." And the fear of the Lord fell on the people, and they went out as one man.... And they entered the [Ammonite] camp during the morning watch, and smote Ammon until the heat of day, so that those that survived were scattered, and no two of them remained together.[70]

Saul wins a great victory by uniting all of Israel "as one man." But how was this great victory achieved? The division of the oxen and their dispatch throughout Israel is intended to remind the Jews of the chilling events surrounding the death of the concubine in Giva. To be sure, by dividing oxen rather than a human being, Saul makes it clear that his rule will be tempered by humanity; even the accompanying threat ("Whoever does not come forth after Saul and Samuel, so shall be done to his oxen") is aimed at property, not at the lives of his subjects, marking a significant improvement over the methods introduced by Gideon and Yiftah. But there can be no mistaking the fact that the unity of the tribes is achieved – as was never the case in the time of the judges – through the introduction of a universal threat of sanction, as a result of which "the fear of the Lord fell on the people." Saul is perhaps more humane than some of his predecessors, but he ultimately achieves the unification of the people through the imposition of a regime of fear of retribution.

But have we not now come full circle? Does not Saul's recourse to threats of violence against the Israelites' property (and by implication, against their lives) not make of him a king just like those of the hated imperial states of antiquity? Is not the Israelite state to be just like Egypt or Babylonia, an imperial state in embryo? Will it not continually build up its might at the expense of its people until the moment when it, too, can make a bid for world empire? What is to prevent it?

Here we come to what is perhaps the most important difference between the theory of the state that is advanced in the Hebrew Bible and that which is familiar to us from the political thought of Early Modernity. In Hobbes and Locke, the social contract that brings the state into being is concluded among the individuals who make up a given nation. There is no party to the agreement other than the people themselves.[71] But the contract that establishes the state in the Hebrew Bible is different: It comes into being as the result of an agreement between the people, on the one side, and God, on the other.

What are we to understand from this? How does the introduction of God into the contract that establishes the state affect the theory of the state?

The biblical narrative clearly supports the idea that the state and the king should be established because the people demand it: The people's desire to be protected from civil disturbances and foreign encroachment is not only understood as being legitimate, but is depicted as taking precedence over other weighty concerns militating against the establishment of a state, such as the risk that the state and the king will become objects of idolatry, and the risk that the king will oppress and enslave his people. Indeed, in portraying God as telling Samuel to *Listen to the voice of the people, in everything that they say to you*,[72] the Hebrew Bible can be seen as going farther in the direction of endorsing democratic rule than any of the classic texts of Greek philosophy. Nevertheless, the biblical authors do not accept the idea that the legitimacy of the king can derive from the consent of the people alone. For what if the people consent to evil? This is no idle question. From the story of the golden calf to the annihilation of the tribe of Benjamin, the biblical narrative has depicted the people as being capable of consenting to great evil.[73] And we ourselves should not doubt this characterization, having witnessed the example of Weimar Germany, for instance, where the consent of the people, as expressed in parliamentary elections, gave birth to one of the basest tyrannies mankind has known and to the deaths of tens of millions of people.[74] No, the legitimacy of the state cannot derive from the consent of the people alone. Something further must be required.

In the story of the establishment of the kingdom in the History of Israel, this additional element is represented by God's will as an independent standard of what is right. Unlike the prophet Samuel, who apparently would have held out against erecting a king until his last breath, God *does* agree to the establishment of a permanent state – a fact that tells us that in the judgment of the biblical narrative, this was, under the circumstances, the right thing to do.[75] Thus while the needs of the people, as they understand them, are taken to be the most pressing consideration in determining the political arrangements under which they will live, these must also be ratified by an independent determination that they have not overstepped the bounds of that which can be considered to be good and right. Moreover, God is here portrayed as a reluctant party to the agreement. And it is precisely this supposition of God's reluctance to enter into the agreement that provides the theological underpinning for one of the most important aspects of the Hebrew Bible's political philosophy, which is the *conditional* nature of the contract that brings the state into being: God does indeed agree to the establishment of the state. But the fact of God's reluctance hangs over the established state, whose rulers must take into account the possibility that if they go too far in the pursuit of evil, God's agreement to the continued existence of their kingdom will be withdrawn.

In order to win over a reluctant God, the contract that establishes the state thus includes a clause that the king must rule not only in a fashion that is (i) consonant with the consent of the people who have established the state; but also (ii) in a manner that is in keeping with what Samuel here calls *haderech hatova vehayeshara* – "the way that is good and right."[76] That is, his rule must be in keeping with an independent standard of justice and goodness, without which the consent of the people will never suffice. As Samuel tells the people upon Saul's anointment as king:

> Behold the king whom you have chosen, and whom you have desired! Behold, the Lord has set a king over you – if you will fear the Lord and serve him, and obey his voice, and do not rebel against the commandment of the Lord, if both you and the king that reigns over you will follow the Lord your God ... I will teach you the way that is good and right.... But if you shall do wickedly, both you and your king shall perish.[77]

We have, therefore, a system of *dual legitimacy*, which responds both to the desires of the people and to a standard of right that is ultimately independent of these desires.[78] It is this system of dual legitimacy that is the basis for the institution of the prophet in the Israelite constitution: While the people and their representatives are constantly seen as making demands on the king in defense of their own interests, the prophet is charged with seeking to press the king toward the good and the right – and in the extreme case, with informing the king that his evildoing has been such that the consent of the God of Israel has been withdrawn from his monarchy.[79]

But what is the content of this independent standard of right? The biblical narrative tells us much about what the Israelite king must do if he is to be judged to have ruled in a manner that is "good and right," and it is not possible to make a full study of the matter here. But I would like to draw attention to the fact that the biblical standard of right is not only concerned with driving idolatry from the land, nor even with elementary moral concerns such as the defense of the widow and the orphan. Perhaps the most important principles describing what it means for the king to follow the right path are those found in the "Law of the King" articulated in the presentation of the Mosaic law in Deuteronomy.[80] There, the Israelite king is described as being bound by the following laws:

> You may appoint a king over you, whom the Lord your God will choose. One from among your brothers shall you set as a king over you. You may not set a stranger who is not your brother over you.[81] But he shall not multiply horses to himself, nor cause the people to return to Egypt to the end that he should multiply in horses.... Neither shall he multiply wives to himself, that his thoughts [*levavo*] not be turned away. Neither shall he greatly multiply to himself silver and gold. And it shall be, when he sits upon the throne of his kingdom, that he shall write himself a copy of this Tora ... and it shall be with him, and he shall read therein all the days of his life, that he may learn to fear the Lord his God, to keep all the words of this Tora and these statutes to do them, that his thoughts [*levavo*] not be lifted above his brothers ... to the end that he may prolong his days in his kingdom.[82]

Thus in the law of Moses, we find that the king is forbidden to amass large quantities of horses; that he is to avoid having many wives; and that he is not to accumulate large quantities of gold. And upon consideration, we can see that these three proscriptions of the Law of the King are really one: For the warning against horses is obviously aimed against maintaining very large standing armies of the kind needed for waging constant warfare. The warning against multiple wives is, similarly, aimed at precluding too great an interest in foreign alliances, of which the accumulation of high-born foreign wives was an important instrument; as well as preventing the kingdom from being drawn into endless intrigues whose source is the ruler's sexual predations and the disputed lines of succession that result. And the warning against the hoarding of gold was aimed against a regime of heavy taxation, impressments, and conquest, such as would be necessary to pay for many horses and many wives at the people's expense.

If we are to state this simply, the Law of the King was laid down to prohibit just that way of life that is characteristic of the great imperial states of the Bible. Instead, it proposes what we might today call a *limited state*: one headed by a king whose life is not consumed in the unending quest for ever greater power, but is instead subject to a law that is higher than his own whims, and whose purpose is the well-being of the nation.[83] And this, of course, is precisely what is represented by the requirement that the king "write himself a copy of this Tora" that he can keep before him always.

In a similar vein, the narrative insists that the state be limited territorially as well. Thus the books of Moses and Joshua include clear boundaries for the land, instructing the Israelites that they are to:

> Come to the mountain of the Emorites, and to all the places near it, in the plain, in the hills, and in the lowland, and in the Negev, and by the seaside, the land of the Canaanites and the Lebanon, as far as the great river, the river Perat.[84]

Perhaps in comparison to the borders of the present Jewish state, the borders stipulated by Moses and Joshua seem generous. But if we compare Israel's ambitions to those of Egypt and Mesopotamia, we see that the biblical narrative is laying down as law the idea that Israel is to be limited in terms of the territories it may seek.[85]

This impression is borne out, too, by God's command that Israel is to keep its hands off of the territories of its neighbors to the east, Edom, Moav, and Ammon. As Moses tells the Israelites before they enter Canaan:

> You are to pass through the border of your brothers the children of Esau.... Take good heed of yourselves therefore. Meddle not with them, for I will not give you of their land. No, not so much a foot's breadth. Because I have given Mount Seir to Esau for a possession.... Do not harass Moav, nor contend with them in battle, for I will not give you of their land for a possession, because I have given Ar to the children of Lot for a possession.... And when you come near, opposite the children of Ammon, harass them not, nor contend with them, for I will not give you of the land of the children of Ammon any possession, for I have given it to the children of Lot for a possession.[86]

Taken together, the Law of the King, the limitation of Israel's borders generally, and the proscription of conquest on Israel's eastern border in particular, afford an understanding that the Israelite kingdom is to be a state different from its neighbors in that it is to be limited in its aspirations – perhaps the first state in the world to have been limited in its might by decree of its own God.

IV. SOLOMON AND THE END OF THE UNITED MONARCHY

The Mosaic Law of the King has been called minimalistic. But I think such a view underestimates the difficulty of what these laws demand of the king, and of the kingdom itself. For just as the laws of sexual purity, dietary restrictions, and Sabbath observance impose a regime of systematic moderation on the appetites of the individual, so too does the Law of the King – which seeks to limit the accumulation of gold, wives, and horses – impose a regime of systematic moderation on the appetites of the state. And for a similar reason: It is the appetites of the state, as expressed in the profligate accumulation of gold, wives, and horses, that is seen as the cause of much of the violence, oppression, and even idolatry that had characterized the states of neighboring peoples. If one could somehow restrain these appetites, a space might be cleared for a regime that would win the consent not only of men, but also of God.[87]

Of course, restraining the appetites of the state means restraining the appetites of the rulers, and the narrative emphasizes that this problem is not one that is intrinsic to monarchy, but haunts all political leadership. Trouble in this vein goes back to Gideon, judge of Israel, who nobly refuses his followers' demand that he make himself king, but who nevertheless exhibits a pronounced taste for quantities of gold and wives – precisely that which the Law of the King proscribes. Neither of these does him much good. The gold permits him to fashion the aforementioned fetish at Ofra, and therefore to lead the Israelites straight into the idolatrous ways of the Canaanites.[88] His many wives, on the other hand, give him seventy sons.[89] And these sons and their mothers immediately begin conniving for succession, so that when Gideon dies, they go about declaring themselves king and murdering one another – a political horror that goes on for several years until the last of the pretenders to the throne is killed and the whole story brought to an end in a bloodbath.[90]

This, however, does not end the story. It only begins it. For the heritage of Gideon to Israel includes an entire tradition of incontinence on the part of subsequent judges, who continued multiplying their own wives, horses, and wealth. Thus we are told that among Gideon's successors, the judge Yair the Giladite has thirty sons who ride thirty horses and live in thirty cities. Ivtzan of Bethlehem likewise has thirty sons, whom he marries off to thirty foreign women, and thirty daughters whom he marries off to thirty foreign men. And Avdon of Piraton has forty sons and thirty grandsons who ride about on seventy horses.[91] All of these examples of profligacy in taking wives, especially foreign wives, and mounting their offspring on horses, are to be seen as indications that the curse of self-glorification and unlimited power continues to hover over the leadership of Israel long after Gideon has departed from the scene.

When the kingdom is established, the focus naturally shifts to the kings of Israel, of whom perhaps only Saul, the first king, hews close to the Law of the King in these matters. David, his rival and successor, is the greater general and better loved by the people, and it is David who succeeds in defeating Israel's enemies all around and bringing peace to the land. But David is also remarkable for his lack of restraint with respect to women. We learn the names of no fewer than eight of David's wives, and there are evidently more whom the narrative doesn't even bother naming.[92] Moreover, he doesn't pause at taking other men's wives, burdening the kingdom with the killing of Uria so he can take Batsheva from him.[93] And while God loves David for his ability to admit his crimes and repent with a whole heart, his deeds nevertheless have consequences that cannot be controlled and shake the kingdom to its foundations. As God tells him, "I will bring against you evil from within your own house."[94] And indeed, the knowledge that David just takes whatever woman he wants infects his sons, with Amnon raping his half-sister, and Avshalom sleeping with his father's wives.[95] Amnon dies too early for us to know whether he would have resorted to murder as well, but in Avshalom's case both bloodshed and treason are mixed up with his inability to control his sexual urges.[96] Moreover, David leaves the succession a shambles amid commitments to his various wives and children, with yet more intrigue and bloodshed as a result.[97] None of this, we are given to understand, could have happened had David had the self-possession to love and remain loyal to but one woman.[98] And one's eyes are drawn, too, to the forced labor that David imposes on the defeated Ammon, and to the brickworks that spring up in their towns in Israel's service.[99]

These events, however, are but a prelude to what is to come during the reign of David's son Solomon. In Solomon's day, the Israelite state reaches the apex of what man can achieve on this earth. Israel has won its wars and now has peace on all sides; it has power and wealth, and is honored among the nations; it has reached its prescribed borders; its ruler is wise, and he brings justice to the state; he is pious, and builds a great Temple to God; under his leadership science and art flourish; and the people are happy.[100] Indeed, it is the success of the early stages of Solomon's reign that serves the prophets as a model of the messianic vision.

Nevertheless, even as Solomon's kingdom reaches the pinnacle of what the state can hope to be, the seeds of its destruction are sown through its incontinence. The state grows painfully distant from the Law of the King:[101]

> Now, the weight of the gold that came to Solomon in one year was 666 talents of gold, besides what he had of the merchantmen, and of the traffic of the merchants, and of the kings of Arabia, and of the governors of the country.

And King Solomon made two hundred targets of beaten gold; 600 shekels of gold went to one target. And he made three hundred shields of beaten gold.... Moreover, the king made a great throne of ivory, and overlaid it with the best gold.... And all King Solomon's drinking vessels were of gold, and all the vessels of the house of the forest of Lebanon were of pure gold; none were silver, for that was considered as nothing in the days of Solomon....

And Solomon gathered together chariots and horsemen. He had 1,400 chariots, and 12,000 horsemen, whom he placed in the cities for chariots.... And Solomon had horses brought from Egypt and from Keve. The king's merchants took the horses from Keve at a fixed price. And a chariot coming out of Egypt would cost 600 shekels of silver, and a horse 150, and so by their hand were they exported to the kings of Hittim and the kings of Aram.

And King Solomon loved many foreign women. Together with the daughter of Pharaoh, there were Moabite, Edomite, Sidonian, and Hittite women – from the nations concerning which the Lord had said to the children of Israel, You shall not go into them, nor shall they come into you, for they shall surely turn your thoughts [*levavchem*] away after their gods. To these, Solomon attached himself in love. And he had 700 wives, princesses, and 300 concubines, and his wives turned his thoughts [*libo*] away.[102]

Attention has often been directed particularly to the matter of Solomon's wives, who "turned his thoughts away" towards foreign gods. This is in keeping with the text that immediately follows, which emphasizes that Solomon built temples in Jerusalem to the gods of all of his foreign wives.[103] But the narrative is not concerned exclusively with the establishment of idolatry in Jerusalem. Rather, there is here a systematic rejection of the Mosaic Law of the King on all three counts – with respect to gold, horses, and wives. It is the influence of Solomon's foreign wives, we are told, that turns his thoughts; but as in the case of Gideon before him, it is the gold that permits him to engage in excesses he might otherwise not have committed, including the establishment of the temples to Kemosh, Molech, and others in Jerusalem.

The Law of the King does not aim only to keep the king's thoughts turned toward God. It has an additional purpose, which is to keep the king loyal to his people and sympathetic to them – in the words of the text in Deuteronomy, "that his thoughts not be lifted above his brothers."[104] We aren't told explicitly that Solomon's thoughts were "lifted above his brothers." But we are certainly meant to wonder: What can a king who will not drink from a silver vessel because it is too lowly know of the sufferings of his people?[105] And how great was Solomon's concern for the burdens imposed on his people when he built himself a palace larger than the Temple he built for God?[106] When he built palaces and shrines for his foreign wives?[107] And we must think of this as well: Is not the forced labor imposed on Israel and on the Canaanite remnant intended to remind us of the forced labor Pharaoh imposed on the Israelites in Egypt?[108]

If we can wonder about these things, then so could Solomon's people. And when Solomon dies, it is precisely the people's sense that the thoughts of the king are no longer with them that is depicted as bringing about the downfall of the kingdom that had been built with so much toil and blood.

The story of the unraveling of the Israelite kingdom is told as follows. Upon acceding to the throne, Solomon's son Rehavam finds himself confronted by a popular leader: one Yarovam ben-Nevat. Yarovam had served as Solomon's minister responsible for forced labor over the northern tribes,[109] and when the king dies, the former taskmaster leads a delegation of the northern tribes seeking to remind the new king that his wives and chariots and vessels of gold are paid for by impressment and taxation – and to demand a reduction in the burden imposed by this burgeoning state. If the tax burden is reduced, the people tell Rehavam, they will serve him willingly:

> Yarovam and all the congregation of Israel came, and spoke to Rehavam, saying, "Thy father made our yoke hard. Now therefore make the hard service of your father, and the heavy yoke which he put upon us, lighter, and we will serve you."[110]

The young king retires to consider what to do. But the men around him swell his head with futile visions of his own growing power:

> The young men who had grown up with him spoke to him, saying, "Thus shall you speak to this people, that has spoken to you saying, your father made our yoke heavy, but you make it lighter for us. Thus shall you speak to them: My little finger shall be thicker than my father's loins. Whereas my father did burden you with a heavy yoke, I will add to your yoke. My father chastised you with whips, but I will chastise you with scorpions."[111]

In the young men's confidence that Rehavam's "little finger" will be "thicker than my father's loins," we find the same soaring arrogance that was the subject of the story of the tower of Babylon. But the young king takes their advice nonetheless, and speaks the evil words that they urge upon him. The result is confrontation and catastrophe:

> And the king answered the people harshly ... saying, "My father did burden you with a heavy yoke, I will add to your yoke. My father chastised you with whips, but I will chastise you with scorpions." And the king hearkened not to the people....
>
> And all Israel saw that the king hearkened not to them. And the people answered the king, saying, "What portion do we have in David? We have no

> inheritance in the son of Jesse. To your tents, Israel. Now tend to your own house, David." ...
>
> Then Rehavam sent Adoram, who was over the taxes, and all Israel stoned him with stones, so that he died. And the king Rehavam made haste to mount his chariot, and to flee to Jerusalem. Thus Israel rebelled against the house of David, to this day.[112]

Upon hearing the young king's brazen message, the northern tribes rise against him, kill the king's minister who has come to collect their taxes, and tear the north of the kingdom away from Judah.[113] In this way, the united kingdom of the Israelite tribes reaches its end.[114]

In this sequence of events, we are permitted a clear view of the manner in which the violation of the Law of the King brings about the downfall of the state. Solomon hoarded wives, gold, and chariots. It was his wives and gold that brought about the establishment of idolatry in the land. It was the taxation and servitude that brought resentment and rebellion. And it was the arrogance of a ruler whose "thoughts were lifted above his brothers" that brought precipitous decline to a kingdom that only a few years earlier had been the envy of all mankind.

But the limited state is not the only political lesson here. It cannot escape notice that the rending of the kingdom of David and Solomon into two is treated by the biblical narrative as a terrible tragedy. This is not an intuition that is original to the book of Kings. It already appears in Genesis, which reaches its climax with the hatred between Joseph and his brothers. After the conquest of the land in the time of Joshua, this same theme appears in the form of recurring civil war. It is the united kingdom of Saul, David, and Solomon that lays the hatred of brothers for one another to rest for a time. And it is Solomon's violation of the Law of the King that is depicted as bringing about the resurgence of this fratricidal warfare in the time of his son, Rehavam. In the years to come, we are told of how the two Israelite kingdoms bleed one another and betray one another to their enemies time and again until finally, weakened unto death by the warfare between them, they fall.[115]

In the History of Israel, a consoling conclusion to this story is only hinted at. But it is found in the orations of the prophets Jeremiah and Ezekiel, who tell of days to come, when the Israelites will again be united under a king of their own, one ruler over all Israel.[116]

V. CONCLUSION

The most important step in seeking the political philosophy of the History of Israel is to recognize that in the biblical narrative, the Israelites are delivered not once, but twice. They are delivered once in Exodus, and once again in Samuel. Their first deliverer is Moses, who redeems them from the tyranny of the state; their second deliverer is David, who redeems them from anarchy. It is in the early stages of his son Solomon's reign that we find the political condition the Bible depicts as the best that can be achieved by man – an achievement that is at once both fleeting and real.

With this in mind, it is not difficult to recognize the political understanding that the narrative was written to teach. The Bible understands the political order as oscillating between the imperial state, as represented by Egypt of the Pharaohs, and anarchy, as represented by Israel in the period of the judges. The first road leads to bondage; the second to dissolution and civil war. Neither alternative, then, can serve as the basis for the freedom of a people. The question with which the biblical narrative wrestles is whether there is a third option, which can secure a life of freedom for Israel in the face of these two mortal threats.

On the political philosophy advanced by the Hebrew Bible, there is such an alternative. If one wishes for political betterment, there is no choice but to establish a state. Yet this state cannot be unlimited in principle, like the states of "all the nations"[117] in the ancient Near East. Rather, it must be a state that will steer a course between the two extremes, seeking "the good and the right." For this, one must have rulers who understand that virtue emerges from limitation of the state: from the limitation of the borders of the state; from the limitation of the size of the armed forces and of what one is willing to do in the name of foreign alliances; from the limitation of the income of the state; and from the limitation of the degree to which the king sees himself as being raised above his own people. It is within the framework of these constraints that both the people and their king are to find the love of justice and of God that characterized the herdsmen who were their forefathers.

The Hebrew Bible thus endorses the integrity of a single, limited state as preferable both to anarchical order and to the imperial state. This limited national state, in which the king will be chosen from among the people and be one of them in spirit, is in fact the biblical ideal. Yet this is an ideal suspended at the midpoint between two competing evils, and the real state that tries to live in light of this ideal perpetually threatens to decline in one direction or the other. In the eyes of the final author who labored to assemble the History of Israel in the shadow of the destruction of Judah and Jerusalem, it was evident that the political mission of man is to steer the state between these twin threats, thereby assuring the sympathies of both man and God, and therefore the political longevity of the kingdom.

6

Jeremiah and the Problem of Knowing

One of the towering figures in the history of Israelite prophecy was Jeremiah ben-Hilikiahu of Anatot (c. 647–572 BCE). Jeremiah warned of the coming destruction of the kingdom of Judah, and ultimately saw it with his own eyes. After the fall of Jerusalem, he continued to be active among the Judean exiles in Egypt. We know his thought principally from his prophetic orations, collected in the biblical book of Jeremiah, as well as from a historical narrative describing the last days of Jerusalem that is appended to them. Traditionally, Jeremiah was also regarded as the author of the book of Kings (the last part of the History of Israel) and Lamentations, and there is reason to think that he, or perhaps one of his students, may have been the final author of the History of Israel as a unified work.[1] But today it is Jeremiah's orations that are most closely associated with his name, and in this chapter I will examine one of the central themes of these speeches: his reflections on the question known to us from Platonic thought as the problem of knowledge and opinion.

In the *Republic*, Plato (c. 428–348 BCE) famously distinguishes between *knowledge* and *opinion*, arguing that on any given question, human beings are found to embrace different opinions, each contradicting the others, as a result of the shifting and illusory nature of our experience of the world. Thus while almost everyone is persuaded that he knows much, in fact he knows almost nothing and spends his days the prisoner of worthless opinions that lead him astray. Knowledge of the things that truly are, Plato suggests, is available only by means of philosophy, which permits the soul to escape this realm of illusion and to enter into a realm of ideas that are eternal and unchanging.[2]

Did the authors of the Bible concern themselves with such questions? Jeremiah certainly did, and the problem of knowledge is at the heart of his orations. Like the Greek philosophers, Jeremiah wrestled painfully with the question of why some men approach a truer understanding of the world than others; and of why an accurate understanding of reality, once it is in hand, can only be transferred to others with such difficulty. In fact, he believed that most people at most times simply do not see things as they are – including wise men, prophets, priests, and those who have studied Scripture with care. What are the reasons for this blindness to the true nature of the things that are before our eyes? Can one escape it, and if so, how? Like most of the biblical authors, Jeremiah is no dualist: He does not believe in the existence of a second "realm" in addition to the world of our daily experience, so he can't answer these questions by referring to a realm of eternal ideas as Plato does.[3] Rather, his answers refer us to the way in which truth emerges in our own experience, paving the way for a conception of knowledge quite different from that familiar from Greek thought.

The book of Jeremiah has three main parts and a postscript: part 1, including chapters 1–36, consists of the collected orations of the prophet;[4] part 2, chapters 36–45, is a historical narrative describing the last days of Jerusalem; and part 3, chapters 46–51, presents prophecies concerning the fate of nine of the nations surrounding Israel.[5] Finally, chapter 52 is a historical postscript almost identical to the end of the History of Israel as it appears in the book of Kings.[6] In my discussion here, I will focus on the orations in part 1 of the book of Jeremiah, which contain most of the material that bears upon the question of knowledge and opinion; and on an important passage from the historical part of the work, which preserves a disputation between Jeremiah and the Judean exiles in Patros in Upper Egypt.

I. SEEKING TRUTH

What is the attitude of the prophets of Israel to independent human search for truth? Jeremiah, at least, takes an unequivocal position on this question, arguing that each and every person is responsible for trying to establish the truth for themselves. This is not a matter of accepting what they hear from wise men, prophets, and priests, since these are only men, and in most cases what they are telling the people of Jerusalem is false and corrupt. Rather, each individual must inquire and examine on their own. And while Jeremiah condemns Jerusalem for its iniquity, and warns that the city's crimes are bringing about its destruction, he also tells the people of the city that if they search diligently for the truth, they may yet save her. Indeed, in one oration, Jeremiah goes so far as to present God as saying that he is willing to forgive the city if *one* man can be found among them who does justice and seeks truth. As he says:

Jeremiah 5:

1. Go up and down the streets of Jerusalem, and see, if you can, and know, and search its broad places: If you can find a man, if there is one who does justice and seeks truth [*emuna*[7]], and I will forgive her.
2. And if they say, "As the Lord lives," it is for nought [*lasheker*] that they swear.
3. Lord, are your eyes not to truth [*le'emuna*]?[8]

In this passage, Jeremiah refers back to Abraham's argument with God over the fate of Sodom,[9] a city about to be wiped from the face of the earth for its evildoing. Abraham asks God whether it is not possible that a handful of righteous men might, by their presence and their deeds, bring God to relent and spare Sodom from destruction. And God ultimately agrees that a city of evildoers may be spared if ten righteous men can be found there. As we are told in Genesis:

Genesis 18:

26. And the Lord said, "If I find in Sodom fifty righteous men within the city, I will spare the whole place for their sakes."...
32. [And Abraham said,] "Perhaps ten will be found there?" And he said, "I will not destroy it for the sake of ten."[10]

In a sense, then, Jeremiah is making a familiar argument, that would have been well known to his audience. He argues that Jerusalem has become akin to Sodom in its deeds, and that the righteous few may yet be able to save the city, if such are to be found. But there is also an important difference between Jeremiah's argument and that which appears in Genesis: While Abraham emphasizes the impact that ten *righteous* men might have on the fate of a city, Jeremiah speaks not merely of men who do justice, but of men who do justice and seek truth: "[I]f there is one who does justice *and seeks truth* ... I will forgive her." It is seeking men, thinking men, that Jeremiah believes are needed to save the city, and he implies that while ten righteous men might save a city from destruction, even *one* just man alone, if he also seeks truth, could be sufficient by himself. For as Jeremiah emphasizes, God's eyes are not focused on the pious oaths that are in men's mouths ("[I]f they say, 'As the Lord lives,' it is for naught that they swear"), but on the truths that stand before them and by which they swear: As he says, *"Lord, are your eyes not to truth ...?"*

What does it mean to say that God's eyes are "to truth"? Why this emphasis on seeking truth, rather than simply supposing, as Abraham does, that for a city to be fit to stand before God it must have men who act justly and righteously? It would seem that Jeremiah does not believe that righteous deeds are ultimately possible in a place in which no man seeks truth. Perhaps in a city in which justice and righteousness are a matter of habit, one may be able to pick them up unthinkingly, simply because it is what everyone does. But where such habits are less common, justice will come to no man without careful consideration. A man will have to inquire, at least, concerning his own deeds, examining them with a critical eye so he can discover the truth concerning them. Without at least this kind of inquiry, a man will always believe that whatever he does is for the best. And this, in fact, is the way in which Jeremiah views the men of Jerusalem. As he writes:

> Jeremiah 8:
>
> 6. I listened and heard: They will not speak rightly. No man regrets his wrong-doing saying, "What have I done?" Each one turns to his own course like a horse charging in battle.

As discussed earlier, much of the work in prophetic argument is performed by metaphors, and this passage furnishes a good example.[11] For Jeremiah, to live without inquiry and investigation into one's deeds is to be like a stallion charging on the field of battle. For the stallion may possess extraordinary strength and ability. But it rushes headlong without reflection, performing whatever deeds it has been commanded to do by whatever foolish rider may be spurring it on. The charge may lead to victory, or the charge may lead to death, but since the horse has never considered the meaning of its actions, it knows nothing of whether it acts from wisdom or folly. No one who lives from one charge to the next can, in Jeremiah's view, come to regret anything, to think about things in the new and different way, or, as he says, to "speak rightly." It is the diligent examination and criticism of one's deeds, which takes place in the pauses between one battle and the next, that is the basis for moral knowledge. Without such inquiry, one cannot hope to know the truth concerning one's actions. And without such truth, one cannot be just.

Jeremiah's position concerning the importance of inquiry is in some respects even more radical than that of Socrates. For Socrates' dispute with the Athenians was not over a demand that everyone in the city should become philosophers. On the contrary, Socrates didn't believe that more than a few had such a capacity, and his demand was ultimately that he be allowed to pursue truth and nurture it with a small band of followers. Jeremiah, on the other hand, makes no such distinction between the few and the many: Failing to find a just man who seeks truth among the mass of the people ("Surely these are poor, so they are foolish"), he resolves to seek such an individual among the great men of the land ("I will take myself to the great ones and I will speak with them") – and fails to find one among these as well.[12] The lowly, then, are for him no different in this respect than the educated and the mighty. As far as Jeremiah is concerned, no individual is exempt from this requirement of independent investigation. All must examine their experiences and their actions with care, lest the deceitfulness of their own thoughts lead them into mistaking wrongdoing for justice.

What role does Jeremiah see the cries of the prophet as playing in the individual's efforts to discover truth and do justice? An important passage teaches that while prophecy can perhaps be of some assistance, Jeremiah sees every man as having the capacity for independent inquiry, and the obligation to pursue it whether he has heard the voice of the prophet or not:

Jeremiah 6:

16. So says the Lord: Stand on the roadways and see, and inquire of the paths of old which way is the good, and walk on it, and find rest for your souls. And they said, "We will not walk on it."
17. And I set watchmen over you, saying: Listen to the sound of the *shofar* [ram's horn]. And they said, "We will not listen."
18. Therefore, hear, O nations, and know, O congregation, what is in store for them.
19. Hear, O land! See how I bring evil upon this people, the fruit of their thoughts.

Let's look, first, at the second verse in this passage, 6.17, which refers explicitly to the place of the prophet in assisting individuals in recognizing the truth. Here, Jeremiah has God saying, "I set watchmen over you" – referring to the role of the prophets by means of the metaphor of the sentries on the city wall, whose job it is to blow the *shofar* as a warning sign when trouble comes.[13] The sentry's blast is not, of course, a substitute for one's own knowledge: To hear the blast of the horn from within the depths of the city is not the same as standing on the wall, as knowing what is actually happening outside the city, as knowing what must be done, as taking action. Indeed, the figure of the watchman suggests only a very limited function that the prophet can perform: He can warn the king and the people of trouble that is coming, drawing their attention to that which is most important when their thoughts would otherwise be elsewhere. In the eyes of Jeremiah, Ezekiel, and others who speak of the role of the prophet in this way, prophecy is understood as having the power to serve as a "wake-up call." But this wake-up call, even where it is effective, is not itself capable of delivering the truth that is needed. It is only a call to get to work, a call to redouble one's efforts, a call to seek the truth now.

Compare this now to the preceding verse, 16.16, in which there is no reference to prophets. Here God speaks directly to the people, as it were, without mediation. And here his message is that the people of Jerusalem, as individuals, *should investigate things for themselves*: "Stand on the road-ways and see," Jeremiah tells them, "and inquire of the paths of old which way is the good." Here, as elsewhere in Scripture, wisdom is to be found in the streets – a metaphor that refers to those experiences in the daily life of a people that are public and accessible to everyone.[14] Everyone has the ability to stand out on these streets "and see" for themselves what path leads to life and the good and what does not. Everyone can inquire into the compara-tive worth among the different paths that have been handed down of old. Finally, everyone can try these roads out themselves, walking on them, and experiencing "rest for your souls." On this view, the quest for truth is once again seen as being *prior* to acts of justice and righteousness: One must first "Stand on the roadways and see," and "inquire of the paths of old which way is the good"; and only then, having seen for oneself and inquired for oneself, can one walk on those paths that are good. Moreover, the quest for truth that Jeremiah here describes is an essentially empirical one. Every person has the capacity to go into the street, open his eyes, and examine dif-ferent ways in which a person can behave, and the different ways in which he can live. The truth will become known to those who stand and look, who inquire and compare. The difficulty lies not in the impossibility of the task, but in the resistance of the people to the very activity of independent inquiry, which alone can save them.

Given this, it is no surprise that when Jeremiah comes to his conclusion three verses later, in 6.19, it is not the deeds of the Jews that he sees as bringing about the evil that is to come, but their thoughts: "*See how I bring evil upon this people, the fruit of their thoughts*." For Jeremiah, it is not the brutal deeds of the men of Jerusalem that are the arena of the real drama that unfolds as the destruction of the city draws near. The real drama is the struggle over their thoughts, over their ability to distinguish in their own minds between that which is really to be relied upon, and counted as knowl-edge, and that which is vain and worthless. What is coming is "the fruit of their thoughts" – of thoughts that might have been found wanting, had they been examined.[15]

II. ARBITRARINESS OF MIND

As we have seen, truth-seeking is so central to Jeremiah's thought that he is willing to suggest that even a single man, if he diligently seeks truth, might be able to save Jerusalem. This is quite an extraordinary statement, raising questions as to what, precisely, Jeremiah understands as taking place in the city. We know that the people *are* interested in knowing the truth, for as Jeremiah himself tells us time and again, they do consult with the wise, with prophets, and with priests.[16] Yet Jeremiah sees all these consultations as being worthless, because the experts do not see things as they are, any more than the people do. Time and again, the prophet criticizes the people and their leaders for their inability to understand the things right before their eyes. And the question of why they do not see well, and how this blindness might be ameliorated, is one of the central themes in Jeremiah's orations. Consider, for example, the following passage, in which Jeremiah directs his attention to the question of what it is that the people see themselves as doing when they offer sacrifices at the Temple in Jerusalem:

Jeremiah 7:

8. See, you rely on false words [*divrei hashaker*] to no benefit to yourselves.
9. Will you steal, murder, commit adultery, swear falsehoods, sacrifice to the Ba'al, and follow after other gods that you knew not,
10. And then come and stand before me in this house, which is called by my name, and say "We are saved," that you may commit all these abominations?
11. Has this house, which is called by my name, become a safe-house for thieves [*me'arat paritzim*] in your eyes? I, too, have seen it, says the Lord.

As elsewhere in Scripture, understanding is here represented by the metaphor of eyesight, and Jeremiah addresses the question of what the people understand by referring to the way the Temple in Jerusalem appears "in your eyes."[17] This is then followed by a sarcastic comment presented as coming from God himself, who responds "I, too, have seen it." What is it, in fact, that Jeremiah describes the people as "seeing"? What is it that he describes God as "seeing"? As we know, the Temple in Jerusalem was constructed by Solomon as a dwelling for God's presence, which is brought to earth when men recognize their misdeeds and bring sacrifices as a token of truly felt regret.[18] But in Jeremiah's assessment of the people's understanding, such a view of the Temple is long gone. The Hebrew expression *me'arat paritzim*, which I've translated as a "safe-house for thieves," literally signifies a cave to which burglars run and hide each time they've committed a crime. Of course, the cave does work to assist the thieves: It affords them protection from being punished for the crimes they really have committed, without being connected in any sense to their having come to regret these crimes. Quite to the contrary: It is precisely because the thieves regret nothing that they come to the cave to seek protection. With this metaphor, Jeremiah argues that the concept of the Temple as a place of atonement has been replaced in the people's understanding with the concept of a criminals' safe-house that can save them even where they do not regret their deeds at all. Thus the people see the Temple ritual not as a means to repentance, but as a mechanism that can grant absolution once a crime has been committed. To this, Jeremiah then has God respond: "I too have seen it" – suggesting that just as the people have come to see the Temple as a safe-house, so too has God come to see the people as nothing more than a pack of thieves looking for an effective hideout.

In other words, everything here is understood to hinge on the way in which the people conceive of what is taking place before their eyes: As Jeremiah emphasizes, it is possible for an entire people to see salvation where there is in fact none at all.

Although Jeremiah speaks here of the way the people "see" things, he more commonly refers to the false conceptions that have taken hold among the people using the standard prophetic term *divrei sheker* – which means both "false words" and "false things." (I discuss the problem of how the term *davar* can mean both *word* and *thing* in Chapter 7.) This expression also appears in the passage above, where it refers to the people's conception of being "saved," and to their understanding of the Temple as a mechanism for granting automatic absolution. The people's conceptions of being saved, and of the Temple itself, are what the prophets of Israel call *false words*, meanings that cannot be relied upon and so do not possess a real existence. Jeremiah uses this expression to refer particularly to the falsity of the people's conception of the Temple in a famous passage earlier in the same oration:

Jeremiah 7:

2. Hear the word of the Lord, all of Judah who come to these gates to bow down before the Lord.
3. So says the Lord of Hosts, God of Israel:
   Improve your ways and deeds and I will cause you to dwell in this place.
4. Do not rely on false words [*divrei hasheker*], saying, "The Temple of the Lord, the Temple of the Lord, the Temple of the Lord are these."

The people can mumble to themselves a thousand times over that they worship in the Temple of the Lord, and are therefore saved. But in Jeremiah's understanding, no such identification can transform the reality he sees into a Temple of God.

A consistent theme in the book of Jeremiah is the recognition that words cannot, in and of themselves, transmit ideas. Time and again, Jeremiah finds that his own understanding of the meaning of a word is different from, and irreconcilable with, the understanding of the same word in the minds of those around him. Jeremiah often seeks to shock his audience into seeing the multiplicity of conceptions that stand behind simple words, as when, in the above passage, he announces in the gates of the Temple that it is a lie to call it by the name "the Temple of the Lord." At other times, he demands that the people stop using otherwise legitimate words that have been corrupted by the bad concepts that have been attached to them. Thus, for example, a Hebrew term for a prophecy is the word *masa*, which can also mean burden. But while the people sometimes inquired after the *masa*, or prophecy, of God, in many cases it was evident to Jeremiah that the people were actually poking fun at him and his God, asking "What is the burden of the Lord?" – with the word of God being understood as nothing but a burden:

Jeremiah 23:

33. Now if this people, or the prophet or priest, asks you, saying, "What is the *masa* of the Lord?" ...
34. ... I will punish that man and his household....
36. And "the *masa* of the Lord" you will mention no more, for should his [God's] word be a burden [*masa*] to man? But you have overturned [*hafachtem*] the words of the living God, of our God the Lord of Hosts.
37. So will you say to the prophet: "What has the Lord replied to you?" or "What has the Lord spoken?"
38. But if you say "the *masa* of the Lord" ...
40. I will place upon you an everlasting shame and everlasting embarrassment that will not be forgotten.

In this passage, Jeremiah accuses the people of purposely "overturning" the words of God, the word he uses for "overturned" being a cognate of the term that appears in Genesis to describe what God does to Sodom: *hafecha* – a turning upside down, a complete ruination.[19] Jeremiah's rhetoric is bitter and his anger surely cannot be fathomed so long as we understand him to be responding only to a few good fellows cracking jokes at his expense. But Jeremiah does not think that what is going on is just some harmless punning. He sees the words in question as those that all Jerusalem must use to parse reality, and as such, he believes they will determine the fate of the city: To overturn a term that might have been used for understanding and for saving many lives, to turn it to another meaning that is worthless just for the sake of a joke, is to purposefully advance the very same corruption of understanding that, as we have seen, has already destroyed the Temple service. Indeed, it is because of such a blindness to the distinction between valuable and worthless meanings of words that Jeremiah believes Jerusalem will be destroyed.

Jeremiah's critique of language is perhaps at its most anguished where the subject is the inability of priests and prophets to understand the words of the Scriptures. For if the words deployed in reading the old texts have themselves already been "overturned" and their intended meanings lost, then those concerned with studying God's word will not have any way of understanding what they are reading. They will not, in other words, know God's word. And this is just as Jeremiah presents it: "[T]hose who grasped my teaching did not know me."[20] And without an understanding of the Tora, much else will go by the board as well. In the following passage, Jeremiah connects the inability to understand the Scriptures with the inability of priest and prophet to draw moral distinctions and to teach others to do so. This being the case, these appointed healers of Israel cannot heal, and the peace that they see in the land is no peace:

Jeremiah 8:

  8. How can you say, "We are wise and the Teaching of the Lord is with us?" Surely, the pen worked in vain, in vain the scribes.
  9. Shamed are the wise men, they have been dismayed and trapped. See how they have rejected the word of the Lord, now what wisdom have they?
  10. Therefore, I will give their wives to others, their fields to those who will possess them. For from the small to the great, they all surely rob. From the prophet to the priest, they all deal falsehood.
  11. And they healed the wounds of my people superficially, saying, "Peace, peace." But there is no peace.[21]

This a frightening picture indeed. It is not that the people are not concerned with God or his teaching, nor that they have lost the desire for peace. On the contrary, priest and prophet remain convinced that it is "the Teaching of the Lord" they uphold, and that it is God's promised "peace" they see in the land. But as with the Temple, the terms in use have been overturned, and what is now understood as the Tora, and what is now understood to be peace, have become detached from the actual things needed for Israel to remain whole and on its land. In this context, the prophets continue to prophesy, but not about anything real:

Jeremiah 23:

  16. The vision their own mind they speak, not from the mouth of the Lord.
  17. They always say to those who despise me, the Lord spoke it, "You will have peace," and to all who walk after the arbitrariness of their mind [*bishrirut libo*] they say, "Evil will not come upon you."[22]

Thus on Jeremiah's view, the prophets of Judah, without any particular ability to penetrate the fog of mistaken conceptions about them, speak words that are, in effect, nothing but "the vision of their own mind." Without that which is truly real to constrain them, they resort to what is easiest: The prophets assure the people that every choice can be for the good, and that in the long run no course can be said to have especially terrible consequences.

Notice that in the passage as I've rendered it, Jeremiah refers twice to the "minds" of the people of Jerusalem and Judah. Jeremiah actually has quite a bit to say about the human mind, but this fact often escapes notice as a result of faulty translation. The Hebrew word *lev* (לב), taken literally, refers to the physical organ we call the heart, and as a consequence most translations use the English *heart* wherever the original Hebrew has *lev*. But in most cases, this translation misses the meaning of the biblical authors, and in many it leads to outright mistakes in translation. Classical Hebrew has no parallel to the later Western dichotomy between the "heart" as the seat of the emotions and the "mind" as the seat of thought. For the biblical authors, sentiments are a part of the process of human thought and of reason, and not something separate from it. And when human beings are thinking, or reasoning, or believing, they do so with their *lev*, which is most directly translated as *mind*.[23]

The fact that most Westerners read the biblical authors as though they are talking about the heart whenever they refer to the mind means that the entire biblical corpus takes on a kind of romantic, sentimental feeling that is absent in the original. And as a byproduct, it makes it almost impossible to understand what the biblical authors have to say about human thought. This is certainly the case for Jeremiah, whose orations regularly use the word *lev* to refer to the mind.[24]

A particularly important concept for Jeremiah is one that appears in the passage I last quoted, that of *shrirut lev* – the "arbitrariness" of the human mind.[25] Jeremiah uses this expression frequently (it is unique to him in the orations of the prophets[26]) to say that men are by nature different from the animals, at least, in this: that man has been uniquely endowed with the capacity to value that which will gain him little or nothing, and to devote himself to its pursuit. This is reflected in the oration from which I quote above, in which the prophets of Israel are depicted as assuring those who act in accordance with the "arbitrariness of their minds" that the things they value will lead them to well-being, and not to ruin. In other passages, we see that this arbitrariness involves "following one's own thoughts," an expression reminiscent of the metaphor of the stallion charging in battle:

Jeremiah 18:

11. Return now, each from his own evil way, and improve your ways and your deeds.

12. And they said, "Give it up! For we will follow after our thoughts [*mah-shevoteinu*], and each will do the arbitrariness of his evil mind [*shrirut libo hara*]."

Elsewhere, Jeremiah refers to arbitrariness of the mind as the capacity, or tendency, to walk away from those things that are true human ends, rather than towards them:

Jeremiah 7:

24. But they did not obey nor did they incline their ears, but walked according to their own counsels and the arbitrariness of their evil hearts [*bishrirut libam hara*], and walked backwards and not forwards.

Thus while other beasts obey the laws of nature and pursue their own good, men do not.[27] They do not see things as they are, but see them in accordance with false words, false understandings that, when relied upon, lead them "backwards" away from their own needs and not "forwards" towards them.

Significantly, it is not only the men of Judah whose minds are arbitrary. Jeremiah believes that the men of other nations are like this as well.[28] Indeed, it would appear to be in mankind's nature to constantly misunderstand the things we see, and to walk away from our own needs without knowing it. These observations bring Jeremiah to a famous, radical conclusion concerning the nature of the human mind as an instrument for attaining knowledge:

Jeremiah 17:

9. The mind is deceitful above all things, and when fatally so, who will know it?

The term for "deceitful" here is *akub*, perhaps related to *akum*, meaning twisted. The nature of the mind is such that it does not "see straight." It entertains false thoughts, leading to false choices. And when the mind grows weak in this way, we have no way of knowing we've been misled. The better part of wisdom, then, will be for every man to suspect the conclusions of his own mind.[29]

III. THE NATURAL LAW

At this point, one may be tempted to impute to Jeremiah some form of fideism. If, after all, the mind is "deceitful above all things," then should not the work of the human mind – that is, *reason* – be set aside in favor of unquestioning faith and blind obedience? Is this not ultimately Jeremiah's message?

Such a reading of Jeremiah's writings must be rejected, for two reasons: First, it must be rejected because there is no way of squaring it with Jeremiah's psychology – with understanding of the mind's nature. Those Christian readings that propose that reason be set aside in favor of faith only become possible once one has embraced a psychology that sees the *mind* and the *heart* as being different faculties, the former being the arena of man's thoughts, while the latter is the seat of belief. If one assumes that these faculties can operate more or less independently of one another, then one can imagine setting aside the corrupt reasonings of the mind in favor of a pure and obedient faith, which believes without trying to understand, and which is located in the "heart." Jeremiah, however, knows of no such possibility, because he knows of no such distinction between the mind and the heart. For Jeremiah, even if the mind is deceitful above all things, it still cannot be set aside in favor of another faculty of belief, for there is no other faculty of belief. To him, the human mind – the very same faculty that does the thinking and reasoning – is also that with which we believe. To say, as Jeremiah does, that the mind as deceitful is just to say that what is believed is the product of deceit. So Jeremiah can hardly be calling on the people to obey and believe instead of going after their deceitful thoughts, for it is precisely their capacity to obey and believe in anything real that he suspects.

Second, Jeremiah cannot be calling on the people to a blind obedience and faith because even if such a thing were desirable, there would be no way to know whom to obey and what to believe. For the problem of knowledge as it appears in Jeremiah's orations is thoroughgoing: It challenges the content of Scripture as it appears to us because those who grasp the Tora may not know its meaning ("Those who grasped my teaching did not know me"[30]); and it challenges the content of prophecy as it appears to us because the prophets may not have God's word ("A vision of their own mind they speak"[31]). This is not because the priests and the prophets are dishonest men, although there are dishonest men among them. It is because the mind is deceitful above all things. And as both the Scriptures and God's word are understood only by means of the human mind, prophet and priest are deceived as to its meaning. But if one cannot rely on the prophet or the priest to get God's word right, then there is nothing at all to be gained by an unthinking acceptance or blind obedience to Scripture or prophecy. If it is not the truth that one is accepting or obeying, then to accept it or obey it is worthless or worse.

All this means that Jeremiah has no recourse but to seek a resolution to the problem of knowledge within the context of a theory that views the mind as being deceitful in the things it presents. If there is a way for human beings to attain truth, it will have to be by way of the flawed mental apparatus with which God has equipped us.

How, then, can men hope to find the truth? This will be possible, it seems, only if reality itself, possessing a certain intrinsic nature, is able to exert some kind of constraint on the arbitrariness of the mind, forcing it into conceptions that are natural and appropriate to men. In Chapter 4, I suggested that the History of Israel understands the deeds of men as being subject to a natural law that derives from the nature of the world itself, which is presented as being accessible to the minds of men, whether in part or in its entirety. This seems like a promising start, for if there is such a law deriving from the intrinsic nature of the world – from the nature of human beings and of the things around them – then it may be that such a law will become known over time, as the true nature of reality gradually forces itself upon the mind of the individual by trial and error. Let's consider where Jeremiah stands on this question.[32]

Jeremiah's orations seem to suggest a view that is much like the one that I have attributed to the History. As far as we can tell, Jeremiah understands everything in the universe as being governed by "laws" that are given by God. For example, Jeremiah considers the fact that the sea is held in check, and cannot rise up and flood the land, to be the expression of a law that governs the physical world:

Jeremiah 5:

22. Will you not fear me, says the Lord, will you not tremble before me, who placed the sand for a boundary to the sea as a law forever, which it cannot pass? And though the waves throw themselves, they cannot prevail, and though they roar, they cannot pass it.

Similarly, the coming of the rains and the growth of the various plants on which the harvest depends is in accordance with the "laws of the harvest":

Jeremiah 5:

24. And they did not say in their mind, "Let us now fear the Lord, our God, who gives rain, the early rain and the later rain in their times, who keeps the weeks of the laws of the harvest for us."[33]

And in the same way, the different species of birds each keep to the seasons and times of their coming, understanding what they need to understand in order to live:

Jeremiah 8:

7. Even the stork in the sky knows its seasons, and the turtledove and the crane and the swallow keep the times of their coming, but my people do not know the law of the Lord.

These passages suggest that everything in the physical world, including the plants and the animals, functions according to regular laws, without which it would come to harm and eventually cease to exist: Without the laws of nature, the solid land would be overwhelmed by the waters, the crops would fail, the birds would die out. And the same is true, apparently, for all things.[34]

What of human beings? Are they also governed by a natural law without which they come to harm and eventually cease to exist? With respect to the nation of Israel, at least, the answer to this question is quite clear. In the last passage quoted above, the laws governing the behavior of the birds are presented as being exactly parallel to the laws that have been made known to Israel: Just as the laws of physics permit the dry land to exist, and the laws of biology permit the birds to live, so too is the Tora to be understood as that "law of the Lord" that would permit Israel their continued existence and well-being, if only they would keep it.[35] Of course, the Jews do not live according to this natural law. Unlike the wheat growing in the fields or the birds in the skies, they go after the arbitrariness of their minds, falling away from their own good into that which leads to their ruin. But this does not change the fact that such a natural law exists – and could, in principle, be discovered and embraced.

But why should there be a natural "law of the Lord" that is fitting only to Israel? The laws that govern the migrations and life cycle of the birds are intrinsic to their natures. But surely the Israelites possess a nature that is extremely similar, if not perfectly identical, to those of the people of other nations? How, then, could the Tora be the "law of the Lord" for Israel, reflecting the way in which the people of Judah and Jerusalem must live if they are to secure life and the good, and yet fail to have the same significance for the other nations, whose nature is on the whole the same as that of Israel? Does Jeremiah think the other nations should also adopt the Tora?

There is evidence that Jeremiah does think something quite similar to this. To begin with, he is explicit in rejecting the laws presently followed by the nations as basically worthless – not just for the Jews, but also for the people who follow them. As he writes:

Jeremiah 10:

2. So says the Lord: Do not learn the ways of the nations, and do not be dismayed by the signs of the heavens because the nations are dismayed by them.
3. For the laws of the peoples are worthless, for they have cut wood from the forest, the work of the workman's hands with the axe....
5. [B]e not afraid of them [i.e., the idols], for they will not harm you. Neither can they do good.

The subject here is astral divination as followed, for example, by the Babylonians, who held that events in the skies were portents revealing the coming fate of men. The Babylonians believed that such portents followed fixed laws, as if they were laws of nature, and kept vast catalogues of the rules they had learned for connecting the omens they had observed with the events they believed must follow.[36] But Jeremiah rejects such astrology, comparing it to the making of idols of wood. Just as the wooden idol is "the work of the workman's hands with the axe," so too are these acts of divination just a making of gods with one's own hands. In each case, Jeremiah says that there is nothing to fear from them, and nothing to be gained, because neither astrology nor carved idols reflect an understanding of the true nature of the world. These "laws of the peoples are worthless," reflecting only men "going after the arbitrariness of their evil minds [*shrirut libam hara*]."[37] And indeed, Jeremiah fully expects that the day will come when not only Israel but all the nations will come to see this, and will abandon the worthless laws they have inherited from their fathers. As he writes:

Jeremiah 16:

19. Nations will come from the ends of the earth and say, "Only lies have our fathers bequeathed us, worthless and with nothing in them to avail.
20. Can a man make gods for himself? They are no gods."

But if the nations are indeed to come from the ends of the earth, saying that the laws of their fathers are "worthless and with nothing in them to avail," what laws are they to turn to? Jeremiah's answer is that the nations of the world should learn "the ways of my people," so that they too "will be built up" together with Israel:

Jeremiah 12:

16. And it will be that if they [the neighboring nations] diligently learn the ways of my people, to swear by my name, "As the Lord lives," as they taught my people to swear by the Ba'al, they will be built up amid my people.
17. And if they do not listen, I will uproot that nation, uproot and destroy it, says the Lord.[38]

We don't have any way of knowing whether Jeremiah proposed that the nations should adopt every part of the Mosaic law, or whether they were only to adopt "the ways of my people" in general, with each nation adapting Israel's laws to their own particular character and needs.[39] But either way, Jeremiah's basic message could not be more direct. Just as there are laws that govern the physical and animal worlds, ensuring that the land is preserved from the forces that would destroy it, and the plants and the birds are kept alive and healthy, so too are there laws that govern the life and well-being of men as well. These laws are the laws of the Tora given by Moses, which instruct us as to what must be done if Israel, or any nation, wishes to live.

IV. PROFIT AND PAIN

As Jeremiah understands it, the natural law is what protects the land from being swallowed up by the sea, and what directs plants and animals to do what they need to do live and flourish. If the laws given Israel by God are the natural law for men, then these laws will teach us what we must do if we want to attain life and the good, as individuals and as nations. By the same token, if we do not obey these laws, we will quickly begin to feel the pain of the disintegration and collapse that will naturally follow. But if this is the case, should not Jeremiah's understanding of the Tora as the natural law offer a solution to the problem of the arbitrariness of men's minds? Should not the pain of disintegration and collapse that follows neglect of the law be sufficient to make it obvious that one has strayed from the path of what is beneficial and good, and force an understanding of the true nature of the world?

Many of Jeremiah's orations point in just this direction, in doing so introducing a term that is significant in this regard in a number of biblical works – Isaiah, Jeremiah, Proverbs, and Job among them: the word *ho'il*, usually translated into English as that which can *profit*, *benefit*, or *avail*.[40] This is a cognate of the Hebrew root *yud-ain-lamed* (יעל), which means to *ascend*,[41] so that when something is described as *ho'il* (past tense; *mo'il* in present and *yo'il* in future tense), it may be understood as that which "raises up" individuals and nations, moving them toward what can preserve and strengthen them. The sense of the term is evident from the following passage from Isaiah:

Isaiah 48:

17. Thus says the Lord, your redeemer, the Holy One of Israel: I am the Lord, your god, who teaches you for your benefit [*leho'il*], who guides you as to the way you should take.
18. Had you listened to my commands, your peace would have been like a river, and your justice like the waves of the sea.
19. Your descendants would have been like the sand, the offspring of your loins like pebbles, not cut off, and his name not destroyed before me.

In this passage God is presented, not as a king demanding obedience, but as a teacher who can instruct Israel in that which is beneficial, and a guide to the roadways who can say which way is best to travel.[42] And we are given a clear view of what it is that stands to be gained from a teaching that is beneficial, or *mo'il*, to man: peace and justice in the land, and a multitude of descendents to bear one's name forward.[43] A similar understanding of God's teaching as instruction and guidance regarding that which can benefit mankind appears in Jeremiah, including in passages we've already seen such as that in which the nations declare that what they received from their fathers was only lies. Here it is again, with some of the relevant Hebrew terms emphasized:

> Jeremiah 16:
>
> 19. Nations will come from the ends of the earth and say, "Only lies [*sheker*] have our fathers bequeathed us, worthless [*hevel*] and with nothing in them to avail [*mo'il*].
> 20. Can a man make gods for himself? They are no gods [*lo elohim*]."

Jeremiah here tells us that the gods of the nations, their ways and their laws, are all to be seen as worthless for gaining an understanding of the way the world actually works, and so have "nothing in them" that can really profit or benefit human beings.[44] The inability of the nations' ways to offer something that can really benefit them is, again, expressed using the term *ho'il*. I have used the English term "worthless" to render the Hebrew *hevel*, which literally means "breath," and is often used as the opposite of that which is *ho'il*, to refer to what is futile and passing and so cannot profit or raise one up.[45] Note, too, the use of the term "no-gods," *lo elohim*, adopted by Isaiah, Hoshea, and Jeremiah to capture the irrelevance of the gods of the nations, since they cannot provide beneficial teachings and guidance regarding the nature of the world.[46] Similarly, in Jeremiah's "safe-house for thieves" oration, the people's reliance on the salvation they believe will come of their sacrifices at the Temple is called *bilti ho'il* – something that is without any benefit to those who do it:

> Jeremiah 7:
>
> 8. See, you rely on false words [*divrei hashaker*] to no benefit [*lebilti ho'il*] to yourselves.
> 9. Will you steal, murder, commit adultery, swear falsehoods, sacrifice to the Ba'al, and follow after other gods that you knew not,
> 10. And then come and stand before me in this house, which is called by my name, and say "We are saved" …?

Here, too, the term *ho'il* is brought to bear in order to tell the people that their thoughts and deeds are just not giving them the things they need to survive and grow strong. They are not such as can profit them, or "raise them upward."

This distinction between those things that can really benefit human beings and those that cannot is the subject of a number of cutting metaphors that Jeremiah uses time and again in his orations. For example, he often compares that which is *mo'il* to water, a rare and precious commodity in a desert land such as Israel – and one without which man dies quickly and in agony. The water metaphor takes us to the heart of the prophetic natural law teaching, because it so forcefully advances the argument that, whatever one may think, there are things that are decreed by nature and concerning which no man has any real freedom. No one, after all, has the power to decide he does not need water, and so no one can just walk away from a reliable source of water with impunity. As Jeremiah tells us:

Jeremiah 7:

13. They that turn away in the land will be inscribed [in the dust],[47] for they have left the source of living water, the Lord.

Jeremiah 18:

14. Would one leave [water] from the rock in the fields, snow from Lebanon? Would one abandon newfound water, cold and flowing?
15. For my people have forgotten me, in vain do they burn incense.

In these and other passages, Jeremiah employs the metaphor of a source of water found in the desert to emphasize that there are certain things that man must have by nature if he is to live, and accuses the Jews of doing precisely that which is forbidden by the laws of nature – of spurning the very water that is needed to keep them alive.[48] Here God's instruction is the water without which man cannot live, and in walking away from it, Israel is walking towards its own very painful death, both physically and politically.

Of course, Jeremiah knows that men, arbitrary though their minds may be, do not *purposely* turn their backs on their most pressing needs, bringing pain and dissolution upon themselves for no reason. They turn away from God's law, which teaches what is required of man by nature, and adopt the laws and customs of the nations precisely because they believe that these will do a better job of bringing them life and well-being. Jeremiah thus extends the metaphor, granting that the Jews believe they have made cisterns for themselves so that they may have water. But these cisterns of man's devising don't work: They are broken and hold no water.[49] Or, in other words, they are not *yo'il* – not able provide any real benefit to man. As he writes:

Jeremiah 2:

8. The priests did not say: "Where is the Lord?" And those who grasped my teaching did not know me, and the leaders committed crimes against me,

and the prophets prophesied by the Ba'al and went after things that will not avail [*lo yo'ilu*].

10. .... See whether there was ever such a thing:
11. Whether a nation abandoned its gods, even if they be no gods [*lo elohim*]. Yet my people exchanged its honor for that which will not avail. [*lo yo'il*] ...
13. For my people have committed two wrongs; They have forsaken me, the spring of the water of life, to dig for themselves cisterns, broken cisterns that hold no water.

In the last part of this passage, Jeremiah provides us with a comparison between the natural law and the artificial laws that men devise for themselves. While reality provides them with a "spring" from which men are able to drink and be saved from the agony of thirst and death, they prefer to "dig for themselves," seeking to supply their needs not from natural sources, but through alternate sources – "broken cisterns" intended to supplant the natural source of water. But this is nothing more than delusion. A broken cistern full of water leads to death just as surely as walking away from the spring and never drinking again. It just takes a bit longer for the results to become known.

Another metaphor of Jeremiah's pursues a similar line of argument from a different angle. In the following passage, Jeremiah compares knowledge of God's law to a tent that provides the shepherd with shelter from the elements, and laments the ruin that comes of permitting this tent to fall. As he writes:

Jeremiah 10:

20. My tent has been ruined and all my cords have broken. My children have left from within me and are gone. No one pitches my tent any more, nor sets up my flaps.
21. For the shepherds have become ignorant, and the Lord they have not sought. For this reason they have not known what to do [*lo hiskilu*] and all their flocks have been scattered.

Here, God's will is compared to a shepherd's tent, which protects the shepherd from the harsh sun, sands, wind, and rain that would otherwise destroy him, his family, and possessions. But the tent is not an edifice that stands of itself. To gain the shelter it affords, one must have practical wisdom, or *haskel*: One needs to know how to "pitch the tent" and "set up its flaps," how to care for the tarp and the cords. Without knowing how to do these things, both the shepherds and their flocks are soon gone. The Israelites, however, have grown ignorant. No longer "seeking the Lord," they "have not known what to do," so they have come to ruin.[50] In this way, Jeremiah directly connects seeking God and knowledge of his will with practical wisdom – with the knowledge that is needed to protect oneself and one's family. Cease your seeking of God, lose hold of the laws and traditions that teach you what to do, and you will soon enough find your life coming to dissolution and grief.[51]

Perhaps even more evocative is the following metaphor, in which God's law is compared to the daylight by which one navigates mountain paths. This metaphor takes Jeremiah's argument onto new ground, explaining to his audience why one cannot simply set aside God and his instructions, and then assume that one will be able to return. For there are psychological factors at work, and one of the natural consequences of setting aside that which is beneficial to man is that *one ceases to be able to recognize what is beneficial*, and so cannot go back. As Jeremiah writes:

Jeremiah 13:

16. Give honor to the Lord your God, before it grows dark, and before your feet stumble on the twilit mountains. And you will hope for light, but he will bring down the shadow of death, extend the mists.[52]

Jerusalem, of course, is a city cradled in a ridge of low mountains, and as the crowds listening to Jeremiah well knew, you cannot reach it without traveling on mountain paths that take you by one ravine after another. A misstep will put you at the bottom of a ravine, and only broad daylight can help you make your way in relative safety. What one needs, then, is daylight by which to see the pitfalls and dangers along the path. When one "gives honor" to God, one can have such daylight, in the form of the ability to see pitfalls and dangers that comes naturally when one understands one's experience through the prism of God's law. But when one turns away, it is as though one is walking in twilight. One's understanding becomes unreliable, and that which is in fact dangerous appears safe. That there is something wrong does become clear, because one begins to stumble – and stumbling by a ravine is not something that can be denied or interpreted away. It is a harsh and undeniable fact. Stumbling, the world becomes unsure and frightening, and one realizes that more light is needed. But by then it is too late. Where one's conceptions have grown false, things only go from bad to worse: Mist and darkness descend, and one's fall becomes inevitable. [53]

We have now seen three versions of Jeremiah's argument that when men depart from that which is beneficial to them by nature, the result is pain and hardship of a kind that even man's arbitrary mind cannot mistake. Time and again, Jeremiah returns to this point, arguing that the undeniable pain which is the natural consequence of having abandoned God's law must "reach into your mind" so that men come to know the bitterness that their deeds have wrought. As he writes:

Jeremiah 4:

> 18. Your way and your deeds have done this to you. It is your evil which is so bitter, which reaches into your mind.[54]

In these and similar passages, Jeremiah tells the people of Jerusalem that their own "ways" and "deeds" are themselves what "ha[s] done this to you" – what has caused the bitterness and hardship that has overtaken them. But precisely because this bitterness is the result of the people's own misconceptions and misdeeds, Jeremiah sees it as having the power of correcting them. In being confronted by the consequences of their way, they will be brought to "know and see" their true cause, which is the departure from God's guidance – "because you left the Lord ... even as he led you in the way":

Jeremiah 2:

> 17. Has not this happened to you, because you left the Lord your God even as he led you in the way? ...
> 19. Your evil will chastise you, and your backslidings will reprove you, and you will know and see that evil and bitter is leaving the Lord your God.

In a famous passage, Jeremiah imagines Efraim, representing the exiles of the northern kingdom, speaking of his wanderings and of the knowledge that has come to him from the destruction of Samaria. As he writes:

Jeremiah 31:

> 18. I have indeed heard Efraim in his wanderings [*mitnoded*], [saying:] "You chastised me and I am chastened like an untrained calf....
> 19. [For] after I was brought to knowledge, I struck my thigh. I am embarrassed and humiliated, for I bear the shame of my youth."

Knowledge, then, is available. Yet its price is experience.[55] A prayer, then, is in order: For a man can walk, but he cannot himself decide whether the ground on which he steps will be firm or not. And so Jeremiah prays that God, who alone knows for certain what will be the results of our actions, will teach us the truth from our actions – but not in the midst of unbearable pain such as that which was the lot of the northern tribes:

Jeremiah 10:

> 22. A sound is heard, here it comes, and a great noise from a north country, to make the towns of Judah a desolation, a haunt of jackals.
> 23. I knew, Lord, that not for man is his way, not for a man as he walks to make steady his step.

> 24. Chasten me, Lord, but with judgment, not with your wrath, lest you diminish me.

V. WHOSE WORD WILL STAND

One of the more remarkable aspects of Jeremiah's theory of knowledge is the emphasis the prophet places on the consequences of maintaining false opinions. Jeremiah repeatedly tells us that false opinion has painful consequences, which bear down upon and punish those whose understanding is false. And this pain is something that cannot be denied. Or can it? Consider the following passage, in which Jeremiah finds, to his astonishment, that the people of Jerusalem can bear the punishment that God inflicts on them for their false opinions. In fact, not only can they bear the punishment – but they do so without feeling anything at all:

> Jeremiah 5:

> 3. Lord, are not your eyes to truth? You have beaten them but they have not felt pain, consumed them but they have refused to take correction. They have made their faces harder than rock, they have refused to return.[56]

Jeremiah here tells us that the people have been "beaten" thanks to their own evildoing – but they don't feel the pain. They have been "consumed" – and yet their opinions and ways change not at all. They are blind not only to impending evil, but even to the evil that has befallen them already. Their faces have been turned "harder than rock," and so they are incapable of learning lessons from the consequences of their errors.[57] Indeed, they taunt the prophets as though nothing has happened, these stone-faced men who feel nothing, jeering: "Where is the word of the Lord? Let it come now!"[58]

We hear the clash of competing conceptions of reality, and see the chasm that has opened up between Jeremiah's understanding and that of the people of the city. How long can this continue? Is there no limit to the damage that can be done before the people come to feel that something has gone wrong with their understanding of the world? In the same oration in which Jeremiah speaks of Jerusalem as Sodom and forbids the people from using words they have "overturned," he asks God how long this grinding of conceptual schemes against one another can continue, with the false prophets anesthetizing the people against the pain they should be feeling, assuring them that they are doing themselves no harm:

> Jeremiah 23:

> 25. I have heard what the prophets have said, those who prophesy falsity in my name, saying: "I dreamed, I dreamed."

26. Until when? Is it in the mind of the prophets, the prophets of falsity, the prophets of the deceit of their own minds?

27. Do they think to make my people forget my name with the dreams that each one tells to his neighbor, as their fathers forgot my name in the Ba'al?

28. Let the prophet who has a dream tell a dream, and he who has my word will speak my word reliably. What has the grain to do with straw? says the Lord.

29. Is not my word like fire, says the Lord, and like a hammer that shatters rock?[59]

To this question, Jeremiah gives an astonishing answer. The people may understand what they will. And the prophets may give eloquent expression to the falsehoods the people have come to see as real. But in the end, the competing realities will collide with great force, and one side will see its end. Note the violence of the metaphors Jeremiah deploys to describe the collision between the two conceptions: The false words (and false things) on which the people rely are like straw, whereas God's words (and the true things to which they give expression) are like fire. In the collision between word and word, that which is of God will explode into flame and burn the false words until they are no more. As for the people's faces, which have become like stone and cannot feel pain in the site of horrifying events, God's words will smash these stone faces until they are rubble. Ultimately, the things that are true will have come forth into the world, and will be known to such an extent that the worthless opinions upon which men had relied will be smashed and burned and will be no longer.[60]

Jeremiah graphically portrays this collision between competing interpretations of reality in a metaphor that also appears in Isaiah and Ezekiel,[61] that of the "cup of fury," the chalice of wine from which the nations will be forced to drink until their understanding is finally cut loose from its moorings. This shocking use of wine as a symbol of Judah's downfall makes its first appearance in the same oration in which Jeremiah compares the false opinions of the people to walking on mountain paths in twilight. Here is what he says:

Jeremiah 13:

12. And you will tell them this word: Thus says the Lord, God of Israel, Every bottle will be filled with wine! And when they say to you, "Do we not know that every bottle will be filled with wine?"

13. Then you will say to them, Thus says the Lord, Behold, I will fill all the inhabitants of this land, even the kings of the house of David who sit upon his throne, and the priests, and the prophets, and all the inhabitants of Jerusalem, with drunkenness.

14. And I will smash them one against the other, the fathers and the sons together, says the Lord. I will not pity, nor spare, nor have mercy, but I will destroy them.

Once again, Jeremiah's speech focuses attention on the fact that the language the people use to interpret reality has been crippled by ambiguity. He begins by announcing to the people of Jerusalem that "Every bottle will be filled with wine!" Yet like other terms we have seen – *peace, saved, burden, Temple of the Lord* – this expression can also be understood in two ways. To the people, the full bottles of wine are an emblem of their pleasure and self-confidence. But for Jeremiah, the vessels that are full of wine are the leaders of the people themselves: kings, priests, and prophets, whose minds are besotted with false opinions and who cannot take a step to save themselves or Judah. In this condition of blindness and foolishness, God will smash them against one another until they fall and can rise no more. It makes no difference that these drunken leaders do not see their end coming. They fall nonetheless.

In another oration, Jeremiah is sent to the rulers of Judah and of the other nations with a cup of wine, which he forces them to drink. Here, too, the imagery of the fallen drunk is deployed, but the metaphor shifts in that the drunkenness that Jeremiah describes is now forced upon Jerusalem against her will:

Jeremiah 25:

15. For so said the Lord, God of Israel, to me:
    Take this cup of the wine of fury from my hand, and cause all the nations to whom I send you to drink....
27. And you will say to them, thus says the Lord of Hosts, the God of Israel: Drink, and be drunk, and vomit, and fall, and rise no more, because of the sword that I send among you.
28. And it will be, when they refuse to take the cup from your hand to drink, that you will say to them, Thus says the Lord of Hosts: You will certainly drink.

Earlier, when Jeremiah had told the people that "Every bottle will be filled with wine," the destruction of Judah and Jerusalem was depicted as resulting from a drunkenness that was, at least in a sense, voluntary. The people of Judah did not, of course, desire the consequences that followed from their thoughts and their deeds, but one still saw how pleased they were with their grasp of reality, and with the actions that follow upon this pleasure.[62] In this oration, however, the rulers of Judah are forced to drink. And while the drinkers wish, after a certain point, to quit ("when they refuse to take the cup from your hand"), they no longer have any choice in the matter and are told, "You will certainly drink."[63] Like the fire that sets straw ablaze and the hammer that shatters rock, God's word is here depicted as having a force and efficacy able to demolish the constructions of men's arbitrary minds: Even the drunks can see Nebuchadnezzar's sword, and there is no way to think it away or refuse its consequences.[64] Regardless of how their minds may writhe, seeking a way to hold on to their earlier understanding, the truth is stronger and must be assimilated ("You will certainly drink"). And when it is, the mind goes into confusion ("be drunk"), then turmoil ("vomit"), and finally collapse ("and fall").

Does this horrifying collapse of the world as the men of Jerusalem knew it result in knowledge? Do the people, once they have been forced to drink of the cup of fury, and the false conceptions in their minds have been brought to naught, come to see reality for what it is? Jeremiah believes that they do, and in his "hammer that shatters rock" oration, he promises the people that these events will indeed bring them, at last, to understanding:

Jeremiah 23:

17. They always say to those who despise me, "The Lord spoke it, you will have peace," and to all who walk after the arbitrariness of their mind [*bishrirut libo*] they say, "Evil will not come upon you."
18. But who has stood in the counsel of the Lord, and seen and heard his word? Who has listened to his word and understood it?
19. Behold, a the storm of the Lord has gone out in fury, a whirlwind, on the heads of the wicked it will fall.
20. The anger of the Lord will not turn back, until he has performed and completed the plans in his mind. In the end [*be'aharit hayamim*], you will consider this and understand [*titbonenu va bina*].

In this oration, the "cup of fury" is replaced by a "storm of fury," which has already gone out into the world, although not many have yet recognized the storm and its course for what they are. The fact that the great majority remain blind, however, does not mean that what is happening is incomprehensible. There is a reality, after all, which is here presented as that which is in God's mind. God has a clear view of what has caused what, and once the storm comes, the people too will gain such a view as well. As Jeremiah tells the people, "In the end, you will consider this and understand."

Here, then, is Jeremiah's answer to the question of whether we can escape the false words and false understandings that result from the arbitrariness of our minds. True, the mind is deceitful, and when it fixes on a mistaken way of seeing things, even painful consequences will not suffice to shake them loose. But God's word is like a hammer that shatters rock. It enters the world and takes on a reality so overwhelming that false conceptions, no matter how tightly we cling to them, are destroyed before it. Once freed from these false conceptions, a new understanding can arise in the minds of men, one that reflects the truth. Knowledge, then, may elude the men of a given time and place. But it is coming. And all men, it would appear, have a chance of attaining it "in the end."

When, precisely, is the "end" of which Jeremiah speaks supposed to come about? The expression Jeremiah uses in this passage, *be'aharit hayamim*, can be read to mean, literally, "in the end of days,"[65] and later readers have often understood this expression apocalyptically, as though Jeremiah were speaking here of the last days of the world. But this is a misreading of the Hebrew, and there is in fact no reason to think Jeremiah has such a distant future in mind. The word *aharit* ("end") is also used, by Jeremiah as well as by other biblical authors, as a term to refer to what happens "in the end" – which is to say, at the end of the particular story being told. Jeremiah uses this term in this way, for example, when he asks the people "What will you do when the end of it comes [*le'aharita*]?"[66] And when he presents God as entertaining, with respect to Israel, "thoughts of peace and not evil, to give you a future [*aharit*] and hope."[67] Jeremiah does not, in these passages, call on the people to think about the end of the world. He just wants them to think about how things are going to turn out, and not just about the way things look today. In the same way, the passage quoted above informs the people: "In the end, you will consider this and understand." This is to say that in the aftermath, once the Babylonians have destroyed the city, the people will understand those things that had been so difficult for them to see before.[68]

The argument that true knowledge is available only "in the end" – or, as we would say today, by way of experience – appears time and again in Jeremiah's writings. For example, Jeremiah endorses the view that the distinguishing mark of the true prophet, as against those prophets speaking falsely, is nothing other than the test of experience: He is a prophet of God if what he says comes true; otherwise, he is not. This empiricist conception of what constitutes prophecy (and therefore of what constitutes God's word) finds its best-known expression in the Mosaic law in Deuteronomy.[69] In Jeremiah, it appears in a public debate that Jeremiah conducts with the prophet Hanania after the exile of Yechonia the king and much of the leadership of Judah. Despite this horrendous event, Hanania presumes to tell the priests and the people that within two years the exiled king and the vessels of the Temple will be returned to Jerusalem. This is a rather remarkable claim to be making: The king of Judah has been taken to Babylonia in chains, as his brother was carried off to prison in Egypt not long before this.[70] Judah is a raped and pillaged land, brutalized and humiliated. And yet Hanania continues to prophesy peace as though nothing much has happened and all will soon be right. Jeremiah is outraged, and tells the people that Hanania's utterances are to be regarded as worthless until such a time as someone has actually experienced them coming true:

Jeremiah 28:

> 9. As to the prophet who prophesies for peace, [only] when the word of that prophet comes, will it be known [*yivada*] whether that prophet has truly been sent by the Lord.[71]

This disputation with Hanania takes place in the Temple in the fourth year of the reign of Tzidkiahu, last king of Judah. Soon Tzidkiahu and his sons will be dead, the Temple in ruins, the kingdom fallen. Yet the priests and the people listen to this debate, quite willing to believe that all will just turn out well.[72] The storm of fury has gone out, but the "end" has not yet come and the Jews' way of thinking has not yet been shattered. But knowledge, Jeremiah tells the people, is coming.

In this context, the historical narrative in the second part of the book of Jeremiah tells an extraordinary story – to my mind, among the most shocking in the Bible. It is roughly ten years later, and those Jews who have not been killed or taken captive by the Babylonians have fled to Egypt. And there in Patros, in Upper Egypt, the survivors of the destruction of Jerusalem engage in a public debate with Jeremiah. These survivors, we understand, *still* cannot find fault with their prior beliefs, and regret only that they have at times weakened in their resolve to serve foreign gods. Here is what they have to say:

Jeremiah 44:

> 15. And they answered Jeremiah, all the people who knew that their wives burned incense to other gods and all the women standing in a great crowd, and all the people living in the land of Egypt in Patros, saying:
> 16. "The word that you have spoken in the name of the Lord we will not hear from you.
> 17. For we will surely do everything that we have vowed to do, to burn incense to the Queen of Heaven and pour libations to her, as we did, we and our fathers and our kings and our princes, in the cities of Judah and the streets of Jerusalem, when we were sated with bread and were well, and saw no evil.
> 18. And from the time we stopped burning incense to the Queen of Heaven and pouring libations to her, we have lacked in everything and ended with the sword and famine."

Thus, even having witnessed the downfall of their nation and the destruction of the Temple, and having fled to Egypt as refugees, the understanding of many among of the Jews continues just as it was before the disaster. To read their account, it is as if there was nothing at all to be learned from the destruction of the kingdom: All had been well in Jerusalem except for Jeremiah's cries to set aside the worship of the Queen of Heaven. The narrator has a little fun with them here, having them say that they "saw no evil" in Jerusalem (which was, in Jeremiah's eyes, precisely the problem!), and that they will not now hear God's word.[73]

Jeremiah, who is horrified that the Jews have gone down to Egypt in search of safety rather than remaining on the land in Israel, sees that they have still learned nothing.[74] And again, he tells them that there is no hope that their understanding of things can hold firm. They will gain knowledge in the end:

Jeremiah 44:

24. And Jeremiah said to all the people, and to all the women: "Hear the word of the Lord, all Judah who are in the land of Egypt....

27. See how I watch diligently [*shoked*][75] over them, for evil and not for good....

28. And the fugitives of the sword who return from the land of Egypt to the land of Judah will be few in number, and all the remnant of Judah that came to the land of Egypt to sojourn there will know whose word will stand, [*devar mi yakum*] mine or theirs.

29. And this will be to you a sign, says the Lord, that I will visit upon you in this place, so you will know that my words will surely stand [*yakumu devarai*] against you for evil.

The terms Jeremiah uses here to describe the clash between God's understanding of things and that of the people are instructive. Here, he uses the Hebrew verb *kam*, literally meaning to *stand* or *arise*, to describe what happens to a word, or an understanding, over the course of time. There are some words, or understandings, that are able to arise and stand as realities in the world. Others come to nothing, having been proved to be mere breath, transient and worthless. In the coming times, Jeremiah has God say, we will learn "whose word will stand" – that of the Jews in Egypt, or that of God himself. In Jeremiah's telling of it, it is as if the rival concepts are pitted against one another in combat, and they will continue to strive against one another until one falls and the other remains standing.[76]

This story of the exiles in Egypt offers stunning evidence that the arbitrariness of man's mind is not to be defeated, and that many human beings simply cannot attain knowledge at all. Given such evidence, we might not have been surprised if Jeremiah had adopted a view such as that of Plato, restricting the attainment of knowledge to the rarest of men – in this case, to the prophet alone. Yet this is not his conclusion, and Jeremiah maintains his account of how knowledge is attained, even in the face of this. Throughout his orations, he steadfastly insists that knowledge is coming, and even describes how it is when individuals come to see that their views have been folly. Here, for example, is a passage from an oration in which Jeremiah tells us of other men of Judah – men who see the coming Babylonian onslaught, and in seeing it experience the dawning of the understanding that Jeremiah believes must come:

Jeremiah 8:

13. I will surely consume them, says the Lord. There will be no grapes on the vine, no figs on the fig tree, and the leaf will whither; and the things I gave them will pass from them.
14. [And they will say:] "Why are we sitting still? Let us gather together and go to the fortress cities, and be silent there. For the Lord our God has silenced us, and has made us drink gall water, for we have sinned before the Lord.
15. We hoped for peace, but no good came, for a time of healing and behold terror....
20. The harvest is over, the summer is ended, and we are not saved."[77]

As in the metaphor of the cup of wine that Jeremiah forces upon the men of Judah, here too we find him comparing knowledge to a drink that is forced upon men ("[God] has made us drink gall water"). Yet in this passage, the people do not fall down senseless. It is only their false understanding that collapses, allowing them to see an entirely different truth that has arisen in its place. And this time, the men of Judah are well aware of the transformation that has taken place in their understanding of the reality about them. *"Let us be silent there"* – they say to one another, the silence of which they speak being nothing other than the collapse of the understanding that used to fill their minds, and of the worthless talk that was built upon it. *"For the Lord has silenced us"* – they continue, because it is the reality that bears down upon them, the events that God has wrought, that have shattered their old understanding as a hammer shatters rock. *"For we have sinned"* – they conclude, speaking of the new understanding that is now before them.

Of especial interest here is the metaphor of the harvest, which we have seen before with reference to the relationship between men's opinions and deeds, on the one hand, and the consequences of these opinions and deeds, on the other: The sowing of the seeds early in the spring is compared to the establishment of certain opinions, or to the taking of certain actions. On this metaphor, there can be carefree days of summer when all one has to do is live on the assumption that what was planted in the spring was good and plentiful. But there can be no arguing with the harvest. As the men of Judah say in this passage: *"The harvest is over, the summer is ended, and we are not saved."* If there were illusions in summer, they are gone in the fall. The same is true for knowledge, which comes in the end, the fruit of experience.

VI. CONCLUSION

As discussed above, Jeremiah's assessment of the value of the individual's independent search for truth is quite radical. While Sodom was destroyed for want of ten righteous men, Jeremiah suggests that if Jerusalem falls, it will be destroyed for want of one man diligently searching for truth. But Jeremiah recognizes that truth is not so easily to be found, and in his orations, he turns to human psychology for an explanation as to why this should be so. On Jeremiah's view, most men, both in Israel and among the nations, live mired in illusions as a result of the arbitrariness of the human mind, which tends to experience reality as being quite different from what it really is, to be pleased with the misconceptions it devises for itself, and to resist all calls for change. Nor is there much help to be had from prophets and priests, since they are often guilty of passing around unreliable interpretations of reality as well, and without diligent inquiry the individual is likely to be led in the wrong direction by false prophets and priests who have been deceived. What hope there is of attaining knowledge, then, comes of experience, which alone has the power to shatter false opinions and replace them with true understanding.[78] And Jeremiah does believe there is hope of this: No man is inherently immune to the reality bearing down upon him. In the end, reality will prove too strong, and overwhelm the false opinions that have held sway for so long. In the end, truth is a hammer that shatters even rock.

Jeremiah's theory of knowledge presents a standpoint that is rather different from those that are familiar from the tradition of philosophy descended from Athenian thought. While his view of reality as being governed by discernible natural laws may at first seem to position him not far from Aristotle's view of our present world as being fixed and intelligible, Jeremiah actually turns out to be much closer to Plato's conception of human beings as constantly set upon by illusions that take hold of them and set their course.[79] In a profound sense, Jeremiah shares Plato's questions concerning man's life amid these illusions, but he resolves them in a very different way: Instead of positing that the realm of our experience is an imitation of another realm of changeless ideas, Jeremiah places the blame on man's psychology, which is deceitful and arbitrary. In this way, he is able to understand reality as a single realm, which is accessible by means of experience. This single realm impinges on one's conceptions in ways that cause pain, so that even those who are happy in their fantasies will ultimately lose them, as the pain inflicted by reality destroys these conceptions and forces the emergence of new ones.

Such a psychologistic view of knowledge has important advantages over those of the philosophical tradition that descended from ancient Greece. It permits us to overcome some of the dualisms that plague much of post-Platonic metaphysics, while paving the way for a realistic approach to the diversity of human viewpoints that is rooted in the functioning of the human mind. Moreover, it shows how the subjectivism frequently associated with such a view can be overcome by referring to the ability of the human mind to advance, under pressure of anomalous events, toward a truer grasp of the world. Not until the modern period do we find significant Western thinkers exploring the problem of knowledge in ways that are broadly comparable to those pursued in Jeremiah's orations.[80] In particular, the principle of human knowledge advancing by way of sudden and radical shifts in worldview does not become a commonplace of Western thought until the twentieth century.[81]

7

Truth and Being in the Hebrew Bible

In the last chapter, we saw that the prophets of Israel could be quite radical in their endorsement of the individual's independent search for truth.
But what did they mean by *truth*? When we come across this term in the
Hebrew Scriptures, does it mean what it does in the writings of the Athenian
philosophers? Does it mean the same thing we mean by the word *truth*
today? These questions are important, because if the Hebrew Scriptures
have a very different understanding of what is meant by truth and falsity
than that familiar from the tradition of thought descended from Greek philosophy, then our readings of the Bible may involve a misunderstanding of
what is meant by man's search for truth, and, indeed, of the nature of prophecy and of God's word more generally. At the same time, if the Bible does
offer us new ways of understanding what is meant by falsity and truth, these
could also have important consequences for Western thought, which has in
recent years become entangled in a seemingly intractable set of difficulties
in its own attempts to gain a clear understanding of what it is we are really
talking about when we speak of the truth.

A famous position in Bible scholarship – one that has cast a long shadow
in academic discussion of the Hebrew Scriptures for over half a century –
suggests that there is not much point in asking the kind of questions I've
just raised. On this view, there can't be many significant differences between
the meanings of basic biblical terms and their Greek- or English-language
equivalents. Reality just is what it is, and the human mind will end up carv-
ing it up, with slight variations, into pretty much the same pieces no matter
what language we're speaking.[1] But I believe this view is misguided, and that
a reader who does not share an a priori commitment to this doctrine should
be able to see that quite the opposite is the case, and that many crucial biblical terms in fact carry very different meanings from the terms usually used

to translate them into English.[2] In the last chapter, for example, I discussed the example of the Hebrew word *lev*, which is almost universally rendered as *heart* despite the fact that it quite plainly refers to the faculty of thought and reasoning – a mistranslation whose effect is to make hundreds of passages throughout the Bible seem to be concerned with the emotions when it is human understanding and reason that are being discussed.[3] And dozens of additional examples could easily be adduced. This means that contrary to what has often been said, the translations of the Hebrew Scriptures in common use are often systematically misleading on many subjects of philosophical significance, and that we really have little hope of understanding the standpoint of the biblical authors if we are unwilling to invest some effort in reconstructing the meanings of the basic terms they used to express their ideas. In this, the study of the Bible is really not any different from the study of the writings of the Greek philosophers, which would likewise be crippled if scholars were unwilling to labor to reconstruct the meanings of the concepts in use in these texts.[4]

In the present chapter, I will therefore set aside the analysis of biblical narrative and metaphor, employing traditional concept analysis as the basis for a discussion of some of the metaphysical presuppositions that characterize much of the Hebrew Bible. In particular, I will look at two of the most important concepts in the Hebrew Scriptures: (i) the biblical equivalent of the word *truth*, which is the Hebrew *emet*; and (ii) the Hebrew term *davar*, which is the main term used in Scripture to refer both to *words* and to *things*. I will suggest that the terms used in the Hebrew Bible for *truth* and *falsity*, *word* and *object*, turn out to have very different meanings than those that are familiar to us from Plato or Aristotle. Their usage is consistent enough to permit concept clarification and philosophical reconstruction in the accepted sense, and such clarification brings us into contact with a metaphysical system that is quite alien to the great approaches to metaphysics known to us from Athenian philosophy.

I. TRUTH AS AGREEMENT WITH REALITY

The traditional point of departure for philosophical discourse concerning truth is often the definition of truth and falsity in Aristotle's *Metaphysics*, which reads as follows:

> To say of what is that it is not, or of what is not that it is, is false; while to say of what is that it is, and of what is not that it is not, is true.[5]

On this view, truth is a quality of things that are said – and in particular, of propositions such as *It is* and *It is not*, which possess this quality if they are uttered with reference to something ("what is") that is in fact, or is not in fact, respectively.[6] Thus, for example, to say of what is a bird, *It is a bird*, or to say of what is not a bird, *It is not a bird*, is to speak the truth. The proposition is therefore assumed to refer to a reality other than itself, which is understood to have an existence independent of what is said about it.[7] (As traditionally understood, that which is said can also be said in thought, so that propositions advanced in thought rather than in vocalized speech can be true or false as well.[8])

In this definition, we already find the basic elements of what is today known as the "correspondence theory of truth,"[9] which has been said to characterize the thought of virtually all philosophers up until recent times, and has given rise to the suspicion that such a conception is perhaps the natural way of thinking about truth.[10] In particular, we see that Aristotle depends on three assumptions that characterize most subsequent discussion of truth in the philosophical tradition:

1. Truth is a quality of speech.[11]
2. True speech is "of" (or "about") a reality independent of itself.
3. True speech is that which agrees with (or "corresponds to") this reality; whereas false speech does not.[12]

The last century has witnessed a series of challenges to the supposition that truth can reasonably be said to be the correspondence of speech to a reality independent of itself. Among other things, these challenges have asked how it can be possible for the individual to escape his own thoughts in order to gain "access" to the independent reality to which speech and thought must be compared; and even if such access can be arranged, what could constitute the desired agreement or correspondence between speech or thought and this independent reality.[13] Yet despite the widespread discomfort with the correspondence view, most discussion of the subject continues to contemplate one or another repair of Aristotle's definition rather than a genuine break with it. Today as yesterday, most philosophers suppose that where there is no speech, there can be no truth; and that true speech is such in virtue of its relationship with the world as it is "in reality."[14] Under these circumstances, it seems a matter of more than antiquarian interest that the Bible offers the Western tradition an entirely different conception of truth that seems not to rely on any of these assumptions.

II. THE TRUTH OF OBJECTS

In what follows I will suggest that the Hebrew Bible employs an alternative understanding of truth, according to which truth is not in the first instance a quality of that which is said, but of objects. I have in mind both conventional, physical objects such as a road, a horse, a seed, or a man, and objects of the understanding more generally, including actions and circumstances.[15] Once I have established what is meant by the term *truth* when it is understood as a quality of objects in general, I will return to the question of truth as a quality of speech, and show that on the biblical understanding, the truth of that which is said is dependent on, and perhaps identical to, that truth which is a quality of objects.

Consider the following examples of the manner in which the Hebrew terms for *truth* (*emet*, אמת) and *falsity* (*sheker*, שקר) are used in the Bible.[16] When Abraham's servant reaches Mesopotamia after a long and treacherous journey, he describes the road that has brought him there as a "true road":

> And I bowed down my head, and worshipped the God of my master Abraham, who has led me on a true road [*derech emet*] to take my master's brother's daughter for his son.[17]

Similarly, when Yitro instructs Moses in how to appoint judges to rule over the people, he teaches that one should seek "true men":

> You shall provide out of all the people able men who fear God, true men [*anshei emet*] hating unjust gain.[18]

And Jeremiah says that God planted Israel as a "true seed":

> And I had planted you a noble vine, an entirely true seed [*zera emet*]. How, then, are you turned into the degenerate plant of a strange vine to me?[19]

We see a parallel usage for the word *false*, as when the psalm says that a "horse is false":

> The horse is false [*sheker*] for safety, and with all his strength, he will not escape.[20]

Similarly, in Proverbs, we find that "attractiveness is false":

> Attractiveness is false [*sheker*], and beauty is fleeting, but a woman who fears God will be praised [by all].[21]

In these and similar passages, true and false are not properties of things that are spoken at all. Instead they are properties of objects and persons. What precisely do the authors of these passages mean when they say that an object – a road, a seed, a man, a horse – is true or false?

In Hebrew, as in other Semitic languages, most words are derived from root-stems, usually three letters long, which can be transformed into all or most of the parts of speech according to a largely consistent morphology.

Each root-stem thus holds together a family of words whose meanings tend to be closely related. In the case of the Hebrew word *emet*, the root is the three-letter sequence *aleph-mem-nun* (אמן) whose cognates can assist us in understanding what the authors of the Bible meant when they spoke of truth.[22] For example, the adjective derived from the passive verbal form of this root is the word *ne'eman*, frequently translated as "faithful." When Isaiah foretells of a great future king of Judah, he speaks of him as a tent-peg fastened in a sure place:

> I will fasten him as a tent-peg in sure [*ne'eman*] ground, and he shall be for a glorious throne to his father's house. And they shall hang upon him all the glory of his father's house, the offspring and the issue.[23]

Thus when the tent-peg has been driven into "sure ground," it will be able reliably to withstand great storms without shifting. The ground is reliable, faithful, certain; and so, therefore, is the peg itself. This same word is used in reference to marital fidelity as well:

> How she has become a harlot, the faithful city [*kirya ne'emana*]! She was full of judgment, righteousness dwelled in her, but now murderers.[24]

In this passage, Jerusalem is compared to an unfaithful woman, who was once reliable and steadfast, but is so no longer. Here we see that the reliability or sureness of the tent-peg can also appear as a quality of persons. Just as the tent-peg could be relied upon not to give way under the strains and stresses of the ropes pulling on it, so too can a faithful woman be relied upon not to give way before the approaches of her suitors.

A similar conclusion arises from considering examples of the use of the cognate term *emuna*, which is often translated as "faithfulness."[25] Like *emet*, this word is a noun-form that is often deployed to describe the quality of an object. This is the case, for instance, in the following passage describing a battle between the Israelites and Amalek in the desert after the departure from Egypt:

> And it came to pass, when Moses held up his hand, that Israel prevailed, and when he put down his hand, Amalek prevailed. But Moses' hands were heavy, and they took a stone and put it under him, and he sat on it. And Aaron and Hur supported his hands, the one on the one side, and the other on the other side, and his hands were steady [*emuna*] until the going down of the sun. And Joshua harried Amalek with the edge of his sword.[26]

The meaning of the term *emuna* in this passage is clear. It is the quality of Moses' hands when they have ceased to waver, when they are steadfast and sure, and can be relied upon to bring triumph to Israel.

From these examples and many others like them, we see that the root *aleph-mem-nun* is employed time and again to refer to things and persons that are reliable, steadfast, and faithful. They refer to the quality of an object or person – a tent-peg or a king, a city or a wife or a pair of hands – that can be relied upon to hold firm under conditions of stress. We can see, therefore, that the Hebrew term for truth derives from a root meaning reliable, steadfast, faithful.

Let us now return to our examples of the use of the word *emet*, and see whether our understanding of the root from which the term is derived assists us in understanding its precise sense when it is used in the biblical text. In the first example, Abraham's servant says that the road that has borne him on his long and dangerous journey is a "true road," by which he means that the road was reliable, bringing him to his hoped-for destination in the face of adversity. The servant was, in other words, counting on the road to do something for him, or to be something for him, as if it were a tent-peg holding up under the strain of the rope. If the road had failed to deliver him to his destination, the servant would have called the road false; but since it did deliver him safely, he says that it is true.

In the same way, we are told that the men Moses chooses to be judges over Israel must be "true men, hating unjust gain." Again, these men must be like the tent-peg, holding firm under duress. In this case, the duress is the natural tendency of men to act in the service of their own interests, and to judge the cases before them so as to advance these interests. Moses is counting on a man he appoints as a judge to hold firm against this tendency, and to deliver up fair judgments nonetheless. A man who can do this is true, because he can be relied upon to hold firm; a man who cannot is false, because he will not hold firm in the face of temptation. Thus the importance of "hating unjust gain": Only a man who loathes unjust gain can be counted upon to hold firm.

The same can be said for other examples. Jeremiah says that God planted Israel as a "true seed" (*zera emet*), which he believed could be counted on, but which instead grew into a corrupt and alien weed; the Hebrew spies tell Rahav the harlot to tie a scarlet thread in her window as a "true sign" (*ot emet*), by which is meant, one she can rely upon to save her life when the Israelite armies approach the city;[27] Proverbs refers to the rewards one receives from doing good deeds as a "true wage" (*sechar emet*), by which is meant a wage one can rely upon;[28] and so forth. On the other hand, we are told that "the horse is false [*sheker*] for safety,"[29] because it cannot be counted upon to deliver its rider from the horrors of battle; that exotic luxuries are a "false bread" (*lehem sheker*), which promise to nourish, but in reality only fill a man's mouth with gravel;[30] and that "attractiveness is false" (*sheker hahen*) in that it cannot be relied upon, as opposed to fear of God, which can.[31]

From these and other examples, we see that in biblical Hebrew, that which is true is something that is reliable, steadfast, faithful; while that which is false is something that cannot be counted upon, or which appears reliable but is not. In these instances, truth and falsity are simply qualities of objects or persons, which parallel the English usage of terms such as reliable, steadfast, or faithful. There is no question, therefore, of truth and falsity referring to any kind of correspondence between speech and reality, for in these cases, there is no speech involved. There are only objects and persons.

Such instances, however, do not exhaust all of the uses of the terms *true* and *false* in the Bible. What of the rest? Most of the remaining uses of truth and falsity appear with reference to actions that are performed by men or God. In these cases we find that someone is to "do truth" (*le'asot emet*) to or for someone else, or else that an action is described as being performed "in truth" (*be'emet*). Thus, for example, when Abraham's servant arrives in Mesopotamia, he meets his master's kinsman, Betuel, and implores him to "do truth and kindness" to Abraham by granting his request that Rebecca return with him to Canaan as Isaac's bride:

> My master made me swear, saying, "You shall not take a wife to my son of the daughters of the Canaanites, in whose land I dwell. But you will go to my father's house, and to my kindred, and take a wife for my son.... And now, if you will do truth [*le'asot emet*] and kindness [*hesed*] to my master, tell me so. And if not, tell me, that I may turn to the right or to the left."[32]

In this passage, we easily understand what it means for Abraham's kinsman to "do kindness" towards him. Abraham has settled in a distant land, and his family has not set eyes on him for many years. To accept the servant's words at face value, and to send his daughter off to be married to Abraham's son, sight unseen, would surely be an act of kindness on Betuel's part. But how is it an act of "truth"? The answer is obvious if we consider the matter from Abraham's point of view. He fears that if his son marries a local woman, he will assimilate to the ways of the Canaanites. He is therefore counting on his kinsman to provide a suitable bride who will prevent Abraham's family from gradually going over to the idolatry of surrounding peoples. His hope, then, is that Betuel will prove reliable, someone on whom he can depend. In this sense, the act of permitting Rebecca to return with the servant to Canaan is not only an act of kindness, but an act of reliability, steadfastness, or faithfulness. It is, in other words, an act of truth. And the one who performs it is said to "do truth" for Abraham, thereby proving himself a true man (or a true kinsman); just as one who does an act of kindness is said to be a kind man.[33] In a similar vein, an action is at times said to be performed "in truth" (*be'emet*), meaning that it is performed such a way that it can be counted on.[34]

From these examples, we see that in the Bible, truth can be a quality of an action if it is understood as evincing reliability, steadfastness, or faithfulness. In this, the truth of an action that is done to or for someone, or the truth of an action when it is performed "in truth," can be seen to differ in no essential respect from the truth that is a quality of objects.

III. WHAT DOES "RELIABLE" MEAN?

As has been said, the truth of objects is in the Bible a kind of reliability, steadfastness, or faithfulness. To be able to rely on something, to be able to count on it – this seems to be the heart of the truth of the Bible. But this is rather vague. Let us see whether we cannot be more precise as to what is meant when we say that something can be "relied upon."

Consider the tent-peg again. When one takes it in one's hand before driving it into the ground, there is no way to know whether it can be relied upon or not. All one has is an expectation, or better yet, a hope of what this object will be able to do. One hopes that it will hold firm in the face of the stresses of the coming storm. Only after the fact, once the storm has passed, can one really say that the tent-peg was reliable, that it was true. The same can be said of Abraham's servant setting out on the road to Mesopotamia. When he first sets foot upon this road, there is no way for him to know that the road is true. All he has is a hope as to what this road can do: He hopes that it will bear him safely through the wilderness, and that it will bring him to the successful completion of his mission. But it is only after these things have come to pass that he actually comes to know that the road was true. In the same way, we know the seed is true only after it has grown into the vine we had hoped it would become; that a man is true only after he has withstood the temptation to corrupt judgment; and so forth. In every case, we find that the truth or falsity of the object is something that cannot be determined when first one comes across it, but only once it has "stood the test of time."[35] To say of an object that it is reliable, or that it is true, then, is to say that the object in question has done what we had hoped it would do despite the hardships thrown up by changing circumstance.

But this is not quite right. For what does the tent-peg really do? To speak of what the tent-peg *does* is an anthropomorphism, a metaphor. In fact, a tent-peg is completely inert. It doesn't *do* anything. It just is what it is – whether at the height of the storm, or when one holds it in one's hand. What we really expect of the tent-peg, our highest hope for it, is not that it will *do* anything, but that it will *be* something. One is tempted to say that what we hope it will simply remain what it is – a whole tent-peg, unbroken – in the face of great stress. But this isn't right either. We actually have no interest in the tent-peg remaining what it is, for what it is may be a peg that will break under pressure because it contains an invisible crack in it, which is presently obscured from our view. What we really hope for when we drive this peg into the ground is something normative: We want it to be what a tent-peg *ought to be* (in our estimation) in the face of the stresses and strains of the storm.

And the same can be said for all other objects. Jeremiah does not present God as hoping the seed will remain what it is in the face of time and circumstance. He hopes that it will be what he thinks a seed ought to be, which is to say, something that grows into a desirable vine and not into a noxious weed. Similarly, Abraham's servant hopes that the road will be what he thinks a road ought to be, which is to say, one that will bear him safely through the wilderness, and that will bring him to the successful completion of his mission. And Yitro hopes Moses can appoint as judges over Israel men who will be what he thinks a man ought to be, namely, someone capable of withstanding the temptation to corrupt judgment. In these and all other cases, an object is found to be reliable when it proves, through changing time and circumstance, to be what we think it ought to be.

I have said that in the Hebrew Bible, that which is true is that which proves, in the face of time and circumstance, to be what it ought; whereas that which is false is that which fails, in the face of time and circumstance, to be what it ought. Is this biblical conception of truth one that can be applied across the board to objects of the understanding in general, including those that are not explicitly called true in the biblical text? I think we can. Suppose, for example, that I see what I take to be a bird in a tree. What would it mean to apply the biblical understanding of truth to this bird? First, we would have to say that whether this bird is true or false cannot be known when first we come across it, just as one cannot know whether a road, a tent-peg, or a seed is true or false when first we come across it. Second, we would know whether the bird was true or false only if it proves to be what we think a bird ought to be through time and circumstance. By this I mean that, for instance, if I walk up to it and push on it, only to find that it falls to the ground and shatters, I can then say that it was a false bird because under pressure from my hand, it failed to be what a bird ought to be. Whereas if I walk up to it, and in doing so, cause it to start and fly away, I can say that it was a true bird, because under pressure of my approach, it nevertheless proved to be what a bird ought to be.

In the same way, the black color of my neighbor's new car when I see it at night is false if it looks dark green the next morning, because under changing time and circumstance, it fails to be what blackness ought to be; whereas it is true blackness if it looks black in daylight just as it did at night. What I take to be the Ninth Symphony of Beethoven is the true Ninth Symphony if the choir sings Schiller's "Ode to Joy" in the fourth movement, whereas it is a false Ninth Symphony if the choir fails to sing as the choir ought to. And the same is the case for all other things. But this is only a different way of saying that that which is truly black is that which is reliably black through time and circumstance; that that which is truly a bird is that which is reliably a bird through time and circumstance; that that which is truly the Ninth is that which is reliably the Ninth through time and circumstance; and so forth.

On the basis of these considerations, it would seem that we have been able to isolate a precise definition of truth and falsity in the Bible, which can be applied to objects of the understanding in general. On this view, that which is true is that which proves, through time and circumstance, to be what it ought. Whereas that which is false is that which fails, through time and circumstance, to be what it ought. We can now proceed to ask whether and how this truth of objects works when applied to speech.

IV. THE TRUTH OF SPEECH

In the Hebrew Bible, the words *true* and *false* are usually used to refer to qualities of objects, persons, and actions. But there are also cases in which *emet* is understood to refer to the truth of speech.[36] Of these, some appear in passages treating judicial matters, in which a claim is made or an accusation leveled, and an investigation must be conducted to confirm or refute the rumor of a crime that has been committed. The following is an example:

> If there be found among you, within any of your gates which the Lord your God has given you, a man or woman who has ... gone and served other gods, and worshiped them, either the sun or the moon or any of the host of heaven ... and it be told to you, and you have heard of it, and have investigated thoroughly, and behold it is the truth [*emet*] and the thing is certain, that this abomination has been done in Israel; then shall you bring forth that man or that woman.... On the testimony of two witnesses or three witnesses shall he be put to death.[37]

In this passage, the authorities receive a report of a man or woman who has gone over to idolatry, and the question at hand is whether the report is true (*emet*) or not. The manner in which the truth of the report is established is evident: A thorough investigation is conducted, as a result of which the report of idolatry can be confirmed and therefore found to be true.

The same pattern can also be found in a number of non-judicial passages such as this one from the book of Kings:

> And when the queen of Sheva heard of the fame of Solomon ... she came to Jerusalem with a very great train.... And she said to the king, "It was a true [*emet*] report I heard in my own land of your acts and your wisdom. But I believed not the words until I came and my eyes had seen it. And behold, the half of it was not told to me; your wisdom and prosperity exceed the fame of which I heard."[38]

In this passage, the queen of Sheva hears a rumor of Solomon's greatness, and the question is whether this report is true (*emet*) or not. Here, too, it is investigation – in this case a visit to Jerusalem by the queen herself – that confirms the rumor, and therefore establishes its truth. And other similar passages in which the truth of speech is at stake work the same way.

Can the terms *true* and *false*, when used in reference to speech, be understood to have the same meaning as when they are used to refer to objects, persons, and actions? If so, then the truth of speech would be no more than a special case of the truth of objects more generally. The question is whether it is possible to understand the truth of speech as referring to reliability, rather than to agreement or correspondence, as required by the philosophical tradition following Aristotle.

Is it possible to understand the truth of speech to mean reliability? At first glance, such a reading seems promising. Indeed, it is precisely the reliability of the words that reach the authorities and the queen of Sheva in the above texts that seems to be tested and proved. That is, where the authorities find that the words of the rumor of idolatry can be relied upon (in that the man or woman who is mentioned is indeed found to have committed acts of idolatry), they are said to be true; and where the queen of Sheva finds that the words of the report of Solomon's greatness that reaches her can be relied upon (in that Solomon proves to be as great a ruler as she has heard), she says that they are true. It does seem, then, that the truth of speech can be understood as its reliability.

On closer inspection, however, this reading seems to run into trouble. For in the last section, in an effort to understand precisely what is meant by reliability, it was concluded that an object is true if it proves, through time and circumstance, to be what it ought; for something to be reliable is for it to prove through time and circumstance to be what it ought. Now, if the truth of speech is the same as the truth of objects, then for a rumor or a report or any other speech to be true, it must be something that remains what it ought through time and circumstance. But this leads immediately to confusion, for the proposal that spoken words should be what they ought to be through time and circumstance seems incoherent. After all, there is hardly something more transient than the spoken word. It lives in a particular breath, and is dead by the next. It would seem that if being what it ought through time and circumstance were the criterion for determining the truth of a word or speech, then no word or speech would ever be true. Indeed, words would be seen as unreliable by their nature, and the Bible would incline to the view that words in general are false. And yet we see that the Bible does attribute truth to certain things that are spoken, and not to others.

We are therefore left with a riddle: If in the Bible, true speech is nothing other than reliable speech, what precisely is meant here by the term *reliable*? Either the reliability of words is something different from the reliability that is characteristic of objects, in which case the distinction must be understood and accounted for; or else the reliability of words is the same as the reliability of objects, but there is something lacking in our understanding of how words work in the Bible, such that they could be what they ought to be through time and circumstance. Either way, we have before us a riddle that must be resolved.

But this isn't the only riddle we have here. Here's another: Consider again what happens when I approach what I take to be a bird on the branch of a tree. In some ways, my understanding of this situation is the same whether my conception of truth is that of the correspondence theory or that of the Bible. For instance, the bird I see before me is the same either way. And in either case, I can appropriately say the sentence *It is a bird* upon seeing it. In these respects, which conception of truth I choose is of no real consequence. Other aspects of this situation, however, do change with my conception of truth. For example, on the correspondence theory, truth or falsity is thought to be a quality inherent in the sentence at the moment it is spoken (or thought). Thus if I say *It is a bird*, the truth or falsity of the sentence is understood to depend on a reality independent of this sentence and pertaining at the moment the sentence is spoken. It would depend, in other words, on whether the object in question is or is not a bird at the moment that the sentence is spoken. On the biblical understanding, on the other hand, to say *It is a bird* is not to say words that are true or false at the moment they are spoken. This is because the truth or falsity of the words is nothing other than the reliability of the words. But this reliability cannot yet be known at the moment these words are spoken since – as in the case of the report of idolatry or the rumor of Solomon's greatness – it depends on whether, upon investigation, the object in question in fact proves to be a bird. On the biblical conception, then, it would seem that the truth or falsity of the spoken word cannot be known until it has proved itself reliable in the course of investigation, which is to say, in the course of time.

The supposition that in the Bible the truth of speech cannot be known except in the course of time is rendered all the more interesting by the following consideration. It was said above that the truth of the bird in the branch cannot be known except in time. If the bird falls and shatters, I say the bird was false; and if it starts and flies away, I say the bird was true. But now it seems that precisely the same is the case with respect to the sentence *It is a bird*, spoken when I first set eyes on it. For if the bird falls and shatters, I will say the sentence was false; whereas if it starts and flies away, then the sentence was true. In other words, the truth or falsity of the sentence *It is a bird* depends directly on the truth or falsity of the bird itself: If the bird proves true, then so does the sentence; and if the bird proves false, then the sentence follows. This is because once it is known whether the bird was true or false, we also know whether the sentence *It is a bird* was true or false. If it transpires that the bird was false, it is the falsity of the bird that, in retrospect, makes the words *It is a bird* into false (i.e., unreliable) words. On the other hand, if it transpires that the bird was true, it is the truth of the bird that, in retrospect, makes the words *It is a bird* into true (i.e., reliable) words.

We find, therefore, that to adopt the biblical account of truth and falsity has the following consequence: that the truth and falsity of speech is found to be dependent on the truth and falsity of the object to which this speech refers. That is, unlike the correspondence theory, in which reality is said to be independent of that which is spoken, in the biblical understanding there is a direct dependence of that which is spoken on that which is in reality. True words are always those that are spoken about true things, whereas false words are always those that are spoken about false things. And indeed, this does seem to be the case. Whenever the biblical authors choose to speak about false words, these are words that refer to false things. Thus Jeremiah says:

> From the prophet to the priest, everyone deals in falsity [*sheker*]. For they have healed the hurt of the daughter of my people superficially, saying "Peace, peace," when there is no peace.[39]

Here the words of the prophets and priests are falsity because the thing that they describe is peace, although there is no peace. That is, the words "peace, peace," are false because they refer to something that appears to be peace but is not what peace ought to be. The words are false, in other words, because they refer to a false peace. Were the peace itself a true peace, then the words would likewise be true. And the same seems to be true in all other cases.

In practice, then, if I apply the Bible's understanding of truth and falsity, I will still say *It is a bird* of what seems to be a bird when I see it. But I will not attribute truth or falsity to what has been said unless I have understood it to have been spoken of a true bird or a false bird, respectively. That is, I will not presume to have knowledge of the truth or falsity of the words until the bird itself has proved to be, or failed to be, what a bird ought to be in the face of time and circumstance.

V. THE OBJECT AS UNDERSTOOD

I ended the previous section with two riddles concerning the meaning of true words in the Bible. First, it was said that on the biblical understanding, when what we say is true, it is because the things to which we refer are true; whereas when what we say is false, it is because the things to which we refer are false. This is troubling because we are accustomed to supposing that the objects to which words refer exist in a reality independent of what is said and thought about them; and the independence of objects from that which is said and thought seems to be violated if the qualities of objects are automatically transmitted to the words or thoughts that refer to them. How it can be that what is said and thought can be dependent on objects in this way requires further explanation. Second, it is uncertain whether the truth or falsity of words, which seems equivalent to the reliability of words, can really be understood as parallel to the truth and falsity of objects, which we have defined as their capacity to be what the object in question ought to be through time and circumstance. As has been said, the proposal that words should be what they ought to be through time and circumstance seems incoherent, since there is hardly something more transient than the spoken word.

If these difficulties are to be resolved, and the relation between the truth of words and the truth of objects rendered clear, we are going to need a more precise understanding of what it is to which the biblical authors refer when they speak of *words*. It is therefore to a discussion of what words are in the Hebrew Scriptures that I now turn. With the completion of this step in my inquiry, I will go back to the two riddles concerning the nature of true speech and see whether they have not been resolved.

The Hebrew term for words, and for spoken things more generally, is *davar* (דבר).⁴⁰ In many cases, a *davar* is undoubtedly understood to be what we would normally call a word or words, as when Moses tells God that he cannot speak before Pharaoh because he is not a man of words:

> And Moses said unto the Lord: "O Lord, I am not a man of words [*devarim*], neither heretofore, nor since you have spoken to your servant, for I am slow of speech and of a slow tongue."⁴¹

Or when Joshua commands the people at Jericho:

> You shall not shout, nor make any noise with your voice, nor shall any word [*davar*] proceed from your mouth until the day I tell you to shout. Then shall you shout.⁴²

But while *davar* does seem to cover all cases of spoken words, its usage is much broader. This is evident, in the first place, from the fact that a *davar* is not only something that is spoken, but also something that is only in one's thoughts. The biblical opposition between that which is "in the mind" [*belev*] and that which is "in the mouth" [*bepeh*] seems precisely to parallel our own opposition between that which is thought and that which is spoken, yet Moses speaks of God's word as a *davar* that can be both "in your mouth" and "in your mind":

> This commandment which I command you this day is not hidden from you ... But the word [*davar*] is very near to you, in your mouth and in your mind, that you may do it.⁴³

That a *davar* in the mind is unspoken is clear from passages such the following warning in Deuteronomy:

> Beware that there not be an unworthy thought [*davar*] in your mind, saying, the seventh year, the year of release is at hand, and your eye be evil against your poor brother, so that you give him nothing.⁴⁴

Similarly, Caleb, recalling his dispute with the other spies over whether Canaan could be conquered, tells Joshua that he bore the *davar* in his mind before speaking it out loud to Moses:

> Forty years old was I when Moses, servant of the Lord, sent me from Kadesh Barnea to spy out the land, and I brought him back word [*davar*] as it was in my mind.⁴⁵

In these and numerous other cases, we see that a *davar* is not necessarily spoken, but can be something that is only in thought.⁴⁶

If the term *davar* were used only in reference to speech and thought, one might be tempted to compare a *davar* to the Greek *logos*, which can be equally speech or thought. In fact, however, the usage of *davar* is broader still, extending to cover not only speech and thought, but all that is embraced by the English term *thing* as well. This includes physical objects, as in the following law prescribed in the book of Numbers:

> Only the gold and the silver, the brass, the iron, the tin, and the lead, every thing [*davar*] that passes through the fire, you shall make it go through the fire, and it shall be clean.[47]

Or in this passage from Deuteronomy:

> You shall not lend on interest to your brother, interest on money, interest on foodstuffs, interest on any thing [*davar*] that is lent on interest.[48]

But a *davar* may also be a thing in the broader sense in which an action, for example, may be a thing, as when the angel tells Lot he cannot destroy Sodom until he has removed himself and his family from there:

> Hasten yourself and escape to there, for I cannot do any thing [*davar*] until you have come there.[49]

Or when God tells Samuel:

> Behold, I will do a thing [*davar*] in Israel at which both the ears of every one that hears it shall tingle. In that day, I will perform against Eli all that I have spoken concerning his house from beginning to end.[50]

Similarly, a *davar* may be a thing in the most general sense, as in the following passage from Leviticus:

> And if the whole congregation of Israel sin through ignorance, and the thing [*davar*] be hid from the eyes of the assembly, and they have done against one of the commandments of the Lord that which should not be done, and have incurred guilt; when the sin, which they have sinned, is known, then the congregation shall offer a young bullock.[51]

And in this one from Ezra and Nehemia:

> Petahya, son of Meshezavel, of the sons of Zerah, son of Judah, was at the king's hand in all things [*davar*] concerning the people.[52]

From these and innumerable other passages, we see that a *davar*, far from being restricted to words and thoughts, can also be any thing at all that is in the world. Indeed, *davar*, the Hebrew term for a word or thought, is also by far the most commonly used term for a thing.[53] So that if we wish to inquire concerning the relation between word and object in the Bible, we discover that these are expressed by a single term, the word *davar*. Thus the most striking aspect of the biblical understanding of the relation between word and object is that the Bible does not normally seem to recognize the distinction between word and object.

It is, of course, possible to insist that the biblical authors must have been able to distinguish words and thoughts, on the one hand, from things, on the other; and that the word *davar* simply has two different usages: At times it is used to describe speech or thought, and at times it is used to describe things.[54] But two considerations militate against simply accepting this argument. First, at the most general level, there is the observation, not easily dismissed, that the biblical authors seem not to feel any need to oppose word and object to one another in the manner of the Greek philosophers. Had they felt the need for such an opposition, it seems likely that they would not have remained satisfied with using a single word to describe both.[55]

Second, at the level of examples, it is clear that the sharp distinction between the two usages cannot be maintained. For in the Bible, the term *davar* appears very frequently in contexts in which there is no way to tell whether it is referring to words or to things. Consider, for example, the following passage from Genesis:

> And Sarah ... said to Abraham. "Cast out this bondwoman and her son, for the son of this bondwoman shall not be heir with my son, with Isaac." And the thing [*davar*] was very grievous in Abraham's eyes because of his son.[56]

Sarah demands that Hagar and Ishmael be expelled from Abraham's household, and he finds the *davar* grievous. But what, precisely, is this *davar*? Is it Sarah's words that are grievous, or is it the thing to which they refer, which is to say, the proposed expulsion of Hagar and Ishmael?

A similar ambiguity is found in the following speech of Moses before the people in Deuteronomy:

> I spoke to you at that time, saying ... "How can I myself alone bear your care, and your burden, and your strife? Take wise men ... and I will make them rulers over you." And you answered me and said, "The thing [*davar*] which you have spoken is good for us to do."[57]

Here, too, there is no way to tell whether the *davar* the people find good to do is the words Moses has spoken, offering for them to select their own judges; or whether it is the thing itself (i.e., the selection of their own judges) they find to be good.

And in this passage from Samuel:

> While they were on the way, the report came to David, saying, "Avshalom has slain all of the king's sons, and there is not one of them left." ... And Yonadav,

the son of Shima, the king's brother, answered and said ... "Let not my lord
the king put a thing [*davar*] in his mind, saying all the king's sons are dead, for
only Amnon is dead."[58]

We know that Yonadav asks David not to put a *davar* in his mind, saying that all his sons are dead. But what, exactly, is the *davar* he is not to
put in his mind? Is it the words of the report that he is not to accept in his
mind, or the thing itself, which is to say, the death of his sons, as it has been
reported?

These are not isolated examples. Rather, the indeterminacy in the meaning of the term *davar* is a fixed feature of biblical language. In reading the
Bible, one is constantly confronted by things that are neither clearly words
nor clearly objects. Given this fact, it seems impossible to conclude that
the term *davar* has two distinct meanings, from which the biblical authors
choose each time they deploy the word. On the contrary, the biblical authors
use the word *davar* as though they see no need to draw a sharp boundary
between word and object.[59]

How are we to understand this? How can one fail to have need of a sharp
distinction between that which is spoken and that to which it refers?

Let us suppose, for a moment, that this blurring of the distinction between
word and object is not an accident of imprecise writing, but is rather a reflection of the biblical understanding, according to which a *davar* is often something intermediate between word and object. Let us suppose, in other words,
that what is meant when the Bible speaks of a *davar* is not a word at all,
but what we might today call an *understanding* of something, by which is
meant the *object as understood*.[60] In this case, when the Bible reports that a
certain *davar* has been spoken, it is describing not something detached from
the object to which it refers, but rather the object itself as it is conceived or
understood by someone. Thus the *davar* that Caleb brings back from Canaan
is neither the words he spoke upon his return, nor the land itself, to which
his words refer. Instead, the *davar* is his conception or understanding of the
land he saw. In the same way, the *davar* Abraham finds grievous is Sarah's
conception or understanding of Hagar's expulsion; the *davar* of which Moses
speaks is his conception or understanding of the selection of judges over the
people; and the *davar* that Yonadav tells David not to put in his mind is the
conception or understanding according to which all his sons are dead.

On this view of what is meant by *davar*, there is no need for the biblical
authors to distinguish between word and object most of the time. When one
speaks of a *davar*, one refers to the understood object, which has no outward expression if one is thinking silently; and which finds expression in
words if one is speaking aloud.

To see how this works in practice, consider, once again, Abraham's servant as he sets out on the road to Haran. Let us say that he speaks or thinks of the road as he begins to walk along it. If one is committed to a radical distinction between thought and object, one may be forced to decide whether the road he has before him is a "real" road independent of his understanding; or, alternatively, whether it is only a representation of this road in his mind. But if one does not embrace such a radical distinction between thought and object – and the Bible, it would seem, does not – the question of whether he walks on the thing itself or on its representation in his mind cannot arise. For in this case, we do not have a thought and an object needing to be distinguished one from the other. There is only the *davar*, the understood object, which is the one road before the servant as he begins to walk.

VI. TRUE AND FALSE *DEVARIM*

I have suggested that the Bible does not possess a clear division between words or thoughts and the objects to which they refer, but rather understands man's reality as consisting of *devarim*, an intermediate category between word and object that may be called an *understanding*, or an *object as understood*. Having made this suggestion, I would like now to return to truth and falsity, and ask what is meant when the biblical authors speak of a *davar* as being true or false.

Suppose again that Abraham's servant sets out for Mesopotamia. Before him is the road on which he travels, as he understands it. If he thinks about it, this road is a *davar* (in English, a *thing*) that is "in his mind." We may now ask whether the *davar* in the servant's mind is true or false. This will depend, as has been said, on whether the *davar*, or thing, in question can be counted on to be what it ought to be through time and circumstance. That is, if the *davar* in the servant's mind proves, through time and circumstance, to be what it ought to be, it will be a *devar emet*, or a true thing; if it fails to be what it ought to be, it will be a *devar sheker*, or a false thing.

What happens if the servant, in addition to having this *davar* "in his mind," also speaks of it? In the language of the Bible, we would say that the *davar* that was in the servant's mind is now, in addition, "in his mouth." But the *davar* now in his mouth is not a different *davar* from the first that was in his mind. Rather, it is the same *davar*, which was perhaps previously hidden in the servant's mind, and is now in evidence in his mouth or on his tongue, as is the case where Joshua says "I brought him back word [*davar*] as it was in my mind"; or where Ezekiel says: "It will come to pass on that day, that things [*devarim*] will arise in your mind ... and you will say, 'I will go up to the land of unwalled villages.'"[61] That this same *davar* is no longer hidden, however, does not change the fact that it is one and the same *davar* – for the servant's understanding of the road has not changed in giving it voice. And since it is still the same *davar* that was previously in his mind, there is no reason to think that the test for whether this *davar* is true or false will have changed. Indeed, the test has not changed at all: If we ask whether the *davar* that is in the servant's mouth is true or false, the answer is still that this will depend on whether the *davar* in question can be counted on to be what it ought to be through time and circumstance or not. That is, if this *davar* that is in the servant's mouth proves to be what it ought to be it will be a *devar emet*, and if it fails to be what it ought to be it will be a *devar sheker*. The fact of its having been vocalized does not have any effect on whether the *davar* in question is a "true thing" or a "false thing."

With this in mind, we can answer the question of whether the Hebrew Bible treats the truth of words as if it were a special case of the truth of objects. The paradigm cases of the truth of words, it will be recalled, are those in which a rumor reaches the authorities, who must investigate in order to ascertain its truth or falsity, as in the following example concerning a rumor of idolatry, quoted above:

> If ... it be told to you, and you have heard of it, and have investigated thoroughly, and behold it is the truth [*emet*] and the thing [*davar*] is certain, that this abomination has been done in Israel; then shall you bring forth that man or that woman.... On the testimony of two witnesses or three witnesses shall he be put to death.[62]

Upon returning to this passage, we now see that the rumor of an act of idolatry is explicitly called a *davar*, a word or thing. But again, we are confronted by a seeming indifference of the term *davar* as between word and object. For what is the *davar* to which this passage refers? Is it the rumor, in which case it is the word that is either true or false; or is it the act of idolatry itself, in which case it is a thing, to which the words refer, that is either true or false? The answer, it would appear, is that this is a false choice forced upon us by the dualism of word and object presupposed by the correspondence theory.[63] In fact, the *davar* in question is the act of idolatry as it is conceived or understood by the authorities upon hearing of it. The question that is being addressed when the authorities investigate the rumor is whether the object before their minds upon hearing the report – the act of idolatry, as they understand it to be – will prove to be what it ought to be in the course of a thorough investigation of the matter.[64] If the investigation proves the *davar* as understood by the authorities to be reliable, by which is meant that it continues to be what was expected in the face of time and circumstance, it is said to have been a true word or thing, *devar emet*. If investigation proves this *davar* to have been unreliable, in that it does not continue to be what it ought to be through time and circumstance, it is recognized to have been a false thing, *devar sheker*.

The same is the case where the queen of Sheva comes to investigate the report she has heard of Solomon's wealth:

> And she said to the king, "It was a true [*emet*] report [*davar*] I heard in my own land of your acts and your wisdom. But I believed not the words until I came and my eyes had seen it."[65]

Here, too, the word that is translated as a "report" is simply *davar*, and here too the *davar* is indifferent as between word and thing. Is it the words the queen heard in her own land that were true, or is it the thing itself, Solomon's greatness, that proved true in the wake of the original report of it? And here, too, we are best off sidestepping this unnecessary dichotomy. For the *davar* in question is the queen's understanding of Solomon's greatness, as it was when she first heard tell of it. It is this understanding that she takes with her to Jerusalem, where she inquires after it. And since protracted experience of this *davar* reveals it to be reliable, she says: *Emet haya hadavar* – "True was the thing" – by which she means that her conception of the thing was *reliable* over the course of time and the circumstances of her inquiry.

VII. A *DAVAR* THAT STANDS

With this understanding before us, it is now possible resolve the two riddles concerning the truth and falsity of words in the Hebrew Bible with which I concluded Section V.

The first of these was the question as to how it is possible for the truth or falsity of words to be dependent on the truth or falsity of the objects to which these words refer, given that words and objects are supposed to be independent from one another. The answer to this question is obviously that in the metaphysical scheme of the Bible, there is no independence of words and things from one another. Rather, the biblical *davar*, which is an understanding or an object as understood, is one and the same whether it is before the mind, or given expression in words. The truth or falsity of a *davar* is determined by whether it can be relied upon to be what it ought in the face of time and circumstance. It is not affected by whether it is merely before the mind in silence, or whether it is also given spoken expression in words. In either case, a reliable *davar* is true, and an unreliable *davar* is false. If we insist on a dualist metaphysics, in which the world as understood and the world as described in speech are forced apart and made to appear as two different things, then a *davar* understood in silence will end up being called a *thing*, whereas a *davar* accompanied by its vocalized expression will end up being called a *word*. In this case, the very act of imposing such a dualism will create the illusion that word and object are two independent things, and we will be surprised to discover that in the Bible, the one cannot be true or false without the other bearing the same quality. But if we do not impose such a dualism, we have no difficulty in seeing that whether the *davar* is held silently before the mind, or whether it is accompanied by an outward vocal expression, it is one and its truth or falsity is likewise one. Whether we then interpret the *davar* to be a word, a thought, or a thing, its truth or falsity will naturally remain unchanged.

The second question that troubled us was how, if the truth of an object is its being what it ought to be through time and circumstance, we can speak of the truth of words, which seem to have no significant duration through time, being uttered in a given moment with respect to a particular circumstance. This question is resolved when we recognize that the biblical *davar* is not really comparable to what in English is called a *word* at all. For when we speak of a word, we tend to think of something that is to a large extent defined by its vocalization: When one stops speaking, the word seems to come to an end. The Hebrew *davar*, on the other hand, is an understanding of things, of which the external vocalization that accompanies it is no more than a sign. And the understanding can endure long after the external sign is gone. Thus it is possible for Jeremiah to say in God's name that:

> All the men of Judah that are in the land of Egypt shall be consumed by the sword and by famine, until there be an end of them. Yet a small number that escape the sword shall return ... and all the remnant of Judah ... shall know whose word [*devar mi*] shall stand, mine or theirs.[66]

Here, the words that are spoken in warning against Judah are uttered at a given moment by Jeremiah. Yet the *davar* spoken by the prophet may "stand" years after the utterance of the words themselves has been completed. Indeed, the *davar* spoken by his opponents may also "stand" for years after it was uttered – and it will so long as the understanding before the minds of these people is not demolished under pressure of events. In other words, it is precisely because the *davar* is not a word that Jeremiah can conceive of the two *devarim* as pitted against one another, striving against one another until one of them falls and the other is left standing.

Much the same can be said concerning the following passage, in which Moses stipulates that a *davar* will be established (that is, it will "stand") in an Israelite court only on the basis of testimony from two witnesses or more:

> One witness shall not rise up against any man for any iniquity or for any sin, in any sin that he may commit. At the mouth of two witnesses or at the mouth of three witnesses shall the thing [*davar*] be established.[67]

Thus in a judicial proceeding, the witnesses will be asked to give testimony, but the words they speak are not the *davar*, but only signs or indications of a *davar* that must be established and remain long after they are done speaking.[68]

In these and other passages, we see that while words come and go in a moment, the *davar* of Hebrew Scripture does not. For the *davar* is the understanding that arises and may endure for years or even for generations, becoming what it ought to be through time and circumstance, and therefore proving itself true; or failing to be what it ought to be, and thereby showing itself to have been no more than a passing illusion.

VIII. CONCLUSION: THE BIBLICAL METAPHYSICS AND OURS

The conception of truth found in the Hebrew Bible is not without parallel in contemporary discourse. Modern English recognizes that an object, person, or action can be true or false across a limited domain of cases, as when we speak of true love, a true friend, a true artist, a heart that is true, or an arrow that flies true. And these expressions seem to conform to the conception of truth as a kind of reliability. Thus when we speak of true love, we speak of a love that proves reliable, which is to say that it is proves, through time and circumstance, to be what a love ought to be; whereas when we say that a friend is false, we mean that he is unreliable, and that, when the chips are down, he fails to be what a friend ought to be. Historically, as well, English and other European languages have made frequent use of such a truth of objects.[69] Moreover, in the philosophical tradition of the West, one does occasionally find mention of the possibility that objects may have the capacity to be true or false.[70] We therefore have at least some evidence that this alternative understanding of truth has had relevance outside of the particular age and worldview of the biblical authors.

But in general, neither the presence of a conception of the truth of objects in Western languages nor the occasional mention of such a conception by philosophers seems to have engendered a systematic effort to try to understand the logic behind the truth of objects, or to develop it as a serious alternative to the conception of truth as a quality of speech familiar from the mainstream of the philosophical tradition. That no such effort has historically been registered in the philosophical tradition seems to be a consequence of the prevalence of dualistic assumptions – even in thinkers not usually labeled dualists – that have made the division between speech and reality seem a natural and obvious one. Once such a division is in place, one can evidently be quite comfortable with a theory according to which (i) *truth is a quality of speech*; (ii) *true speech is "of" (or "about") a reality independent of itself*; and (iii) *true speech is that which affirms (or "corresponds to") this reality*.

The last hundred years, however, have brought a long series of critiques of dualist philosophies and their conception of a reality independent of that which is spoken or thought. Calls to overcome such dualism have been registered time and again. In philosophy, these criticisms have been felt as an increasing discomfort with the correspondence theory of truth. Although critics of the correspondence theory are not always individuals who have broken with the dualism of word and object, their arguments can generally be seen as reflecting an inability to make the dualist metaphysics work. This is evident, for example, in the various versions of the "access" argument. On this argument, truth cannot be adequately described as an agreement or correspondence between that which is thought or spoken and that which is in reality, because there is no way one can escape one's own thoughts in order to gain access to a reality independent of them; and if no such access to a reality independent of the mind is available, then it seems impossible that any individual can make the comparison between thought and reality that is necessary to establish correspondence, and therefore truth. This challenge comes in many variations, and is registered with many hesitations, some of them reasonable.[71] Nevertheless, it cannot be refuted because it points to a flaw in the dualism on which the correspondence theory rests. This flaw is the assumption that the object before the understanding – the object visible before us – is itself not "real," but only indicates or represents some other, mind-independent object that is not the one before us. So long as this assumption continues to stand, one must rely on the metaphysical construction of an absent "thing-in-itself," which alone is capable of rendering this dualism plausible; and which then permits the advancement of the correspondence theory. But the assumption of the "thing-in-itself," it seems, will ultimately have to be abandoned. And when it goes, so too will the correspondence theory, which is based on it.

Against this philosophical backdrop, it seems particularly appropriate to consider the very different conception of truth that is found in the Hebrew Bible, which appears to do entirely without the dualist premises upon which the correspondence theory was constructed. Unlike the philosophical tradition descended from Athenian thought, the biblical authors do not base their understanding of truth on a dualism of word and object. They do not, in other words, imagine real objects to exist in a realm of their own, independent of what is said or thought. As a consequence, there are, in the Bible, no words that can correspond or fail to correspond with objects or states of affairs already existing in reality. On the biblical understanding, truth is a quality of objects, which they are known to possess only once they have proved themselves reliable – by which is meant, once they have proved to be what they ought to be through time and changing circumstance. Our understandings or conceptions of objects, on the other hand, are not a separate kind of being in a distinct realm of their own. Instead, they are themselves the actual object as understood by us, or *davar*. Thus the truth or falsity of our conception of a given object is all there is to say about the truth or falsity of this object. There is no other object other than the one before us. On this scheme, my speech is nothing other than my conception of the object in question, albeit accompanied by vocalization that permits me to communicate this conception. This is why true words always seem to be said of true things, and false words of false things. The words express the object as understood by the speaker, which is all the reality he has. If the conceptions expressed by the words are reliable and therefore true, then the things being discussed are themselves reliable and therefore true.

If this is correct, it means that the authors of the Hebrew Scriptures were not dualists.[72] They were able to do with one realm alone, in which true understandings of things are distinguished from false ones by their ability to stand the test of time within the confines of this one realm. This means that in the Hebrew Bible, truth does not seem to exist in the given moment, but only in the course of subsequent events, which are what make an understood object, or *davar*, into something true or false. Indeed, in Deuteronomy, the test of whether the words of a prophet can be considered true is explicitly said to be their capacity to prove themselves in time:

> I will raise them up a prophet from among their brethren ... and put my words in his mouth.... And if you say in your mind, "How shall we know the word [*davar*] which the Lord has not spoken?" Know that when a prophet speaks in the name of the Lord, if the thing [*davar*] follow not, nor come to pass, that is the thing [*davar*] which the Lord has not spoken, but the prophet has spoken it out of presumption.[73]

Today, most are very far from being able to imagine what it must have been like to live in a world whose objects were understood to have been created by the speech or thought of God. But we do have some ability to imagine what it means to live in a world consisting of objects as understood, in which there is no reality that is genuinely independent of our own mind. The criticism that is always leveled against such an interpretation of our experience is that it necessitates a thoroughgoing subjectivism; that it can have no truth in it. The biblical authors, however, seem to have maintained just such an understanding while at the same devoting themselves to the quest for truth, seeking it and even, as it seems, finding it. To work through what they meant when they spoke of *truth* seems, therefore, to be an endeavor that can perhaps be of assistance at a time when the dualist metaphysics familiar to us is set upon with difficulties, and when our understanding of what is meant by truth is threatened along with it.

8

Jerusalem and Carthage

Reason and Faith in Hebrew Scripture

In recent years, it has again become popular to speak of Jerusalem and Athens as representing contradictory and irreconcilable ways of interpreting reality and determining the conduct of our lives.[1] Historically, this insistence on an absolute opposition between the Bible and the philosophy of ancient Greece has been most closely associated with the Church Father Tertullian, who famously asked "What indeed has Athens to do with Jerusalem? What concord can there be between the Academy and the Church? What between heretics and Christians?"[2] But Tertullian was hardly alone in this. His Jerusalem–Athens dichotomy launched an entire discourse within the Western tradition based on two premises that are by now often presented as if they were self-evidently correct and in need of no further discussion. These are the assumptions that:

(i) "Faith" and "reason" name distinct and opposed aspects of mankind's mental endowment; and that
(ii) The tradition of thought found in the Bible represents and encourages the first of these, whereas Greek philosophy embraces the second.

These premises have been extraordinarily fruitful in the history of the Christian West, inspiring some to defend faith against reason, others to champion reason against faith, and yet others to argue that the two can be reconciled – all of this within the framework established by Tertullian and while treating his two premises as an appropriate basis for discussion. Nevertheless, my own view is that both of these premises are almost certainly false: I do not believe the dichotomy between faith and reason is very helpful in understanding the diversity of human intellectual orientations. I say this, among other reasons, because I think it is an empirical fact that the faithful are in many cases quite reasonable individuals, whereas those who are most intransigent in their unreason are often the most unfaithful. And I do not believe that either the tradition of inquiry preserved in the Hebrew Scriptures or the tradition of discovery represented by the writings of Plato and Aristotle are particularly well suited to play the roles usually assigned to them in the often facile debate that ensues once the supposed opposition between faith and reason is taken as a point of departure.

In the present chapter, I will consider one aspect of this topic: the question of whether the Bible can reasonably be seen as representing the position labeled "faith" in the Tertullianic disputation between faith and reason. Tertullian, of course, champions a very specific kind of Christian faith. And it is to this kind of Christian faith that he and many others after him have been pleased to give the name "Jerusalem." In my view, this nomenclature derives from Tertullian's rhetorical posture with respect to those he was debating in his home city of Carthage, and can teach us next to nothing about the thought of Jerusalem. Indeed, I wish to suggest that the kind of faith that bears the label "Jerusalem" in the discourse inspired by Tertullian cannot be found in the Hebrew Bible at all. To study the Hebrew Scriptures is to encounter an entirely different worldview (or rather, a complex or school of worldviews) from that which is so often called "faith" – a worldview as easily opposed to that emanating from Carthage as it is to the thought of Athens. To speak intelligently about the thought of the Hebrew Bible and its place in the history of the West, we must therefore learn to think in terms of an unaccustomed and very different opposition, that between Carthage and Jerusalem.

What follows, then, is a preliminary exploration of the opposition between Carthage and Jerusalem. I begin with a brief recapitulation of the opposition between Jerusalem and Athens as it appears in the writings of Tertullian and of those who follow his lead. I then turn to an investigation of the place of human reason in the Hebrew Scriptures; and inquire in what sense, and to what extent, it can be said that the biblical authors see faith as a virtue. I conclude that the Tertullianic conception of "Jerusalem" cannot be reconciled with the texts of Hebrew Scripture in regard to either reason or faith, but must be considered another position altogether, which may be represented by the city of Carthage.

I. TERTULLIAN'S JERUSALEM AND TERTULLIAN'S ATHENS

Quintus Septimius Florens Tertullianus was born in 155 CE in Roman Carthage (in present-day Tunisia), where he was raised a pagan and became a convert to Christianity. He was the first significant Christian thinker to write in Latin, and is for this reason sometimes called the Father of the Latin Church. According to most accounts, he eventually left the Church after concluding that it was heretical.[3] His last works date from no later than the year 222.

Tertullian lays out a view according to which the faith of a Christian and the philosopher's pursuit of truth are seen as irreconcilable and mutually antagonistic. I will touch on three aspects of his thought that are especially significant in this regard. These are, first, his adoption of an authoritative catechism by means of which a Christian can gain access to needful knowledge; second, his disavowal of the worth of a life devoted to seeking truth; and third, his endorsement of the idea that what a Christian is called upon to believe is in some sense absurd, and therefore antithetical to reason.

I turn first to Tertullian's advocacy of catechism. In *Prescription Against Heretics*, Tertullian argues that Christians must abstain from the philosophers' quest for truth because the restless seeking for understanding is precisely that which leads to heresy. Christians are to concern themselves only with what he calls a "rule of faith" (or "law of faith"), which is a kind of catalogue of the things a Christian needs to believe. Tertullian's rule of faith reads as follows:

> Now the rule of faith ... is unquestionably that wherein our belief is affirmed that there is but one God, the Selfsame with the Creator of the world, Who produced all things out of nothing through His Word sent down in the beginning of all things; that this Word is called His Son, Who in the Name of God was seen under divers forms by the patriarchs, was ever heard in the prophets, and lastly was brought down by the Spirit and Power of God the Father into the Virgin Mary, became Flesh in her womb, and being born of her lived as Jesus Christ; that thereafter He proclaimed a new law and a new promise of the Kingdom of Heaven, wrought miracles, was crucified, and on the third day rose again, was caught up into the heavens, and sat down at the right hand of the Father; that He sent the Vicarious Power of the Holy Spirit to lead believers; that He will come with glory to take the saints into the enjoyment of life eternal and of the heavenly promises, and to adjudge the wicked to fire perpetual, after the resurrection of both good and bad has taken place together with the restoration of their flesh.[4]

Tertullian thus argues that there is one definitive body of knowledge that man must acquire. Moreover, this body of knowledge is not itself in any sense the result of some kind of human quest for truth. Rather, it consists of teachings that Jesus received directly from God, and handed down directly to his apostles, who then made them known through the apostolic churches. Regarding the question of how one is to know which is the proper doctrine,

Tertullian argues that this can be known because it is the doctrine of those churches whose lineage can be traced directly back to the apostles:

> [A]ll doctrine which agrees with the apostolic churches ... must be reckoned for truth, as undoubtedly containing that which the [said] churches received from the apostles, the apostles from Christ, Christ from God. Whereas all doctrine must be prejudged as false which savors of contrariety to the truth of the churches and apostles of Christ and God.[5]

The question of how mankind can gain access to truth is thus for Tertullian a matter of ensuring that one has gained access to authoritative doctrine by receiving it from an apostolic church. The possibility of real disagreement among such churches cannot even arise, because the truth is one and evident. As Tertullian tells us, "Where diversity of doctrine is found, there ... must the corruption both of the Scriptures and [of] the expositions thereof be regarded as existing."[6] Simply stated, the rule of faith, being one, authoritative, and perfectly clear, is able to put an end to human questioning and seeking with respect to matters of ultimate significance. As Tertullian says, "This rule [of faith] ... was taught by Christ and raises among ourselves *no other questions* than those which heresies introduce."[7]

What, then, are we to make of that famous exhortation of the Gospels, "Seek and ye shall find"?[8] For Tertullian, this call to seek truth refers only to those who have not yet found Christ's rule of faith. Once this rule of faith is found, all other seeking is to come to an end. As he writes:

> I lay down this position: That there is some one, and therefore definite, thing taught by Christ, which the Gentiles are by all means bound to believe, and for that purpose they "seek," in order that they may be able, when they have "found" it, to believe. However, there can be no indefinite seeking, for that which has been taught [is only one] definite thing. You must "seek" until you "find," and believe when you have found. Nor have you anything further to do but to keep what you have believed, and therefore nothing else is to be sought, after you have found and believed what has been taught by [Christ,] who charges you to seek no other thing than that which he has taught.... What you have "to seek," then, is that which Christ has taught, [and you must go on seeking] ... until you find it. But you have succeeded in finding when you have believed.[9]

Thus for Tertullian, one should seek only until one has found the rule of faith. This having been found, all other seeking for knowledge should in principle come to an end. Indeed, he insists that beyond what is taught by Christianity, there is no truth of significance to be sought:

> We want no curious disputation after possessing Christ Jesus, no inquisition after enjoying the Gospel! With our faith, we desire no further belief. For this is our ... faith: That there is nothing we ought to believe besides.[10]

Tertullian does not, of course, expect that Christians will cease to have questions, but he urges that the only proper outlet for such questions is the study of the Gospel with Christian teachers. All other seeking must be seen as endangering the rule of faith:

> Let our "seeking," therefore, be in that which is our own [teaching], and from those who are our own, and concerning that which is our own – that and only that ... can become an object of inquiry without impairing the rule of faith.[11]

And if one were to complain that such a worldview, in effect deriding all seeking of truth other than the study of the Gospel, would condemn mankind to a life of blind ignorance, Tertullian says he is willing for men to remain in ignorance of other things so that they learn nothing that might undermine their faith. As he writes:

> [I]t is better for you to remain in ignorance, lest you should come to know what you ought not, because you have [already] acquired the knowledge of what you ought to know.... To know nothing in opposition to the rule [of faith] is to know all things.[12]

We thus have from Tertullian an extraordinarily extreme statement of the relationship between the Christian and the search for knowledge. On his view, there is some "one, and therefore definite" thing to be pursued – and this is the teachings of Christ, which can be known easily and fully by consulting an authoritative source. Beyond this, there is simply no point in inquiry and argument. There is simply no other knowledge worthy of being sought after.

It is in this context that Tertullian declares himself to be opposed to philosophy and asks, famously, "What has Athens to do with Jerusalem? What concord can there be between the Academy and the Church?" And in this context, the reasons for Tertullian's understanding of Athens as being fundamentally hostile to Jerusalem are plain. Having already said that a Christian had best remain ignorant, "lest he should come to know what he ought not," there is nothing left to be gained by reading the writings of the pagans. And indeed, in *The Soul's Testimony*, Tertullian argues that a Christian should have nothing to do with the literature and teaching of the pagans, including even the works of philosophers who argue that there is only one God. "Let it be granted," he writes, "that there is nothing in heathen writers which a Christian approves."[13] More specifically, the Christian – whose only concern should be "to keep what he has believed" – can gain nothing from the philosopher's art "of building up and pulling down" beliefs. All such an art can do is to propose reasons for pulling down the Christian's rule of faith.

In *Prescription Against Heretics*, Tertullian thus declares philosophy to be inimical to Christianity. As he writes:

> Unhappy Aristotle! Who invented for these men dialectics, the art of building up [arguments] and pulling [them] down; an art so evasive in its propositions, ... so productive of contention – embarrassing even itself, retracting everything, and really treating of nothing! ... [W]hen the apostle would restrain us, he expressly names philosophy as that which he would have us be on our guard against. Writing to the Colossians, he says: "See that no one beguile you through philosophy and vain deceit, after the tradition of men."[14] ... He had been at Athens, and had in his interviews [with the philosophers] become acquainted with that human wisdom which pretends to know the truth, while it only corrupts it.... What indeed has Athens to do with Jerusalem? What concord can there be between the Academy and the Church? What between heretics and Christians?[15]

We have seen, then, that Tertullian calls upon Christians to reject philosophy,[16] and to cease the pursuit of truth once they have come to believe in the Gospel, which is the only belief a Christian needs. This would already seem to be a hard-core antiphilosophic position, granting the rule of faith an unchallengeable and exclusive rule in the soul. But for Tertullian, even this is not quite enough – as it leaves open the possibility that faith in Jesus is ultimately something reasonable, in the sense that it can somehow be made to square with what human beings call reason. Tertullian rejects even this, arguing that the things the Gospel asks Christians to believe are, if judged by any worldly standard, just so much foolishness. What is asked of the Christian, he says, is to hold fast to faith, even though that which is to be believed is absurd. He lays out this view in a famous passage in *The Flesh of Christ*:

> [C]onsider well this Scripture, if indeed you have not erased it: "God hath chosen the foolish things of the world, to confound the wise."[17] Now what are those foolish things? ... Will you find anything to be so "foolish" as believing of a God that has been born, and of a virgin, and of a fleshly nature too, who wallowed in all the ... humiliations of nature? ... There are, to be sure, other things also quite as foolish.... For which is more unworthy of God, [and] which is more likely to raise a blush of shame: That *God* should be born, or that He should die? That He should bear the flesh, or the cross? Be circumcised, or be crucified? Be cradled, or be coffined? Be laid in a manger, or in a tomb? *Talk of "wisdom"!* You will show more of *that* if you refuse to believe this [concerning his death] also. But, after all, you will not be "wise" unless you become a "fool" to the world, by believing "the foolish things of God":... The Son of God was crucified – I am not ashamed, because men must be ashamed of it. And the Son of God died – it is by all means to be believed, because it is absurd. And He was buried and rose again – the fact is certain, because it is impossible.[18]

In this passage, the opposition between faith and reason is elevated to an absolute, inasmuch as God has chosen to ask mankind to believe things that are frankly and simply repugnant to reason. Just as God chooses to use the weakness of the Christians to defeat what is, by human standards, considered powerful on this earth, so too does God choose the foolishness of the Gospels to defeat what is, by human standards, considered wisdom. By any measure that the human mind is capable of devising, what God asks us to believe must be regarded as foolishness. Tertullian thus argues for a kind of Christian faith that is irreconcilable with human reason, and in fact repugnant to it.

Tertullian's views are those of a fanatic. But this has not prevented them from exerting a powerful influence on later Christian thought. An important strand within Christianity has always applauded this posture, and its echoes continue to be heard down to our own day. We find a similar position, in which Christian faith is taken to be "an absurdity to the understanding," being advanced in the writings of Kierkegaard:

> What, then, is the absurd? The absurd is that the eternal truth has come into existence in time, that God has come into existence, has been born, has grown up, etc., has come into existence ... as an individual human being.... [In other words,] the absurd is precisely the object of faith, and only that can be believed.... Christianity ... has required the inwardness of faith with regard to what is ... an absurdity to the understanding.[19]

In the same vein, C. S. Lewis speaks of the things that Jesus asks mankind to believe, if judged by human standards, as "asinine fatuity" and "lunacy":

> [Y]ou will see that what this man said was, quite simply, the most shocking thing that has ever been uttered by human lips.... Asinine fatuity is the kindest description we should give.... In the mouth of any speaker who is not God, these words would imply what I can only regard as a silliness and conceit unrivalled by any other character in history.... A man who was merely a man and said the sort of things Jesus said ... would either be a lunatic – on a level with a man who says he is a poached egg – or else he would be the Devil of Hell.[20]

It is with some discomfort that I quote these passages. But we need to look such texts in the eye if we are to understand why Tertullian's opposition between Jerusalem and Athens continues to have so much traction. It is not only opponents of religion who permitted themselves to speak of the biblical teachings as absurd, as asinine fatuity. These things come from the mouths of leading Christian thinkers. It is this recurring trope, according to which Christian faith requires belief in things that are repugnant to human reason, that permits contemporary commentators to speak of Scripture as though it purposely stands in opposition to the dictates of human reason.[21]

II. THE HEBREW BIBLE AND THE IDEA OF A "RULE OF FAITH"

Tertullian knew little about Jews and Judaism.[22] He never set foot in Jerusalem. Yet he appropriated the name of that distant, Jewish city as the symbol of his radical brand of Carthaginian Christianity. In this way, the name of Jerusalem was made to stand for a faith of catechism, and for the renunciation of man's search for truth in favor of a willful belief in that which is understood to be asinine and absurd.

I cannot speak for others. But I find this association of Jerusalem with these things painful. And each time I encounter this kind of Christian faith, I am moved to wonder anew: *What has any of this to do with Jerusalem? What concord can there be between the faith of Carthage and the teachings of Hebrew Scripture?*

I would like to share a few considerations as to why the claim that the Hebrew Bible in some way partakes of Tertullian's faith must be rejected.

Let us begin with the crux of Tertullian's religion, the assertion that there exists a certain paragraph, consisting of a list of concrete propositions, which encompasses all that must be believed – all the knowledge that must be acquired – if humanity is to attain its highest end.[23] In laying down this rule of faith, it is possible to argue that Tertullian is following the example of Paul.[24] But it is not possible, I believe, to argue that he is following an example or precedent that can be found in the Hebrew Scriptures. Indeed, in the entire vast corpus of texts that make up the Hebrew Bible, we find nothing that presents itself as a definitive catalogue of beliefs (or actions) considered necessary and sufficient for the attainment of salvation. Neither the Ten Commandments, nor Moses' stirring summation of what God requires of us in Deuteronomy ("And now Israel, what does the Lord your God require of you ..."[25]), nor the passages collated and recited in the prayer *Shema Israel*[26] presents itself as such a definitive catalogue encompassing everything that mankind (or the Jews) must believe. Even the most concrete of these texts, the Ten Commandments, is not in any sense complete as a guide to proper action, much less belief. The Bible offers us no catechism.[27]

But I would like to take this a step further. For I think it is not merely a matter of contingency or happenstance that the Hebrew Bible offers no catechism. I believe that the Hebrew Bible positively *defies* catechism – that it was purposely structured so as to make catechism difficult, if not impossible. While the first half of the Hebrew Bible can be regarded as a single narrative ultimately assembled by a single hand,[28] the same cannot be said of the twenty-six additional works that comprise the second half of the Hebrew Bible. As I discussed in Chapter 1, these present us with a broad spectrum of opinions even on essential issues – from the disagreements between Daniel and Esther on the efficacy of religious observance in the political realm, to those between Isaiah and Micha concerning the ideal that will find expression in the coming age, to that between the History of Israel and Ezekiel on the question of whether children are punished for the deeds of their parents.[29] To understand the Hebrew Bible requires, then, that we recognize it as an artful compendium, whose teaching is not to be found in one brief and sharply delineated understanding, but by way of a family or school of viewpoints, each of which approaches truth from a different place. It is therefore impossible for the reader of the Hebrew Bible to say, together with Tertullian, that where diversity of doctrine is found, there must be "corruption ... of the Scriptures and the expositions thereof." It is of the essence of what we mean when we speak of something as being *biblical* in character, that it presents its truth by means of a diversity of views.

That the Hebrew Scriptures are of this form results in part from the political character of biblical Judaism, which consciously aims to embrace an entire nation, and must be broad enough in its reach to do so. But the biblical defiance of catechism goes deeper than this. Biblical religion must be skeptical with respect to attempts at imposing a "rule of faith" or catechism due to the Bible's oft-repeated observation that ultimate knowledge of God's thoughts is beyond the powers of man, which are by nature fallible and frail.[30] This is so even with respect to Moses himself, who seeks repeatedly to gain a clear view of God's name, his face, his ways. Yet even Moses, the greatest of the prophets, can apparently do no better than to stand in the cleft of a rock, covered by God's hand, and to catch a glimpse of God's back after he has passed.[31] And this same impression of an elusive God returns time and again elsewhere in the Bible – in Elijah's quest at Sinai, which ends in silence's thin voice; in Isaiah's vision of God on his throne in a hall filled with smoke; and so on.[32]

Moreover, this elusive character of God's presence in the world refers to the *best* case, in which an individual has been gifted with relative clarity of vision and the personal strength to accept and assimilate what has been seen. For the individual who does not possess the prophet's gifts, the challenge is much greater. Consider, for example, the encounter between Israel and God at Sinai. There, God himself appears before each and every Israelite – and yet the people gain almost no knowledge from this encounter. Why? Because the people flee from insight: At first they cry out in terror and beg for Moses to receive God's word in their place; and shortly thereafter they have lost any sense or meaning that God's presence may have had for them and run to make themselves a bovine god of gold.[33] The lesson here is bitter and abundantly clear. Human beings do not necessarily have the strength of character to accept the truth, even when it is before their eyes.

It is no surprise, then, that the biblical authors so consistently depict the common Israelite, who has had no such direct experience of God, as being adrift on a sea of conflicting opinions as to what God wants. The orations of Isaiah and Jeremiah depict Jerusalem as being awash with the views of well-meaning idolaters arguing on behalf of the traditional gods of the land; and of confused prophets, who see only the goodness of the present time and cannot imagine its end; and of blinkered priests, who study the Scriptures with great care, and yet cannot get past the shallowness of their own interpretations to find the word of God buried in their texts.[34] In the writings of these prophets, we find that every route to knowledge has become difficult in the extreme: Tradition, prophecy, and Scripture are all of them corrupted, so that it is not at all obvious how or when the truth will come to be known.

In the Hebrew Bible, God's word is thus seen as present in the world. To find it, however, one must hack one's way through an epistemological jungle and try and break free to something that is enduring and true. In the absence of success in such efforts, the relationship between the many things that are said in God's name and what one is in fact to think, to believe, to do, remains chronically unclear.

In the religion of Tertullian, the Christian message possesses an unsurpassed clarity. One has it in a paragraph. It "raises among ourselves no other questions." Biblical religion, for all its astonishing beauty, possesses no such clarity. The form of the Hebrew Bible reflects the pessimistic – one may also say realistic – epistemology, or theory of knowledge, of the biblical authors.[35] The very existence of a Bible such as we have reflects the elusive nature of knowledge concerning man's salvation, which cannot be trapped in a paragraph and must be sought through multiple approaches.

III. THE BIBLE AND "UNASSISTED" HUMAN REASON

In Section II, I argued that both the form and the content of the biblical teaching are such as to deny the possibility of catechism. But if this is right, the implications must be far-reaching. For it means, among other things, that man has no option of embarking on a one-time quest for truth that comes to a permanent end once he has discovered God's teaching – as Tertullian proposes. Indeed, on the biblical view, almost the opposite is the case. Those who wish to learn from the Hebrew Bible have no choice but to embrace what is of necessity a lifelong search for the truth.[36] Those who assembled the biblical canon evidently lived such lives themselves. And while their search must have been different in various ways from the philosophical quest of the Athenian tradition, its rejection of the possibility of authoritative catechism means that it has next to nothing in common with the faith of Carthage. Indeed, the entire purpose of Tertullian's catechism is to put an end, once and for all, to the epistemic jungle that characterizes the universe of the Hebrew Scriptures, in which one's search for truth is of necessity a lifelong search.[37]

In this section and the one that follows, I would like to look more closely at how the biblical authors understood this search for truth.

It is often said that a distinction must be drawn between philosophy and the tradition of inquiry we find in the Hebrew Scriptures because the former represents the free and "unassisted" use of reason, whereas the latter represents a fettered reason "assisted" by God's commands. I am not sure that such a distinction is even coherent. But it does suggest that we should take an especial interest in the following question: What is the Bible's view of individuals who reason and take action in the absence of anything that can be recognized as "assistance" from God, or from a human being speaking in God's name? What does the Bible really think about the "unassisted" search for the truth?

Consider some examples:

1. *Shifra and Pua.* Look first at the case of the Hebrew midwives in Egypt. Pharaoh commands that the male children of Israel be put to death, but the midwives, Shifra and Pua, refuse his order. Later, we are told that God rewards them for this. But they have no decree from God to the effect that the murder of infants is wrong. The reasoning here is entirely their own.[38]

2. *Yocheved, Miriam, and Pharoah's daughter.* Similarly, the infant Moses is saved by his mother Yocheved, who sets him adrift on the Nile, by his sister Miriam, who risks her life to track the basket, and by Pharaoh's daughter, who draws him out of the river and raises him in contravention of her father's commands. None of these women has a decree from God or his prophets to teach them that to save the child is right. The reasoning that leads them to this is entirely their own.[39]

3. *Moses.* We are told that Pharaoh's daughter gives Moses his name and raises him as her son. Other than this, the first thing we learn about him is that when he has grown, he goes out to his brothers and sees their suffering. Coming across an Egyptian beating a Hebrew slave, he kills him and buries him in the sand. No word of God suggests to

him that it is right to inquire after one's people, or that one should slay their oppressors. The reasoning that leads him to these things is entirely his own.[40]

And what is said concerning these examples can be said of many others. Indeed, the Bible is filled from end to end with stories of individuals who exercise their own reasoning and judgment in the absence of "assistance" from God or of those speaking in his name.[41] What are we to make of this? On the face of it, the sheer volume of such examples seems to suggest that the Bible has a well-established position concerning free human inquiry and the actions taken as a result of such inquiry. The Hebrew Bible – in this regard, nearly all of its very different authors – appears to take individuals who seek truth and do justice on their own initiative as exemplars for a human life properly led. More than this, there are biblical works in which such seeking for truth is explicitly presented as the foundation of the good life for the individual and for that state. I have already discussed Jeremiah's declaration that even a single man, if he seeks truth and does justice, may be sufficient for God to spare a corrupt city.[42] Indeed, Jeremiah is unambiguous in his view that the search is not one that requires any special instructions from God:

> So says the Lord: Stand on the roadways and see, and inquire of the paths of old which way is the good, and walk on it, and find rest for your souls. And they said, "We will not walk on it."[43]

This motif of searching out truth by standing on the highways is significant in itself. The different roads that are open to us are there to be compared. If we can look at them and discern "which is the good way" almost empirically, without need for God's instructions, it is because the evidence is there to be discovered by those who look. A similar motif appears in the book of Proverbs:

> Wisdom cries aloud in the street. She sounds her voice in the squares. She cries in the chief place of the concourse, at the entrances to the city gates, in the city she speaks her message: "... I have called and you refused. I have stretched out my hand and none regarded."[44]

What kind of wisdom are we talking about exactly, which the book of Proverbs insists is available in the streets? The Bible offers various examples of the kind of reasoning that can be employed by women and men to escape from the depravity of their illusions, and to break free to an understanding of the truth. Here is an example, concerning drinking:

> Look not upon the wine when it is red, when it sparkles in the cup.... In the end, it bites like a snake, and stings like a viper. Your eyes will behold strange

things, and you heart will utter perverse words. You will be like one who lies down in the ocean, like one who lies down atop a mast. They have struck me, but I was not harmed, they have beaten me, but I felt it not. When will I awake? I will seek it yet again.[45]

And here is another example, concerning adultery:

[K]eep you from an evil woman, from the smoothness of a strange tongue. Lust not after her beauty in your heart, nor let her take you in with her eyelids. For ... the adulterous wife hunts your precious soul. Can a man take fire in his breast, and not be burned? Can one walk on hot coals, and his feet not be scorched? So it is for him that goes in to his neighbor's wife. Whoever touches her will not go unpunished.... He who commits adultery with a woman lacks understanding; he destroys his soul.... For jealousy is the rage of a man, and he will not spare you on the day of his vengeance. He will accept no compensation, and will not rest content, though you give him many gifts.[46]

And another, from Isaiah, concerning idolatry:

They have not known nor gained understanding, for he [God] has prevented their eyes from seeing, and their minds from thinking right [*mehaskil libotam*]. And none considers in his mind, none has knowledge and none reason to say: I have burned half of it in the fire, and have even baked bread on its embers, roasted meat and eaten. And with the remainder will I now make an abomination? Will I prostrate myself before a block of wood? ... An overthrown mind has deceived him, and he cannot save his soul, and cannot say: Is there not falsehood [*sheker*] in my right hand?[47]

In these examples, the wisdom that is available in the streets is seen to be nothing other than reasoned argument as to what things are truly of value. Thus the biblical authors argue that one should not drink because one can see that it dulls one to pain and is addictive; and that one should not commit adultery because we know from experience that a man will have his vengeance. Similarly, the argument against idolatry from Isaiah calls upon the people to reason from experience so that they may uproot falsehoods from their minds. As we are told: *You already know that half of this block of wood in your hand has already been tossed into the fire. You know, therefore, that it has no power even to defend itself from destruction, much less to answer your prayers and deliver you. To believe now that the other half of this same block of wood can save you, so that you should throw yourself down before it and beg it for assistance, is therefore to embrace falsehood.*

In these and other similar cases, the biblical authors appeal to arguments based on experience that is available to all Israel and to all men, whereas fools are consistently said to be those who pay no heed to the counsel of experience, and so proceed in the direction of their own ruin and that of their nation.[48] Here the distinction between the biblical search for truth and that of the philosopher becomes exceedingly vague, bordering on non-existent.

No wonder, then, that in the orations of the prophets of Israel, wisdom gained from experience, and from reasoning based on this experience, at times becomes interchangeable with having heard God's voice. Consider, for example, the following passage from Jeremiah:

> And I will make Jerusalem a ruin, a lair of jackals, and I will make the cities of Judah a desolation, without inhabitant. Who is the man so wise that he can understand this, and to whom the mouth of the Lord has spoken, that he may explain it: On what account is the land lost, withered like a desert, without anyone to pass through it?[49]

Here, "the man so wise that he can understand this" is invoked in parallel with the man "to whom the mouth of the Lord has spoken," as if the appearance of understanding in the mind of the individual is the same as God's speech.[50] We find a similar construction in Isaiah, who looks forward to the coming of the future king, upon whom will rest the spirit of God. And yet this "spirit of God," as Isaiah understands it, is itself indistinguishable from wisdom, understanding, and the ability to judge wisely and with justice:

> And the spirit of the Lord will rest upon him: The spirit of wisdom and understanding, the spirit of good counsel and bravery, the spirit of knowledge and of the fear of the Lord, and his delight shall be in the fear of the Lord.[51]

IV. SEEKING TRUTH IN GOD'S PRESENCE

The authors of the Hebrew Bible view the individual's "unassisted" search for truth in a consistently favorable light. In particular, the Hebrew Bible sees the individual as being – much of the time – at a substantial remove from accessible sources of knowledge concerning God's word, and sides with those women and men who struggle to obtain knowledge of that which is true wherever and however it can be found.

Of course, this is only a part of the picture. The Bible also describes many direct encounters between man and God, encounters in which truth is, if not perfectly manifest, at least evident enough. But even here, it is difficult to reconcile the submissive faith of Tertullianic religion with the picture of interaction between man and God that is presented in the Hebrew Scriptures. In this regard, consider again the opening passages in Exodus. The story of the Israelites' escape from Egypt is the paradigm case of overt intervention by God in the affairs of man. And yet upon examination, it turns out that this story is told as though God only *reacts* in the wake of extensive and "unassisted" human reasoning and action based on such reasoning: It is only due to the deeds of Shifra, Pua, Yocheved, Miriam, and Pharaoh's daughter that Moses is born, survives, and grows to manhood. It is only due to Moses' own unguided choices that he kills the Egyptian, flees Egypt, and takes up life as a shepherd in the desert. Indeed, even God's appearance at the burning bush is depicted as taking place only after Moses sets out to find him:

> Now Moses kept the flock of Yitro his father-in-law, the priest of Midian. *And he led the flock beyond the desert, and came to the mountain of God,* to Horev. And the angel of the Lord appeared to him in a flame of fire out of the midst of a bush. And behold, the bush burned with fire, but the bush was not consumed. And Moses said, "I will turn aside and see this great sight, why the bush is not burned." *And when the Lord saw that he turned aside to see, God called to him* out of the midst of the bush and said, Moses, Moses.[52]

If what we are looking for is unilateral acts of God, this is pretty strange stuff. For it turns out that even God's appearance at the burning bush is in response to Moses' seeking: First, Moses drives his herd deep into the wilderness. Only *after* he reaches "the mountain of God" is he presented with a distant sight that draws him in. And only *after* taking up the challenge and turning aside to pursue it, does God finally respond.[53]

Other first encounters between the prophets and God exhibit a similar quality, as though God speaks in response to human searching. I have already mentioned Elijah's quest to Sinai in search of an apparently absent God. No less striking in this regard is the call of Isaiah, which begins not with a command but with a question:

> In the year that king Uziahu died, I saw the Lord sitting on a throne.... And I heard the voice of the Lord, saying, "Whom shall I send, and who will go for us?" And I said, "Here am I. Send me." And he said, "Go."[54]

As in Moses' encounter with God at the burning bush, there is in this passage a distinct hesitation on God's part. Isaiah does not see God as seeking man out in order to command him. Instead, God raises a question: *"Whom shall I send, and who will go for us?"* Only after Isaiah rises to this challenge (*"Here am I, send me"*) does God turn to him and tell him what to do. And what if Isaiah had not responded as he did? The implication here is that God might have continued asking *"Whom shall I send, and who will go for us?"* for quite a long time, awaiting the man who would step forward.[55]

A similar impression arises from Jeremiah's account of his first prophecy as a young man, which also depicts God, not as issuing commands, but as posing a question:

> Then the word of the Lord came to me, saying: "Jeremiah, what do you see?" And I said, "I see the rod of an almond-tree." Then the Lord said to me, "*You have seen well,* for I watch over my word to perform it." And the word of the Lord came to me a second time, saying: "What do you see?" And I said: "I see a seething pot, and the face of it is to the north." Then the Lord said to me, "Out of the north the evil shall break forth upon all the inhabitants of the land."[56]

Here, too, God poses a question – *"Jeremiah, what do you see?"* Why does God play this game? Why does he not simply tell Jeremiah what he sees? The answer, it seems, is that prophecy does not work this way. At least sometimes, God's role is to initiate a question and not an answer. In responding to this question, the prophet can "see well," as God says here, or he can see less well.[57]

It is of course the case that biblical figures do hear God's voice without any prior human search being reported to us. Even so, the evidence that prophetic insight is often the result of a human search is too abundant to be ignored. Especially striking is the case of Abraham, because here we have the first instance of Hebrew prophecy, and it would appear to be one in which God's message – to leave Babylonia and go to found a nation in Canaan – is unprovoked, out of the blue. But even here, the narrative is careful to inform us that God's approach to Abraham follows after an unexplained, but also unambiguous, case of human initiative: that of his father Terah, who himself conceives of a journey to Canaan and even sets out on it.[58]

Against this backdrop, we are more easily able to understand the famous lines of Jeremiah, in which God himself calls upon man to seek and quest for knowledge:

> Moreover the word of the Lord came to Jeremiah a second time, while he was yet shut up in the court of the guard, saying: … Call unto me, and I will answer you, and I will tell you great things, and hidden, which you knew not.[59]

In this passage, it is God himself who longs for Jeremiah's searching for knowledge. The fact that God promises that if called upon, he will tell Jeremiah things "which you knew not" seems to rule out any relationship based on a fixed catechism that is to rule in the prophet's soul. If the relationship between man and God were supposed to consist of man's acceptance of a paragraph of propositions that "raises among ourselves no other questions," there would be no sense at all in God's promising that if man inquires and seeks, he will be told "great things" that had until now been hidden.

As these examples suggest, the God of the Hebrew Bible is not in the business of demanding belief in some fixed body of propositions. The biblical God is portrayed as revealing his truths and unleashing his deeds in response to man's search for truth. He even longs for man's questioning and seeking. Indeed, his preference for human beings who seek and question is such as to have given rise to an entire tradition of biblical figures questioning God's decrees, conducting disputations with God, and at times even changing God's mind – including Abraham's argument with God over the justice of destroying Sodom; a series of occasions in which Moses challenges God's intentions to destroy Israel; Gideon's questioning whether God has not abandoned Israel; David's anger over what he sees as God's unjust killing of one of his men; and the arguments of Isaiah, Jeremiah, Ezekiel, Havakuk, Jonah, and Job questioning God's justice.[60] In all of these cases, man is shown as able to challenge God's decrees and yet have the respect of God as a consequence. In the cases of Abraham and Moses, it would appear that a view presented by a human being can prevail even over that which God initially sees as right. And as I suggested in Chapter 4, the capstone of this tradition is the story in which Jacob struggles all night with God himself and in the morning receives a new name – the name Israel: *"Your name will no more be called Jacob, but Israel, for you have striven with God and with men and have prevailed."*[61]

The implications of these stories are so far-reaching that it seems many readers would prefer to forget them. Certainly, if we take them seriously, we are left without the possibility of seeing Hebrew Scripture as calling for man to adopt a life of submissive belief in a catechism we regard as repugnant to reason. On the contrary, it would seem that from the perspective of biblical authors, the proper human standpoint involves such daring in argument and action that even what appears to be God's truth is not always permitted to stand unchallenged. As Job tells his companions:

> Let me alone that I may speak, and let come on me what will.... Though [God] may slay me, yet will I trust him. But I will maintain my own ways before him. This also will be my salvation: For a flatterer will not come before him.[62]

V. THE BIBLE AND HUMAN WISDOM AND FOOLISHNESS

It is significant, in this context, that there are no texts in the Hebrew Scriptures in which God's word is referred to as "foolishness" or "absurd," after the example of Tertullian and those who follow his cue. True, one can propose a charitable reading of the Christian texts in which such characterizations of God's word appear, according to which God's wisdom is only called foolishness or absurd because it appears so from the perspective of human beings as they are today. But such an approach only serves to emphasize the point at issue, which is this: The authors of the Hebrew Bible are *never* tempted to say that the word of God is "foolishness" or "absurd" by the standard of human beings. This is because in the Hebrew Scriptures, God's wisdom and truth are, in principle, recognizable as such by human beings, according to the standards of the present world.[63] To be sure, there are times and places in which human beings do not see the truth and wisdom in God's word. Indeed, there are many such. But the biblical authors themselves cannot go very far in sympathizing with this failure, because to them it is obvious that the wisdom presented by the prophets as the word of God is itself precisely the wisdom that is sought by human beings for the present, human world.

We see this in a variety of contexts. Perhaps the most famous is Moses' assessment, in his address to the Israelites in Deuteronomy, that the law that he has taught them can be understood to represent wisdom to the members of all other nations who would care to look:

> For this [teaching] is your wisdom and your understanding in the sight of the nations, who will hear these laws and say: "Surely this great nation is a wise and understanding people." For ... what nation is so great that it has laws and statutes as just as all this teaching I set before you this day?[64]

If Moses believes, as he says in this passage, that the nations will be able to see the wisdom in the law he teaches Israel, then this law must reflect a standard independent of itself – a standard that many among the nations may be able to access after their own fashion.[65] This is not, of course, to say that there are not nations that are corrupt and deceived concerning what is wisdom and understanding. Nevertheless, we see that Moses believes that there exists such a worldly standard according to which God's teaching should in principle be recognized as wise. As Moses tells the people: "I set before you this day the path of life and the good."[66]

This is precisely the lesson of the story of Bilam, a non-Israelite seer who calls himself "the man whose eyes are open."[67] In Numbers, Bilam is commissioned by the king of Moav to curse Israel. But when he comes to see Israel for himself, he concludes that this people has in fact been blessed: Living according to God's law, they are a just people, without iniquity or perversity, flourishing like trees by the riverside. Seeing all this with his own eyes, Bilam tells his king that he cannot curse whom God has not cursed, and declares: "Let me die the death of the just, and let my end be like his!"[68]

As it turns out, Bilam's end is not like Israel's.[69] But the prophets of Israel repeatedly describe other nations as being able to do just what Bilam could have done, coming to see the wisdom in Israel's ways and adopting them. We have already seen Jeremiah predict that nations will eventually come to understand that there is nothing to be sought in their own laws, saying "Only lies have our fathers bequeathed us, worthless and with nothing in them to avail";[70] and that they will, as God says, "diligently learn the ways of my people ... [that] they will be built up."[71] The predictions in Isaiah are even more startling in this respect:

> And it will be in the course of time, that the mountain of the Lord's house will be established ... and all the nations will stream to it. And many peoples will go to it, saying, "Come, let us go up to the mountain of the Lord, to the house of the God of Jacob, and he will teach us from his ways, and we will walk in his paths." For out of Zion will go forth instruction [*tora*], and God's word from Jerusalem.[72]

> [F]or instruction [*tora*] will go out from me, and my law will be kindled as a light for the peoples.[73]

From these and similar passages, we see that the prophets understand Israel's teachings as holding out something that the nations should be able to recognize as desirable, advantageous, and true, and that eventually they will see this.[74]

In Chapter 6, we saw that the standard by which Isaiah and Jeremiah judge God's word is its ability to bring "profit" to man.[75] A similar understanding of the law of Moses as bringing practical benefit to those who observe is be found repeatedly in Psalms and Proverbs as well. They are the means by which any man can become wise if he applies himself:

> The laws of God are reliable, making the simple wise.[76]

Similarly, in the famous Psalm 119, the poet cries out to God to give him understanding: "Give me understanding that I may live!"[77] But the understanding he is talking about is that which one gains by studying the law and living in its light. As he writes:

> Oh how I love your law! All day long I consider it. Your commandments make me wiser than my enemies, for they are ever with me. I have more understanding than all my teachers, for your laws I consider. I understand more than my elders, because I have kept your commands. I have restrained my feet from every evil way, because I observe your word. I have not turned from your laws, for you have instructed me. How sweet are your words unto my palate! Sweeter than honey to my mouth! From your commands I gain understanding.[78]

In these and many similar passages, we see that in the eyes of the prophets and scholars who composed the Hebrew Scriptures, God's word instructs us as to how to live well and flourish in our own world. In this sense, God's wisdom and truth must be seen, not as something fundamentally different from that of man, but rather as something that is continuous with man's wisdom. God's wisdom is, we may say, that which the individual would have if he could to "see to the end" of things – that is, if he had sufficient experience and knowledge, and could reason well enough on the basis of this knowledge, so as to know the future results of his actions. Man tends to "see to the end" only rarely and dimly, which is the reason that he finds it so difficult to know the truth as to what will profit him and what will be worthless or worse. How he can overcome this debility and, to some extent, attain God's wisdom is, in a sense, the subject of the Hebrew Scriptures. But the wisdom that is sought in the Bible, which is called God's wisdom, is not something repugnant to human wisdom and reason or alien to it. God's wisdom is precisely that understanding of things which would lead mankind to well-being and flourishing in this world were mankind to possess it. It is, in other words, precisely that which human wisdom and reason aspire to attain.

In the conception of biblical authors, then, God's wisdom is not antithetical to human wisdom. It is not inherently "foolishness" or the "absurd" from the perspective of human wisdom and reason. On the contrary, it is precisely that which human wisdom and reason are supposed to be – that which can guide us to those truths that are genuine, enduring, and capable of bringing mankind to well-being. To say this is, however, to let go of the Tertullianic prejudice that what is of interest to the biblical authors is something that is simply of a different order from human wisdom and reason. From the standpoint of Jerusalem, it is precisely because the word of God is continuous with human wisdom and reason that human beings – Jews and gentiles alike – are capable of recognizing it as wisdom.

VI. THE FAITH OF JERUSALEM

I opened this chapter with the question of whether the Hebrew Bible can reasonably be seen as representing the position labeled "faith" in the Tertullianic disputation between faith and reason. On the basis of what we've seen, I think the answer clearly has to be negative.

Tertullian's conception of faith is one that finds expression in (i) a fixed catechism of propositions. And this catechism is understood as (ii) making a life of truth-seeking unnecessary and even injurious, since (iii) God demands the unconditional surrender of man's faculties to him, and so requires us to embrace even those propositions of the catechism that, by the standards of human reason, must be considered absurd. But what the authors of the Hebrew Bible were seeking was something entirely different: They reject and defy catechism, presenting us instead with Scriptures so variegated and vast that they leave no alternative, if we are to take them seriously, but to engage in a lifelong search to understand what is in them and what they require of us. Moreover, the purpose of the quest initiated and described in the Hebrew Scriptures is precisely the attainment of "what the world calls wisdom": a knowledge of that which gives life and the good to individuals and nations. What the authors of the Hebrew Bible wished to bequeath to Israel and to the nations, then, is not what is repugnant to human reason or absurd. On the contrary, they hoped to point the way to that which is reasonable – to that which human reason, when it is at its best, will know to be right.

This means that the teachings of the Hebrew Scriptures are diametrically opposed to those of Tertullian's "rule of faith." The opposition between these two standpoints is that which I have characterized as the clash between Jerusalem and Carthage.

But what, it will be asked, of the *faith* of Jerusalem? Even granting that the standpoint of the Hebrew Bible is one that rejects unequivocally the faith of Carthage, surely the Hebrew Scriptures are not *only* about seeking that which truly confers life and the good on man. They also enjoin us, time and again, to heed God's voice and keep the law of Moses. And such observance also involves a kind of faith – if not that which has been falsely imputed to the Hebrew Scriptures, then at least some other kind. We may ask, then: What is the faith that is called for in the Hebrew Scriptures and Jewish tradition?

Passages from the History of Israel that speak of faith in God are relatively rare, but the ones we have stand out in their importance. For example, Abraham is described as having belief in God, late in life, in the following text in Genesis:

> After these things, the word of the Lord came to Avram in a vision, saying, "Fear not, Avram. I am your shield, and your wage will be very great...." And he brought him outside and said, "Look now, toward heaven, and count the stars if you can count them," and he said to him, "So will your seed be." And he had faith [*vehe'emin*] in the Lord, and he [God] considered it as righteousness in him.[79]

The Israelites as a people are also described as believing in God after they witnessed the defeat of Egypt at the Red Sea:

> And the Lord saved Israel that day from the hand of Egypt, and Israel saw Egypt dead on the sea shore. And Israel saw the great work that the Lord performed against Egypt, and the people feared the Lord, and they believed [*vaya'aminu*] in the Lord and in Moses his servant.[80]

In these two passages, we are told that Abraham and the Israelites "believed in the Lord," or "had faith in the Lord." It is obvious, however, that the verb *he'emin*, which in these passages is used to speak of *believing* or *having faith* in God, does not refer to the belief that God exists, which is what is most commonly understood as what it means to "believe in God" today.[81] Nor does it refer to the acceptance by Abraham and the Israelites of any other proposition whose content could easily be fit into a catechism. Rather, the faith in God described in both of these passages is what we would, more precisely, call *trust in God*.[82] It refers to a belief – by which I mean a feeling or a sense[83] – that God can be counted on to protect Abraham and his descendants and bless them as he said he would. This is evident from the context, in which God promises Abraham that his wage (sometimes translated *reward*) will be great and that his seed will be numerous as the stars of the heavens, and Abraham finds that he believes him; and in which God saves the escaped slaves from certain death at the hands of Pharaoh's chariots, so that they find themselves trusting that God and Moses would in fact deliver them to Canaan as promised. And it is evident from the word *he'emin* itself, which is a cognate of the word *truth* (*emet*) discussed in the last chapter. Words in this family tend to refer to that which is *reliable, steadfast, faithful*, and the term here under discussion is no exception. When the narrative speaks of Abraham as having faith in God, it refers to his belief that God can be relied upon. And when it speaks of the Israelites as believing in God and Moses, it means, again, that they felt they could rely upon them. From these passages, then, it would appear that the "faith" of Hebrew Scripture is the belief that the God of Israel can be *relied upon*, or *trusted*.

The same can be said of texts from the History in which belief in God fails: It was the failure of Israel to believe in God (*lo ya'aminu bi*) when he sent them into battle in Canaan that led to their being sent into the wilderness for forty years.[84] It is the failure of Moses and Aaron to believe God (*lo he'emantem bi*) that is given as the explanation for God's decision not to allow them into the promised land.[85] Likewise, the failure to believe God's warnings as delivered by the prophets (*lo he'eminu*) is one of the ways in which the failure of the House of Israel is described in explaining the exile of the northern kingdom.[86] In these passages, as well, it is the fact that the people did not rely upon God to perform that which he promised – or, in the last case, warned – that is described as their not having faith.

It is significant, in this context, that Moses himself emphasizes the fact that Israel's God can be relied upon or trusted in speaking before the Israelites as they are about to enter the land of Canaan in Deuteronomy. As he says:

> Know, therefore, that the Lord, your God, is God, the faithful God [*ha'el hane'eman*], who keeps the covenant and remains generous to those who love him and keep his commandments to a thousand generations.... And [therefore] you will keep the commandment and the laws and the statutes that I command this day, to do them.[87]

Moses here calls the God of Israel "the faithful God," using the Hebrew term *ne'eman* (נאמן), another cognate of *emet* meaning *loyal, faithful*.[88] In saying that Israel's God is "the" faithful God, he informs the people that the God of Israel, alone among the gods, is loyal or faithful. Or in other words, the God of Israel, alone among the gods, can be relied upon to deliver on the promises that have been made in his name.[89]

And what has the God of Israel promised? After Sinai, the concern with God's promises is principally connected with God's law, and the promise that Israel will have life and the good if they will keep this law. To call God *the faithful God*, then, is to say that if one keeps God's law, then God will grant one life and the good. And to have *faith in God* is, likewise, to feel that if one keeps God's law, God will grant one and one's nation life and the good.

In addition to the History of Israel, other biblical works that explicitly speak of faith in God as a virtue include Isaiah, Jeremiah, Psalms, Proverbs, and Chronicles. Thus Jeremiah tells us that faith will strengthen us ("Blessed is the man who trusts [*yivtah*] in the Lord, for the Lord will be his stronghold"[90]), and a central teaching of the Psalms is that trust in God has the power to save us ("I trusted [*batah*] in him and I was helped"[91]). Similarly, in Chronicles, King Yehoshafat of Judah tells his people before battle that trust in God is the key to victory:

> And they rose early in the morning and went out to the wilderness of Teko'a, and as they went out, Yehoshafat stood and said: "Hear me, Judah and the inhabitants of Jerusalem. Have faith [*ha'aminu*] in the Lord your God, and you will be established [*vete'amenu*]! Have faith [*ha'aminu*] in his prophets and you will succeed [*vehatzlihu*]."[92]

Isaiah goes farther, calling on men to have faith at all times:

> Trust [*bithu*] in the Lord always, for in the Lord God we find an everlasting rock.[93]

And of course there are other works in the Bible – Esther immediately comes to mind – that have quite a bit to say about faith even if the word *faith* does not appear in them anywhere.

Nevertheless, faith in God isn't emphasized to the same degree in different biblical works. Only in Isaiah, Psalms, and Proverbs do we seem to find faith in God as a kind of universal imperative – something that we should all have at all times.[94] The History of Israel treads more carefully, as do Jeremiah and other biblical works. The Mosaic law, for example, which repeatedly enjoins the people to *fear God* and to *love God*, does not command faith in God. In the History, as we've seen, there is an explicit reference to the fact that God saw Abraham's faith as righteousness in him – but this hardly amounts to a universal call to faith. And the History also describes the people's lack of faith in God as part of the picture that brought about the destruction of the northern kingdom. Yet this is mentioned as one item among a great many in an indictment seventeen verses long, in which the question of trusting in God bears no special emphasis.[95] Lack of faith is not mentioned at all in the History's description of the sins for which Judah and Jerusalem are destroyed.[96]

I conclude from this that while the Hebrew Scriptures do regard trust in God – that is, the sense that one can rely on God's promises as we have them – as something that is obviously to be desired, many of the biblical authors do not make faith in God an imperative that must always be in the first rank of our concerns, as is the case, say, in the New Testament and in much of subsequent Christian tradition.

Why not? In Deuteronomy, Moses could not be more emphatic or more direct in informing the people that God will grant life and the good, in this world, to individuals and nations who keep his commands and his laws.[97] This is without question what Moses believes. And he thinks Israel should believe this too. So why not insist on this belief outright? Why not command faith in God "with all your mind and all your soul and all your heart?"[98]

VII. MOSES AND GOD'S NATURE

The Mosaic law itself offers little help in answering this question. But you can get a good sense of why faith in God is not commanded by looking at what the biblical narrative has to tell us about Moses' experiences in trying to get God to speak to him unequivocally on this subject.

Moses is, as has often been said, unique among the prophets in the ease and clarity with which he seems to be able to communicate with God. The narrative tells us that Moses speaks to God "face to face, as a man will speak with his neighbor,"[99] and indeed, we get to see Moses speaking quite forcefully with God on a number of occasions, trying to persuade him, and even threatening not to carry through with the charge God has given him. And at times he succeeds in changing God's mind.[100] Yet for all this, Moses is still a man, and when he turns his attention to trying to understand God's nature – or in biblical language, God's *name*, his *ways*, his *honor* – this proves to be quite a difficult task. This is not a simple subject, but it's crucial to touch on it here because when, after repeated attempts, Moses finally does get a glimpse of God's nature, it turns out that what he sees is a version of the same proposition that is here under discussion.

The story of Moses' attempts to understand God's nature goes back at least as far as Jacob, who has lifelong and pressing questions concerning the nature of the God who promised his mother Rebecca that he would triumph, but then seemingly abandoned him.[101] Jacob's questions appear in a powerful form in the story of his wrestling with God through the long night before his brother Esau finally catches up with him. In this story, we learn not only that God asks Jacob his name, and gives him a new name reflecting his true nature, but that Jacob responds *by asking God to reveal his own name*. As we are told:

> And Jacob was left alone, and a there wrestled a man with him until the breaking of the dawn.... And he said to him, "What is your name?"
>
> And he said, "Jacob."
>
> And he said, "No longer will no longer be Jacob, but Israel, because you have struggled with God and with men and have prevailed."
>
> And Jacob asked him, saying, "Tell me, please, your name."
>
> And he said, "Why is it that you ask my name?" And he blessed him there.[102]

Often in biblical stories, names are taken as reflecting natures, and Jacob's names are no exception: The name Jacob (*ya'akov*) invokes the word *ekev*, referring to the heel of a man's foot; and reflects, as it seems, Jacob's dogged attempts to recoup after others have got ahead of him – apparently by grabbing another's heel from behind so as to bring him down.[103] The name Israel (*yisra'el*), as we see in this passage, refers to the change that takes place in Jacob's character as it transpires he has it in him not just to clutch at his adversaries' heels, but actually to "struggle with God and with men" and to overcome them all. And once God has spoken to Jacob of his own nature, by way of the name he has given him, Jacob returns the favor by demanding to know God's name as well. But Jacob seems to receive no answer. His question is gently rebuffed with another question – *Why is it that you ask my name?* Jacob, who can wrest a blessing from God himself, nevertheless finds God's nature a closed book before him.

The man who will gain such knowledge is Moses. And when Moses, having sought out the God of Israel in the desert of Sinai, finally approaches him at the burning bush, he too asks to know God's name, as his forefather had:

> And Moses said to God, "But when I come to the children of Israel and say to them, 'The God of your fathers has sent me to you,' they will say to me, 'What is his name?' What will I say to them?"
>
> And God said to Moses, "I will be what I will be" [*ehi'eh asher ehi'eh*]. And he said, "So will you say to the children of Israel, 'I will be' [*ehi'eh*] sent me."[104]*

Of course, the Israelite slaves in Egypt are not really interested in God's name.[105] It is Moses himself who is concerned with this question. And he

---

* Many English-language Bibles translate God's *ehi'eh asher ehi'eh* (אהיה אשר אהיה) as "I am that I am," and the subsequent *ehi'eh* (אהיה as "I am"). These translations follow the Septuagint, which renders *ehi'eh asher ehi'eh* using the Greek expression *ego eimi ho on* (ἐγώ εἰμι ὁ ὤν), meaning roughly, "I am the one who is." This is then echoed by other Greek-language texts such as Philo, *Life of Moses* 1. 74–75 and *On Dreams* 1.230–231; and the New Testament, in which Jesus refers to himself using similar expressions at John 8:24, 28, 58. See also Revelation 1.8. In this way, the text in Exodus is made to fit more or less into the Greek tradition going back to Xenophanes, Parmenides, and Plato that associates God with *being*. See Louis H. Feldman, *Judaism and Hellenism Reconsidered* (Leiden: Brill, 2006), p. 62.

To my mind, this tradition of adjusting the translation of *ehi'eh asher ehi'eh* to bring it into line with Greek thought is problematic in three ways. First, it misrepresents the literal meaning of God's answer to Moses, because the verb *ehi'eh* is in the future tense, and in its other appearances in Hebrew Scripture, it means simply "I will be." Look, for example, at Genesis 26.3, where God tells Isaac, "Live in this land and I will be [*ehi'eh*] with you and I will bless you." Or Exodus 3.12, immediately preceding our text, where God tells Moses, "I will be [*ehi'eh*] with you." Second, it misrepresents the context in which the question of God's name arises in the Jacob and Moses narratives, which are concerned not with whether God exists (that is, with whether God is or has being), but with whether he can be relied upon to fulfill what has been promised. Third, it misrepresents the broader biblical metaphysics, which is very far from associating God with *being*.

For these reasons, I have preferred the much more straightforward "I will be what I will be." Compare the Aramaic translation of Onkelos, as cited by Nahmanides on Exodus 3.13–14, which similarly glosses: "I will be with whom I will be," meaning that God will be faithful to whom he chooses. Similar readings are suggested by Michael Fishbane, *Biblical Text and Texture* (Oxford: Oneworld, 2003 [1979]), pp. 67, 71; and Jon D. Levenson, *Sinai and Zion* (New York: Harper & Row, 1985) p. 22. On this point see also Benno Jacob, *The Second Book of the Bible: Exodus*, Walter Jacob, trans. (Hoboken: Ktav, 1992), pp. 71–77; Martin Buber, *Moses: The Revelation and the Covenant*, with intro. by Michael Fishbane (Amherst, N.Y.: Humanity Books, 1998 [1946]), pp. 51–54.

gets an answer better than the one Jacob gets – although it, too, is to no small extent a rebuff. For in this passage, too, names reflect natures. And the name *I will be what I will be* bespeaks a very particular kind of nature. It describes a nature that can become anything at all, that is entirely arbitrary and free, fluid and changing. Like the waters from which the earth itself had been brought together, God appears to man, on this view, as being entirely devoid of nature or direction, and therefore as something that cannot be relied upon to be anything, and or to do anything, at all.

Moses is not, however, willing to accept this answer. After God's confrontation with Pharaoh, and his giving the law at Sinai, and his anger over the golden calf, Moses knows that a better answer must be forthcoming. And after climbing Sinai the third time, Moses again asks God, with much greater insistence this time, to show himself – his ways and his glory. This time Moses gets a different answer. God tells Moses that he will permit him to look upon him, and to know his name. Or at least, this is a *part* of what God tells him. Here is what God says:

> And Lord said to Moses, "I will also do this thing that you have spoken, for you have found favor in my eyes and I have known you by name." … And he said, "I will make my goodness pass before you, and I will proclaim the name of the Lord before you, and I will be gracious to whom I will be gracious, and I will have mercy on whom I will have mercy."[106]

This is a rather shocking response. On the one hand, God finally agrees to present Moses with his name, thereby permitting him to approach knowledge of his nature. He agrees, that is, "to proclaim the name of the Lord before you." Yet in the very same sentence in which God tells Moses that he will reveal to him his name, he concludes with "and I will be gracious to whom I will be gracious, and I will have mercy on whom I will have mercy." As is bitingly evident in the Hebrew, "I will be gracious to whom I will be gracious" (*vehanoti et asher ahon*) and "I will have mercy on whom I will have mercy" (*verihamti et asher arahem*) are little more than recapitulations of what God said to Moses at the burning bush: "I will be what I will be" (*ehi'eh asher ehi'eh*). What appeared there as an intimation that God has no nature at all, and that his will is perfectly arbitrary, appears here again in a form that is perhaps even more extraordinary: *I will be gracious to whom I will be gracious, and I will have mercy on whom I have mercy.*[107] What can this mean? Will not the judge of all the earth do justice? The very agreement to provide an intimation of God's true nature is presented as bearing with it the imprimatur of the arbitrary and the meaningless – as if there were no justice or purpose to be found in this world at all.

Moses hews a second set of tablets from stone, as God instructs him. And when he is done with the work, God places Moses in the cleft of a rock, covers him with his hand so that he is all but blind, and then, as promised, passes before Moses and proclaims "the name of the Lord" before him. Here's the way this event is described:

> And the Lord descended in a cloud, and stood with him there, and proclaimed the name of the Lord. And the Lord passed before him and proclaimed, "The Lord, the Lord, a God merciful and gracious, longsuffering, and abundant in giving and truth [*emet*], storing up [the results of] righteousness to thousands [of generations], bearing iniquity and transgression and sin; but who will certainly not pardon [the guilty], visiting the iniquity of the fathers on the children, and on the children's children, to the third and fourth generation."[108]

This is the fourth time that God is depicted as addressing the question of his name in response to man's inquiries – but only the first in which it is possible to discern anything more than arbitrariness and chaos in his responses. Step by step, the narrative takes us upward and inward, peeling back the layers of reality until finally we reach this, the moment in which Moses comes to know the most man can know of God's nature and his ways.[109] And to the extent that the "name of the Lord" that is described here is taken as a clear and unequivocal pronouncement concerning God's nature and his ways in governing the world, we can see why Moses believes what he does, and why he speaks to Israel as though what he believes is right. For what Moses comes to understand from this is that despite layer after layer of outward appearances that tell us precisely the contrary, God can indeed be relied upon to reward justice with much grace ("storing up [the results of] righteousness to thousands [of generations]"), and injustice with punishment ("visiting the iniquity of the fathers on the children"). Moses has faith in God because he can see that God is "the faithful God."[110]

But this is not all that must be taken into account here. I have said that *to the extent that the "name of the Lord" that Moses learns at Sinai is taken as a clear and unequivocal pronouncement concerning God's nature and his ways*, we can see why Moses believes what he does, and why he thinks Israel should have faith in God as well. But is the "name of the Lord" that God proclaims before Moses really *a clear and unequivocal pronouncement* concerning God's nature? Let's look again. God here tells Moses that crimes will certainly be punished – but that the consequences of evildoing may not be visible until the second, third, or even fourth generation after they have been performed. And he says that he is abundant in his generosity and can be relied upon to "store up" the results of righteousness for thousands of generations, but it is uncertain when that which has been accumulated in God's storehouse will be released so that it can actually be felt by mankind.[111] This is not, then, an unequivocal statement that the judge of all the world will do justice for individuals and nations *now*, as Abraham seemed to think he could. It only says that God will do justice *in the end* – an end that those who are being asked to heed the law of Moses may never see in their lifetimes, and cannot even rely upon for the lifetimes of their own children. This fits well with the experience of the slaves in Egypt, whose cries God did not hear for two centuries while their blood was being spilled like water. And if this is so, then our text is telling us that we must be prepared for a significant dilution of what is meant when we say that the God of Israel can be *relied upon* to grant life and the good, in this world, to individuals and nations who keep his commands and his laws. From the perspective of the individual looking only to his own lifetime, the acts of "the faithful God" may end up looking very much as though he will be gracious to whom he will be gracious, and will have mercy on whom he will have mercy. He may, in other words, look very much like a capricious reality without tendency or direction at all.[112]

Beyond the troubling nature of the "name of the Lord" that Moses comes to understand at Sinai, the passage we are discussing in Exodus also seems to qualify the *degree* to which Moses has in fact gained knowledge of God, and this to an astonishing extent. I mentioned above that when God proclaims the "name of the Lord" before Moses, he is "passing" in front of him while Moses is wedged in a crevice in the mountain with the palm of God's hand covering him so that he can see but little. Here is the text describing how Moses is positioned when God passes him by:

> And [God] said, "You will not be able to see my face, for no man can see me and live." And the Lord said, "Here, there is a place by me, and you will stand upon the rock. And it will be, when my glory passes by, I will put you in the cleft of the rock, and I will cover you with my hand until I have passed. And I will remove my hand and you will see my back, but my face you will not see."[113]

Now in the passage quoted above we were told that "the Lord descended in a cloud, and stood with [Moses] there, and proclaimed the name of the Lord. And the Lord *passed before him* and proclaimed." The proclaiming or crying out (*vayikra*) of the name of the Lord is, in other words, not static in nature. It is something that is extended over time, involving God's *passing* before the mind of man. In the present passage, we learn more about the nature of this passing by, which turns out to involve (i) God's approach, in which man, were he to look upon God, would see him coming and thus "see his face"; (ii) God's passing by, during which man would still see God's face from the side; and (iii) God's having passed, at which time "you will see my back," but his face can no longer be seen. Only with respect to this last stage, when God is receding and all that is left to see is his back, is Moses able to gain an unobstructed view. The "name of the Lord" that Moses receives at God's proclamation is thus depicted as having been revealed to Moses in a manner that is exceedingly imperfect and unclear. If we are to take the metaphor of God's passing at face value, it would seem that what is known concerning "the name of the Lord" is known with any kind of sharpness and certainty *only where God has already passed by* – that is, only with respect to those of God's actions that are already in the past. No such clairvoyance is vouchsafed concerning anything having to do with the future, for such a sharpness and certainty concerning the future would require Moses to stare directly into God's face as he approaches. And this no man can do.

Moses, we are to understand, came closer to grasping God's nature and his ways than any man ever has, or ever will. And yet the narrative in Exodus is quite radical in restricting Moses' understanding to that which is knowable by human beings. The "name of the Lord" as we have it does not overcome the limits of Moses' constitution as a human being. It bears the mark of Moses' human mind and its limitations. It therefore constitutes a limited and imperfect vision.[114]

The narrative parts of the History thus count as virtuous the belief that God can be relied upon to grant life and the good to those who keep his commands. But they do not provide us with an unequivocal message as to whether such faith is *possible* for human beings, given the limitations on what we can understand and know of God's nature and his ways. Moses is depicted as striving mightily to gain sufficient knowledge of God's ways to see that trust in God is in fact justified. In this Moses is depicted as succeeding, but only partially, the very passages that depict this success being written in such a way as to undermine our certainty as to what it actually means. The fact that God *"will be gracious to whom I will be gracious"* keeps ringing in our ears. The fact that Moses sees only God's passing and not his coming makes us shiver for the future. Can God really be relied upon? The story of Moses at Sinai is written to leave us thinking that he can. But it is also written to leave us wondering whether this is really so.

Which brings us back to the question of why the Mosaic law does not command faith in God. Had the Hebrew Bible consisted only of a legal codex, together with some supplementary material aimed at persuading its readers that the law was to be obeyed, then this supplementary material could easily have commanded that all strive to have perfect faith in the swift rewards and swift retribution that would come of failing to live up to God's law. But as discussed in Chapter 2, the prophet or scholar who labored to compose the final version of the History of Israel in the shadow of the destruction of Judah and Jerusalem didn't leave us anything like that. Instead, he decided to assemble a law book embedded in a much more extensive *tora*, or teaching, whose concern is to advance general arguments of a much broader nature, providing us with a framework for understanding the place of the law in our lives and in world history that far outstrips anything that could have been treated in the preamble of a traditional Near Eastern legal codex. Seeking that which is above and beyond the will of mere men, their man-made laws and their man-made gods, the final author of the History wished to persuade his readers that there exists a law whose force is of a universal nature, because it derives from the way the world itself was *made*, and therefore from the natures of the men and nations in this world. More than this, he wished to persuade them that the law of Moses was the very first systematic expression of this natural law, written down for the benefit of Israel and of all mankind. And that the God of Israel, *even if he is entirely invisible, possessing only a king in chains in a dungeon and no armies with which to enforce his law, would still end up destroying those who reject his ways and rewarding the just – because this is the way the world has worked since its creation.*

So in the History, Moses presents us with a law that is described categorically, as every law must be. But this law is accompanied, in the narrative portions of the *tora*, by a philosophical investigation as to how this law has come to be, the reasons for keeping it, and its meaning is for mankind – an investigation conducted in stories such as those just discussed concerning Moses' efforts to gain a clear understanding of God's nature. And these philosophical purposes are not necessarily conducive to the kind of untempered calls to faith that might easily have been appended to any lesser law. For example, if Moses himself is depicted as having failed to achieve a perfect clarity and certainty concerning God's nature, including especially the fact that he can be relied upon, then how can such perfect clarity and certainty be demanded as a law that all others must take up and obey? Indeed, the entire series of texts discussed in Chapter 4, which emphasize God's love of individuals who will take a risk and "wrestle" with him over the betterment of their own station and that of mankind, would appear to stand in tension with a categorical command to trust God: After all, does Abel's turn to shepherding not proceed from a certain *lack* of trust in God, who has sent Adam to serve the cursed soil from which he was taken? Does not Abraham's *Will the judge of all the earth not do justice?* bespeak a certain lack of faith? And what of Jacob's *I will not let you go until you bless me*? And Moses' *If you will not forgive their sin, erase me from your book?*[115] Do these not also proceed from a certain *lack* of trust in God? It is not a belief that all God's judgments are at all times for the best that motivates these challenges. It is a sense that God has misjudged, and would wish to be challenged and persuaded to change his course by man.

It has sometimes been said that faith in God is not commanded in the Mosaic law because only actions can be commanded, and not thoughts or feelings. But this is not the standpoint of the law itself, which is straightforward in commanding the "fear of God."[116] And indeed, the biblical authors are, as far as I am aware, unanimous in seeing the fear of God as an imperative for all men, at all times. The reason is that in the language of Scripture, the expression "fear of God" refers, as has been said, to a dread of the consequences of wrongdoing. It is the sense that if one acts wrongly, terrible things may very well follow. The command to fear God is, in other words, also a command to fear that we may have misunderstood, that we may have miscalculated, that we may be wrong and about to do something terrible. And this sense, once it burns in one's soul, can be the spur and the engine that permits man to seek that which is true and right and to do it even in the face of great hardship. As this is expressed in Psalms: "The beginning of wisdom is the fear of God."[117]

Likewise, Moses repeatedly calls on Israel to "love the Lord, your God,"[118] which in Scripture is usually another name for serving God and keeping his commandments "with all your mind and all your soul and all your might."[119] This may sound, upon first hearing, like a command wholeheartedly to perform actions along a steady prescribed course in accordance with fixed and undoubted beliefs. But it is nothing of the sort. The History of Israel most often associates love of God with individuals such as David (whose "mind was whole [*levavo shalem*] with the Lord his God"[120]) and Josiah ("who turned to the Lord with all his mind [*bechol levavo*] and all his soul and all his might"[121]) – individuals who have taken the lead in pursuing a significant reassessment and change of heart, personally and nationally. Here again, the constant mistranslation of *lev* as "heart" has done us a significant disservice. For it is with their "whole mind" that these individuals served God – achieving repentance and improvement because they "sought God"[122] with "open mind,"[123] and so were able to accept new considerations that had not come up before, and to accept a change in their own understanding, and to accept and then lead a change in course. The History thus sees the love of God, like the fear of God, as a force that can serve as a spur and an engine for seeking the true and the right and doing it.

The fear and love of God, then, are commanded by Moses, and are inscribed in his law. But these qualities, as they are understood in the History of Israel, are shepherd's virtues, which can serve as a source for individual inquiry, for challenging the existing order and the decreed course of events. Not so the trust in God, which is a genuine virtue as well – but a farmer's virtue, a virtue of men such as Cain and Noah, Isaac and Joseph, who are never portrayed as questioning the fate God has decreed for them, no matter how harsh their road has become. To recognize faith as a virtue is one thing. To command it categorically is something else again – something that Moses, who is himself depicted as exhibiting an inappropriate lack of faith at the waters of Meriva, does not do in giving the law to his people.[124]

VIII. JERUSALEM RECONSIDERED

It is common to say that Christianity is "a faith." To say this is to reduce a complicated phenomenon to just one of its elements. But in Christianity, belief in certain propositions is so central that such a reduction may perhaps be justified. Certainly this is Tertullian's view, and quite a few passages in the New Testament can be read as supporting such a reduction as well: Thus the Gospel of John teaches that "God ... gave his only son, that everyone who has faith in him may not die but have eternal life";[125] Paul writes that "[T]he Gospel is the saving power of God for everyone who has faith";[126] and so on.

There is no similar justification for calling what is found in the Hebrew Scriptures, or in Jewish tradition more generally, "a faith." The biblical faith in God is an important virtue, as loyalty is a virtue. Moreover, it has the power to strengthen us for the trials ahead, and to bring us to observance and understanding. But faith in God is not commanded in the law of Moses. And the narrative sections of the biblical History suggest time and again that an unblemished trust in God may not be feasible, and that, where feasible, it may lead to consequences that are not to be desired by either man or God. Indeed, the fact that figures such as Abel, Abraham, Jacob, and Moses are portrayed as lacking such an unblemished trust in God, while others seem to have such trust, speaks volumes. Even biblical works such as Psalms and Proverbs, which urge faith in God more or less unequivocally, are as interested in many other subjects, and do not come close to making trust in God their principal focus.

No, the Hebrew Scriptures cannot be reduced to "a faith" without perverting and destroying them. And this remains so even after we discard Tertullian's definition of faith – the likes of which can be found nowhere in the Hebrew Bible – and replace it with the conception of faith that was familiar to the biblical authors. The supposed contest between Jerusalem and Athens, in which Hebrew Scripture is made to stand in a corner labeled "faith" in a disputation with Athenian "reason," is a spectacle that evokes cheers of pleasure in many quarters today. But for the contest to be so entertaining, it requires just this perversion and destruction of Scripture.

I realize that for many readers, the view that I am proposing, in which the Bible is recognized as calling individuals to a life of independent judgment in search of truth and the good, will be especially difficult to accept because of the central place of the Mosaic law in the biblical corpus. For there is a powerful impulse within the Western tradition that sees law as standing in opposition to reason, and as an ally of the faith of Carthage. According to this understanding, law, *by its very nature*, requires an unthinking obedience to authority. And such obedience is the very opposite of a life conducted in light of one's own independent reason. Such a demand for unconditional obedience was, after all, the demand made by the laws of Athens in Plato's *Crito*, and it was this unconditional obedience that they used to put Socrates to death. What better proof might one want for the claim that law is opposed to philosophy and reason than this? Tertullian, too, when he wishes to say that certain beliefs are to be accepted on authority, speaks of a "rule of faith" or "law of faith." And many other examples could easily be adduced. And once one has subscribed to this view, the endorsement of the law of Moses by the biblical tradition and its rabbinic interpreters is easily taken to be yet another indication, if not the decisive one, that the Bible demands an obedient faith and rejects reason, the search for truth, and philosophy.

But this inclination to see an opposition between law and reason is misguided, and should be rejected as well, both as regards law in general and with respect to the place of the law of Moses within biblical and later Jewish tradition. It is of course true that a system of laws requires obedience if it is to achieve its aims. And it is also the case that as an instrument of collective judgment, law will always require things that *someone* thinks are unreasonable.[127] But neither of these evident facts establishes an opposition, or a contradiction, between law and reason. And two important considerations suggest that law is, or at least can be, consonant with the search for truth and with the free exercise of reason: The first is that most philosophers, beginning with Plato, have insisted that reason requires obedience before the laws of the state or society in which one lives, even in cases in which such obedience poses a grave hardship for us.[128] The explanation for this is that reason admits of ends that are greater than the well-being of the individual at a given moment, and that of one's state or society is often seen as being such an end.[129]

The second consideration is in a sense more significant, although it is less frequently discussed. This is that law is itself an *instrument of reason*. It is a tool that the reasoning individual uses as a means of confronting present needs with the reasoning that has already been done by others in the past. Reason would not require such an instrument if we could somehow found our state and our society anew every day, as Socrates founds a city in speech in a single evening in the *Republic*. But we cannot found our state and our society anew every day. We know from experience that the enterprise of building up a human society requires a great measure of stability and continuity in terms of forms and practices. And this means that a relevant process for seeking what is reasonable and what is best must be one conducted with great care, in a manner that gives a very great weight to established precedent and custom. We do not, therefore, say that we accept the established precedent and custom that has been handed down from previous generations *on faith*, even where we think they might have been framed in a manner that makes better sense to us. Rather, we understand this inheritance as the consequence of a process of *reason*, taking its provisions as our point of departure and applying ourselves to learning the legal reasoning of past generations which brought us to this point; and only then, once we have entered into the discourse of the preceding generations from a standpoint of knowledge and respect, do we consider what adjustments must nonetheless be made in the accepted interpretation of the laws on the basis of wisdom gained through experience, and in response to changing circumstances. All this is, as I say, in accord with reason, as an English common lawyer, for example, will attest. But it involves a certain process of reason that, for good reasons, prefers consistency and stability wherever change has not been shown to be necessary.

I have said these things with respect to law in general, but it is no different in the case of the law of Moses. This law is not given a central place in Hebrew Scripture with the intention of contravening human reason – any more than the law of any nation is taught with the intention of contravening human reason. On the contrary, this law is presented in the History of Israel as one that should be adopted for the benefits that it will bring to individuals and to Israel as a nation, which will be kept alive, both on its land and in exile, by the observance of this law. In the Orations of the Prophets, Proverbs, and Psalms, this is often said to be an empirical matter – one can simply compare a life lived in accordance with the law and see that it is better. One may disagree, of course, considering the biblical authors to have been mistaken on this point. But in disagreeing, the individual does not reject an absurd proposition, to which one is expected to assent only because God is its author. He rejects a system of laws that is proposed to him by men who thought human reason would endorse them as worthy of being taken up.

What is left, I suppose, is to argue about all those "And God said"s that appear throughout the Mosaic law: One can say that from the moment that God's name is invoked, the law is no longer a matter to be adjudicated by reason. One *has to obey* because God said so.

I've heard this said many times, but I've never been able to make sense of it. The fact is that no one *has to obey* because God said so. From the story of Adam in Eden, through almost every page of Scripture, and down to our own time, people choose to live as they choose to live. Some live in accordance with what seems reasonable to them, and *do not* live in accordance with God's law; others live in accordance with what seems reasonable to them, and *do* live in accordance with God's law. The choice is entirely in human hands. This is why Moses has to urge Israel to "choose life."[130] Moses has to urge this on them and on us precisely because *no one has to obey because God said so.*[131] Indeed, the principle that no one *has to obey* is pretty close to heart of the biblical worldview – and of what the authors of Scripture are trying to teach.

The confusion on this point stems, I think, principally from an insistence on reading the Mosaic law – and thinking and speaking about "the Law" – as though it were capable of being understood without reference to the narratives in which it is embedded. Torn from the context in which they appear, the laws are just laws, and one's imagination can run wild inventing explanations as to what it means for someone to say God commanded them. But the Mosaic law is not presented in the History of Israel as a text that can be read independently. It appears in the midst of narratives that have much to tell us about the giving of the law, and in fact, one does not have to read too far to realize that *the law of Moses is dependent on these narratives for its force and for its significance.*[132] It is in the context of these narratives that we are taught to see the laws not as mere commands, but as part of a covenant between ourselves and God – a covenant that has two sides to it, and which a vulnerable God needs as much as we need it. And it is in the context of these narratives that we learn to see the law of Moses as the natural law, the will of the one God who created mankind and all creatures, and who for this reason comprehends man's needs and what must be done to secure them. It is in the context of these narratives, in other words, that the law becomes, not a command, so much as a gift to Israel, and to all mankind.

At the same time, the narrative sections of the History raise important questions concerning the law of Moses as we have it – questions that can be seen as challenging and weakening the force of the law. As discussed, Moses is depicted as showing us the road to life and the good, and the road to death and evil, and urging us to choose one over the other. But the stories included in the History also teach us that no man, not even Moses himself, can know God's nature with perfect certainty. This means that man does not know, with perfect certainty, whether God can in fact be relied upon to keep faith with those who obey his commands. We may understand from this that Moses cannot know with a perfect certainty whether the road he proposes will in fact profit us, and whether it can be relied upon to grant us life and the good, any more than that road which he urges against. Perhaps there is no road that can be relied upon to grant individuals and nations life and the good?

These, then, are two sides of the same coin: The extraordinary strengthening of the Mosaic law, which is seen as natural law, deriving from the very nature of God's creatures; and the weakening of the law, which is seen as being something less than perfectly certain, due to the limitations of man's understanding – are both a consequence of the History's presentation of the law of Moses as that which men should want to embrace according to the standards of human reasoning, which are the standards of this world. The narratives, then, permit us to position the law, and our observance of it, within a life lived according to reason. They are the philosophical investigations that serve to explain the law and qualify it, so that we retain an understanding of why observance of this law should be something we should want – and that all men should want. So far as I know, no other national law in history has been promulgated together with such an extensive philosophical commentary whose purpose is to explain and qualify it. That such a thing is even conceivable is the achievement of Jerusalem's search for truth and justice, for life and the good.[133]

It bears repeating that Jerusalem's search for truth is in many ways very different from that of Athens. But Jerusalem is not different from Athens in the way that Tertullian and his followers suggest. The Hebrew Scriptures are not about the question of whether one is "assisted" or not in one's search for truth. It is not to answer this question that the God of Israel appears in our Scriptures as speaking to man and acting on his behalf. The women and men depicted in these texts and the authors who wrote them are troubled by other, and to my mind far more important, things. First and foremost, they see themselves as seeking to discover that which is reasonable – that which is true and just, and that which would give life to man on this earth. And they understand that that which is reasonable for mankind is not immediately evident, and in fact not evident at all to many. So they struggle with the question of how one is to find that which will stand and that which can be relied upon to benefit mankind in the face of an epistemic jungle – a confused and frightening reality in which such knowledge is chronically distant. They believe that such wisdom can be found in the world, because they believe that God has spoken it. To find it is the difficulty, and the subject of a lifelong quest.

Far from subscribing to the faith of Carthage, what the biblical authors want, then, is precisely "what the world calls wisdom." In this, Jerusalem is not so terribly far from Athens – and remote indeed from Carthage. The time has come to draw a sharp distinction between Jerusalem and Carthage, so that Jerusalem may begin to speak in its own voice. Only once this has been achieved will comparisons with Athens, Rome, and others become a serious possibility.

PART III

CONCLUSION

9

God's Speech After Reason and Revelation

Not too long from now, it may be possible to write a comprehensive work on the ideas of the Hebrew Scriptures. But for now, such a work remains out of reach – at least for me. This book was meant to be something much more modest. It's an introduction. And in it, I've tried to accomplish two things: I've suggested a methodological framework I believe can permit a more rapid advance in the direction of a well-articulated understanding of the philosophical content of the Hebrew Scriptures than we've seen so far. And I've conducted a number of investigations into the philosophical concerns of the biblical authors that make use of this framework as a basis. My hope is that this methodological framework and these investigations together will suffice to make the case that the philosophical exploration of Hebrew Scripture is both possible and much needed; and that this project will now seem more plausible both to those who have been skeptical about it, and to those who have been interested and excited by the prospect of such a project but have wanted a clearer sense of what it would involve.

At this point, I'd like to put my pen down and hear what others have to say, and especially to see what others can contribute to this, our joint project. But there is one other subject I should touch upon before closing – the question of whether we wouldn't be better off discarding the reason–revelation dichotomy entirely in reading the Hebrew Bible. I will say a few words about this now.

This book was written to answer the question of whether the Hebrew Scriptures can be profitably read as works of reason, rather than revelation. In the Introduction to the book, I wrote that if we are forced to choose between reading the Hebrew Scriptures as reason or as revelation, we'll get much farther in understanding what these texts were intended to say to us if we read them as works of reason. And nothing I've seen in the course of preparing my manuscript has suggested that I was mistaken in this. In reading the Hebrew Scriptures as philosophical works, whose purpose was to assist individuals and nations looking to discover the true and the good in accordance with man's natural abilities, we unlock the texts in a way that immediately brings to light many ideas that had been largely invisible when these works were read as revelation.

But at the same time, I also wrote that I don't actually think the "reason" side of the Christian reason–revelation dichotomy is capable of doing full justice to the content of these texts either. The reason–revelation distinction is alien to the Hebrew Scriptures, and ultimately this framework is going to have to be thrown out as a basis for interpreting the Hebrew Bible. Even after we've come to understand the teachings of these texts as they appear when read as works of reason, there will still be a second step that needs to be taken – one that involves discarding the reason–revelation distinction completely, and learning to see the world as it appeared to the prophets of Israel, before the reason–revelation distinction was invented. A few words, then, about this second step. The rest I will leave for another work.

The traditional distinction between reason and revelation was based on the medieval model of what human reason is. On this view, reason involves deducing perfectly certain propositions from other propositions taken to be self-evident, or derived from immediate sensation. In the wake of the successes of Newtonian science, this understanding of what reason is all about pretty much collapsed. But despite the passage of centuries, no consensus has emerged as to what is to replace it. Philosophy and the cognitive sciences still await an account of what we are talking about when we speak of *reason* that will have a fraction of the support that the medieval conception of reason had in its day.[1] And at this point, the suggestions being made are only getting wilder. In the last few decades, scholars studying the mind have suggested that the emotions may be directly implicated in the normal processes of human reason.[2] Others have concluded that reason depends, at its foundations, on metaphor and analogy.[3] Yet others have proposed that mental operations such as "insight" or "intuition" will be needed to make sense of human reason.[4] I won't try to evaluate any of these claims here. But the trend is obvious to anyone who cares to look. What is happening is that many of the mental phenomena that the Western philosophical tradition had had pegged as being "opposed to reason" are now being proposed for rehabilitation – not because anyone is in favor of irrationality, but because these operations of the mind may simply turn out to be a part of the picture of what rationality really is.

With respect to revelation, we at first seem to be in better shape. But I'm not sure how long this impression is going to last, either. Medieval philosophy was based on an Aristotelian metaphysics that made answering the question of what "revelation" is look deceptively easy. As discussed in Chapter 7, this was a view that required the division of reality between two realms – one "outside" the mind and another "inside" the mind or in speech. This outside–inside scheme offered an easy way of recognizing revelation: Whatever is outside is "reality," which is identical with God's understanding of things. If knowledge of what is outside the mind, in reality, suddenly appears inside the mind, yet without any process of human reasoning taking place to bring this about, then one could think of this as a miracle, a *revelation*. Revelation is thus conceived as a unilateral *inpouring* of the truth from outside, an inpouring that is unilateral on God's part, an act of divine grace.

But what we've seen of the metaphysics of Hebrew Scripture causes serious problems for this view of what revelation is all about. Chapters 6–7 suggested that the metaphysics of some of the biblical authors, if not all of them, is radically monistic – that it defines *knowledge* and *truth* in terms of only one realm, without recourse to Aristotle's outside–inside distinction.[5] True words (understood also as "things") are those that stand, or hold good, through time in this one realm. God's words (understood also as "things") are those that stand, or hold good, above all others. On the face of it, this seems to mean that when Isaiah or Jeremiah speaks of "God's words," he is not talking about something he recognizes as coming from "outside" of him. It's not an inpouring that is being described, then. Nor is he talking about something coming from "inside," as Schleiermacher wanted us to believe. It's something else.

What exactly is it that Jeremiah was experiencing on those occasions when God's speech filled his mind? Unfortunately, his orations are not intended to capture the phenomenology of prophecy. In fact, none of the prophets are much interested in sharing this kind of information with us. In Jeremiah's writings, for example, virtually the only passage offering us an explicit account of what his exchanges with God are like is his description of his first encounter with God as a youth. This passage opens with an extended "calling," in which the young man is told to stand and speak to the nations of their rise and fall,[6] which is presented as God's own words. But when it comes to the actual content of the prophecy that Jeremiah is to deliver, the text shifts gears and we encounter something quite different. God now *asks* Jeremiah what it is that he sees:

Jeremiah 1:

11. And the word of the Lord came to me saying: What do you see, Jeremiah? And I said: "I see an almond [*shaked*] stick."

12. And the Lord said to me: You have excelled in seeing, for I am watchful [*shoked*] to accomplish my word.

13. And the word of the Lord came to me a second time saying: What do you see? And I said: "I see a seething pot, and its face is to the north."

14. And the Lord said to me: From the north, evil will break forth upon all the inhabitants of the land.

Twice, God asks Jeremiah what he sees, and twice the young prophet responds with a metaphor that cuts to the heart of the condition of Judah and Jerusalem.[7] First, Jeremiah sees an almond tree, which in winter appears as a barren stick with neither leaves nor fruit, but is called a *shaked* in Hebrew – a cognate of the verb *shakad* meaning "to be diligent" – because it blossoms in January and bears fruit within three weeks, the first of the trees in Israel to awaken from its barrenness and fulfill its hidden promise each year.[8] Jeremiah looks upon the kingdom, endangered and troubled, but sees the fulfillment of God's promise that Jerusalem will flower and bear fruit. This is a difficult metaphor to extract from the events of Jeremiah's day, and God responds to Jeremiah's metaphor by telling him he has "excelled in seeing." Jeremiah's second metaphor, a seething pot with its face to the north, depicts Jerusalem in a manner that is closer to home: The cauldron roils with moral decay and political instability, and Jerusalem, bounded by steep precipices on all sides but the north, can only be militarily conquered from that direction.[9] This is a metaphor that invokes not the future hope of the city, but its slide toward destruction.

If we consider this give-and-take between God and man as an example of prophecy as Jeremiah experiences it, a few points stand out. First, contrary to the common understanding of the prophet as a passive vessel into which God's message is poured from on high, it is difficult to escape the emphasis on Jeremiah's own role in the shaping of his prophecy. In this exchange between Jeremiah and God, the term used in describing what Jeremiah is doing is not a specific term for prophecy, but the Hebrew word *ro'eh*, which is the conventional term used for seeing.[10] God asks Jeremiah not what he prophesies, but simply what he sees when he looks out at Jerusalem. Moreover, while this prophecy does begin with an approach from God, this approach is not in the form of God holding forth on a subject of concern to him. Rather, it is in the form of a *question*: God asks what it is that Jeremiah sees, and after Jeremiah has given an answer, God responds to what Jeremiah has said by telling him that he has "excelled in seeing." Obviously, there would be no point in God telling Jeremiah that he had "excelled in seeing" if Jeremiah's role here were simply to look at ready-made images that God has placed before him. In that case, it would

be God who had excelled in presenting. But here the emphasis is unambiguously on Jeremiah's own capacity for vision, for seeing the truth when he
looks upon the city.[11]

Looking more closely at this passage, we see that Jeremiah's experience of
prophecy is in fact in three parts, two of which are depicted as deriving from
God, whereas the third comes from Jeremiah himself:

(i) God asks: Jeremiah becomes aware of a difficulty in understanding
reality as it presents itself before him.

(ii) Jeremiah sees: Jeremiah discovers a metaphor, a concept from his
previously existing stock of everyday terms, which appears to him
most truly to describe the reality that has presented itself to him.

(iii) God confirms: Jeremiah understands that his analogy, when measured against reality, provides a deeper, more accurate truth concerning the nature of reality.

We therefore see Jeremiah's prophecy as being in the form of a cycle. God
does indeed initiate. But what he brings into the prophet's mind is, in the
first place, not an answer but only a question: Jeremiah becomes aware that
his experience is in some sense inexplicable, and he is called upon to give
an answer of himself.[12] In the second stage, it is Jeremiah's seeing, which
is praised for its acuteness, that provides the answer. Only thereafter, once
Jeremiah has hit upon the metaphor that holds the key to understanding
the reality before him, does the prophet hear God's voice confirming and
answering.

In Chapter 3, I suggested that the prophet's reliance on metaphor is related
to the need to be able to present difficult arguments to a broad audience.[13]
Arguments made by way of analogies drawn from common experience – the
stallion, the watchmen, the seething pot – would be more readily understood by the prophet's audience than the same argument couched in abstract
terms. I think that this is right, and that the claim that prophetic metaphor
is intended to obscure the argument of the prophet, so that only some might
be able to understand it, is obviously wrong. But considering what we've
seen here, it doesn't seem to give us the whole picture. For Jeremiah, it
appears that argument by metaphor is not merely a convention adopted for
the sake of the crowd. It is, as the report of his first prophecies suggests, the
primary mode of his "seeing," and that which permits him to cut to the heart
of the reality before him and to see things as they *really are*: It is in seeing a
man *as* a charging stallion, in other words, and a prophet *as* a watchman on
the city wall, that he is able to see these things for what they really are, and
to understand them as they should be understood.[14]

I am not here suggesting that when Jeremiah hears God speak, this is not really revelation or miraculous knowledge – just as I was not trying earlier to suggest that when we incorporate sentiment, metaphor, and insight into our model of what the human mind is doing when we think straight, this means that we are no longer talking about reason. We may still wish to recognize God's speech as revelation, and we may still want to call our normative thought processes, when they're doing what they're supposed to do, reason. But without the metaphysical scheme that was used to underwrite the medieval conception of revelation, I'm afraid this term just isn't going to be left with much meaning to it. Like the definition of reason, the definition of revelation looks as if it is in danger of slipping to the point where we no longer really know what we're talking about when we speak of it.

I have said that if we wish to understand Hebrew Scripture, we will ultimately have to give up on the reason–revelation distinction. Perhaps the reasons for my saying this are now clear. Given that the biblical metaphysics does not appear capable of sustaining the Greek-style conception of revelation as an inpouring from another realm, we will have need of a new conception of *revelation* that is an outgrowth of, and compatible with, what we know of the biblical metaphysics. This we will eventually succeed in obtaining, just as we will ultimately settle on a better understanding of what is meant by *reason* than what we have to work with now. What is not clear at all is to what extent our understanding of God's revelation to man in Hebrew Scripture, and our understanding of reason, once both of these terms have become clear and firm, will remain things that are possible for us to hold apart and keep distinct from one another.

Appendix

What Is "Reason"? Some Preliminary Remarks

In this book I have used the terms *reason* and *philosophy* without attempting to provide formal definitions for them, and without trying to defend my understanding of the way these words should be used against the many other interpretations that are possible. This is not because I think such definitions and such a defense are unimportant. On the contrary, I think we are going to find it very difficult to come to an understanding of what the Hebrew Bible is about and what it does (and does not) have to teach us without a precise understanding of what reason is. But after a number of attempts at introducing such formal definitions into the body of this work, I came to the conclusion that I couldn't integrate this material without creating more problems – for myself and for my readers – than I was solving. In particular, I found that an extended elaboration and defense of my views on the nature of reason necessarily led me far from the main subjects this book was intended to cover. Whereas a cursory discussion could only leave readers with the impression that what I have to say on this subject is superficial and fails to do it justice.

Nevertheless, because of the importance of the topic, I don't feel right completely abandoning those readers who feel they need a more sharply drawn picture of what I am talking about when I speak of *reason* and *philosophy*. For those readers, I've included this appendix, whose content is precisely a superficial treatment of the subject that fails to do it justice – no more and no less. These few pages are aimed only at providing the barest outline of what I think needs to be said about what I take to be the nature of human reason. They give a general direction, which a few readers, perhaps, may find useful. Filling out this bare outline in a way that is systematic and persuasive is something I will have to do elsewhere.

Due to considerations of space, this appendix will not deal with the definition of *philosophy* as something distinct from reason. I do agree that in principle, it is desirable to distinguish philosophical discourse as a subset of the universe of instances of human reason. There are, for example, plenty of activities in which we employ at least aspects of reason to get at the truth of a particular matter, but in which we only make use of rigidly predefined concepts, and of operations conducted by rote (consider the multiplication of large numbers). And philosophy, I think, should in some way involve deriving, clarifying, challenging, or improving the concepts we employ, and not only applying them mechanically. But for the present discussion, I don't believe that working out the exact boundaries between philosophical and nonphilosophical reason will be all that helpful. What matters is to understand, if possible, something concerning the nature of reason. If that were in hand, many things concerning the nature of philosophy would, I think, quickly follow.

The term *reason* is often used, in a broad sense, to refer to the operation of those faculties of the human mind by which man is naturally able to gain knowledge of that which is true and good. But this broad usage of the term, when examined more closely, turns out to be confused and confusing. For what exactly *are* the mental faculties that man naturally relies upon to gain knowledge of the true and the good? I'm not sure anyone has a very good answer to this question. And without one, all talk of "reason" (as well as distinctions drawn between reason and other things, such as "revelation" or "faith") risks becoming a game played with empty words.

It was not always the case that the term *reason* was so ill defined. Medieval philosophy possessed a conception of reason that was relatively clear and well defined. Relying on Euclid's geometry as a model, medieval philosophers understood *reason* as beginning with propositions whose truth is self-evident (or which derive indubitably from the evidence of the senses), and proceeding from these to other propositions deduced from them with absolute certainty.[1] Even Descartes thought something similar to this, arguing that from the supposedly self-evident fact that *I think*, one could deduce with perfect certainty much of what one might want to know about the nature of the world. In both its Scholastic and its Cartesian versions, the self-evident nature of the premises and the absolutely certain nature of valid deductive inference was supposed to permit the human mind to reach conclusions that could be known with perfect certainty, as was thought to be the case in geometry and other branches of mathematics.

But this conception of reason doesn't command the kind of following it once did. In part, this is because of developments within mathematics itself. In the wake of the development of non-Euclidean geometries in the nineteenth century and their subsequent introduction into science to describe physical space, it has become difficult to defend the idea that reason does in fact begin with things that are indisputable and evident to everyone. In fact, the mathematics of the last century has distanced itself from the view that its premises are necessarily true, preferring instead to see them as postulates for the sake of argument.[2] And this shift is, I think, representative of a more general trend. In philosophy, too, many seem to have come to the conclusion that what is perfectly evident to one individual is, in general, not so evident to others. And so there has been a move – at times explicit, but often made implicitly – toward a view of reason as consisting of the "working out" of the implications of premises that are held to be "basic" for various reasons, even if the origins of these premises are at times quite obscure. As the philosopher Nicholas Wolterstorff has written:

> Once upon a time, lasting until not long ago, philosophers assumed that philosophy … had to be rationally grounded in certitudes.... [Today, however, the philosopher] finds himself believing in many things, both large and small. Perhaps he believes in physicalism. He then regards the challenge facing him as a philosopher not to be that of discarding all those convictions unless he can rationally ground them in certitudes; the challenge facing him is that of working out the nature and implications of his physicalist convictions in various areas of thought, doing so in such a way as to cope not only with the complications that arise in his own mind but with the objections lodged against his line of thought by others. In principle these objections might prove so powerful that he gives up his physicalism.[3]

On this view, the self-evident propositions that used to stand as the foundations for medieval and Cartesian reasoning are seen as being replaced by beliefs "both large and small" whose origins are uncertain. These basic propositions may, as Alvin Plantinga suggests, be derived from "having experience of a certain sort" – by which is meant non-propositional experiences such as feelings or sensations of different kinds.[4] The basic propositions that emerge from this background then serve as the basis for chains of deductions, much as was the case in medieval thought. But these basic propositions are no longer treated as absolutely certain, and so the conclusions deduced from them are also not thought to be certain either. These are held only probabilistically or hypothetically, to be overturned when some unspecified weight of objections has been brought to bear against them.[5]

Moreover, it is not only among mathematicians and philosophers that we now find it said that different individuals will argue on the basis of different and often mutually contradictory premises whose origins are unknown or unimportant; and that despite the obscurity of their origins, many or all of these premises can be seen as the basis for "reason" so long as they are not embraced dogmatically (i.e., in the face of an overwhelming argument to the contrary).[6] We encounter similar views in a variety of other disciplines, as well as in descriptions of the way reasoned argument should be conducted in matters of politics or religion, or in making private decisions. Although I can't here provide the evidence that would be needed to make a compelling case for this, my sense is that it is now possible to speak of the increasingly widespread acceptance of a kind of neo-Scholastic conception of rationality – one that does away entirely with the medieval conceit that a properly framed argument should be able to compel universal assent; but shares with its medieval predecessor the intuition that whatever reason is, it must be primarily concerned with making arguments by deducing propositions that compel assent from other propositions taken as fixed or given.

This neo-Scholastic conception of reason is, I think, a mixed blessing. The abandonment of the supposition that certain propositions are self-evidently certain is to my mind a welcome one. But together with this, there has also been a disturbing tendency to give up on truth as the aim of reason. The fact that the premises are no longer certain – and that they seem to arise out of all sorts of barely understood psychological processes whose relationship to rationality is unknown – militates in the direction of settling for valid deduction as basically the only thing we have left that can we can give the name of "reason." And valid deduction, if it proceeds from premises that aren't known to be true, is an activity that has no relationship to actually seeking the truth. It's just a kind of game, in which you deduce from your premises and I deduce from mine, without either of us knowing that all these deductions are getting us anywhere. As one philosopher recently said to me, "I don't really care whether philosophy brings us any closer to the truth. What matters to me is to make a good argument." My impression is that more than a few philosophers are today inclined to say something like this. And this only makes sense: If you don't have a great deal of confidence in your premises, and you see reason as consisting of nothing more than valid deduction from these premises, then you won't think reason has that much to do with advancing toward the truth!

I don't think this is a very good place to be. If it is not to advance toward truth that we engage in reason, I'm not sure why we should reason at all. Moreover, there are cases in which the exercise of human reason has brought us closer to the truth in a manner that I think is difficult to deny. For instance, Newton's *Mathematical Principles of Natural Philosophy* (1687; hereafter, the *Principia*) succeeded in bringing the motions of celestial bodies, terrestrial projectile motion, the rise and fall of the tides, the movement of the pendulum, and the shape of the earth's surface all under a single set of laws. To me this seems to be a most impressive example of human reason successfully being applied to advancing us toward truth. Why not use examples of this kind as the basis for a revised conception of what reason is?

The *Principia* is not only of interest because it is such a good example of how the exercise of human reason can bring us closer to truth. As Newton emphasized in his preface to the *Principia*, in the "Rules for the Study of Natural Philosophy" he appended to the second edition of this work, and in queries appended to his *Opticks*, his purpose in composing the *Principia* was precisely to provide us with examples of proper reasoning – and thereby to overthrow the accepted modes of reasoning that had been inherited from medieval and Cartesian philosophy. In this sense, the *Principia* speaks directly to us about our own present quandary: It gives us a view of what human reason can really do, precisely in order to get us to understand that reason is something different from what it had often been taken to be. So what was the conception of reason that Newton sought to advance?

Newton's science was, of course, what we now call empirical science, meaning that its results are derived from experience rather than from propositions taken to be self-evident. But to describe Newton simply as an empiricist is more than a little misleading, in that it obscures the revolution he sought to introduce into our conception of rationality. For Newton doesn't discard entirely the deductive method of medieval philosophy as others had tried to do before him. On the contrary, the method of deductive proof proceeding from definitions and axioms is so important to the *Principia* that in many respects it looks and feels as if it were a sequel to Euclid's *Elements*. Nevertheless, Newton's approach to reason is revolutionary in that he sees deductive sciences such as geometry *as being based on axioms that are themselves carefully derived from experience*. Thus in Newton's mind, Euclid's geometry is understood not as beginning with its axioms, but rather as beginning in a prior procedure of abstraction that establishes these axioms in light of broad experience.[7] Newtonian rationality, as exhibited in the *Principia*, likewise involves a two-step procedure based on abstracting axioms (for example, Newton's "laws of motion") from experience; and then deducing propositions from these general laws. What gives the axioms the right to stand *as true* is their twofold contact with experience: First, the axioms are consciously abstracted from experience as the first stage of human reasoning. Second, the axioms are considered to hold good only because of the support they gain from their successful application to far-flung domains of experience,[8] which reconfirms the framing of the axioms originally proposed and establishes them as reliable – and therefore true.[9]

Such a view of reason certainly constitutes a break with medieval and early modern rationalist philosophy. But Newtonian rationality is not less of a challenge to the neo-Scholastic view of reason that has become increasingly popular in our own day. Even a view such as that advanced by present-day philosophers such as Plantinga and Wolterstorff – who accept that the truth of one's premises ultimately depends on the tenability of the conclusions deduced from these premises – would not, I think, qualify in Newton's eyes as an example of the proper exercise of human reason. This is because in the absence of a prior procedure of abstraction that seeks to establish our premises (or basic propositions) in light of broad experience, and then reconfirms the framing of these premises by way of their successful application to far-flung domains of experience – in the absence, that is, of a Newtonian form of reasoning – the premises that are being taken as basic will have to be seen as being to a greater or lesser extent arbitrary. And for Newton, as for his predecessors, "arbitrary" meant irrational.

Let's suppose that Newton's position as I've described it is correct, and that human reason, when it is working well, does involve such a two-stage procedure. What do we know about the first stage in the process of human reason? Unfortunately, the answer is: not a great deal. Newton himself is inconsistent in the terms he uses in discussing this stage of reason, and the descriptions and examples he offers don't amount to more than fragments of an account. Today philosophers refer to the operation Newton discusses in treating this first stage of reason as *abductive* or *retroductive inference*, or *inference to the best explanation*.[10] But as far as I can tell, a really good account of this aspect of human reason does not yet exist either in philosophy or cognitive science. So for now, I'll just point to a few features of Newtonian abductive inference that I think can be helpful in the context of the present discussion.

First, it is important to notice that while the end-product of Newton's abductive procedure is a system of definitions and axioms in propositional form – among them the "laws of motion" that serve as the axioms in the *Principia* – what Newton struggles to derive from experience is not, in the first instance, propositions. They are rather abstract objects (or qualities of objects) such as *force* and *mass*, which he treats as the "general causes"[11] of the observed phenomena in the domain being treated. These can be seen as the subject matter of the propositions that serve as his definitions and axioms.

Second, Newton does not rely on well-established usage in deploying these terms. While one can find certain precedents in the work of earlier natural philosophers, the fact is that both *force* and *mass* are to a significant degree transformed in their Newtonian usage.[12] Indeed, we will not be far from the mark if we say that terms such as *force* and *mass* are in the first instance brought to bear in the domain Newton is studying only as metaphors or analogies, rather than as literal descriptions of what it is he is seeing. At first, the abstractions that Newton is dealing with are only *like* forces and masses as these had been previously understood. But these likenesses are good enough to serve as the basis for Newton's attempts to understand the operative causes in the domain in question. And once these metaphors are in play, they are reworked and adjusted until they can be cleanly interrelated within the context of a system of axioms or premises. It is only the habit of subsequent generations, which come to see terms such as *force* and *mass* as being defined exclusively by the laws in which they are embedded, that obscures the metaphorical or analogous nature of the abductive work that originally brought these laws into being – just as it has obscured the origins of the terms that appear in Euclid's axioms.

The prominence of metaphor and analogy in the abductive first stage of Newtonian rationality should ring some bells – or sound some alarms. This is because of the prominent part that metaphor and analogy have played and continue to play in an ever-growing literature in fields such as philosophy, history of science, psychology, linguistics, and anthropology challenging the sufficiency of deductive inference from premises as a model for describing the functioning of sound human reason. The literature on this question has been diverse, some of it focusing on the centrality of metaphorical representation in much of human thought.[13] Other studies have focused on the place of "models" – theoretical constructs typically consisting of spatially extended and moving parts – at the heart of modern scientific reasoning.[14] Yet others have drawn attention to the use of type-contrasts or typologies in narrative prose to reason about subjects not easily framed in terms of propositions.[15] But amid the profusion of approaches, I think a common thread can be discerned. The bottom line that emerges from these studies is that whatever human reason is, it involves operations of the conscious mind that are in some important sense more fundamental than those that are at the fore when we are deducing propositions from other propositions. Just how this more fundamental part of conscious human reasoning works, and the precise nature of its relationship to the kind of deductive argument from "basic" propositions that has so often been equated with reason, are questions that must be regarded as wide open at this time.

As suggested above, this is not the place to enter into a detailed discussion of how these questions are to be answered. But I do want to say enough to give the reader a sense of the considerations that lead me to use the term *reason* in the way I do. So here's what I can say for now: A metaphor, analogy, or model is not propositional in form. So it cannot itself serve either as a definition or as an axiom; nor is it a representation of something that can serve as a definition or an axiom. Instead, the metaphors that are deployed in abductive inference are intended to point to general causes (or "natures"[16]) that, although they are general in character (that is, transcending the individual instances from which they have been abstracted), nevertheless in important respects resemble the concrete objects or circumstances from which they are abstracted. In particular, just as a concrete object or circumstance is infinite in terms of the qualities that can be correctly ascribed to it, so too can an infinite number of qualities be ascribed to that general cause or nature that the metaphor, analogy, or model of abductive inference is intended to represent to us. Indeed, it is precisely the fact that metaphors are unlimited in the number of qualities that can correctly be attributed to them that makes them such useful tools in establishing the new abstract terms needed in abductive inference.

Only once we have learned reliably to recognize a given general cause or nature in experience is it then possible to begin trying to establish a partial description of it in terms of propositions. Definitions and axioms employ propositions to attempt to capture and to draw out, in a form that is as precise as possible, that which is implicit in the general causes or natures that have already gained a measure of use. These propositions necessarily involve a simplification (or "idealization") of the general cause in question, but they contribute a precision to the discussion that often makes the trade-off worthwhile.[17] Thus deductive inference from propositions should be regarded, as it is by Newton, as being able to bring us to true conclusions so long as the definitions and axioms are right. But the possibility of adjustment in these definitions and axioms always remains open, since even an apt metaphorical representation of a general cause or nature may be poorly or overly simplified in the transition to a propositional rendering.

All this is quite preliminary and sketchy. Nevertheless, I suspect it is closer to being a just description of what is involved in human reason than other conceptions, still quite popular, based principally on a deductive inference. If I'm right, this means that when we do finally get to a good characterization of what man's mental faculties do, it's going to turn out that what we call *reason* will need to be defined as something like *the exercise of those operations of the human mind by which general causes are derived from experience, elaborated as laws and principles that are likewise general in character, and applied to particular cases.*

On this understanding of reason, the *application* of the general to the particular serves a twofold purpose: On the one hand, it permits us to gain what, at least in the first instance, appears to be knowledge concerning a particular case that we did not have before. Newton, for example, is able to predict the oblate shape of the earth based on a series of deductions from his premises. On the other, the confirmation or disconfirmation that is attained when our deductions are confronted with actual experience – with, say, the actual shape of the earth as it appears to us through careful observation – is ultimately what provides the basis for holding our premises as true.

It is this definition I have relied upon throughout this book in discussing *reason* and *philosophy*.

With respect to the texts of the Hebrew Scriptures, then, the question of whether they can and should be read as works of reason or philosophy takes the following form: Do they engage in the effort to derive and make known to us the general causes or natures of the things encountered in human experience? Are these general natures used in attempts to establish principles or laws of general applicability concerning the world of our experience? And do these find application in particular cases and circumstances, whether to import knowledge into particular instances, or to substantiate the truth of the principles and laws in question?

As soon as one recognizes, as I have suggested, that metaphor, analogy, and typology are in fact means by which the author of a work can establish positions with respect to general causes or natures, it becomes much easier to see that the great majority of the biblical authors, and perhaps all of them, are indeed engaged in reason; and that it is the exercise of reason they hope for, as well, in their readers. It is this exercise of reason, which we find almost everywhere in the Hebrew Bible, that I've sought to depict in my inquiries into the ethics, political philosophy, epistemology, metaphysics, and faith of the Hebrew Scriptures as presented in Part II of this work.

Notes

Introduction: Beyond Reason and Revelation

1. There were, of course, important voices dissenting from this view. Perhaps most important among the Church Fathers is Justin Martyr, who seeks to place Jesus' resurrection within the order of that which is considered possible by the philosophers. See, for example, Justin Martyr, *On the Resurrection 6*. The neo-Platonist Origen also presents a more complex view. Many centuries later, the humanist strain within Reformed Protestantism largely rejects the distinction between reason and revelation as well. For further discussion of this issue, see Steven Grosby, "Hebraism: The Third Culture," in Jonathan Jacobs, ed., *Judaic Sources and Western Thought* (New York: Oxford University Press, 2011), pp. 73–96; Eric Nelson, *The Hebrew Republic: Jewish Sources and the Transformation of European Political Thought* (Cambridge, Mass.: Harvard University Press, 2010); Yoram Hazony, "Judaism and the Modern State," *Azure* 21 (Summer 2005), pp. 33–50; Fania Oz-Salzberger, "The Jewish Roots of Western Freedom," *Azure* 13 (Summer 2002), pp. 88–132. Yet despite these and other significant variations in the Christian position, I think it is fair to say that a sharp distinction between reason and revelation became normative in early Christianity, and has remained a potent force shaping Christian doctrine down to our own day. The best-known exponent of this rigid distinction between reason and revelation was the Church Father Tertullian, whose views I discuss in Chapter 8.
2. Immanuel Kant, *Religion Within the Limits of Reason Alone*, Theodore M. Greene and Hoyt H. Hudson, trans. (New York: Harper & Row, 1960), p. 116.
3. Exodus 7.1 and many other examples.
4. Isaiah 7.7 and many other examples.
5. Plato, *Sophist* 241d.
6. On the theological and religious character of Parmenides' poem see Werner Jaeger, *Theology of the Early Greek Philosophers*, Edward S. Robinson, trans. (New York: Oxford University Press, 1947); W. K. C. Guthrie, *History of Greek Philosophy* (Cambridge: Cambridge University Press, 1965), vol. II; Sarah Broadie, "Rational Theology," in A. A. Long, ed., *Cambridge Companion to Early Greek Philosophy* (Cambridge: Cambridge University Press, 1999), pp. 205–224.

Guthrie, for example, emphasizes that Parmenides and other philosophers of the period wrote in epic verse, as Homer did. Homer had emphasized that the goddess was speaking through him, and in general, "to a Greek the gift of poetry meant that he was not writing unaided.... This was not metaphor, but reflected a genuine belief in an inspiration whereby the poet is granted deeper insight into the truth than other men" (Guthrie, *History of Greek Philosophy*, vol. II, p. 6).

7. Parmenides' poem appears in A. H. Coxon, *The Fragments of Parmenides* (Assen, Netherlands: Van Gorcum, 1986). The quotes are from Fragment 1, pp. 44, 48.

8. Parmenides, Fragments 9–11, pp. 80–84.

9. Parmenides, Fragment 12, p. 86.

10. Parmenides, Fragment 8, p. 74.

11. Parmenides, Fragment 13, p. 86.

12. Parmenides, Fragment 5, p. 54.

13. Parmenides, Fragment 8, p. 76.

14. Parmenides, Fragment 5, p. 54.

15. Parmenides, Fragment 8, p. 78.

16. Empedocles' poem appears in Brad Inwood, *The Poem of Empedocles* (Toronto: University of Toronto Press, 2001). The passage quoted is from Fragments 9 (3) 10 (131), pp. 214–215.

17. Heraclitus' fragments appear in Charles H. Kahn, *The Art and Thought of Heraclitus* (Cambridge: Cambridge University Press, 1979). This quote is Fragment 118, p. 83.

18. Heraclitus, Fragment 57, p. 55.

19. Guthrie's view, for example, is that "Parmenides was at one with Heraclitus in claiming a prophetic or apocalyptic authority for his teaching" (Guthrie, *History of Greek Philosophy*, vol. II, p. 6).

20. The first Greek philosopher, Thales, lived in Miletus in what is now Turkey. According to one tradition, Thales had himself come to Miletus together with a refugee from Phoenicia – that is, from roughly what is now Lebanon. He was said to have had for teachers only the priests of Egypt, and to have said that the world was "the most beautiful of things, for it is the work of God"; as well as that the gods are aware of all actions of men (Diogenes Laertius, *The Life of Thales* 1, 6, 9). The similarity of his teachings to those of ancient Israel has been frequently remarked upon.

21. Plato, *Apology* 31d, 40a–b. Later readers, concerned to make sure that Socrates' philosophy is kept clean of this divine speech, have sought to limit the action of this god to practical matters. But note in this passage that Socrates himself describes the god as interfering even in the middle of his speeches, so that there is no reason to think it did not also affect his philosophy.

22. Plato, *Apology* 33c; cf. 30a. In the *Theaetetus* Socrates describes his philosophical activity as midwifery, and explains that he has been "compelled" to do this work by the goddess (150c; cf. 150d).

23. For Socrates calling upon gods for assistance in his philosophy, see Plato, *Philebus* 25c; *Symposium* 237a; *Republic* 432c. See also *Laws* 893b; *Timaeus* 27b–d. A famous case in which Socrates explicitly describes his philosophical insight as coming in the wake of an intervention by a divine voice is in *Phaedrus* 242b–d.

24. For further discussion, see Mark McPherran, *The Religion of Socrates* (University Park: Pennsylvania State University Press, 1999); B. Darrell Jackson, "The Prayers of Socrates," *Phronesis* (1971), pp. 14–36.

25. Bertrand Russell, *The History of Western Philosophy* (New York: Simon & Schuster, 1945), pp. 38–58, 89–90.

26. If we refused to study a great thinker every time he disagreed profoundly with our own intuitions, there would be no great philosopher left to study. Think of Plato, with his divine voices, his realm of ideas, his acceptance of infanticide, and his communism. Or Newton, with his alchemy, his belief in the growth of matter, his absolute time and space, his God deducible from the laws of physics. Or Kant, with his claims to have discovered a pure reason independent of human minds, his mystical transcendental deduction, his denial that it is right to lie to save the life of one's friend. Or of William James's belief in the occult, or Nietzsche's assertion that our every action is repeated in an eternally returning cycle. The first thing we learn in reading the great works of the past is that tolerating the counterintuitive is basic to the enterprise.

27. I do not mean to suggest that Christianity was alone in this. In the Middle Ages, Islamic and Jewish thinkers embraced this distinction as well. For example, the great Jewish philosopher Sa'adia Gaon, writing in Baghdad in the year 933, begins his principal philosophical work by introducing a sharp distinction between reason and revelation, and much of subsequent medieval Jewish thought follows Sa'adia in this. See Sa'adia Gaon, *The Book of Beliefs and Opinions*, Samuel Rosenblatt, trans. (New Haven: Yale University Press, 1948), pp. 26–33. Interestingly, Sa'adia suggests that everything that is known by revelation can be attained by way of reason. Nevertheless, he does insist that reason and revelation are entirely different things.

28. This discussion is based on Yoram Hazony, "Judaism and the Modern State," pp. 34–37, 40–42.

29. Wilhelm von Humboldt, "Decline and Fall of the Greek Republics" (1808). Available from the Schiller Institute, http://www.schillerinstitute.org/transl/humboldt_gk_pns.html.

30. Immanuel Kant, *Religion Within the Limits of Reason Alone*, pp. 116, 118. Both the emphasis and the parenthetical "(Greek)" are in the original. Notoriously, Kant argued for a "pure moral religion" as "the euthanasia of Judaism." See Immanuel Kant, *The Conflict of the Faculties*, Mary J. Gregor, trans. (Lincoln: Nebraska University Press, 1992 [1979]), p. 95. For a thorough and chilling account of the role played by anti-Semitism in Kant's philosophy see Michael Mack, *German Idealism and the Jew* (Chicago: University of Chicago Press, 2003), pp. 1–41.

31. "Speaking generally, we have properly only two epochs to distinguish in the history of philosophy … the Greek and the Teutonic. The Teutonic philosophy is the philosophy within Christendom.... [T]he Christian-European people … possess collectively Teutonic culture; for Italy, Spain, France, England, and the rest, have through the Teutonic nations received a new form.... The Greek world developed thought as far as to the Idea; the Christian Teutonic world, on the contrary, has comprehended thought as Spirit" (Georg Wilhelm Friedrich Hegel, *Lectures on the History of Philosophy*, E. S. Haldane, trans. [Lincoln: Nebraska University Press, 1995], vol. I, p. 101).

32. Hegel, *Lectures*, vol. III, p. 22.
33. See Jonathan Sacks, *Crisis and Covenant: Judaism After the Holocaust* (Manchester: Manchester University Press, 1992), pp. 260–270.
34. George H. Sabine and Thomas L. Thorson, *A History of Political Theory* (Hinsdale, Ill.: Dryden Press, 1973).
35. Leo Strauss and Joseph Cropsey, *History of Political Philosophy* (Chicago: University of Chicago Press, 1987); Sheldon Wolin, *Politics and Vision: Continuity and Innovation in Western Political Thought* (Boston: Little, Brown, 1960).
36. To be fair to Rutgers, my teacher Carey McWilliams did think and write more than others about the Bible's impact, by way of Calvin and the Puritans, on America's founders. See, for example, his 1984 essay "The Bible in the American Political Tradition," included in an edited volume by another teacher of mine at Rutgers, Myron J. Aronoff, ed., *Religion and Politics* (New Brunswick, N.J.: Transaction, 1984), pp. 11–45. My dissertation advisor at Rutgers, Gordon Schochet, later became one of the moving figures behind the reconsideration of the Hebrew Bible's place in the history of Western political ideas. See *Hebraic Political Studies* (Shalem Press), the journal Gordon co-edited with Arthur Eyffinger.
37. Sheldon Wolin, *Politics and Vision*, p. 97.
38. Sheldon Wolin, *Politics and Vision*, p. 96.
39. To back himself up, Wolin is satisfied with citing a single passage in the Bible, Daniel 7.9–27. But compare Micha 4.3–6: "Nation will not lift up sword against nation.... But they will sit every man under his vine and under his fig tree, and none will make them afraid ... for let all people walk everyone in the name of his god, and we will walk in the name of the Eternal our God for ever and ever."
40. I refer here to general histories of Western philosophy. Some of the specialized works treating the history of Greek philosophy are actually more alert to the similarities between classical Greek thought and the thought of the Bible.
41. Bertrand Russell, *History of Western Philosophy*, p. 25.
42. As for what Judaism contributed to the history of the West, Russell lists the following items: sacred history; "the existence of a small section of mankind whom God specially loves"; a new conception of "righteousness" ("almsgiving, for example"); part of the Hebrew law ("for instance the Decalogue"); the messiah; and "other-worldliness" (Bertrand Russell, *History of Western Philosophy*, pp. 308–309). But none of these merits further attention in Russell's history of philosophy. As reason, it is all barren. Even the new conception of "righteousness" Russell mentions, which sounds as if it might have had a significant influence in the area of moral philosophy, disappears from the narrative and is lost.
43. Anthony Kenny, *A New History of Western Philosophy* (New York: Oxford University Press, 2007), p. 86.
44. Here is Kenny's summary of the teachings of the Hebrew Bible: "The framework of Jesus' teaching was the world-view of the Hebrew Bible, according to which the Lord God Yahweh had created, by mere fiat, heaven and earth and all in them. The Jews were God's chosen people, uniquely privileged by their

possession of the divine law revealed to Moses" (Anthony Kenny, *New History of Western Philosophy*, p. 86).

45. I suspect that these scholars may feel that they actually *are* dealing with the Bible when they touch on the subject of God as a concept of potential relevance to ethics. Harman, for example, mentions that you can have a "divine law theory" of ethics "which says that right and wrong derive from God's law.... [I]n this view, we care about right and wrong because we care about whether we are going to Heaven or Hell" (Gilbert Harman, *The Nature of Morality: An Introduction to Ethics* [New York: Oxford University Press, 1977], p. 92). And Williams devotes a brief chapter to the question of whether the concept of God adds anything to ethics, coming to the conclusion that it does not because it is "incurably unintelligible" (Bernard Williams, *Morality: An Introduction to Ethics* [Cambridge: Cambridge University Press, 1972], p. 72). But if this is the case, then Harman and Williams are mistaken. Neither of these discussions comes close to touching on the actual ethical teachings of the Hebrew Bible. (On this subject see Chapter 4 in this book.) And I suppose this silence is preferable to philosopher Simon Blackburn's *Being Good: A Short Introduction to Ethics*, which makes no mention of any real contribution (or potential contribution) of the Bible to moral thought either, but does open with two pages on what he calls the "shortcomings" of the Bible's moral conception. His conclusion is tongue-in-cheek, but instructive nonetheless. As he writes: "All in all, then, the Bible can be read as giving us carte blanche for harsh attitudes to children, the mentally handicapped, animals, the environment, the divorced, unbelievers, people with various sexual habits, and elderly women. It encourages harsh attitudes to ourselves, as fallen creatures endlessly polluted by sin, and hatred of ourselves inevitably brings hatred of others" (Simon Blackburn, *Being Good: A Short Introduction to Ethics* [New York: Oxford University Press, 2003], pp. 10–13). I'm sure that if he wished, a scholar of Blackburn's abilities could write a paragraph of this kind ridiculing the morals of Aristotle or Kant as well.

46. John Deigh, *An Introduction to Ethics* (Cambridge: Cambridge University Press, 2010), p. 124. Emphasis added.

47. This explains how it can be that as late as 1987, one Bible scholar could publish a paper proposing the establishment of an academic discipline whose purpose would be "to inquire in a critical academic framework what Tanach [i.e., the Hebrew Bible] is all about" (M. H. Goshen Gottstein, "Tanach Theology: The Religion of the Old Testament and the Place of Biblical Theology," in P. Miller, P. Hanson, and S. D. McBride, eds., *Ancient Israelite Religion: Essays in Honor of Frank Moore Cross* [Philadelphia: Fortress Press, 1987], p. 622; see also pp. 627–628).

48. This way of looking at the Hebrew Scriptures appears to begin with Spinoza, who argues that "the word of God is faulty, mutilated, tampered with, and inconsistent." See Benedict Spinoza, *A Theologico-Political Treatise*, R. H. M. Elwes, trans. (New York: Dover, 1951), p. 165.

49. See Julius Wellhausen, *Prolegomena to the History of Israel* (Atlanta: Scholars Press, 1994 [1885]). Recent years have seen a good deal of source-critical scholarship that retreats from adherence to this rigid scheme of sources. But this

change has had little effect insofar as the study of the ideas of the Scriptures is concerned.

50. Solomon Schecter, "Higher Criticism – Higher Anti-Semitism," in *Seminary Addresses and Other Papers* (Cincinnati: Ark Publishing, 1915), pp. 35–40; Joseph Blenkinsopp, *Prophecy and Canon: A Contribution to the Study of Jewish Origins* (Notre Dame, Ind.: Notre Dame University Press, 1977), pp. 19–20; Jon Levenson, *The Hebrew Bible, the Old Testament, and Historical Criticism: Jews and Christians in Biblical Studies* (Louisville, Ky.: Westminster John Knox, 1993), pp. 1–61.

51. Even the academic discipline of Jewish studies has until now largely avoided the scholarly investigation of the ideas of the Hebrew Bible, usually taking up its pen roughly in the time of Philo.

52. The historian Donald Harman Akenson has pointed out that on the question of the place of biblical ideas in the history of the West, there is no way to get a straight answer from his profession: Ask about it and "soon the query is lost in a squid-like cloud of academic hedging, qualification, redefinition and virtuoso havering" (Donald Harman Akenson, *Surpassing Wonder: The Invention of the Bible and the Talmuds* [New York: Harcourt Brace, 1998], p. 3). Akenson attributes the systematic unwillingness to confront the West's biblical past to "a certain vague and unconscious snobbishness," which prefers "to be descended from patrician slaveholders and master intellectuals than from disputatious Semites" (Donald Harman Akenson, *Surpassing Wonder*, pp. 3–5). The philosopher Walter Kaufman, a leading Nietzsche scholar of the last century, concurred that the story of "the impact of the Hebrew Bible on Western thought and art and literature has never yet been told" because so "much that was Hebrew originally has long been absorbed with such complete success that one no longer thinks of it as having any source at all" (Walter Kaufman, *From Shakespeare to Existentialism* [Princeton: Princeton University Press, 1980], p. 89).

53. Robert Alter, *The Art of Biblical Narrative* (New York: Basic Books, 1981); Meir Sternberg, *The Poetics of Biblical Narrative* (Bloomington: Indiana University Press, 1985).

54. Brevard Childs, "The Old Testament as Scripture of the Church," *Concordia Theological Monthly* 43 (1972), pp. 709–722; Brevard Childs, *Introduction to the Old Testament as Scripture* (Philadelphia: Fortress Press, 1979). See also James A. Sanders, *Tora and Canon* (Eugene, Oreg.: Wipf & Stock, 1999).

55. John Barton, *Understanding Old Testament Ethics* (Louisville, Ky.: Westminster John Knox, 2003); Daniel Elazar, *Covenant and Polity in Biblical Israel* (New Brunswick, N.J.: Transaction, 1995); Michael Walzer, *Exodus and Revolution* (New York: Basic Books, 1985); Aaron Wildavksy, *Moses as Political Leader*, with intro. by Yoram Hazony (Jerusalem: Shalem Press, 2005 [1984]).

56. Joshua Berman, *Created Equal: How the Bible Broke With Ancient Political Thought* (New York: Oxford University Press, 2008); Mary Douglas, *Leviticus as Literature* (New York: Oxford University Press, 1999); Lenn Goodman, *God of Abraham* (New York: Oxford University Press, 1996); Steven Grosby, *Biblical Ideas of Nationality* (Winona Lake, Ind.: Eisenbrauns, 2002); Leon Kass, *The Beginning of Wisdom: Reading Genesis* (New York: Free Press, 2003); Mira Morgenstern, *Conceiving a Nation: The Development of Political Discourse in*

the Hebrew Bible (University Park: Pennsylvania State University Press, 2009); Eleonore Stump, *Wandering in Darkness: Narrative and the Problem of Suffering* (New York: Oxford University Press, 2010); Shmuel Trigano, *Philosophy of the Law*, with intro. by David Novak, Gila Walker, trans. (Jerusalem: Shalem Press, 2011 [1991]); Gordon Wenham, *Story as Tora: Reading Old Testament Narrative Ethically* (Grand Rapids, Mich.: Baker Academic, 2000). I would also include among these Yoram Hazony, *The Dawn: Political Teachings of the Book of Esther* (Jerusalem: Shalem Press, 2000 [1995]).

1. The Structure of the Hebrew Bible

1. I discuss some my reasons for saying this in Chapter 9.
2. Many academic Bible scholars would say that the works I have just mentioned are themselves collections of smaller works (or of parts of smaller works) written by different authors at different times. In this book, I will for the most part avoid entering into controversies concerning the compositional history of the various books of the Bible. For my purposes here, it is sufficient that each of these books can be read as a finished unity, and that this implies the existence, at some point, of a final author or editor ready and able to produce such a completed work out of the sources available.
3. This three-part division is similar, but not identical, to the division of the rabbis into (i) *Tora*, (ii) *Prophets*, and (iii) *Writings*, which appears in the Talmud. The Tora only includes the first five of the sequence of nine works that constitute the History of Israel – the five books whose authorship is traditionally attributed to Moses. The second half of the History is then included in the anthology of the Prophets. See the listing of the works included in the section of the Prophets at Talmud *Baba Batra* 14b.
4. I do not mean that any of these texts is literally a "commentary" on the history, in the sense that it is entirely dependent on it for its substance and meaning. My intention is to use the term much more loosely, to refer to works that appear to have been assembled as comments, reactions, or additions to the History, including amendments and criticism of it. This appearance can of course be quite misleading since some of the material seems to predate the existence of the History as a unified work. Nevertheless, as we have them now, these are works that, as it seems to me at least, are edited and positioned so that they appear to depend on the History and respond to it.
5. Exodus 17.8–13.
6. There is no reason to think that the Orations and the Writings were added to the Bible at the same time. It is entirely possible that the collection of the Orations was added first as a set of commentaries on the History, and that the structure of the Orations was later imitated when the Writings was added. Other hypotheses could be devised that would make sense as well. My intention is only to point out that in the Hebrew Bible as we have it, the Orations and the Writings appear, structurally, as parallel compilations.
7. Exodus 20.18f. The subject of the relationship between the narrative and legal parts of the History is discussed throughout this work, but especially in Chapter 2, Section I; Chapter 3, Section III; and Chapter 8, Sections VI–VIII.

8. For systematic treatment of the question of the coherence of the historical narrative from Genesis to Kings, see David Noel Freedman, *The Unity of the Bible*, pp. 1–39; Donald Harman Akenson, *Surpassing Wonder: The Invention of the Bible and the Talmuds* (New York: Harcourt Brace, 1998). An earlier treatment is G. Hoelscher, *Geschichtsschreibung in Israel* (Lund: Gleerup, 1952).

9. On this view, Moses wrote Genesis, Exodus, Leviticus, Numbers, and most of Deuteronomy; Joshua wrote the very end of Deuteronomy and the book of Joshua; Samuel wrote Judges and the book of Samuel; and Jeremiah wrote Kings. See Talmud *Baba Batra* 14b.

10. An excellent summation of the vast professional literature on the question of the sources used in composing the History is Richard Elliott Friedman, *Who Wrote the Bible?* (New York: Harper Collins, 1997 [1987]). The classic critique of this approach is Umberto Cassuto, *The Documentary Hypothesis*, with intro. by Joshua Berman (Jerusalem: Shalem, 2006).

11. Meir Sternberg, *The Poetics of Biblical Narrative* (Bloomington: Indiana University Press, 1985), p. 13. Sternberg does not, of course, object to historical criticism in principle. In another passage he emphasizes that: "In principle, to be sure, there is nothing illegitimate about the endeavor [of trying] to identify the historical writer(s) with a view to locating the narrative in its proper sociocultural matrix.... Unfortunately, however, this line of inquiry has yielded over the centuries a prohibitive ratio of fantasies to findings, let alone explanations – and not for want of trying or ingenuity but of data on which to exercise them.... The sad truth is that we know practically nothing about biblical writers – even less about the process of writing and transmission – and it looks as though we never will" (Meir Sternberg, *The Poetics of Biblical Narrative*, p. 64).

12. R. N. Whybray, *The Making of the Pentateuch*, p. 15. Or as another scholar puts it: "A purely historical analysis of the [Old Testament] literature cannot yield satisfactory results. Efforts to specify dates for biblical books and to examine them according to their historical sequence are doomed from the start. It has become increasingly clear that no satisfactory history of the literature can be written.... Thus far, no satisfactory criteria exist by which to separate later glosses from early writings" (James Crenshaw, *Story and Faith: A Guide to the Old Testament* [New York: Macmillan, 1986], p. 2). In surveying the scene, Edward Greenstein concludes: "Many contemporary Biblicists are experiencing a crisis in faith.... [We are losing] faith in believing the results of our study. The objective truths of the past we increasingly understand as the creations of our own vision.... [M]odern criticial approaches are no more or less than our own midrash" (Edward Greenstein, *Essays on Biblical Method and Translation* [Atlanta: Scholars Press, 1989], p. 23).

13. In other words, I believe that the academic study of the Hebrew Bible should be conducted in much the way that, say, the study of Aristotle's texts is conducted: Historians specializing in the compositional history of the texts can conduct research of this kind without this necessarily preventing philosophers and political theorists from studying the finished texts as we have them. Such an approach to the Bible has been successfully adopted since the 1980s especially by scholars of political philosophy seeking to understand the political teachings

of the biblical texts, and it has continued to prove its worth in subsequent studies of the philosophy of the biblical texts. On this subject, see the methodological comments of Michael Walzer, *Exodus and Revolution* (New York: Basic Books, 1985), pp. 7–8; Aaron Wildavsky, *Moses as Political Leader*, with intro. by Yoram Hazony (Jerusalem: Shalem Press, 2005 [1984]), pp. 10, 20; Daniel Elazar, *Covenant and Polity in Biblical Israel* (New Brunswick, N.J.: Transaction, 1995), pp. 54–55; Leon Kass, *The Beginning of Wisdom: Reading Genesis* (New York: Free Press, 2003), p. 14; Joshua Berman, *Created Equal: How the Bible Broke With Ancient Political Thought* (New York: Oxford University Press, 2008), pp. 8–9.

14. The outline of this story through to the division of the kingdom in the time of Solomon's son Rehavam is discussed in Chapter 5. The two Israelite kingdoms war against one another and betray one another until finally Israel falls at 2 Kings 17.6, 189–11. The story of the horrifying destruction of Judah's kings at the hands of Egypt and Babylonia is told at 2 Kings 23.29–25.21. See also Ezekiel 19.1–9. This end also appears in Moses' discourses at Deuteronomy 28.36, 29.27. Note that the Bible includes an epilogue containing a further historical account about the years immediately after the fall of Jerusalem in Jeremiah 36–45. This epilogue reads as though it may originally have been intended to serve as the conclusion of the History of Israel.

15. There are scholars who place the composition of most of the narrative before the final destruction of Judah, during the restoration under the Judean king Josiah. See, for example, William M. Schniedwind, *How the Bible Became a Book* (Cambridge: Cambridge University Press, 2004). On this view, it is only the tail end of the story that is written in exile, and then tacked onto an already existing narrative – an approach that doesn't work very well for readers who see the History as an integrated unity whose teachings throughout reflect the end of the story as we now have it. To make a plausible case for this view, it would be necessary to describe the ending that was previously contemplated in the time of Josiah, and to explain how this ending fits together with the teachings of the rest of the work until this point. So far as I can tell, such a proposal has not yet been advanced.

16. Modern scholars have also pointed to Jeremiah or his close associate and disciple Baruch as the central figure associated with the compilation of the unified History. Richard Elliott Friedman, for example, sees Jeremiah, in collaboration with Baruch, as the author of the unified sequence of five books extending from Deuteronomy to Kings. See Richard Elliott Friedman, *Who Wrote the Bible?*, pp. 146–149. David Noel Freedman sees the unified History in its entirety as the work of Baruch. See David Noel Freedman, *The Unity of the Bible*, pp. 70–71. I agree with Meir Sternberg that we do not possess information of the kind that could actually permit us to give a final answer to the question of whether the author was himself Jeremiah, or Baruch, or someone else close to their circle whose name we do not know. See Meir Sternberg, *The Poetics of Biblical Narrative*, pp. 67–68.

17. I don't have any reason to think that the text was initially of much interest to non-Jews, few of whom must have known Hebrew. Like most others, my impression is that this is a text that was written to be read by Jews. But since it

is, as I say, a product of the exile, it is also a text that is keenly aware of what the surrounding nations might have to say.

18. I have adopted the term *Orations of the Prophets* to distinguish the works of prophetic oratory included in this part of the Bible – works such as Isaiah and Jeremiah – from historical works that have traditionally been attributed to prophetic authors, such as Judges, Samuel, and Kings. Traditionally, the historical works that make up the second half of the History of Israel have been called the "Former Prophets" (*nevi'im rishonim*) and the collections of prophetic oratory the "Latter Prophets" (*nevi'im aharonim*).

19. Genesis 20.7. This is the first time the word *navi* is used in the Bible.

20. On the prophet as social critic, see Michael Walzer, *Interpretation and Social Criticism* (Cambridge, Mass.: Harvard University Press, 1993), pp. 69–94.

21. Deuteronomy 18.15–18.

22. Judges 5.14–18. We are told explicitly that before the establishment of the kingdom prophecy was "rare in those days, and vision was not widespread." See Samuel 1.3.1.

23. Modern scholarship has understood Isaiah as in fact being two works, due to the apparently contemporaneous references to the Babylonians in the second half of the book. This view appears in the medieval Jewish commentator Ibn Ezra, who follows R. Moses ibn Chiquitilla in this opinion. See Uriel Simon, "Ibn Ezra Between Medievalism and Modernism: The Case of Isaiah 40–66," *Supplement to Vetus Testamentum* (1985), pp. 257–271. For discussion, see Benjamin Sommer, "The Scroll of Isaiah as Jewish Scripture, Or Why Jews Don't Read Books," in *Society of Biblical Literature 1996 Seminar Papers* (Atlanta: Scholars Press, 1996), pp. 225–242.

24. Sid Z. Leiman, *The Canonization of Hebrew Scripture* (New Haven: Connecticut Academy of Arts and Sciences, 1991), p. 28.

25. On Ezra as a single work including the Nehemia narrative, see Talmud *Sanhedrin* 93b. See also Talmud *Sanhedrin* 38a, where Nehemia is identified with Zerubavel.

26. "Wisdom literature" is a technical term used by scholars of the Bible and the ancient Near East to associate certain works of the Bible, especially Proverbs and Kohelet, with a genre of Egyptian and Mesopotamian treatises and poems seeking worldly wisdom that can be seen as a precursor to Greek philosophy. For an excellent summary and survey of the non-Israelite sources in question, see Michael V. Fox, *Proverbs 1–9: A New Translation With Introduction and Commentary* (New Haven: Yale University Press, 2000), pp. 17–27. In this book I have not used the term "wisdom literature" or the scheme of categories that it establishes. This is not because there is anything wrong with finding a strong resemblance between an Egyptian manual on ethics and, for example, the book of Proverbs. There isn't. But the fact that Proverbs may indeed be similar *in form* to an Egyptian manual on ethics does not mean that it is any more of a work of "wisdom literature" than Genesis or Judges, Jeremiah, or Esther. All these works are works of "wisdom literature," in that they were composed largely in an effort to attain and inculcate worldly wisdom. But this fact ends up being obscured because of a nomenclature that singles out two or three books of the Bible as "wisdom literature," while the entire rest of the biblical

corpus is implicitly held to be something else (non-wisdom literature? anti-wisdom literature?). In this way, the reason–revelation dichotomy ends up being imported into the Bible itself as an instrument for distinguishing a few biblical works from all the rest. I believe this approach to categorizing biblical works should be resisted, along with the common assumption that if it is reason or philosophy one is looking for in the Hebrew Scriptures, then Proverbs and Kohelet must have some kind of special place in the discussion. I do not say this out of any lack of interest in, or affection for, the books of Proverbs and Kohelet. I simply do not see that they can compete with the biblical narratives and prophetic orations, which are by far the largest and most important blocks of material in the Bible, together constituting perhaps five-sixths of the biblical corpus. It is these works that I believe we have to consider first if we wish to study the philosophy of the Hebrew Scriptures. Indeed, I look forward to a time when most of the Hebrew Bible, if not all of it, will be recognized as "wisdom literature."

27. I again use the term *author* loosely to refer to the final author or editor of the works in question. Psalms, for example, is a collection of poems written by at least a number of different authors.

28. Isaiah 2:2–4; Micha 4:2–5.

29. Joel 4:9–12.

30. This view is in some respects similar to that which appears in works such as Benjamin Sommer, "The Scroll of Isaiah as Jewish Scripture, Or Why Jews Don't Read Books," and Israel Knohl, *The Divine Symphony: The Bible's Many Voices* (Philadelphia: Jewish Publication Society, 2003). As Sommer writes, "as one utilizes the findings of modern scholarship, one renews an essential characteristic of Jewish learning. Biblical exegesis in rabbinic and medieval Judaism has always focused on debate and variety.... [T]he post-modern Jew revels in the diverse voices and counter-voices [discovered by critical Bible scholarship] so reminiscent of Talmudic and contemporary dialectic" (p. 238). I do think the Hebrew Scriptures present us with a diversity of voices, and that the editors of the biblical corpus sought such diversity. But my own sense is that in accepting as historical fact the hypothetical compositional histories of the biblical texts proposed by modern scholarship, Sommer and Knohl build their case for the internal diversity of the Bible on documents whose existence cannot be proved, while losing sight of what are in many respects the most important and authentic voices in the biblical corpus – those of the final authors who gave us the History of Israel and other biblical works in the form we now have them – and of the diversity of viewpoints that the corpus of these final works was meant to represent. For alternative views focusing on the works of the final authors, see Brevard Childs, *Introduction to the Old Testament as Scripture* (Philadelphia: Fortress Press, 1979); James Sanders, *Canon and Community* (Philadelphia: Fortress Press, 1984); Dale Patrick and Allen Scult, *Rhetoric and Biblical Interpretation* (Sheffield: Sheffield Academic Press, 1990), pp. 130–139.

31. However, I do not believe that the heart of the biblical teaching is reducible to some one principle or concept, such as covenant, the holiness of God, God's lordship, or any of the other candidates advanced by academic Bible scholars as the putative "center (*Mitte*)" of Old Testament theology. On this, see Jon D. Levenson, *The Hebrew Bible, the Old Testament, and Historical Criticism: Jews*

and Christians in Biblical Studies (Louisville, Ky.: Westminster John Knox, 1993), pp. 54–56. My meaning here is only that it is possible to distinguish those biblical teachings that are emphasized by the authors of the Bible and command relatively broad agreement among them from those that do not.

32. For a compelling presentation of this view, see James Kugel, *The God of Old* (New York: Free Press, 2003), pp. 5–36.

33. Indeed, one may wonder whether the Orations of the prophets would have survived at all had they not been associated at some point with the History.

34. Ezekiel 18.1–23. I don't know that Ezekiel was familiar with the full text of the History as we have it. But if he had known only the text of Deuteronomy, he would have found this theory elaborated there at length.

35. See Yoram Hazony, *The Dawn: Political Teachings of the Book of Esther* (Jerusalem: Shalem Press, 2000 [1995]), pp. 123–143.

36. See, for example, Sara Japhet, *The Ideology of the Book of Chronicles and its Place in Biblical Thought* (Winona Lake, Ind.: Eisenbrauns, 2009).

37. Again, it is worth remembering that not all of the "later" materials postdate the composition of the History. The orations of Amos or Isaiah may have been written later than some of the sources upon which the History is based. But anything written by these prophets would have predated the composition of the History as a unified work.

38. Additional legal material appears in Ezekiel 43.18–48.35.

39. The distinction between the law and the philosophical investigations that surround it is a familiar one in the Talmud. See, for example, Talmud *Hagiga* 14a; *Suka* 28a.

40. On this point, see also David Noel Freedman, *The Unity of the Bible*, pp. 7–9.

41. Ur and Haran may not actually have belonged to an entity called Babylonia in the time of Abraham. But this is not an important fact for the final author of the History, who refers to the city of Ur as "Ur of the Chaldees." See Genesis 11.28, 31. The Chaldeans are the Babylonians, and are referred to using this name repeatedly when they appear as Judah's destroyers in Kings.

42. (1) Genesis 3.23–24; 2 Kings 24.14–16; (2) Genesis 11.1–9; 2 Kings 25.4–10; (3) Genesis 12.1–7; 2 Kings 24.14–16, 25–11; (4) Genesis 22.1–19; Judges 11.30–40; (5) Genesis 34.13–29; 2 Kings 10.15–28; (6) Genesis 37.26–28; 2 Kings 17.1–6, 18.9–11; (7) Exodus 4.1–5, 7.19, 14.15–29; 1 Samuel 17.38–47; (8) Exodus 11.2; 2 Kings 24.13; (9) Exodus 32.4; 1 Kings 12.28; (10) Exodus 33.12–34.7; 1 Kings 19.8–12.

43. This is more difficult to do if one is reading a Christian Old Testament, most versions of which arrange the books of the Bible in a different order from the one I've been discussing. In many Protestant Bibles, for example, the first seventeen works of the Old Testament appear as follows: Genesis, Exodus, Leviticus, Numbers, Deuteronomy, Joshua, Judges, Ruth, 1 Samuel, 2 Samuel, 1 Kings, 2 Kings, 1 Chronicles, 2 Chronicles, Ezra, Nehemia, Esther. This means that the History of Israel, which I have proposed should be seen as the primary literary structure in the Hebrew Scriptures, does not really exist as an evident unity in most Christian Bibles. By proceeding from Kings straight into Chronicles, Ezra, Nehemia, and Esther, the History loses its sharply defined end, blurring into seemingly redundant historical material whose point of view is often quite

different from that of the History. Similarly, the interpolation of the book of Ruth in the middle of the History breaks it up at a crucial juncture and makes it harder to recognize it as a unified story. By the same token, the position of Moses' address to the people in Deuteronomy as the centerpiece of the History is likewise lost. Most important, the concatenation of the competing history of Chronicles directly after Kings basically eliminates the special status that the History is awarded in the Jewish Bible, where it is permitted to stand alone as a clearly defined historical work at the front of the compilation.

2. What Is the Purpose of the Hebrew Bible?

1. As Meir Sternberg writes: "Like all social discourse, biblical narrative is oriented to an addressee and regulated by a purpose or set of purposes involving the addressee. Hence our primary business as readers is to make purposive sense of it" (Meir Sternberg, *The Poetics of Biblical Narrative* [Bloomington: Indiana, 1985], pp. 1–2).
2. It is common to find the Church Fathers saying that the meanings of the Hebrew Scriptures are obscure. Thus, for example, Justin Martyr writes that in the Jewish Bible there is much that is "expressed mysteriously in metaphorical or obscure language or ... hinted at by symbolic actions" (Justin Martyr, *Dialogue with Trypho*, Thomas B. Falls, trans., rev. with intro. by Thomas P. Halton, Michael Slusser, ed. [Washington: Catholic University of America, 2003 (a. 135 CE)], p. 106). Similarly, Origen argued that there is "no taint of human eloquence ... mingled with the truth of the doctrines" of Scripture. As he writes, "If our books had attracted men to belief because they were composed with rhetorical skill or philosophical cleverness, our faith would undoubtedly have been supposed to rest in the skillful use of words and in human wisdom, and not in the power of God" (Origen, *On First Principles*, G. W. Butterworth, trans. [New York, Harper & Row, 1966], p. 267). But are the Hebrew texts in question really any more obscure than the writings of Homer or Plato? I doubt it. Part of the obscurity may be the result of poor translations into Greek and Latin. And part of it is, I believe, a result of the fact that the Church Fathers were already quite removed from the purposes for which these texts were written.
3. Paul Ricoeur, *Essays on Biblical Interpretation*, ed. with intro. by Lewis S. Mudge (Philadelphia: Fortress Press, 1980), p. 50.
4. For example: "From the outset it was clear that, although the Scriptures were held in common with Jews, Christians were claiming a different way of reading them. The old writings had taken on a new meaning in light of the Gospel. Paul contrasted the 'letter which kills' with the 'spirit which gives life' (2 Corinthians 3.6). The Bible had become for the Christian Church a new book" (Brevard Childs, "The Old Testament as Scripture of the Church," *Concordia Theological Monthly* 43 (1972), pp. 709–722, at p. 712).
5. John 1.6–7. Although the tradition of the Church says that the disciple intended in this passage is John the Apostle, this is now disputed. At any rate, the text claims that it was written by a disciple very close to Jesus, as John was.
6. John 21.20, 24.
7. Luke 24.36–37, 46–48.

8. Acts 1.8.
9. 1 Corinthians 15.1–18.
10. This way of presenting the biblical teachings continues to be central to Christian theological discourse in our own time. For example, Brevard Childs writes that "The Christian faith is tied to a particular historical witness.... Our faith is established on the witness of the prophets and apostles, not to history *per se*, [and] not to general philosophical insights available to all men alike" (Brevard Childs, "The Old Testament as Scripture of the Church," pp. 713–714).
11. Dru Johnson has pointed out to me that my description of the New Testament here is most apt with respect to those books associated with Luke, John, and Paul. These texts, however, could be seen as representing a later Christian teaching within the New Testament corpus – one that establishes the framework of witnessing and testimony as normative and then encourages readers to approach the earlier texts of Matthew and Mark in its light. Such a distinction between later and earlier New Testament teachings may be important for Christians who wish to retrieve the earlier (and so perhaps more authentic) Christian teaching, which might not have been as concerned to establish the facticity of Jesus' resurrection, but rather to pursue other agendas (such as convincing Jews that Jesus is the final prophet greater than even Moses). I agree with Dru that the New Testament can be read in this fashion, and that something like this may be the best reading of the early Christian texts. But even if this is right, I don't see this as a challenge to my overall description of the New Testament corpus as we now have it. This corpus is dominated by the framework established in the writings connected with Luke, John, and Paul. Indeed, it is just this framework that is usually meant when Christians speak of the teachings of the New Testament.
12. See, for example, John 8.12–19.
13. Notice that this juridic metaphor sets up a very particular kind of relationship between the text, presented as testimony, and its reader. In this relationship, the position of the reader is that of a judge, as in a court of law, and his role is to evaluate the quality of the witnesses so as to determine whether or not the witnesses' account of what happened is to be believed. Christian readers tended to judge the witnesses credible, to accept their testimony, and to believe their account of events. But when one sits in judgment, one also has the option of concluding that the witnesses are not credible. And this is precisely the path taken in the nineteenth century by the Protestant scholars who developed a school of thought to the effect that the texts of the Hebrew Scriptures had to be seen as being "corrupt" – by which they meant that the biblical texts were (i) seen to contain historical inaccuracies, and (ii) to be internally contradictory. Moreover, the reasons for these inaccuracies and contradictions are imputed to (iii) the impure motives of the authors, who are thought to have tampered with the available testimony to advance petty interests of different kinds. What all three of these criteria have in common, of course, is that they are manifestly juridic in character. They are the kinds of criteria that would be used to disqualify a witness in a court of law. It is precisely this kind of argument that was applied by the new biblical criticism to demonstrate that the testimony of the biblical witnesses could not be credited. In this sense, source criticism of the Bible continued to embrace the juridic paradigm of the New Testament as

the principal framework for studying the Bible. Indeed, what one reads in these books is still the same juridic discourse so familiar from the Gospels: Who are the witnesses? How many are there? How credible are their accounts? Whom should we believe?

14. In this context, it is worth comparing Plato's contempt for individuals who spend their time in law courts. See Plato, *Theaetetus* 172d–173b.

15. Ephesians 3.2–9. Paul's authorship of this letter has been widely disputed by contemporary New Testament scholars.

16. 1 Corinthians 2.6–10. See also 1 Corinthians 4.1; Romans 16.25–27; Ephesians 1.8–10; Colossians 1.25–27, 2:2–3. This Pauline doctrine finds an echo in the Gospels' talk of the "secret of the kingdom of God," at Matthew 13.11, Mark 4.11, and Luke 8.10.

17. This is not to say that Paul presents Christian teaching as consisting only of such hidden secrets that have not been accessible to the human mind. In a number of well-known passages, Paul writes that aspects of God's teaching have been available to man from the creation of the world. For example, in his Letter to the Romans, he writes of the wicked that: "[A]ll that may be known of God by men lies plain before their eyes; indeed God himself has disclosed it to them. His invisible attributes, that is to say, his everlasting power and deity, have been visible, ever since the world began, to the eye of reason, in the things he has made. There is therefore no possible defense for their conduct; knowing God, they have refused to honor him as God, or to render him thanks." Similarly, he writes that: "When Gentiles who do not possess the law [of Moses] carry out its precepts by the light of nature, then, although they have no law, they are their own law, for they display the effect of the law inscribed on their hearts. Their conscience is called as witness, and their own thoughts argue their case on either side, against them or even for them" (Romans 1.19–22, 2.14–15). Such passages make it clear that Paul believed that at least parts of the Jewish teaching, both with regard to God's nature and with regard to the Mosaic law, have been available to men by way of reason, which he also calls "the light of nature." However, the metaphysical and moral insights that he says have always been available to men do not, in these passages, include the hidden secrets that have come to light in the Gospel.

18. It may be asked whether there aren't events in the Hebrew Bible that are also depicted as being of an entirely singular nature, and therefore beyond the reach of reasoned inquiry based on generalization from experience. Ryan O'Dowd, for example, argues that in the History of Israel, "Israel is led to conclude that no such acts as the Horeb revelation or the Egypt deliverance have occurred since creation" (Ryan O'Dowd, *The Wisdom of Tora: Epistemology in Deuteronomy and the Wisdom Literature* [Göttingen: Vandenhoeck and Ruprecht, 2009], p. 41). And understood in a certain way this is right: There is a sense in which the biblical account does leave one with the understanding that the exodus from Egypt and the giving of the law at Sinai are earth-shaking events, and that they are best understood as introducing something new into the history of mankind. This way of looking at the story of the Jews is backed up at times by God himself, as when he tells Moses that "I will do wonders that have not been made anywhere on earth or for any nation." This passage appears at Exodus 34.10.

See also Deuteronomy 4.34. Nevertheless, I think it is a mistake to read Hebrew Scripture as presenting these events as utterly without parallel, and therefore beyond the scope of man's capacity to reason from experience, as John and Paul seem to do with respect to the coming of Jesus. In the Hebrew Bible, the History itself tells us that the giving of the law at Sinai was not unique: There had been a previous "giving of the law" in the time of Noah, which is described in Genesis 9.1–17. And once you notice this other earlier giving of the law, you can see that God's giving laws to mankind is in fact something of a pattern. Adam, after all, receives laws from God, as does Abraham, and Moses also receives laws from God prior to Sinai. So the giving of the law is perhaps better understood as being different from mankind's earlier experience in degree rather than in kind. And the same, I think, is true of the exodus from Egypt: The stories of Abraham in Egypt and Jacob in Aram are both written so as to serve as precedents for the exodus from Egypt – as well as for the ultimate return of the exiles to their land after the destruction of Judah in the time of Jeremiah and Ezekiel. Moreover, the understanding that God may have brought about other exoduses for other nations is explicit in the orations of the prophets, as when Amos writes: "Are you not as the Ethiopians are to me, sons of Israel? says the Lord. Did I not bring Israel out of the land of Egypt? And the Philistines from Caphtor? And the Arameans from Kir?" (Amos 9.7). Similar parallels between the exodus and the history of other nations are drawn in Deuteronomy 2.19–23 and elsewhere.

19. I see this interpretation as having been dominant in the Christian Church from very early in its history and down to our own day, and for this reason refer to it as a Christian reading of the Hebrew Scriptures. Nevertheless, it is important to note that by the Middle Ages, a similar reading of Scripture can be found among Jews as well. Thus Sa'adia Gaon argues that it is the credibility of the eyewitness accounts to God's miracles reported in the Bible that requires us to accept the teachings of Jewish tradition and obey God's laws. See Sa'adia Gaon, *The Book of Beliefs and Opinions*, Samuel Rosenblatt, trans. (New Haven: Yale University Press, 1948), pp. 29–33. In support of this importation of the juridic paradigm into Jewish philosophy, Sa'adia cites Isaiah 44.8, discussed in note 20. But I doubt this passage in Isaiah can support the weight that Sa'adia places on it. A single oration of Isaiah can hardly be sufficient to establish the supposition that the Hebrew Scriptures generally aim to provide eyewitness testimony to the occurrence of miracles so that the belief in the God of Israel and his law may be justified. Not only is the apparent absence of such passages in the rest of the biblical corpus striking, but Isaiah 43–44 is itself hardly unequivocal evidence in support of Sa'adia's argument. After all, what Isaiah is calling upon the Jews to "witness" to in this passage is that "I, I am the Lord and beside me there is no deliverer"; and that beside God, "there is no Rock, none I have known" (Isaiah 43.11, 44.8). There is no reference here to miracles or to the need to bring forward eyewitnesses to miracles in order to authenticate God's teaching and his law. Isaiah's point is only that the God of Israel and his law have in the past brought them well-being and that the Israelites know this, whereas the gods of the nations have done nothing for them and are worthless. One has to go rather far to make of this an actual call to bear witness to God's miracles so that a belief in God may be in this way justified.

20. As far as I am aware, something resembling this juridic metaphor, in which the Jews are called upon to serve as witnesses on behalf of God, appears in the Hebrew Bible itself only in the later part of the book of Isaiah at 43.10, 12, 44.8, and 55.4. In these passages, the Israelites are indeed called upon as witnesses for God in a kind of disputation with the idolaters. The parallel with the New Testament teaching is quite strong here, and it may well be that these verses were the inspiration for the juridic paradigm deployed by the New Testament authors and the Church Fathers. But I don't think that these passages should be considered sufficient to establish the juridic paradigm as an appropriate framework for reading the Hebrew Bible. First, notice that this metaphor would appear to have been deployed by only one of the biblical authors. Its absence from the rest of the Hebrew Scriptures seems to suggest that the other authors of the Hebrew Bible believed their writings could be understood quite well without any reference to witnessing or testifying on behalf of the God of Israel. Second, even these passages in Isaiah only resemble the New Testament juridic paradigm in certain respects. For instance, none of them reads like a call for actual witnesses to miracles literally to step forward and tell of what they have seen, as we find in the New Testament. Rather, the reference seems to be figurative – referring to the Jews as speaking out on behalf of the God of Israel and his law as reliable and beneficial to man, as opposed to the gods of the nations that "cannot profit" in any way (44.10). By the same token, none of the passages in Isaiah refer to Scripture as testimony. Their point seems simply to be that the Jews have experience and arguments on their side that can make the God of Israel and his law plausible in the eyes of the nations.

21. Scholars have argued that the anonymity of the biblical author is intended to dramatize the fact that the speaker is in effect God himself. See Eric Auerbach, *Mimesis: The Representation of Reality in Western Literature* (Princeton: Princeton University Press, 1953 [1946]), pp. 14–16; Meir Sternberg, *Poetics of Biblical Narrative*, pp. 32–34, 46–47, 84f. This is a bold and impressive thesis, but there is no evidence in the text to support this supposition. Indeed, it is doubtful whether any Israelite writer would have presumed to write from God's perspective. Nor is it obvious to me that the authorial voice in the biblical narratives is any more omniscient than that of, say, Homer in the *Iliad*. A better approach to the question of the biblical author's omniscience is Jacob Wright's argument that the anonymous authorial voice of the History was intended to be the voice of the nation. See Jacob Wright, "A Nation Conceived in Defeat," *Azure* 42 (Autumn, 2010), pp. 83–101, at pp. 88–89. Interestingly, when you look closely at the texts of the four Gospels of the New Testament, it turns out that none of them present the identity of their author unambiguously either. This is even true in the Gospel of John, where the author, claiming to be an eyewitness and a personal disciple of Jesus, is assumed to be John himself. Thus the form of the New Testament as a series of eyewitness accounts in which we know the names of the witnesses is to an extent an appearance introduced by the later editors of these works. This is as opposed to the letters of Paul and Peter, whose witness and testimony is associated with letters written in their own names. Thanks to Dru Johnson for pointing this out.

22. Chronicles, for example, reports that the prophet Isaiah wrote an account of the reign of King Uziahu. See 2 Chronicles 26.22.

23. The most obvious exception is Moses' discourses in Deuteronomy, which are explicitly attributed to him by name. Moreover, these discourses do emphasize to the Israelites (presumably the forefathers of latter-day readers of this work) that the wonders of the exodus from Egypt and the giving of the law took place "before your eyes" (4.34–35, 5.2–4, 6.22) so that they might know that the God of Israel is ruler of the world; and assert that the covenant that is based on them is one that is made not only with "him that stands with us here this day ... but also with him that is not with us this day" (29.13–14). With respect to these passages, one can make the case that the History of Israel takes upon itself the task of bolstering the Jews' acceptance of the responsibilities of keeping the law by emphasizing that their own forefathers were witness to certain great events, and accepted the covenant on behalf of them. But even in these passages, in which the Hebrew Scriptures are at their closest to functioning as texts of testimony and witness, they are still quite removed from what we have in the declarations of Paul, who tells us we must either believe the testimony of the witnesses or else give up our faith as null and void. The discourses of Moses in Deuteronomy and the related texts in Joshua make no such declarations. Nor would they have been appropriate. For the covenant between the Jews and the God of Israel does not actually depend on the Israelites having witnessed God's might in the exodus (although this helps). In fact, it does not even depend on the Israelites having accepted the covenant at Sinai, for the simple reason that the Jews have the opportunity to renew the covenant now, in their own time and place, even if they are uncertain as to what actually took place at Sinai. Indeed, this is precisely what happens in subsequent generations, when the people of Israel feel the need to make the covenant with God again, as in the days of Joshua, Yehoiada the Priest, and King Josiah, each of whom was able to effect a restoration of the ancient covenant and its renewed acceptance by the people. See Joshua 24.16–28; 2 Kings 11.17, 23.1–3. For related texts, see Daniel J. Elazar, *Covenant and Polity in Biblical Israel* (New Brunswick, N.J.: Transaction, 1995), pp. 212–213. This, I would suggest, is the actual purpose of the final author of the History, who brings this series of accounts of the renewing of the covenant throughout the generations because he seeks the renewal of the covenant in the exile, in his own day.

24. Jacob Wright, "A Nation Conceived in Defeat," pp. 94–95.

25. See William M. Schniedwind, *How the Bible Became a Book* (Cambridge: Cambridge University Press, 2004), p. 45. But see the alternative view presented by Oded Bustenay, *Mass Deportations and Deportees in the Neo-Assyrian Empire* (Wiesbaden: Ludwig Reichert Verlag, 1979), p. 74.

26. Jeremiah 44.15–18. Compare Deuteronomy 31.17, which holds out the hope that the exiles will reach the opposite conclusion, saying "Are not these evils come upon us because our God is not among us?" Echoes of the people's belief that the God of Israel has forsaken them appear at Isaiah 50.2 and Ezekiel 9.9.

27. Compare Ezekiel 3.11: "And go, get you to the exiles, to the children of your people, and speak to them and tell them thus says the Lord your God, and [see] whether they will listen to you or refuse." A similar view of the exilic background to the biblical texts appears in Edward Greenstein, *Essays on Biblical Method and Translation* (Atlanta: Scholars Press, 1989), pp. 46–47.

28. As discussed in Chapter 1, Section I, my assumption is that the History was composed in the decades immediately after the destruction of Jerusalem. But the argument presented here does not depend on this dating. The concerns discussed here could as easily have been those of an author writing a century later or more.

29. Meir Sternberg, *The Poetics of Biblical Narrative*, p. 31.

30. On the History as a work intended to constitute a community in exile and prepare for the return from it, see Dale Patrick and Allen Scult, *Rhetoric and Biblical Interpretation* (Sheffield: Sheffield Academic Press, 1990), pp. 51–54, 77–78.

31. Genesis 13.1, 33.18; Joshua 3.17.

32. Similarly, the fact that this identity is described as having been forged, not in the land of Israel, but in exile, in the wilderness of Sinai; and that the Jews are therein shown as having possessed an illustrious history as a people, in Joshua and Judges, even without a kingdom, makes the History a work that could offer hope to a people that might otherwise have been convinced that all had been lost. See Jacob Wright, "A Nation Conceived in Defeat," pp. 92–93. Considering the course of subsequent events, there is reason to think that the History achieved its aims. We know that in the century and a half after 538 BCE, tens of thousands of exiles returned to rebuild Jerusalem and Judah under the leadership of Zerubavel, Ezra, and Nehemia, and others. It is possible that for many of them, the enthusiasm to participate in such a cause derived in large measure from their having grown up from childhood in the ways of thought established by the History of Israel.

33. For further discussion, see Chapter 3, Section III, especially note 122.

34. As Isaiah says, "Lord of Hosts, God of Israel ..., you are he who alone is God of all the kingdoms of the earth, for you made the heavens and the earth" (Isaiah 37.16). In the History, too, Solomon, in dedicating the Temple, expands his vision to the men of all nations, suggesting that those who "come from a distant land" to sacrifice and pray at the Temple in Jerusalem, having heard that the God of Israel rules the world with a strong hand, will be heard and forgiven and granted their requests just as if they were Israelites. See 1 Kings 8.41–43. For the Mosaic law as a law for all the nations, see discussion later in this chapter.

35. See my discussion in Chapter 3, Section III; and in the Appendix.

36. Deuteronomy 7.7.

37. The simple answer to the question is that in Deuteronomy, Moses tells the Jews that God has made a covenant with their ancestors and with them; and that even in the depths of exile, he will ultimately hear their cries and return them to their land if they will hold fast to his law. But the biblical narrative is not content to present only the simple version of its teachings. I am here concerned with the broader answer that stands behind this simple answer. See my discussion in Chapter 3, Section III.

38. Genesis 12.1–3. Emphasis added.

39. Genesis 18.19. Emphasis added. Compare the similar promise made to Isaac at Genesis 26.4, and to Jacob at 28.14. When Abraham hears this blessing, God is praising Abraham's understanding of justice. When Isaac hears it, however, God is praising Abraham's obedience: "I will multiply your seed as the stars of

heaven, and will give to your seed all these lands, and in all your seed will the nations of the earth be blessed, because Abraham obeyed my voice, and kept my charge, my commandments, my statutes and my laws." This is in keeping with the tendency of the narrative to see Isaac as being closer to the type of the farmer, Cain, for whom obedience is a principal virtue; than to that of the shepherd, Abel, whose character is recognized in Abraham, Rebecca, and Jacob. See also Bilam's view at Numbers 24.9.

40. In the Bible itself, different theories are presented, the most famous of which is Isaiah's vision of the nations coming to Jerusalem to learn how to govern themselves and lead a righteous life, and to seek judgments in their disputes that will substitute for decisions made through war. See Isaiah 2.2–4; Micha 4.1–5. Interestingly, the classical rabbinic commentators are divided on the subject. R. Nehemia argues that the Jews are meant to become advisors to the nations (*Genesis Raba* 39.12); R. Elazar suggests that the reference is to the converts of all nations who will become part of Israel (Talmud *Yevamot* 63a); and another view suggests that those who are distant from God will be brought closer to him (*Genesis Raba* 39.11). Readings similar to mine appear in Benno Jacob, *The First Book of the Bible: Genesis*, Ernest I. Jacob and Walter Jacob, ed. and trans. (Jersey City: Ktav, 2007 [1974]), pp. 86–87; and Umberto Cassuto, *A Commentary on the Book of Genesis* (Jerusalem: Magnes, 1997 [1949]), vol. II, pp. 313–315. Cassuto is right that the expression *venivrechu vecha* can only be read "will be blessed in you," among other reasons because otherwise the parallel passage in Genesis 18.18 doesn't make sense.

41. Many authors have suggested that the purpose of Genesis 1–11, before the appearance of Abraham as the founder of the Jewish people, is to present a general theory of man's nature. See, for example, Leon Kass, *The Beginning of Wisdom: Reading Genesis* (New York: Free Press, 2003), pp. 9–10. This approach has much to recommend it. Genesis 1–11 does indeed serve as a kind of prologue that permits the reader a general understanding of the world in which Israel is situated. However, we have to be very careful not to assume that this prologue is in any sense a complete entity that can stand alone. Much that appears in Genesis 1–11 is presented only in embryonic form, receiving reinforcement and elaboration in subsequent stages of the History. I would therefore suggest that Genesis 1–11 provides us with a preliminary sketch of man's nature. The general theory of man's nature is perhaps more rightly said to be a project of the History as a whole.

42. I make this point here only in brief. A detailed discussion appears in Chapter 4.

43. Genesis 4.4.

44. Genesis 6.9.

45. Genesis 18.19.

46. In addition to the many examples of just and unjust deeds that are treated as such in Genesis without reference to explicit instructions from God, we have one example of God giving an explicit law to man that presages the Mosaic law. This is the law given to Noah as part of his covenant with God after the flood at Genesis 9:4–7, which reads as follows: "But flesh as it lives, with its blood, you will not eat. And I will surely demand the blood of your lives. At the hand of every beast will I demand it, and at the hand of man. At the hand of every man's

brother will I demand the blood of man. Whoever sheds a man's blood, by man will his blood be shed. For in the image of God did he make man." This brief law makes Noah a precursor to Moses, in that he is depicted not only as living according to vague intuitions of what is right and wrong, but as conceiving of the world in terms of a covenant with God, in which God protects the world from destruction in exchange for man living according to laws that improve the world for men and beasts.

47. Deuteronomy 4.6, 8. Compare Deuteronomy 6.24: "And the Lord commanded us to perform all these laws, to fear the Lord our God, that it might be good for us always, to preserve us alive as on this day." See also Maimonides on these verses in *Guide for the Perplexed* 3.31, p. 321; Leon Kass, *The Beginning of Wisdom*, p. 14.

48. Numbers 24:3. The meaning of the expression *shtum ha'a'in* is unknown, but it would seem to be parallel with *glui einaim* in 24:4, which means that Bilam's eyes are open to see.

49. Numbers 23.8–10, 20–21, 24.5–6. But things don't end so well; the narrative later implicates Bilam in trying to turn Israel from its God. See Numbers 31.16.

50. For discussion of the law of Moses as intended for all mankind, see Chapter 6, Section III; Chapter 8, Section V.

51. Talmud *Yoma* 28b.

52. Talmud *Avoda Zara* 2b.

53. Nevertheless, there are in fact aspects of the Mosaic teaching that are considered too difficult for men – namely, those that relate to God's nature. See my discussion in Chapter 8, Section VII. Thus there may be a distinction to be drawn between metaphysical questions, which could well be beyond our abilities even in principle, and moral and political ones that we have a right to expect men will be able to understand. This distinction in the biblical teaching was first pointed out to me by Joshua Berman.

54. Deuteronomy 29.28, 30.11–15. A parallel passage exists in Isaiah 45.19, in which God is depicted as emphasizing that he has not spoken in secret.

55. This is the subject of Chapters 6–7.

56. The murder of God's prophets is reported in 1 Kings 18.4, 13, 19.10.

57. On man's soul in the Hebrew Bible, see Ethan Dor-Shav, "Soul of Fire: A Theory of Biblical Man," *Azure* 22 (Autumn 2005), pp. 78–113; Ethan Dor-Shav, "Ecclesiastes: Fleeting and Timeless," *Azure* 18 (Autumn 2004), pp. 67–87.

58. Hebrews 1.1f. There are many commentators today who continue to be troubled by precisely this. A common view is that monotheism requires a "comprehensive, consistent revelation.... An inconsistent or fragmentary communication from God would undermine the capacity to be trusting and obedient" (Dale Patrick and Allen Scult, *Rhetoric and Biblical Interpretation*, p. 136). But this approach is an extension of that of the New Testament. The Hebrew Scriptures do not, as it seems, deride the inconsistent or the fragmentary view of God, just as they do not unequivocally insist on trust and obedience. On trust and obedience, see Chapters 4 and 8.

59. Exodus 33.18–23. This issue is taken up at length in Chapters 7–8. On Moses' attempts to understand God's nature, see especially Chapter 8, Section VII.

60. In the Talmud, the rabbis point out that when Isaiah saw the angels about God's throne, they had six wings each, but that Ezekiel describes them as having only four. See Talmud *Hagiga* 13b. As R. Isaac observes in Talmud *Sanhedrin* 89a, "No two prophets prophesy in the same style." Also relevant here is Robert Alter's argument that biblical narrative itself is "a process of studied contrasts between the variously limited knowledge of the human characters," one in which "the characters generally have only broken threads to grasp as they seek their way." Moreover, this is true of prophets as well as other men. As Alter emphasizes: "Dedication to a divinely certified career of visionary leadership is itself no escape from the limitations of human knowledge" (Robert Alter, *The Art of Biblical Narrative* [New York: Basic Books, 1981], pp. 157–158).

61. For a related view, see Mira Morgenstern, *Conceiving a Nation: The Development of Political Discourse in the Hebrew Bible* (University Park: Pennsylvania State University Press, 2009).

3. How Does the Bible Make Arguments of a General Nature?

1. It is often assumed that in order to be able to advance clearly drawn ideas, a narrative work must become intolerably didactic. Thus, for example, the novels of Ayn Rand will resort to characters that are little better than black-and-white personifications of particular virtues or vices, plot devices that spell out the consequences of any given action as inevitable and unambiguous, and – as if this weren't enough – speeches by characters that unequivocally express the general argument that the characters and plot were intended to expound. That biblical narrative is capable of being instructional without resorting to such crass didacticism is one of the principal burdens of Meir Sternberg's *The Poetics of Biblical Narrative* (Bloomington: Indiana University Press, 1985). On this subject, see especially pp. 35–41.

2. John Barton, *Understanding Old Testament Ethics* (Louisville, Ky.: Westminster John Knox, 2003), pp. 24–25. Emphasis in the original.

3. John Barton, *Understanding Old Testament Ethics*, p. 25. See Gordon Wenham's discussion, *Story as Tora: Reading Old Testament Narrative Ethically* (Grand Rapids, Mich.: Baker Academic, 2000), pp. 1–4.

4. Thus, for example, the great German Bible critic Hermann Gunkel believed that the biblical author heartily approved of Abraham lying about Sarah being his wife, and of Jacob's trickery in stealing the birthright from Esau. See Hermann Gunkel, *Genesis*, Mark E. Biddle, trans. (Macon, Ga.: Mercer University Press, 1997), pp. 170, 310–311. Gordon Wenham discusses these examples in *Story as Tora*, pp. 76–77.

5. Martha Nussbaum, *Love's Knowledge: Essays on Philosophy and Literature* (New York: Oxford University Press, 1990), p. 5.

6. I do think there is truth to the claim that narrative is better suited for making fine-grained observations than abstract theoretical discourse. But I don't see this as implying that narrative cannot also handle large-scale abstractions.

7. For discussion of typological categorization in narratives and its implications for philosophy, see Eleonore Stump, *Wandering in Darkness: Narrative and the Problem of Suffering* (New York: Oxford University Press, 2010), pp. 39–81.

8. Genesis 3.17–19, 23, 4.2–4.
9. See my discussion in Chapter 4, Section I.
10. For example, Genesis 12.1, 14.1–24, 18.20–33. On Abraham more generally, see my discussion in Chapter 4, Section II.
11. For example, Exodus 2.11–22, 5.1, 32.11–14.
12. Exodus 12.3–13.
13. Genesis 37.1–50.26.
14. On the type contrast among Joseph, Judah, and Levi, see Shmuel Trigano, *Philosophy of the Law*, with intro. by David Novak, Gila Walker, trans. (Jerusalem: Shalem Press, 2011 [1991]).
15. Genesis 37.2–14.
16. Reuven, Shimon, Levi, and Judah are all shown as failing in their loyalty to their father. Shimon and Levi thrust their father aside and make the decisions against his will when their sister is raped in Genesis 34.1–35.5; Reuven sleeps with Bilha, his father's concubine, at Genesis 35.22. Judah joins in with his brothers in selling Joseph, his father's favorite son, at Genesis 37.18–35 – a scene in which only Reuven tries unreservedly to save Joseph from his fate. Judah's "going down from his brothers" to take up with Canaanite friends and a Canaanite wife, at Genesis 38.1–2, are also hardly positive signs of loyalty to his father, even if there is some regret over Joseph's fate to be found in this apparent withdrawal from his family. Only many years later does Judah redeem himself, in part, by offering to remain a bondsman to Joseph in Egypt in exchange for Benjamin's freedom to return to his father Jacob. See Genesis 44.18–34.
17. See Genesis 39.1–6, 20–23 for Joseph's success with Potifar and the master of the prison. For Joseph's relationship with Pharaoh, see Genesis 41.1–50.26 throughout.
18. See my discussion in Chapter 4, Section III.
19. Genesis 34.1–35.5, 37.18–35.
20. Genesis 46.31–47.4.
21. Exodus 2.1, 11–21.
22. Exodus 32.25–28.
23. Numbers 25.1–15.
24. Joshua 13.33. See also Numbers 18.20, 24; Ezekiel 44.28.
25. Genesis 49.5–7.
26. Joshua 19.1–9.
27. We get to see Joseph's political abilities in pretty much everything but warfare. In this, Moses prefers the abilities of Joshua, who is descended from Joseph's son Efraim, to those of Caleb, who is head of the tribe of Judah. I understand the political leadership of Joseph and Joshua as foreshadowing the superiority of the northern kingdom (that is, the "house of Joseph") over the southern kingdom (the "house of Judah") in political affairs.
28. Genesis 38.11–26.
29. Genesis 44.18–34.
30. Solomon says that in his day not a word has failed of all that God has promised Moses. See 1 Kings 8.56. There is some truth in this. But notice that it is Solomon, and not God, who says it – a pattern that we've seen before in Joseph's pronouncements concerning God's will.

31. Joseph's Egyptian marriage is at Genesis 41.45; Solomon's at 1 Kings 7.8. For Joseph's expropriation of the land of Egypt and the possessions of the people, see Genesis 47.13–26; compare Solomon's enslavement of the Canaanite population, 1 Kings 9.17–23. The advances of the Queen of Sheba, too, appear to recapitulate the story of Potifar's wife's interest in Joseph. Joseph, however, refuses. Whereas Solomon, who we are told "loved many foreign women" as a matter of foreign policy, also "gave the Queen of Sheba her every desire, whatever she asked, besides that which he gave her of his royal bounty." See 1 Kings 1.10.13, 11.1.

32. See my discussion of Solomon and the downfall of the kingdom in Chapter 5, Section IV.

33. 1 Kings 11.28.

34. 1 Kings 12.28–30. It is interesting that while the History mostly blames the establishment of the northern kingdom on the excesses of Solomon and his son, it is merciless in recalling Yarovam's crime of establishing those golden calves. This is idolatry, to be sure, but the reason that this particular act of idolatry becomes a benchmark for the evildoing of the northern kingdom is because of the treason involved: Yarovam manipulated the people's idolatry to ensure that there would never be a reunification of the two kingdoms.

35. Leon Kass goes so far as to suggest that the biblical narrative calls for the rejection of Joseph outright, to the extent of arguing that Jacob, before he dies, decides "the name of Joseph will no longer live in Israel," and "destroys the tribe of Joseph and removes Joseph from among his sons and inheritors" in *The Beginning of Wisdom: Reading Genesis* (New York: Free Press, 2003), pp. 640–659. These quotations are from pp. 641, 645. This conclusion seems to me to be misplaced. A long list of texts throughout the History, the Orations of the Prophets, Psalms, and Chronicles suggest that Joseph not only retains an honored place in Israel, but in fact remains one of the three most important tendencies – together with Judah and Levi – that the biblical authors wish to see allied in the leadership of the nation. Joseph and his name do indeed live on in Israel, as one can see, for example, in the blessings heaped on Joseph in Genesis 49.22–26 and Deuteronomy 33.13–17, in the vision of the reunification of Judah and Joseph in Ezekiel 37.15–22, and in the frequent references to the "house of Joseph," the tribes of the "children of Joseph," and related terms in Numbers 1.10, 32, 13.11, 26.28, 37, 34.23, 36.1, 5; Deuteronomy 27.12; Joshua 14.4, 16.1, 4, 17.14, 16–17, 18.5, 11, 24.32; Judges 1.22–23, 35; 2 Samuel 19.21; 1 Kings 11.28; Amos 5.6, 15, 6.6; Ovadia 1.18; Zecharia 10.6; Psalms 77.16, 78.67, 80.2; 1 Chronicles 5.1–2, 7.29. See also Ezekiel's description of the rebuilt Temple, which includes gates named after each of the twelve tribes, including a gate named for Joseph, at Ezekiel 48.32.

36. The momentary alliance between David and Avner ben-Ner, the Benjaminite head of Saul's armies, is portrayed as being an overture to such an alignment between a Judah-like king and a Joseph-like general. The powerful tradition that God denied David the right to build the Temple due to the blood he had shed would seem, in part, to be directed to his toleration of the murderous Yoav as the head of his armies. Yoav murders Avner, among others, thereby preventing such a consolidation, at 2 Samuel 3.6–39. See Joel Rosenberg, *King and*

Kin: Political Allegory in the Hebrew Bible (Bloomington: Indiana University Press, 1986), p. 168.

37. And indeed, it is the reuniting of Judah and Joseph in some future kingdom that the prophets dream about when they look beyond the exile to some future time of well-being. See Isaiah 11.13–14; Jeremiah 3.18, 30.21; Ezekiel 34.23, 37.15–24; Hoshea 2.2.

38. *Midrash Tanhuma*, Lech Lecha 9; Nachmanides, commentary on Genesis 32.4.

39. Exodus 32.1.

40. Exodus 32.4. This shocking declaration is repeated by Yarovam when he makes the golden calves the northern kingdom is to worship in place of the God of Israel. See 1 Kings 12.28.

41. Judges 6.1–8.21.

42. Judges 8.23.

43. Judges 8.24–27.

44. We need not assume that just because no one makes gods of gold anymore, there are no such gods being made in our own time.

45. Another story that refers to the taking off of earrings is the rape of Dina, which ends with the women and children of Shechem who have been taken captive taking off their earrings and giving them to Jacob. But in contrast with the other two stories, Jacob takes these and buries them under a tree. See Genesis 35.4.

46. See my discussion of these stories in Chapter 5, Section II.

47. Genesis 24.55.

48. Genesis 29.19.

49. Genesis 45.16–20. See my discussion in Chapter 4, Section III.

50. Judges 19.3–10.

51. 1 Kings 11.21–22.

52. Compare Exodus 18.27.

53. Corrupt though Giva was, it was only one town in Benjamin. See Judges 20.1–21.25.

54. Genesis 22.1, 46.2; Exodus 3.4; 1 Samuel 3.4. Notice that in each of these four cases, God speaks the name of the individual he is addressing twice: "Abraham, Abraham," "Moses, Moses," and so forth. See also Genesis 22.11, 27.1, 31.11, 37.13; 1 Samuel 1.3.16; 2 Samuel 1.7.

55. Genesis 22.7. See also Genesis 27.18, where Isaac uses this same charged expression in response to a no less fateful approach from his own son, Jacob. Here, however, the term is loaded with irony, which is delivered by the words interposed between *hineni* and *beni*.

56. Genesis 22.1, 11.

57. See my discussion of this passage in Chapter 4, Section II.

58. Genesis 22.4, 13, 33.1. On this term, see James Diamond, "The Biblical Moment of Perception: Angelic Encounter as Metaphysics," paper delivered at the Shalem conference on Hebrew Bible, Talmud and Midrash, Jerusalem, June 26–30, 2011.

59. Genesis 19.27, 20.8, 21.14, 22.3, 28.18, 32.1; Exodus 24.4, 34.4; Joshua 3.1, 6.12, 7.16, 8.10; Judges 19.8; 1 Samuel 15.12, 17.20.

60. Deuteronomy 4.28, 28.36, 64, 29.16; 2 Kings 19.18; Isaiah 37.19; Jeremiah 3.9.

61. Deuteronomy 12.8; Judges 17.6, 21.25; 2 Samuel 19.7; Proverbs 12.15, 21.2.

62. Numbers 20.5; Deuteronomy 8.8; 1 Kings 5.5; 2 Kings18.31; Jeremiah 5.17; Isaiah 36.16; Hoshea 2.14; Joel 1.7; Micha 4.4.

63. 1 Samuel 12.21; Jeremiah 2.8, 11, 7.8, 12.13, 16.19, 23.32; Isaiah 30.5, 6, 44.9, 10, 47.12, 48.17, 57.12; Havakuk 2.18.

64. Leon Kass, *The Beginning of Wisdom*, pp. 10, 54. Already in the Bible itself, what happens to the fathers is held up as a model for imitation by future generations, as at Isaiah 51.1–2. This doesn't mean that these narratives aren't history as well, for there is no reason that a historical work can't also be instructional narrative. Indeed, many famous works of history, from Thucydides' *History of the Peloponnesian War* to Winston Churchill's *The Second World War*, are written with the aim of transcending the mere recounting of events in order to develop principles for understanding the course of events in general.

65. Robert Alter, especially, has warned against "the condescending preconception that the [biblical] text is ... bound to be crude or simple." As he writes, "[T]he supposedly primitive narrative is subjected by scholars to tacit laws like the law of stylistic unity, of non-contradiction, of non-digression, of non-repetition, and by these dim but purportedly universal lights is found to be composite, deficient, or incoherent.... Attention to the ancient narrative's consciousness of its own operations ... will reveal how irrelevant these complacently assumed criteria generally are" (Robert Alter, *The Art of Biblical Narrative* [New York: Basic Books, 1981], p. 21); see also Tzvetan Todorov, *The Poetics of Prose*, Richard Howard, trans. (Ithaca: Cornell University Press, 1977), pp. 53–65.

66. I've taken this scheme of categories from Barton, on the question of whether the biblical narrative expects us to think that Abraham should have told Pharaoh that Sarah was his sister. As he writes: "As for the writer [of the narrative], he may mean us to approve of the deceit because of the excellent purpose it serves, or to disapprove of the deceit but marvel at the mystery of a God who can bring good out of evil, or to be amused and intrigued but to pass no moral judgment, or to register the change in *mores* since the heroic age in which the nation began. We cannot say with confidence what is the author's intention" (John Barton, *Understanding Old Testament Ethics*, p. 26).

67. My argument in the next three paragraphs largely follows Meir Sternberg, *The Poetics of Biblical Narrative*.

68. Genesis 27.1–45, 29.20–26. Compare the prophet Hoshea's denunciation of Jacob's treatment of Esau at Hoshea 12:2–3.

69. Genesis 37.31–35.

70. Genesis 34.1–35.5, 37.13–36.

71. Judges 11.34–40, 19.26–30. Compare Judges 11.40 with 19.30.

72. R. Nehemia, quoted in the Jerusalem Talmud, *Rosh Hashana* 58:4.

73. Genesis 32.29. See my discussion below in Chapter 4, Section IV.

74. Most strikingly, as discussed above, by God's depriving both the tribes of Shimon and Levi of the right to possess a territory of their own. See Genesis 49.5–7; Joshua 13.33, 19.1–9.

75. Genesis 35.5. Jacob's fear of what the people of the land will do to him ("I being few in number, they will gather themselves together against me and slay me") is pitted against the brother's concern for justice ("Will he treat our sister like a prostitute?") in Genesis 34.30–31. The brothers' moral argument is thus

opposed to Jacob's argument from prudence, which is immediately proved mistaken in the subsequent verses in which we are told that "the terror of God was on the cities around them, and they did not pursue the children of Jacob" in the aftermath of the massacre.

76. The narrative depicts Judah and Joseph as being tempted sexually in consecutive stories, with Joseph successfully resisting, while Judah fails the test. See Genesis 38.11–27, 39.7–20.

77. For Joseph's failure to resist Pharaoh, see my discussion in Chapter 4, Section III.

78. Talmud *Megila* 14a.

79. The Hebrew Bible places Daniel in the Writings together with such works as Proverbs and Kohelet, indicating that the editors of the Bible were well aware that this was not a prophetic work. But many Christian editions of the Bible move Daniel into the same section as the prophetic writings.

80. Mark 4.3–20. Similar passages appear at Matthew 13.1–23; Luke 8.4–15.

81. Augustine, *On Christian Doctrine*, D. W. Robertson, trans. (Indianapolis: Library of Liberal Arts, 1958), 4.8.22. This is in keeping with the style of "esoteric" teachings, which distinguish between the initiates, who are supposed to be able to understand the secrets being divulged, and those who are intentionally left "outside" the circle of the initiated.

82. Much later, this line of argument is picked up by Maimonides, who also writes that the analogies in the Bible are meant as a sort of riddle, which hides the profound and secret teachings that must remain hidden from the multitude: "You must know that if a person, who has attained a certain degree of perfection, wishes to impart to others, either orally or in writing, any portion of the knowledge which he has acquired of these [esoteric] subjects, he is utterly unable to be as systematic and explicit as he could be in a science of which the method is well known. The same difficulties which he encountered when investigating the subject for himself will attend him when endeavoring to instruct others.... For this reason, great theological scholars gave instruction in all such matters only by means of metaphors and allegories.... If we were to teach in these disciplines, without the use of parables and figures, we should be compelled to resort to expressions both profound and transcendental, and by no means more intelligible than metaphors and similes.... The full comprehension of all that the prophets have said is found in the knowledge of the figures, their general ideas, and the meaning of each word they contain" (Maimonides, *Guide for the Perplexed*, Introduction, pp. 4–5). Abravanel goes further, writing of prophetic metaphor with some disdain. See his commentary on Exodus 19.1–3, section 2.7.

83. See Meir Sternberg, *The Poetics of Biblical Narrative*, pp. 49, 51.

84. Note, however, that my subject here is the use of metaphor in the Orations of the Prophets, where metaphor is used in the service of making an argument. There are riddles in the Bible, such as Samson's riddle to the Philistines at Judges 14:14, which are indeed intentionally opaque. But this riddle is not part of a prophetic oration intended, principally, to offer instruction to its audience. The prophets also do occasionally present an opaque metaphor in order to build suspense, and then immediately interpret the metaphor for the audience, as in

2 Samuel 12.1–7; Ezekiel 17.1–24, 37.16–22. This technique is something else entirely from the purposive presentation of metaphors so that part of an audience will not be able to understand as in the New Testament. The position presented here with regard to prophetic metaphor is extended and modified in Chapter 6, Section II, and in the Appendix on the nature of reason.

85. Isaiah 17.11.

86. Compare Proverbs 14.12: "There is a way that appears just to man, and its end is ways of death."

87. See the next verses in Isaiah 9.19–20, in which Isaiah extends his argument both to individuals ("no man spares his brother") and the level of the tribes of Israel ("Menasheh against Efraim, and Efraim against Menasheh; and they both together against Judah"). The passage reads: "No man spares his brother. He snatches on the right but remains hungry, and eats on the left and is not sated, each eating the flesh of his own arm: Menasheh against Efraim, and Efraim against Menasheh; and they both together against Judah."

88. Isaiah 9.17–18.

89. Matthew 13.13–14.

90. Isaiah 6.8–11.

91. 2 Kings 20.1–6; Isaiah 38.1–6. Other examples include Genesis 6.6–7; Exodus 32.14, Numbers 14:11–20; 1 Samuel 14.11, 15.35, 2.30–31; Jeremiah 42.10; Hoshea 11.5–9; Jonah 3.10. Interestingly, both Bilam and Samuel argue that God is not a man, and cannot change his mind: See Numbers 23.19; 1 Samuel 15.29. But the view advanced by these figures is not accepted by the biblical narrative. Samuel's case is especially interesting, since he well knows that God had chosen Saul as king over Israel, and then changed his mind about this. In fact, our text tells us a second time that God changed his mind in the case of Saul only six verses after Samuel informs Saul that God is not a man and doesn't do such things! It may be that Samuel is not being fully truthful with Saul here. In any case, the view that seems normative in the History is that God does change his mind. This view is presented explicitly by Jeremiah: "At a given moment I may speak concerning a nation or kingdom, to uproot it and to pull it down and to destroy it. But if that nation, against whom I have pronounced, turn from their evil, I repent of the evil that I thought to do to them. And at a given moment, I may speak concerning a nation or kingdom, to build and to plant. But if they do evil in my sight, and do not heed my voice, then I change my mind concerning the good I said I would bestow upon it" (Jeremiah 18.7–10). But Jeremiah also accepts the view of the History to the effect that God's judgment is often delayed so that the effects of evil or good appear only in the time of one's children or later. See Jeremiah 32.18.

92. Deuteronomy 18.21–22. See also 13.1–6. For further discussion of this empirical aspect of prophetic thought, see Chapter 6, Section V.

93. As in E. Jenni and Claus Westermann, eds., *Theological Lexicon of the Old Testament*, Mark Briddle, trans. (Peabody, Mass.: Hendrickson Publishers, 1997 [1971]), p. 1154.

94. Genesis 4.3. Emphasis added.

95. For further discussion, see Chapter 6, Section V.

96. Isaiah 11.6, 65.25.

97. Isaiah 19.23–25. Compare Ezekiel 34.25–31.
98. For discussion of the issues surrounding the categorization of these works as "wisdom literature," see Chapter 1, note 25.
99. The mistaken translation of the term *tora* as "law" goes back to the Septuagint edition of the Bible, which usually translates *tora* as *nomos*, the Greek term for law (although *nomos* itself has significantly broader terms and is often better translated into modern English as "custom"). On the difficulties of the Septuagint's translation of the term *tora*, see Louis H. Feldman, *Judaism and Hellenism Reconsidered* (Leiden: Brill, 2006), pp. 58–59.
100. See R. Isaac on Genesis 1.1 in *Midrash Rabah*; Rashi on Genesis 1.1. Abravanel is particularly emphatic on this point, distinguishing between law and *tora*. Law is that which is found in the legal codices of the nations, as well as in the law of Moses. But *tora*, or teaching, is directed to developing man's beliefs. What we have from Moses is thus in two parts, that part which is the law (*dat*), and that part which is the teaching (*tora*). See Abravanel, commentary on Exodus 19.1–3, section 3.
101. These are certainly not the only such metaphors, although they are perhaps the most common. Another is the metaphor of the biblical tradition as the "tree of life," as in Proverbs 3.18; and that of Scripture as nourishment, as in Ezekiel 3.1–3.
102. Jeremiah 5.22, 24, 8.7; Psalms 148.3–6. For discussion of this point, see Chapter 6, Section III.
103. For discussions of the metaphor of the covenant in Hebrew Scripture, see Jonathan Sacks, *Radical Then, Radical Now* (New York: Continuum, 2000), pp. 73–88; David Novak, *The Jewish Social Contract: An Essay in Political Theology* (Princeton: Princeton University Press, 2005), pp. 30–90; Joshua Berman, *Created Equal: How the Bible Broke With Ancient Political Thought* (New York: Oxford University Press, 2008), pp. 15–49.
104. There has been much discussion of the question of whether the model for the biblical covenants is really a voluntary covenant or one that is coerced. For the purposes of my discussion here, it makes little difference. Even when a king forces his conquered subjects to enter into a covenant with him, he is recognizing that without their assistance he will not be able to rule.
105. On God's love for Abraham and Israel more generally, see Deuteronomy 4.37, 7.8, 13, 23.6; Isaiah 43.4, 63.9; Jeremiah 31.2; Tzefania 3.17; Malachi 1.2; Psalms 47.5. The classical rabbinic sources return frequently to the participation of Israel in doing the work that God has not yet completed. For example, R. Berachia suggests that the meaning of Genesis 12.2–3, in which God tells Abraham that the nations of the world will be blessed in him, is that until then God alone has been responsible for bringing blessings to the nations, and from now on Abraham will have this responsibility. See *Genesis Raba* 39.11, as well as *Midrash Tanhuma* 68.
106. For this use of the word *brit*, see Ezekiel 16.8; Malachi 2.14.
107. See Isaiah 1.21, 54.5–8, 57.3–10, 61.10–11, 62.4–5; Jeremiah 2.2, 20, 3.1–25, 13.27, 23.10; Ezekiel 16.1–63, 23.1–49; Hoshea 2.4–10. The Jewish tradition of *kabala*, too, is especially sensitive to the matter of God's vulnerability, and his need of man's assistance.

108. See Joshua Berman, *Created Equal*, pp. 40–46.
109. Proverbs 1:8. See also Proverbs 3.1; Psalms 78.1. The father's teaching at Passover is called "God's *tora*" at Exodus 13.9.
110. On the role of the father as instructor, see, for example, Exodus 13.9; Deuteronomy 32.7, 46–47, 1 Kings 2.2–3; Isaiah 38.19; Psalms 78.3–8; Proverbs 23.22–26, 27.3.
111. The metaphor of God as a father and teacher appears at Deuteronomy 8.5; Jeremiah 3.4, 19, 31.8, 17–19; Isaiah 1.2, 30.20–21, 63.16–17; Hoshea 11.1–5; Psalms 90.12, 132.12; Proverbs 3.12.
112. Genesis 1.26. See also 9.6.
113. Genesis 2.19.
114. Genesis 2.15.
115. Genesis 1.28.
116. Genesis 1.26–28.
117. Genesis 1.29, 2.16–17.
118. See my discussion in Chapter 4.
119. Yehezkel Kaufmann suggests that man's freedom to make moral choices, whether right or wrong, is that which sets the Bible apart from the religions of the ancient Near East. See Yehezkel Kaufmann, *The Religion of Israel: From Its Beginnings to the Babylonian Exile* (New York: Schocken, 1972 [1960]), p. 76.
120. As far as I can tell, the Bible makes no claim to the effect that God is perfect being. The argument for God's perfection enters the Western tradition through the philosophy of Greek thinkers such as Xenophanes, Parmenides, and Plato (in the *Timaeus*). For the incompatibility of the doctrine of God's perfection with the Bible, see Eliezer Berkovits, *God, Man and History* (Jerusalem: Shalem, 2004 [1959]), pp. 58–67. The idea of God's perfection is, perhaps, compatible with a reading of Scripture as law. But the concept of the covenant, which depends essentially on recognition of God's weakness, cannot, so far as I can see, be reconciled with the doctrine of God's perfection under any circumstance.
121. On mankind's partnership with God in the creation of the world, see Talmud *Shabat* 10a. See also Joseph Isaac Lifshitz, "Secret of the Sabbath," *Azure* 10 (Winter 2001), pp. 85–117.
122. The dynamics of these relationships are sometimes reported in the Bible, as when the king of Moav succeeds in defeating Israel in battle, as it appears thanks to the timely sacrifice as a burnt offering to his god of "his eldest son who should have reigned in his stead" (1 Kings 3.26–27). King Hezekiah of Judah and the victorious king of Assyria, too, point to the similarity between God's promises and those made by the gods of the various nations that the Assyrians have already defeated at 2 Kings 19.17–18; Isaiah 36.18–19. Joshua Berman's study of this point emphasizes that among Israel's neighbors, covenants were established between a god and the king who served him, but virtually never between a god and a people as is the case in Hebrew Scripture. Berman suggests that there may be a single parallel case known to scholars among the Phoenicians, but he is skeptical even of this. See Joshua Berman, *Created Equal*, p. 187 n. 101. I am not sure Berman is entirely correct in his interpretation of the facts available.

A famous stele of a Moabite king known as the "Mesha Stele," for example, records the sentiment that "Omri was king of Israel and he oppressed Moab for many days because Kemosh was angry with his land." The anger of the Moabite god is directed here not only against the king of Moav but against the entire land. See William Foxwell Albright, *The Proto-Sinaitic Inscriptions and their Decipherment* (Cambridge, Mass.: Harvard University Press, 1969), pp. 320–21. The king of Moav may therefore be the partner of the Moabite god in this treaty, and yet the land of Moav enters into the matter anyway because the king of Moav is not acting as a private person. I don't think Berman needs to prove this point in order for his own argument concerning the uniqueness of the God of Israel's direct covenantal relationship with each and every Israelite to be accepted. He is right on this. But I do not think we need to go so far as to insist that Near Eastern gods stood in a relationship with their kings as individuals, and not with their kings as representing the nations over which they ruled.

123. Jeremiah 44.15–19.
124. See note 100.
125. The reasons given for the Noahide covenant relate to the problematic nature of all of mankind. See Genesis 6:5, 8:21. These reasons provide the most general basis for the Noahide law of Genesis 9:3–7; see also Talmud *Yoma* 28b.

4. The Ethics of a Shepherd

1. This assumption dominates the academic literature on the ethics of the Hebrew Bible. See, for example, Walter Eichrodt, *Theology of the Old Testament* (London: SCM Press, 1967), vol. II, p. 316; Johannes Hempel, *Das Ethos des Alten Testaments* (Berlin: Verlag Alfred Töpelmann, 1964), pp. 189–192; Eliezer Schweid, "The Authority Principle in Biblical Morality," *Journal of Religious Ethics* 8 (1980), pp. 180–203. Even Genesis is read by biblical scholars as a kind of treatise on obedience. As Brevard Childs writes, "The life of obedience is illustrated in these [patriarchal] narratives – given long before the Law – which call for unswerving trust in the faithfulness of God.... God's revelation of himself to the fathers is an act of pure grace which calls forth the required stance of faithful obedience" (Brevard Childs, "The Old Testament as Scripture of the Church," *Concordia Theological Monthly* 43 [1972], pp. 709–722, at p. 718).

    This reading of the Bible is the counterpart to a position in recent analytic philosophy called Divine Command Ethics. See, for example, Robert M. Adams, "A Modified Divine Command Theory of Ethical Wrongness," reprinted in *The Virtue of Faith* (New York: Oxford University Press, 1987 [1973]), pp. 97–122; Philip L. Quinn, *Divine Commandments and Moral Requirements* (New York: Oxford University Press, 1978); Philip L. Quinn, "The Recent Revival of Divine Command Ethics," *Philosophy and Phenomenological Research* 50 Supplement (Autumn 1990), pp. 345–365. Philosophical introductions to the study of ethics likewise leave the impression that biblical ethics is about divine commands and obedience. See, for example, Gilbert Harman, *The Nature of Morality: An Introduction to Ethics* (New York: Oxford University Press, 1977), pp. 92–93; John Deigh, *An Introduction to Ethics* (Cambridge: Cambridge University Press, 2006), pp. 123–125.

2. Genesis 4.10–12.
3. Genesis 6.5–8, 13 and 18.20f. Additional examples of the God of Israel as judging the nations, although they have presumably not received commands from
   God concerning his laws, include Genesis 15.14, 16, 20.4; Deuteronomy 8.5,
   18.12, among many others.
4. Genesis 3.12, 9.20–21, 9.22.
5. Genesis 19.30–36, 34.1–4, 29.13–31.43; Exodus 1.8–15.
6. Genesis 18.25.
7. The view that the biblical narrative reflects such a natural law teaching that
   is accessible to human reason is a common one in traditional Jewish exegesis. See, for example, Nachmanides on Genesis 6.1, 13; Hizkuni on Genesis
   7.21; Yehuda Halevi, *Kuzari* 2.48; Netziv of Volozhin, Introduction to *He'emek
   Davar*; R. Moshe Feinstein, *Igrot Moshe*, "Yoreh De'ah," 2.130 on Genesis
   3.12. See also discussion in David Novak, *Natural Law in Judaism* (Cambridge:
   Cambridge University Press, 1998). Nevertheless, a familiar reading of the history of Western thought sees natural law theories as having originated with Stoic
   texts such as Cicero (106–43 BCE), *De Legibus* 1.58, 2.11. The most prominent
   academic scholar arguing for a biblical natural law teachings has been John
   Barton, *Understanding Old Testament Ethics* (Louisville, Ky.: Westminster John
   Knox Press, 2003). Barton's argument is focused on the prophetic orations.
8. See my discussion in Yoram Hazony, "The Jewish Origins of the Western
   Disobedience Tradition," *Azure* (Summer 1998), pp. 17–74.
9. The only explicit instructions given to man prior to the advent of the conflict
   between farmer and shepherd in Genesis 4 seem to be the command to multiply
   and master the earth (Genesis 1.28); the command to till the garden and preserve it (Genesis 2.15); and the command to refrain from eating from the fruit
   of the tree of knowledge of good and evil (Genesis 2.16).
10. Exodus 19.16, 18; Joshua 6.5. See also 1 Samuel 13.3.
11. Exodus 13.5, 16.3.
12. Numbers 14.33. This verse is unfamiliar to English readers because it is usually
    translated as "And your children will wander [*yihiu ro'im*] in the wilderness
    forty years." But *ro'im* literally means "shepherds," and the verse should actu-
    ally read: "And your children will be shepherds in the wilderness forty years,"
    just as Moses was a shepherd in Midian forty years before he found God. See
    the commentaries of Rashbam, Ibn Ezra, and Hizkuni.
13. References to David as a shepherd include 1 Samuel 16.11, 19, 17.15, 20, 28,
    34, 40, 54; 2 Samuel 5.2, 7.8. The young David's unfamiliarity with good weap-
    ons is not particular to him, for we are told that at that time, the Philistines,
    who knew metallurgy, would only sharpen the Israelites' farming tools. Israel
    had neither sword nor spear to fight with. See 1 Samuel 13.19–22.
14. Genesis 46.33–47.3.
15. 1 Samuel 17.28, 40, 54.
16. Modern Bible scholarship has taken notice of the prevalence of shepherding
    imagery in the Hebrew Bible, often concluding that ancient Israelite texts deploy
    the shepherd as the symbol of the benevolent political ruler, who successfully
    cares for his people as a shepherd cares for his obedient flock. This is the way
    that this symbol is thought to have been used in ancient Mesopotamia, Egypt,

and Greece, and the metaphor of the shepherd is also used this way in the Bible, especially in the Orations and the Writings. See, for example, Ezekiel 34.1–31, where the benevolent political ruler is the God of Israel. See Jack Vancil, "Sheep, Shepherd," in David Noel Freedman, ed., *Anchor Bible Dictionary* (New York: Doubleday, 1992), vol. V, pp. 1187–1190. Vancil notes that in the Greek pastoral poetry of Theocritus (third century BCE), the shepherd also functions as a symbol of the retreat to nature, and of resisting the allure of the city. But he recognizes no biblical parallel.

17. Genesis 3.17–19, 23.
18. The curse appears again in Genesis 4.11, 5.29. R. David Kimche argues, correctly I think, that the curse on the soil here is meant to be a curse that is still in place in our own time. See his comment on Genesis 4.12.
19. Compare Genesis 2.15, where God places man in the garden of Eden "to work the garden and keep it." God's conception of man as being tied intrinsically to agriculture thus runs much deeper than the exile from the garden and the curse on the soil. I am indebted to James Diamond for this observation. But note that the word *avoda* is also the principal biblical term for worship, so the expression "serve the ground" is also heavy with connotations of idolatry. This connotation goes back to the use of the same term with reference to Adam's work in Eden.
20. Genesis 4.2.
21. There is reason to think that the killing of Abel is not premeditated, since the punishment of exile, rather than death, is prescribed in the Mosaic law for manslaughter. See R. David Kimche on Genesis 4.12.
22. See Michael Fishbane, *Biblical Text and Texture* (Oxford: Oneworld, 2003 [1979]), pp. 24–25, 31.
23. The explanation often offered is that in reporting that "Abel also brought from the firstborn of his flock and from their fatty parts" (Genesis 4.4), the text intends to signal that Abel brought the best of his flock, while Cain brought less desirable parts of his produce. See, for example, R. David Kimche on Genesis 4.3. But this can't be right. The "also" (which in Hebrew, *gam hu*, carries a double emphasis) just as easily suggests that Abel was bringing from the first of his flock just as Cain had brought from the first of his produce when he sacrificed.
24. This is implied by the Hebrew "Abel became [*vayehi hevel*] a keeper of sheep" – Abel turned into a shepherd, whereas Cain stayed what his family had been, namely, farmers.
25. See Rashi on Genesis 4.2, which links Abel's decision to the curse on the soil. See also Seforno's comment on Genesis 4.2, to the effect that shepherding requires more intelligence, and so is a turn away from the menial labor involved in farming. Abravanel on Genesis 4.1–8 likewise recognizes that Abel's choice involves a rebellion against the constant involvement with man's material needs, the coarse and the vulgar, and sees him as a slave of the soil. The turn to shepherding, on the other hand, reflects an effort at self-improvement. But Abravanel's reading of shepherding as being a turn toward the political life of man seems to me to have little or no resonance in the History. As discussed, this understanding of the shepherding metaphor does appear in the Orations of the Prophets and in the Writings. But I think it is a mistake to introduce it here.

In the type contrast advanced by the History, it is farming that represents the great political empires of the Near East, whereas shepherding is to an extent an escape from this. Indeed, it is quite significant that the most political of Jacob's sons, Joseph, is the one who is attracted to agriculture.

26. Jonathan Silver has pointed out to me that Rousseau makes almost exactly this distinction between shepherds and farmers, and reads the conflict between them as appearing in the biblical story of Cain and Abel as I do here. As Rousseau has it: "Human industry expands with the needs that give rise to it. Of the three ways of life available to man, hunting, herding, and agriculture, the first develops strength, skill, speed of body, courage and cunning of soul, it hardens man and makes him ferocious. The land of the hunters does not long remain that of the hunt. Game has to be pursued over great distances, hence horsemanship. Game that flees has to be caught, hence light arms, the sling, the arrow, the javelin. The pastoral art, father of repose and of the indolent passions, is the most self-sufficient art. It almost effortlessly provides man with food and clothing: It even provides him with his dwelling; the tents of the first shepherds were made of animal skins: so were the roofs of the ark and the tabernacle of Moses. As for agriculture, it arises later and involved all the arts; it introduces property, government, laws, and gradually wretchedness and crimes, inseparable for our species from the knowledge of good and evil. Hence the Greeks viewed Triptolemus not merely as the inventor of a useful art, but as a founder and a wise man to whom they owed their first education and their first laws. Moses, on the other hand, appears to have disapproved of agriculture by attributing its invention to a wicked man and making God reject his offerings: The first tiller of the ground would seem to have proclaimed by his character the bad effects of his art. The author of Genesis had seen farther than had Herodotus" (Jean-Jacques Rousseau, "Essay on the Origins of the Languages," in Victor Gourevitch, ed., *The Discourses and Other Early Political Writings* [Cambridge: Cambridge University Press, 1997], pp. 247–299, at pp. 271–272).

27. On Abel's turn to shepherding as self-improvement, see Abravanel on Genesis 4.1–8. Compare Hermann Gunkel, *Genesis*, Mark E. Biddle, trans. (Macon, Ga.: Mercer University Press, 1997), pp. 42–43.

28. Genesis 4.6–7.

29. Abel's sacrifice also finds an echo in Abraham's sacrifice of a ram on Mount Moria, which frees man from human sacrifice. See Section II. Similarly, it prefigures Moses' command to the Hebrew slaves in Egypt, who have also become "servants of the soil," to sacrifice a sheep and be free. See Exodus 12.3–11, 21–23.

30. Genesis 4.16–17.

31. Scholars have traditionally used the name "Babylonia" only for the southern part of Mesopotamia, and "Assyria" for the northern part. But see Jean Bottéro, *Mesopotamia: Writing, Reasoning and the Gods*, Zainab Bahrani and Marc van de Mieroop, trans. (Chicago: Chicago University Press, 1992 [1987]), pp. 1–2, 48. Bottéro argues that Assyria "was always culturally dependent on Bablylonia, even starting in the mid-second millennium.... Our sources, from the earliest moment that we have them, reveal nothing but one coherent civilization." In this civilization, "history was centered around the city of Babylon from about

1,760 on." Because the Hebrew Bible purposely associates the Babylonians who destroy Judah and Jerusalem with Abraham's place of origin in Babylonia, I will use this term loosely and interchangeably with the term "Mesopotamia," which is preferred by scholars.

32. See Karl A. Wittfogel, *Oriental Despotism: A Comparative Study of Total Power* (New Haven: Yale University Press, 1957). A relevant parallel appears in the following passage from the Hindu scriptures: "The whole world is kept in order by punishment.... If the king did not, without tiring, inflict punishment on those worthy to be punished, the stronger would roast the weaker like fish on a spit: The crow would eat the sacrificial cake and the dog would lick the sacrificial viands, and ownership would not remain with anyone, and the lower ones would usurp the place of the higher ones.... Punishment alone governs all created beings, punishment alone protects them, punishment watches over them while they sleep.... Punishment is ... the king" (*The Laws of Manu*, G. Bühler, trans. [Delhi: Motilal Banarsidass, 1962], book 7, sections 16–22, pp. 219–220).

33. Genesis 11.1–4.

34. Genesis 43.32, 46.34. Kass suggests that for the Israelites the word *to'eva* ("abomination") refers to "those activities that deny or efface the fundamental distinctions of creation: Child sacrifice, which makes a child into an animal; bestiality, which makes an animal into a human being; homosexual sodomy, which makes a man into a woman; and idolatry, which makes an animal or some other creature or object into a god" (Leon Kass, *The Beginning of Wisdom: Reading Genesis* [New York: Free Press, 2003], p. 625). But this same word is attributed to the Egyptians as they view shepherds in general, and Israel in particular. For Egypt, it would seem that *to'eva* is that which refuses the order and obedience imposed by god and king.

35. See John W. Flight, "The Nomadic Ideal in the Old Testament," *Journal of Biblical Literature* 42 (1923), pp. 158–226, esp. pp. 213f.; Jon D. Levenson, *Sinai and Zion* (New York: Harper & Row, 1985), pp. 19–23.

36. The biblical narrative's hesitations concerning farming are reflected in *Genesis Raba* 22.3.

37. Genesis 11.31–32; Nahmanides on Genesis 12.1. Nevertheless, God says he brought Abraham out of Ur in Genesis 15.7.

38. Genesis 15.7.

39. God changes Abraham's name from Avram (Abram) to Avraham (Abraham) in Genesis 17.5.

40. Genesis 12.1–3.

41. Genesis 12.8.

42. Genesis 18.18–19. See also 22.18, 26.4.

43. Genesis 24.1. We need not accept the assessment of Eleazer of Damascus, who in trying to impress Abraham's kinsmen counts these blessings in terms of livestock, servants, silver, and gold. See Genesis 24.35.

44. Genesis 12.11–13, 16.1–6, 17.17–18, 20.2.

45. Genesis 18.18–19. See also 22.18.

46. Genesis 13.9–11, 18.1–8, Abraham's generosity to guests being the opposite of what was to be found in Sodom, for which it was destroyed; compare Rebecca, Genesis 24.18–20.

47. Genesis 14.11–17, 18.23–25, 21.11.
48. Genesis 14.21–24, 21.25–30, 23.6–20.
49. Genesis 12.7, 8, 13.4, 18, 17.23, 21.33. Abraham's trust in God is mentioned at Genesis 15.6; compare with Hagar at 16.13–14. On the subject of Abraham's trust in God, see Chapter 8, Sections VI–VIII.
50. Genesis 21.22.
51. Genesis 19.1–9.
52. Genesis 14.21–24.
53. Genesis 21.25–30.
54. Genesis 23.6–20.
55. 1 Samuel 1.12–17, 22–25, 8.1–3; 1 Kings 21.1–24.
56. Genesis 15.8.
57. Genesis 14.13.
58. Genesis 21.25. This is in contrast to Isaac, who is much less inclined to take a hard line, and goes and digs more wells when the Philistines fight him for them. See Genesis 26.17–22.
59. See Genesis 16.1–16, 21.1–21. The willingness to expose one's wife or daughter to the sexual predations of others is central to both of the story of the destruction of Sodom and that of the concubine in Giva. In both, this trait is seen as indicating that the evil of the city has risen to such a point that it must be destroyed. It therefore seems unlikely to me that there is any point in seeking to justify Abraham's behavior. I believe, rather, that this story of Abraham's treatment of Sarah is punished by Sarah's willingness to abuse Abraham by thrusting her bondwoman upon him – an act that results in much suffering for both.
60. Examples of such strife are the fights between Abraham's men and Lot's in Genesis 13.7; between Abraham's and Avimelech's in 21.25; and the constant fighting between Isaac's men and Avimelech's in 26.20–21.
61. Leon Kass, *The Beginning of Wisdom*, p. 322.
62. Genesis 24.15–20.
63. Genesis 24.29–30.
64. Genesis 18.25.
65. I do not know of any case in which a biblical figure is struck down for what he says to God. The Hebrew Bible seems not to think of God as taking people's lives for what they say in conversation with him. But the God of Israel does take the lives of individuals guilty of sacrilege, as at 2 Samuel 6.6–7.
66. See Leviticus 18.21, 20.2; Deuteronomy 12.31, 18.10; Judges 11.34–40; 2 Kings 3.27, 16.3, 17.17, 21.6, 23.10; Isaiah 57.5; Jeremiah 7.31, 19.4–6; Ezekiel 16.20–21, 36, 20.26, 23.37–39; Hoshea 13.2; Psalms 106.37–38. On child sacrifice in extra-biblical sources, see Lenn Goodman, *God of Abraham* (New York: Oxford University Press, 1996), pp. 19–20.
67. Genesis 12.12, 20.1–2.
68. 1 Samuel 22.9–19; 2 Samuel 11.14–17.
69. These phrases are drawn from Edward Kessler, *Bound by the Bible: Jews, Christians and the Sacrifice of Isaac* (Cambridge: Cambridge University Press, 2005), p. 5.
70. For discussion, see Jon D. Levenson, *The Death and Resurrection of the Beloved Son: The Transformation of Child Sacrifice in Judaism and Christianity* (New Haven: Yale University Press, 1995).

71. Most obviously in Abraham's challenge: "Will not the judge of the entire world do right?" and in the destruction of Sodom for its sins.

72. Ze'ev Levy, "On the Aqedah in Modern Philosophy," *Journal of Jewish Thought and Philosophy* (2007), pp. 85–108; Lenn Goodman, *God of Abraham*, p. 21.

73. Genesis 22.13. See *Genesis Raba* 56.9, opinion of R. Bunai quoted by R. Judan. The prophet Hoshea pungently describes the alternative: "[T]hey who sacrifice men, kiss calves" (Hoshea 13.2). The context for the prophet's speeches is the downfall of the northern kingdom, whose symbol was the two golden calves that Yarovam made for his people, so that it may be these calves Hoshea has in mind. But either way, the image accuses Israel of having reversed the tradition of Abraham, in which one sacrifices the animal and kisses the child.

74. Genesis 22.1.

75. Circumcision, as Leon Kass, puts it, is a form of "partial sacrifice." See Leon Kass, *The Beginning of Wisdom*, p. 334.

76. Abraham once again demonstrates that he is willing to sacrifice Sarah's chastity to save his own life in Gerar at Genesis 20.1–2. See also the bread and water that he sends away with Hagar and Ishmael at Genesis 21.14, in a passage that parallels the binding of Isaac in a number of ways.

77. Genesis 22.2.

78. Leviticus 18.21, 20.2; Deuteronomy 12.29–31, 18.10.

79. *Midrash Raba* 56.8 cites the view of R. Aha that at Moria, God tells Abraham: "Did I tell you to slaughter him? No. I said to 'take him up' [*veha'alehu*]. You have taken him up. Now take him down." I don't believe the point here is that God was actually playing word games. Rather, the rabbis emphasized that God never intended for Abraham to slaughter his son. Similarly, see Talmud *Ta'anit* 4a. I haven't yet seen an opinion in the rabbinic literature that dissents from this view.

80. This horrifying line of argument has gained currency in part because the New Testament appears to be committed to this view, with the Letter to the Hebrews suggesting that Abraham believed he could slaughter his son since God has the power to resurrect the dead: "By faith, Abraham offered up Isaac ... his only son.... For he reckoned that God had the power even to raise from the dead – and from the dead, he did, in a sense, receive him back" (Hebrews 11.17–19). This consideration of Isaac's possible resurrection comes from the implicit parallel drawn here between Isaac and Jesus: Just as God was willing to sacrifice "his only son," so too was Abraham. And because Jesus was then resurrected from the dead, it becomes plausible to think that Isaac might have been. This view is defended, among others, by Eleonore Stump, who argues that Abraham could only pass God's test if he had perfect faith that "even if he sacrifices Isaac, Isaac will live and flourish.... Abraham has to also believe that in sacrificing Isaac, he will do Isaac no harm" (Eleonore Stump, *Wandering in Darkness: Narrative and the Problem of Suffering* [New York: Oxford University Press, 2010], p. 300). I am afraid that in introducing this New Testament trope, advocates of this view risk missing the entire point of the story, which is that the God of Israel, unlike other gods of Canaan, would never will the murder of an innocent person. The sacrifice of children is, as I've said, described in Leviticus and Deuteronomy as that which God hates, that for which the Canaanites are to be

expelled from their land and, indeed, put to death. Hebrew Scripture knows of no happy results that can come about after Isaac is dead.

81. Genesis 22:5–8. The famously compressed language of the Hebrew Scriptures is compressed here as well, just as Eric Auerbach says it is. See *Mimesis: The Representation of Reality in Western Literature*, Willard Trask, trans. (Princeton: Princeton University Press, 1953 [1946]), pp. 3–23. But the sparseness of detail permits something that Homer's text, for example, does not, which is a very great precision in communicating to the reader which details are important enough to merit consideration. Auerbach misses this point, and thus understates the extent to which the biblical authors are able to make precise statements concerning the implicit intentions of the figures in the narrative, as is the case in the description of Abraham's journey to Moria with his young men.

82. The biblical author's choice of the word "walked" is also charged with meaning: the Hebrew *vayelchu*, from *halach*, being a term that the biblical authors use to refer to the moral aspect of the way one leads one's life. That they are said to walk together, twice, seems clearly to signal that Abraham's intentions and Isaac's have not diverged in a material way.

83. Genesis 22.13–14.

84. The end of Genesis 22.14 reads, "... whence we now say, 'On the mount, the Lord will reveal himself.'" This, at any rate, is Lenn Goodman's beautiful translation. Goodman suggests that the meaning of this is that in seeing to the ram, God revealed his true nature. See Lenn Goodman, *God of Abraham*, p. 22. Note that Mount Moria is also mentioned in 2 Chronicles 3.1 as the site of Solomon's Temple.

85. Genesis 22.12, and also 22.16.

86. R. Levi suggests that Sarah dies of grief in the aftermath of the binding of Isaac. See *Genesis Raba* 58.5. Similarly, the rabbis suggest that damage that was done to Isaac on the altar is responsible for the failing eyesight that is ascribed to him in the story of Esau and Jacob at Genesis 27.1. See *Genesis Raba* 65.10. Of course, the blindness is ascribed to Isaac at the end of his life, many years after Moria. The argument seems to be this: that because of the harm done to him at Moria, Isaac could never see properly again with respect to certain matters, including his relationship with his sons.

87. Genesis 22.19. "Where was Isaac?" the rabbis ask. See *Genesis Raba* 56.11.

88. Genesis 24.62.

89. Genesis 25.9. The text also leaves open the possibility that Isaac's "blindness," which prevents him from loving Jacob, is somehow a consequence of what Abraham did to him on the mount of Moria. See *Midrash Raba* on Genesis 27.1, which argues for this point.

90. See Genesis 16.14 for Hagar's naming the place, which means in Hebrew "Well of the Living One Who Sees Me." Isaac is said to live "on the way" to this place at Genesis 24.62, and to live "near" there at Genesis 25.11. This is apparently not only a physical closeness. When Esau wants to please his father, his idea for how to do it is to take one of Ishmael's daughters as his (third) wife. See Genesis 28.8–9. For a haunting discussion of the parallels between the stories of Ishmael and Isaac in relation to their father, see Eleonore Stump, *Wandering in Darkness*, pp. 286–299.

91. This translation fits well if one wants to see a parallel between Isaac and Jesus, but otherwise it is problematic.

92. Compare Genesis 20.6, where God spared or saved Avimelech from sin by turning his thoughts away from Sarah; and 1 Samuel 25.39, where Avigail spares or saves David from sin by appeasing his anger against Naval.

93. Does Abraham emerge stronger from this trial, and able to undertake self-sacrifice as he must? The narrative wishes us to believe that he does. When Eliezer, upon leaving for Aram to find a wife for Isaac, asks Abraham if he may promise to bring Isaac to visit Mesopotamia in order to secure a wife for him, Abraham now knows the right answer, and responds unambiguously: Even if Isaac's happiness, and Abraham's dreams of future greatness, are to be sacrificed, Eliezer must swear not to take Isaac back there (Genesis 24.5–6). And when Sarah dies, and Abraham has children by Ketura, the one wife of his old age, he knows how to do what he did not before – how to restrict his heirs to the children of a single wife, although it certainly pains him greatly to do so by sending Ketura's children away. Only this time, Abraham sends them away generously, as he did not know to do with Ishmael (Genesis 25.1–6). In old age, Abraham has learned to do what is right, even where his own interests and longings dictate otherwise.

94. Genesis 12.10. See also 26.1, 41.54, 42.2.

95. Genesis 13.6–7. They are crowded out by the Canaanites. Compare Esau's departure from Canaan for similar reasons in Genesis 36.6–8.

96. He would apparently have gone down to Egypt, had God not intervened and told him "Sojourn in this land, I will be with thee." Thereupon Isaac sows grain and succeeds at farming. See Genesis 26.1–3, 12.

97. Genesis 42.1–2. See also Judges 6.3–6, 11; Ruth 4.21; 2 Samuel 21.1; 1 Kings 17.1; 2 Kings 8.1–3; Amos 4.6–8.

98. Genesis 47.4.

99. Genesis 37.2–4 and Seforno on this verse. The Hebrew phrasing *ro'eh et ehav* means "shepherds with his brothers," but it is worded so as to have a second meaning as well, that he "shepherds his brothers" rather than the sheep. Compare to David's shepherding Israel as its king at 2 Samuel 5.2.

100. Genesis 37.8.

101. Even as adults in Egypt, Joseph continues to attempt to impose order and unity on the brothers. See Genesis 43.33, 45.24. This aspect of their relationship can be understood as foreshadowing the anarchy among the tribes in the period of the Judges, in which Joseph's efforts are parallel to the demand for the imposition of a central authority at the hands of a king.

102. See Jean Bottéro, *Mesopotamia*, pp. 105–124. Other than Joseph, the only other Israelite who interprets dreams in the Bible is Daniel. As R. Levi argues, when the brothers say, "Look, here comes the dreamer," what they are really driving at is: "Here comes the one who would ensnare them into serving foreign overlords." See *Genesis Raba* 84.14, on Genesis 37.20.

103. As taught in a parable of the school of R. Ishmael, Joseph's father appears to him in the window over Potifar's bed, saying: "Your brothers will have their names inscribed upon the stones of the priestly garments [in the future Jerusalem] and yours among theirs. Do you wish to have your name erased from among theirs in order to be called a patron of harlots?" See Talmud *Sota* 36b.

104. This success is in contrast with his older brothers, Reuven and Judah, who are unable to overcome such temptation. Reuven sleeps with one of his father's concubines at Genesis 35.22. Judah becomes badly entangled because of a visit to a harlot at Genesis 38.1f.

105. R. Johanan, in the name of R. Meir, suggests that this earns Joseph his place as a Jew: "From this was he worthy to be made a shepherd." See Talmud *Sota* 36b.

106. "Why did Joseph die before his brothers? Rabi and the rabbis disagree. Rabi said: Because he embalmed his father. The Holy One, may he be blessed, said to him: Can I not protect My righteous ones? … But in the opinion of the rabbis: Nearly five times did Judah say: 'Your servant, my father,' 'your servant, my father,' yet he heard it and kept silent." See *Genesis Raba* 100.3.

107. "In the opinion of the rabbis: Nearly five times did Judah say: 'Your servant, my father,' 'your servant, my father.' Yet he [Joseph] heard it and kept silent." See *Genesis Raba* 100.3. Judah says this four times himself, Genesis 44.24, 27, 30, 31, and once with his brothers, Genesis 43.28.

108. And they referred to Joseph as "bones," the symbol of living death in exile; and as a cask of wine that had been emptied of its contents: "R. Judah said in the name of Rav: Why was Joseph referred to as 'bones' while he yet lived (Genesis 50.25)? Because he did not intervene to protect his father's honor when his brothers said to him: 'Your servant, our father' (Genesis 44.31), but made no reply to them. R. Judah also said in the name of Rav, although others say it was R. Hama ben R. Hanina: Why did Joseph die before his brothers? Because he conducted himself with rulership." See Talmud *Sota* 13b. Both of these criticisms are aimed at Joseph's understanding of his own place in the world as a result of his position in the Egyptian state: He considered it acceptable to participate in a system in which Jacob and his God, as well as the rest of the world, were understood to be servants. See also *Brachot* 55a. Cf. Ezekiel's comparison of the people Israel in exile to a valley filled with bones at Ezekiel 37.1f. The figure of the wine cask belongs to one of the greatest of the aggadists, R. Levi, whose view is recorded at *Exodus Raba* 20.19. Even an ostensibly supportive commentator remarks that Joseph's great achievements as a Jew take place in private: According to R. Hanin ben Bizna in the name of R. Simeon the Pious, Joseph sanctified God's name in private in the trial of Potifar's wife – as opposed to Judah, who sanctified God's name in public by admitting the wrongs he had committed against Tamar. See Talmud *Sota* 10b.

109. Yoram Hazony, *The Dawn: Political Teachings of the Book of Esther* (Jerusalem: Shalem Press, 2000), pp. 123–143.

110. Genesis 41.14, 41.28–36, 41.45, 41.42, 41.42, 41.42, 42.6, 42.15, 41.45, 50.2, 50.26.

111. Genesis 41.51.

112. Genesis 41.37.

113. Even in his greatest moment of righteousness and selflessness, when he spurns the advances of Potifar's wife, he thinks first and most naturally of the earthly master whose interest he would be betraying, and only then of the sin itself, saying: "Behold, my master does not inquire after what I do in his house, and he has placed all that he has in my hand. There is no one greater in this house than I, and he has not withheld anything from me but you, since you are his

wife. How, then, can I do this great wrong – and sin against God?" (Genesis 39.8–9).

114. Genesis 45.5–8.

115. Genesis 45.9–11.

116. Genesis 50.20–21.

117. Amenemhet I, quoted in Harold Nicolson, *Monarchy* (London: Weidenfeld & Nicolson, 1962), p. 20. Amenemhet I served as vizier to the last Pharaoh of the Eleventh Egyptian Dynasty, whom he probably overthrew in order to become the founder of the Twelfth Dynasty. He ruled Egypt from 2000 to 1970 BCE, approximately 200 years before the time of Abraham.

118. Genesis 47.29–31.

119. Genesis 45.19.

120. Genesis 46.1. Pharaoh's intention is to increase their dependence on the Egyptian state.

121. "Why did he not call Reuven or Judah? Reuven was the firstborn and Judah was king, yet he disregarded them and called Joseph. Why? Because Joseph had the means of fulfilling his wish" (*Genesis Raba* 96.5).

122. Genesis 50.4–5.

123. The Moses story is the reverse image of Joseph's failure: When Moses approaches Pharaoh two centuries later with the request that the Jews be allowed to go up from Egypt for a religious rite, he refuses Pharaoh's offer to go without the children and herds. See Exodus 10.9–12, 24–26.

124. The incongruity of it brought the rabbis to jest at Joseph's expense, saying: "To whom did he speak? To the queen's nurse, asking her to persuade the queen, who in turn should persuade the king." See *Genesis Raba* 100.4.

125. For this reason the rabbis observed that "as soon as Jacob our father died, the enslavement of Egypt began for Israel." See *Genesis Raba* 96.1.

126. Genesis 50.24–25.

127. Genesis 50.16.

128. Exodus 1.8, 10, 13–14, 22.

129. See Paul Rahe's chapter "The Primacy of Politics in Classical Greece," in *Republic Ancient and Modern* (Chapel Hill: University of North Carolina Press, 1994), vol. I, pp. 14–40.

130. Plato, *Crito* 50a–51c.

131. Aristotle, *Nichomachean Ethics* 1094a17–1094b12.

132. See Yoram Hazony, *The Dawn*, pp. 69–82. An important exception is David, whose refusal to harm Saul even as his king tries to murder him is a striking example of loyalty to the state and its ruling figures in the face of injustice. See 1 Samuel 24.1–8.

133. Note that the Temple is an expression of the wealth and power of the state as well. Nothing resembling it could have been contemplated before the establishment of the kingdom. See Joshua Berman, *The Temple* (Northvale, N.J.: Jason Aronson, 1995), pp. 57–81.

134. In this regard, see especially Jeremiah 35.1–19, where the prophet explicitly holds up the Rechabites, a tribe of nomads that has sworn to live in tents with neither fields nor vineyards for all time, as an example of moral rectitude to be emulated by Judah. These Rechabites are the descendents of the

same Yehonadav ben-Rechav who joins with Yehu in the destruction of the evil house of Ahav, king of Israel. See 2 Kings 10.15f. The prophet Hoshea also speaks of a life in tents as an ideal. See Hoshea 12.10–11.

135. Despite my use of the pronoun "his" here, I do not see any evidence that the biblical authors saw the slightest difference between the responsibilities of the father and that of the mother in this regard. Sarah, Rebecca, and Rachel are examples of women who are depicted as being deeply involved in setting the course that will be followed by their households. Rebecca, in particular, deserves attention in this regard, for it is her deeds, at Genesis 27.5–16 and 27.46–28.5, that set the course of the rest of Jacob's life.

136. As we see, for example, in the string of disobedience stories with which the narrative of the redemption from Egypt begins, starting with the midwives' refusal to obey Pharaoh's command to murder the male infants of the Israelites. See Exodus 1.17–2.17, and my discussion in Chapter 8, Section III.

137. By presenting Joseph as succeeding, at least once, in defying the corruption of Egypt, the History holds out the possibility that a Jew, even if he is immured in the ways of Pharaoh's court, may succeed in resisting and redeeming himself and his people. The hope that this is so is the basis of the stories of Esther, Daniel, and Nehemia.

138. On at least three occasions, we get to see Moses arguing with God and persuading him not to destroy Israel: Exodus 32.9–14; Numbers 14.11–20, 16.19–23. But after the sin of the golden calf, Moses also insists that God's presence enter the camp and accompany Israel up into the land. On this point God refuses, directly commanding Moses to desist from his demands and take the people up without the divine presence, at Exodus 32.34, 33.1. However, Moses does not go up as he is commanded, instead pitching a tent to meet God outside the camp (33.7) and continuing the argument: "And Moses said to the Lord, 'Look, you tell me to take this people up, but you have not made known to me what you will send with me'" (33.12). Moses even explicitly states his refusal to take the people up without God's presence (33.15). This is not just an argument, but an actual fight between Moses and God, which continues until at last Moses prevails and God, as it seems, agrees to journey with the Israelites in Exodus 40.33–38.

139. Leviticus 10.16–20.

140. Different interpretations are possible, but the simplest reading is that God commands the public killing of those individuals who have been mixing sex and idolatry in their pursuit of Moabite woman and their worship of Ba'al-Pe'or; whereas Pinhas kills a man in private who has taken to bed a Midianite woman whose relationship to this idolatry is uncertain. Pinhas's excess of zeal would appear to bring about a reckless imprecision in the application of God's command. This recklessness would seem to be what motivates God to take Pinhas and his line out of political and military affairs by giving them the priesthood. But God's pleasure in the results of Pinhas's action is nonetheless unmistakable. See Numbers 25.1–16. Notice that the purpose of the priesthood, as we are told, is "to distinguish between the sacred and the profane, and between the pure and the impure" (Leviticus 10.10) – something at which Pinhas evidently excels.

141. Numbers 27.1–11; Joshua 17.3–4.
142. Genesis 32.25–30, and see Rashi on this verse.
143. Genesis 25.23.
144. Jacob himself compares Esau's face and that of God in Genesis 33.10; and Hoshea 12.4 likewise suggests that the struggle was with God. The view of Jacob as having struggled with God his entire life appears as well in Michael Fishbane, *Biblical Text and Texture*, pp. 54–55. Note also Leon Kass's observation that Jacob's attempt to extract a blessing from the angel by force recalls his attempt to win the birthright from his brother by extortion; and his later attempt to gain his father's blessing by trickery. See Leon Kass, *The Beginning of Wisdom*, p. 459.
145. But one does not struggle with God with impunity. The old trick that Jacob and his mother Rebecca played on his blind father was in the service of the right end, for we know Esau as a killer and not the man who should have inherited from Isaac. The text emphasizes this in reporting Esau's vow to murder his brother because of his parents' favor for him, at Genesis 27.41, which reprises Cain's murderous hatred for Abel. In addition, we are told of Esau's taking two Canaanite wives, as opposed to Jacob's obedience in following his parents' instructions not to take a wife of Canaan. See Genesis 27.28–28:9. But it was a great wrong nonetheless. Indeed, even Jacob's haggling with a famished Esau over a pot of lentils is in stark contrast to the generosity of his grandfather Abraham, who did business without trying to take advantage of another's momentary weakness. And for the wrong he inflicted on his father, Jacob suffers his whole life. He is exiled for fear of his brother, and then tormented, deprived of his wages and of Rachel. The seven years that he lives with Leah and without Rachel are years lived in the shadow of Lavan's devastating remark: "In our place it's not a thing that is done, marrying off the younger before the firstborn" (Genesis 29.26). And the worst is yet to come. For Jacob will soon lose Rachel; and then Rachel's son Joseph, his favorite, to trickery at the hands of his sons that again reminds us of the trickery Jacob himself inflicted on his own father. Jacob has struggled with God and has prevailed. But the metaphor of God's maiming him in the struggle – only partially a metaphor, since Jacob never walks properly again after this – is worth considering well before one decides to wrestle God.
146. Genesis 23:4. The Hittites tell Abraham, on the contrary, "A prince of God you are among us" at Genesis 23:6. Isaac, too, tells his son Jacob that he is still a "sojourner" in the land although they have both lived there their entire lives! See Genesis 28:4.
147. A similar account with slightly different points emphasized appears in Leon Kass, *The Beginning of Wisdom*, pp. 461–463.
148. For Noah and Isaac as farmers, see Genesis 5.29, 9.20, 26.12. Notice that Isaac, the only one of the patriarchs who is described as a successful farmer, is also the only one who is able to maintain himself in the land of Israel all his life. The message here seems to be that if Israel is ever to be rooted in the soil of its own land, this will come about only through an increased emphasis on the virtues of the farmer that Isaac represents. Unlike Abraham – but like Noah – Isaac is never, as far as I can tell, depicted as arguing with God or disobeying him. On this

point see also the remarkable comment of the *Zohar*, which reads God's angry demand that Moses leave him alone that he may destroy Israel in Exodus 32.10 as pleading with Moses to be obedient and compliant like Noah for a change. This reading is based on the Hebrew text, which says *ata haniha li*, meaning "Now let me be," but which the *Zohar* takes to mean "Now be like Noah to me." This counterpoint between the two types does not end with the books of Moses, but continues to the end of the History of Israel. Thus Joshua, who is of the line of Joseph, displays a simple devotion to God's will that allows him to be the conqueror of the land (e.g., Joshua 11.15); and like Cain he goes on to build a city (Joshua 19.49–50). Whereas Moses' much more skeptical and defiant shepherd-character gets him into trouble with God, who accuses Moses of not believing in him at Numbers 20.12; but see Chapter 8 for further discussion. The contrast between farmers and shepherds appears, too, in the contest between Saul and David, which presents Saul as a farmer at 1 Samuel 11.4–7; as opposed to David, who is depicted as a shepherd repeatedly, as at 1 Samuel 16.11, 19, 17.15, 20, 28, 34, 40, 54. Solomon, David's son, is a man of many and extraordinary virtues, but they are, again, the virtues associated with Cain and Joseph, not those of his father. And the prophet Elijah is in the end too difficult for God, who replaces him with his disciple Elisha, whom we are told was a farmer at 1 Kings 19.19. The references to oxen in these passages should not be confused with shepherding imagery. The shepherds in the biblical narratives may own some cows. But in general, cattle-raising is associated with the agrarian economy, in which oxen are used, wherever possible, to plow fields. Thus Pharoah, for example, has dreams of grain and cattle – see Genesis 41.17–24. Similarly, in the passages just cited, Saul is depicted as tending cattle and asses, and Elisha as plowing a field with oxen. Indeed, the reference to Saul following after cattle ("And behold, Saul followed after the cattle from the field") is a painful allusion to what is to come.

149. For related views concerning the relationship established in the History between the Mosaic law and the narratives in which it is embedded, see Diana Lipton, *Longing for Egypt* (Sheffield: Sheffield Phoenix Press, 2008), pp. 174–176; Ze'ev Maghen, "Dancing in Chains: The Baffling Coexistence of Legalism and Exuberance in Judaic and Islamic Tradition," in Jonathan Jacobs, ed., *Judaic Sources and Western Thought* (New York: Oxford University Press, 2011), pp. 217–237. On the relationship between the law and the biblical narratives more generally, see Chapter 3, Section III; and Chapter 8, Section VIII in this book.

5. The History of Israel, Genesis–Kings: A Political Philosophy

1. An earlier version of this article appeared as Yoram Hazony, "Does the Bible Have a Political Teaching?" *Hebraic Political Studies* (Winter 2006), pp. 137–161.

2. See Jeremiah 44.15–18. See Chapter 3, Section I.

3. The caveat "had they been made early enough" is crucial. The History does not suggest that God will automatically save anyone who mends his ways. It is the decisions made earlier in the history of the kingdom that have the greatest weight.

4. As discussed in Chapter 3, Section III.

5. Abravanel, commentary on 1 Samuel 1.8.

6. Genesis 4.17. See Leon Kass, *The Beginning of Wisdom: Reading Genesis* (New York: Free Press, 2003), pp. 144–147, 217–243; and Chapter 4, Section I.

7. Genesis 11.1–9.

8. On the tower of Babylon as a critique of the imperial state, see Daniel Gordis, "The Tower of Babel and the Birth of Nationhood," *Azure* 40 (Spring 2010), pp. 19–36; Yoram Hazony, "On the National State, Part 1: Empire and Anarchy," *Azure* 12 (Winter 2002), pp. 27–70, at pp. 34–35, 39; Michael Fishbane, *Biblical Text and Texture* (Oxford: Oneworld, 2003 [1979]), p. 37. Notice that Isaiah uses the story of the tower of Bablyon as a critique of the Israelite state as well. See Isaiah 14.13–14.

9. See, for example, Ezekiel 28.1–10, 29.3, 9.

10. Even Darius, one of the better-loved imperial rulers in the Bible, is presented as accepting the idea that supplication before God should be forbidden for thirty days, so that all requests in the empire should be directed to him alone. See Daniel 6.8–10.

11. Judges 1.7.

12. For this reason, I don't see that the History recognizes a difference, in principle, between the great imperial states of the ancient Near East and the petty states. Only with the introduction of the Mosaic regime of government limited by law does the narrative recognize a distinction of principle.

13. The biblical narrative speaks explicitly of God as having taken Abraham out of the land of the Chaldeans, another name for the Babylonians. This reference to Abraham as coming out of Babylonia is perhaps anachronistic. But it ties Abraham to the tower of Babylon, as well as to the destruction of Jerusalem at the hands of the Babylonians many centuries later.

14. On the anarchic tendency in the biblical political teaching, see John W. Flight, "The Nomadic Ideal in the Old Testament," *Journal of Biblical Literature* 42 (1923), pp. 158–226, esp. pp. 213f.; S. N. Eisenstadt, "Israeli Politics and the Jewish Political Tradition: Principled Political Anarchism and the Rule of the Court," reprinted in *Explorations in Jewish Historical Experience* (Leiden: Brill, 2004 [1986]).

15. Genesis 12.15, 20.2, 26.17–18, 14.11–12, 34.1–2.

16. This pattern is already established in Abraham's time. See Genesis 12.10.

17. It is important to note that as a consequence of this economic argument, a powerful dissent is registered against the anarchic ideal within the text of Genesis itself. This dissent is represented in Genesis by Joseph, a Hebrew herdsman who, as a boy, dreams of harvesting grain and ruling the heavens (Genesis 37.9). By the time he emerges as Pharaoh's minister, Joseph appears to have been won over to the view that man cannot survive without the state, and that God himself wishes men to be saved by it (for example, Genesis 45.5–8). For discussion of Joseph's politics of engagement with the state and its subsequent treatment in the Hebrew Bible, see Aaron Wildavsky, *Assimilation Versus Separation: Joseph the Administrator and the Politics of Religion in Biblical Israel* (New Brunswick, N.J.: Transaction, 1993); and Chapter 4, Section III. For this reason, I am unable to accept the argument of Moshe Weinfeld and others, to the

effect that the establishment of the Israelite state "contradicts" the earlier traditions of Israel. The critique of anarchy within the biblical narrative is imma-
nent in the very first presentation of the anarchic vision, in Genesis. Neither the
violence nor the economic dependence on Egyptian agriculture represented by
Joseph permits us to accept anarchy as a simple and unalloyed ideal. The rejection of the preferences of Gideon and Samuel represents the understanding of
the biblical narrative that Joseph's critique of anarchy is in large measure correct. For Weinfeld's view, see his essay "The Transition from Tribal Republic to
Monarchy in Ancient Israel," in Daniel J. Elazar, ed., *Kinship and Consent: The
Jewish Political Tradition and its Contemporary Uses* (New Brunswick, N.J.:
Transaction, 1997), pp. 216–232.

18. See Aaron Wildavsky, *Moses as Political Leader*, with intro. by Yoram Hazony
(Jerusalem: Shalem Press, 2005 [1984]); Michael Walzer, *Exodus and Revolution*
(New York: Basic Books, 1985).

19. Exodus 1.15–21.

20. Exodus 1.22–2.10.

21. Exodus 2.11–12.

22. Exodus 3.1f. On the place of initiative in the Bible's conception of man's relationship with God, see Chapter 8.

23. Deuteronomy 7.19; Exodus 6.6. The passivity of the Hebrews is, in Exodus,
attributed to their enslavement. See, for example, Exodus 13.17–18, where God
tells Moses that he should not take the slaves straight up to Canaan lest they see
war and become so fearful that they demand to return to Egypt.

24. Exodus 12.3–13, 21–23. Amon, the god of the Egyptian capital of Thebes, was
represented as a ram. By the time of the enslavement of the Jews, Amon had
become the most powerful and prominent god in the pantheon, under whose
standard the Egyptian armies waged war. Moses himself tells Pharaoh that what
the Hebrews sacrifice is the "abomination of Egypt," and that if they were to
sacrifice it before the Egyptians, they would kill them (Exodus 8.22). The rabbis are even more explicit, having God tell Moses: "As you live, Israel will not
depart from here before they slaughter the Egyptians' gods before their very
eyes" (*Exodus Raba* 16.3; also 16.2). Notice, too, that the sacrifice of the sheep
in place of a human being is the symbol of Abraham's faith. For discussion, see
Chapter 4, section II.

25. For Egypt as the "house of bondage," see Exodus 13.3, 14, 20.2; Deuteronomy
5.6, 6.12, 7.8, 8.14, 13.6, 11; Joshua 24.17; Judges 6.8; Jeremiah 34.13. The
public consumption of the false god as the minimum display of loyalty to the
God of Israel is repeated at Exodus 32.20, where Moses grinds the golden calf
into powder and makes Israel drink it.

26. Judges 8.22–23.

27. Judges 9.7–15.

28. 1 Samuel 8.11–18.

29. Biblical Hebrew uses the term *eved* to mean both *servant* and *slave*. In its usage
as *slave*, it is touched with connotations of idolatry as well.

30. See in particular 1 Samuel 12.1–25, in which Samuel presents an interpretation
of history contrary to that favored by the narrative itself. On Samuel's view, the
judges Gideon, Yiftah, and Samuel are listed in one breath as having "delivered

you out of the hand of your enemies round about, and you dwelled secure" (1 Samuel 12.11). Moreover, Samuel insists that although "I am old and grey-headed," nevertheless "my sons are with you" (1 Samuel 12.2). Against the narrative's determination that the sons of Samuel had taken bribes, Samuel makes his famous speech: "Whose ox have I taken? Whose ass have I taken? Whom have I defrauded?" (1 Samuel 12.3). In addition, as a demonstration of Israel's vulnerability, now that they have followed after the ways of Joseph, choosing an earthly ruler and becoming dependent on agriculture, Samuel threatens (with God's help) to destroy the wheat harvest and bring all Israel to starvation (1 Samuel 12.17–19). Thus the narrative, while sympathetic to Samuel's longing for anarchy, does not support him in his views: Both the continual violence in the land and the corruption of his own sons testify against his forgiving view of anarchy.

31. See especially Joshua 1.16–18, 24.16–21, 31.

32. Judges 2.7, 10. These words are intended to invoke the opening passage of Exodus, in which the Hebrews are enslaved in Egypt. See Exodus 1.8. This parallel between Exodus and Judges sets up the twin dangers of empire and anarchy. It is worth noting the additional message that is packed into this matter of political forgetfulness. Indeed, the subject of the *transmission* of wisdom may be said to be one of the most pressing political questions raised by the biblical narrative.

33. On this progression as representing a decline in civic virtue, see Gordon Wenham, *Story as Tora: Reading Old Testament Narrative Ethically* (Grand Rapids, Mich.: Baker Academic, 2000), pp. 54, 59–69; Daniel J. Elazar, *Covenant and Polity in Biblical Israel* (New Brunswick, N.J.: Transaction, 1995), pp. 290–291. See also Martin Noth, *The Deuteronomistic History* (Sheffield: Journal for the Study of the Old Testament Press, 1943), pp. 72–76, 122–123; D. W. Gooding, "The Composition of the Book of Judges," *Eretz-Israel* 16 (Jerusalem: Israel Exploration Society, 1982), pp. 70–79; and J. P. U. Lilley, "A Literary Appreciation of the Book of Judges," *Tyndale Bulletin* (1967), pp. 94–102. This view is opposed by Martin Buber, who recognizes no such decline, and sees in the last two episodes "a monarchical book appear[ing] at the side of the anti-monarchical book of Judges, or rather, in opposition to it" (Martin Buber, *Kingship of God*, Richard Scheimann, trans. [Atlantic Highlands, N.J.: Humanities, 1967], pp. 77–84). It remains difficult to see how this view can be reconciled with the plain meaning of the text. A newer reading that sees the book of Judges as a struggle among competing voices can be found in the essays in Michael Walzer, Menachem Lorberbaum, and Noam J. Zohar, eds., *The Jewish Political Tradition* (New Haven: Yale University Press, 2000). See in particular Michael Walzer's introduction to the chapter on "Kings," pp. 109–116; and Moshe Halbertal's essay on "God's Kingship," pp. 128–132.

34. Judges 3.11, 3.30, 5.31. At 3.30, the land was quiet for not forty but eighty years. The fourth episode, concerning Gideon, likewise ends with the claim that "the land was quiet for forty years." See Judges 8.28.

35. When Deborah asks the northern strongman Barak to muster for battle, he responds, rather cryptically: "'If you will go with me, then I will go. But if you will not go with me, then I will not go.' And she said: 'I will surely go with you'" (Judges 4.8–9).

36. Judges 5.14–18.
37. For the first time a judge in Israel is explicitly described as the son of a man who owns an altar to Ba'al. See Judges 6.25.
38. The narrative, however, leaves open the possibility that Efraim would have followed Gideon had he summoned him at the outset of the war. Instead, he only calls on Efraim after victory is already at hand. It is apparently his own fear of the greater tribes that prevented him from issuing the summons. See Judges 7.23–8.1.
39. The tribes that go with him are Menasheh, Zevulun, Naftali, and Asher. See Judges 6.34–36. His troubles with Efraim and Gad are described at 8.1–9.
40. Judges 8.16–17.
41. Judges 8.24–28.
42. Judges 9.1–57.
43. Until the end of the Gideon episode, the narrative had begun each time with "the children of Israel cried up to the Lord"; and each time, God heeded their cries by raising up a judge to deliver them from their enemies. See Judges 3.9, 3.15, 4.3, 6.6. But in the fifth episode, when the children of Israel cry up to the Lord, they are met with despair. As God tells them: "You have forsaken me and served other gods. Therefore I will deliver you no more. Go and cry to the gods that you have chosen. Let them deliver you in the hour of your troubles" (Judges 4.8–9). And indeed, the last two of Israel's judges are not precisely redeemers.
44. Judges 11.3.
45. Yiftah's discourse on Kemosh appears in Judges 11.23–24. Compare to Joshua's prohibition on speaking the names of the gods of Canaan: "Brace yourselves, therefore, very much ... that you come not among these nations that remain among you. Neither make mention of the names of their gods, nor swear by them, nor serve them" (Joshua 23.7). See also Exodus 23.13; Hoshea 2.19; Psalms 16.4. It is noteworthy that the narrative describes the followers of Kemosh as continuing to sacrifice their children to him at 2 Kings 3.26–27.
46. Yiftah's sacrifice of his daughter to the God of Israel is described in Judges 11.30–31, 34–39. On the "Molochization" of the God of Israel implicit in his act, see Martin Buber, *Kingship of God*, pp. 68, 116. Precisely such an act was envisioned and proscribed by Moses: "Take heed of yourselves, that you not be ensnared into following them, after they are destroyed before you. And that you do not inquire after their gods, saying 'How did these nations serve their gods? I too will do likewise.' You will not do likewise on behalf of the Lord. For every abomination to the Lord, which he hates, have they done for their gods. Even their sons and their daughters have they burned in the fire to their gods" (Deuteronomy 12.30–31). Similarly: "There must not be found among you anyone that makes his son or his daughter to pass through the fire.... Because of these abominations the Lord thy God drives them out before you" (Deuteronomy 18.9–10).
47. The first four episodes explicitly speak of peace having been returned to the land. The last four, beginning with Yiftah, do not describe peace as having been returned to the land.
48. Judges 12.1–7. The bloodshed between Gad and Efraim finally brings to a head an internal tension between Israel and the tribes east of the Jordan, which both

Moses and Joshua struggled to subdue. In particular, Joshua had insisted that the men of the east bank remain with the Israelite armies until the west bank had been subdued, and only then retire to their own homes (Joshua 1.12–18). They are released from their pledge, after years of war, in Joshua 22.1–6. Already by Joshua's day, there had been a move by the tribes of the west bank to wage war against the east, but it had been defused (Joshua 22.9–34). Compare Yiftah's failure in this regard with Gideon's success in defusing a similar situation in Judges 7.23–8.3.

49. Judges 16.20–21, 25. The passage that dominates the entire Samson episode is the proscription of Joshua: "For if you should at all turn back to attach yourselves to the remnant of these nations, these that remain among you, and shall make marriages with them, and go in unto them, and they to you … they shall be snares and traps to you, and a scourge in your sides, and pricks in your eyes, until you perish from off the good land which the Lord your God has given you" (Joshua 23.12–13). Note, in particular, the chilling foreshadowing of Samson's eyes being put out.

50. Judges 17.6. Compare 18.1.

51. Tellingly, Dan's enemies are defeated in battle by the Efraimites, who choose to make them tributaries, rather than giving Dan their land. See Judges 1.34–35. Thus the Efraimites directly profit from the suffering of the Danites – and this despite the explicit prohibition on making covenants with the peoples of the land. See Judges 2.2.

52. Judges 18.5–10, 27–28.

53. Compare this episode with Moses' exhortations: "Neither shall you bring an abomination into your house, lest you become accursed like it, but you shall utterly detest it, and utterly abhor it" (Deuteronomy 7.26); "Take heed of yourself that you forsake not the Levite as long as you live upon the earth" (Deuteronomy 12.19).

54. Judges 18.30. Look at the Hebrew text for this verse, in which the letter *nun* in the name "Menasheh" (מנשה) is suspended above the rest of the word; if this letter is ignored, the text reads "Mosheh" (משה) – Moses. That this is the intention is evident from the fact that Moses' son was Gershon, a Levite; whereas Menasheh has no such son, and is not a Levite.

55. Compare Deuteronomy 12.19: "Take heed of yourself that you forsake not the Levite as long as you live upon the earth."

56. Judges 19.15–28.

57. Judges 20.1–21.48. In the aftermath, Israel goes up to the settlement of Yavesh Gilad in Gad, which again had been remiss in participating, and conducts an additional massacre there (Judges 21.8–12). These atrocities are then compounded by Israel's sanctioning of the abduction and forced marriage of the young women of Yavesh Gilad and Shiloh to the surviving Benjaminites (Judges 21.12–23). This would appear to involve rape, at least in some of the cases, raising questions about how far superior the tribes are to the Benjaminites they had warred against.

58. Genesis 19.1–13.

59. C. F. Burney, *The Book of Judges* (Eugene, Oreg.: Wipf & Stock, 2004 [1918]), pp. 444–445. See also Susan Niditch, "The 'Sodomite' Theme in *Judges*

19–20: Family, Community, and Social Disintegration," *Catholic Bible Quarterly* 44 (1982), pp. 365–378. Like Sodom, Giva becomes a byword for sin in the Bible. See Hoshea 10.9.

60. Judges 2.19. Noth suggests that this is likewise the meaning of the expression *veyosifu la'asot hara* at Judges 3.12, 4.1, 10.6, and 13.1, which is then read "And they did even worse in God's eyes" (Martin Noth, *Deuteronomistic History*, p. 72).

61. Of course, there is an important difference between the two cases. In Giva, it is man that judges and punishes, and not God. Like much else in the book of Judges, this matter is ambiguous. On the one hand, we have to see the attempt to restore justice in an unjust land as being praiseworthy. In this sense, man is expected to emulate God. On the other hand, the Israelites do not really succeed in this effort. For in Sodom, God is depicted as sparing the just, whereas the just of Benjamin die together with the wicked. Moreover, the subsequent slaughter of the men of Gad seems utterly gratuitous. We are pressed to draw the conclusion that under conditions of anarchy, even the effort to bring justice to the land must end in mob rule and injustice. Note that Giva, like Sodom, becomes a byword in the prophetic literature for depravity so deep that it is worthy of being wiped from the earth. See, for example, Hoshea 10.9.

62. Judges 17.6, 21.25. Also 18.1, 19.1. Compare Deuteronomy 12.8: "You shall not do after 'All the things we do here this day,' each man what is right in his own eyes."

63. An important suggestion by Leon Kass is that we read the story of the Flood in Noah's day as reporting God's response to the anarchic condition of man prior to the first laws against bloodshed in Genesis 9.1–7. See Leon Kass, *The Beginning of Wisdom*, p. 162. If this reading is accepted, then the book of Judges must be seen as recapitulating in much greater detail a version of a lesson that has already appeared in the story of Noah.

64. The History is aware that not all states are ruled by kings. See Daniel Elazar, *Covenant and Polity*, p. 242. But the issue of interest in the Bible's treatment of kingship is not the difference between, say, monarchy and oligarchy; or hereditary and elected kingship. The Bible is concerned with the principle of a standing government with a standing army, with all that this implies in terms of taxation and coercion of the people. This is, for the biblical authors, the difference between having a king and "There was no king in Israel."

65. 1 Samuel 8.4–5. The reference here to Samuel's sons not following his ways alludes to their accepting bribes. See 1 Samuel 8.2. The story of Samuel's sons is paralleled by the subversion of the priesthood a generation before by the sons of the high priest Eli, as described at 1 Samuel 2.12–26. Compare Numbers 19.32: "[N]or will you pollute the sacred donations of the sons of Israel, lest you die."

66. For Samuel's opposition to the establishment of the state, see 1 Samuel 8.10–20, quoted in Section II of this chapter.

67. 1 Samuel 8.7. But see the very different use of the expression "as in all the nations" made by Ezekiel once the kingdom is tottering on the edge of destruction and many of the Jews are already in exile in Babylonia (Ezekiel 20.32–33, 25.8). See also Hoshea 13.9–11, written concerning the fall of the northern kingdom.

68. 1 Samuel 10.21–26.

69. I am indebted to Ari Gontownik for his remarks concerning this passage.
70. 1 Samuel 11.1–14.
71. Thomas Hobbes, *Leviathan*, Edwin Curley, ed. (Indianapolis, Ind.: Hackett, 1994), ch. 18, pp. 110f.; John Locke, *Two Treatises of Government*, Peter Laslett, ed. (Cambridge: Cambridge University Press, 1960), vol. II, sections 95–99, pp. 330–333; Jean-Jacques Rousseau, *On the Social Contract*, Roger D. Masters, ed., Judith R. Masters, trans. (New York: St. Martin's Press, 1978), 1.4, pp. 53–54. See Otto von Gierke, *The Development of Political Theory* (New York: W. W. Norton, 1939).
72. This passage is parallel to Genesis 21.12, in which Abraham does not want to drive out Hagar and Ishmael, but God tells him, "In all that Sarah says to you, listen to her voice." The implication is that, here too, God acquiesces in what is necessary, although in some sense also obviously wrong.
73. But at times, the common sense of the people also saves the day, as when Saul seeks to murder his son Jonathan, who is rescued by the people. See 1 Samuel 14.24–45.
74. The fact that it is the consent of the people that brings the establishment of tyrannies was well known to Plato as well. See Plato, *Republic* 565d.
75. God's will in the Hebrew Scriptures can usually be understood as reflecting an objective standard of right. But there are enough exceptions for this principle to be applied only with care.
76. The standard of "the way that is good and right" is the standard that is used to judge the kings of Judah and Israel throughout the rest of the narrative. In the book of Kings, especially, the term "right" apparently refers to the achievement of a minimally decent society; whereas the "good" refers to the attempt to serve God with a whole heart. A discussion appears in Ofir Haivry, "The Way of the World," *Azure* 5 (Autumn 1998), pp. 44–53.
77. 1 Samuel 12.13–14, 23, 25. Compare Yehoshafat the king's instructions to the Levite judges in 2 Chronicles 19.11: "[S]trengthen yourselves to perform it, and the Lord will be with the good."
78. The institution of prophecy can be seen as the expression of this system of dual legitimacy in the political understanding of ancient Israel, and in the political philosophy of the Bible.
79. As Abravanel emphasizes in his commentary on Exodus 19.1–3, section 2.6, no prophet ever ruled over Israel as its king, and only Samuel did so even as a judge. Moses can perhaps be considered an exception, but the fact that Moses' son does not succeed him suggests that such a supposition would be mistaken. For an instance in which the prophet pronounces God as having withdrawn his consent, see, for example, 1 Samuel 15.28. For discussion of the role played by the people, see Michael Walzer, "Biblical Politics: Where Are the Elders?" *Hebraic Political Studies* (Summer 2008), pp. 225–238.
80. The Mosaic "Law of the King" is not to be confused with the speech of the prophet Samuel informing the people of the custom of the king, which is known by the same name. See 1 Samuel 8.11–18. In this chapter, I use this term exclusively to refer to the Mosaic law in Deuteronomy.
81. Although there were prophets of other nations, Israel were to heed prophets from their own people. See Deuteronomy 18.15, 18.

82. Deuteronomy 17.14–20. I have translated "his thoughts" for *levavo*, which is usually translated "his heart." For a discussion of this issue, see Chapter 6, Section II.

83. This may be seen as the basis of constitutional government. For discussion, see Joshua Berman, *Created Equal: How the Bible Broke With Ancient Political Thought* (New York: Oxford University Press, 2008), pp. 53–80; Alan L. Mittleman, *The Scepter Shall Not Depart from Judah: Perspectives on the Persistence of the Political in Judaism* (Lanham, Md.: Lexington, 2000), pp. 95f.; Daniel Elazar, *Covenant and Polity*, p. 313.

84. Deuteronomy 1.7. Compare Deuteronomy 11.24, 32.8; Joshua 1.4.

85. See Steven Grosby, *Biblical Ideas of Nationality: Ancient and Modern* (Winona Lake, Ind.: Eisenbrauns, 2002).

86. Deuteronomy 2.4–6, 9, 19.

87. It is relevant that in the rabbinic retelling, the first kingdom of the Israelites was destroyed as a result of idolatry, bloodshed, and sexual impropriety. See Talmud *Yoma* 9b. This account would appear to be parallel to the biblical categories of gold, horses, and wives. I am indebted to Ofir Haivry for this observation.

88. The prophets complain bitterly over the fact that when God blesses Israel with gold, they use it to make idols. The most troubling example is the gold the Hebrews took out of Egypt at God's behest, which they then used to make the golden calf. The story of Gideon here repeats this pattern, again depicting Israel as taking gold that has been won from Israel's enemies with God's help, and turning it to the creation of a fetish. As the prophet Hoshea says in God's name: "And she did not know that it was I who … multiplied silver for her and gold, which they used for the Ba'al" (Hoshea 2.10).

89. "He had many wives," at Judges 8.30, follows precisely the language of the proscription in Deuteronomy.

90. Judges 8.30–9.57.

91. Judges 10.3–4, 13.8–9, 13.13–19.

92. David already has six named wives in Hebron, each of them having children. See 2 Samuel 3.2–5. In 2 Samuel 5.13–15, we are told that once in Jerusalem he took yet more wives and concubines, and the narrative doesn't even bother to name them anymore. Ten concubines are mentioned in 2 Samuel 15.16. See also 1 Chronicles 3.1–9, which names seven of David's wives, but leaves out Saul's daughter, Michal.

93. 2 Samuel 11.1–12.23. See also 2 Samuel 3.12–16.

94. 2 Samuel 19.11.

95. 2 Samuel 13.1–13, 16.20–22.

96. Avshalom's murder of his brother Amnon at a sheep-shearing at Ba'al Hatzor on the way to Shechem is another replay of the story of Joseph and his brothers, which takes place in much the same place. See 2 Samuel 13.23–29.

97. 1 Kings 1.5f.

98. The institution of taking more than one wife seems, in the Hebrew Bible, to be depicted only in a negative light. As R. David Kimche observes in his commentary on Genesis 4.19, marital strife appears in the biblical narrative only after Lemech takes two wives. In fact, the addition of a second wife is consistently depicted in the History as a source of suffering and trouble. In addition,

Abraham's accepting Hagar is depicted as a terrible mistake. See Genesis 16.1–16, 21.1–21. And Jacob's four wives are the background for the murderous hatred among the brothers of different mothers, as well as for Reuven's sleeping with one of his father's wives at Genesis 35.22, 37.1–20. See also the painful rivalry between Hannah and Penina in 1 Samuel 1.6–8. So far as I know, no son sleeps with his father's wife or daughter in the Bible in a case in which his father is married only to his mother. On Abraham's "giving up his harem" in banishing Hagar and Ishmael, see Leon Kass, *The Beginning of Wisdom*, p. 290.

99. 2 Samuel 12.31. The occupation of Ammon would appear to be in violation of the law of Moses quoted above, and mention of forced labor and brickworks harks back to the suffering of Israel in Egypt.

100. 1 Kings 3.3–28, 4.20–5.22.

101. See Joseph Blenkinsopp, *Prophecy and Canon* (Notre Dame, Ind.: Notre Dame University Press, 1977), p. 51.

102. 1 Kings 10.14–11.4. This picture parallels Isaiah 1.6–7. I have again translated *lev* as "thoughts." See my discussion in Chapter 6, Section II.

103. "Then Solomon did build a high place for Kemosh, the abomination of Moav, on the hill that is before Jerusalem, and for Molech, the abomination of the children of Ammon. And he did likewise for all his foreign wives, who burned incense and sacrificed to their gods. And the Lord was angry with Solomon, because his heart was turned from the Lord, God of Israel, who had … commanded him concerning this thing, that he should not go after other gods. But he kept not that which the Lord commanded" (1 Kings 11.7–10).

104. Deuteronomy 17.20. It is particularly important that study of the Tora is supposed, not only to turn the king toward God, but also to prevent the evil of his feeling too high above his brothers.

105. 1 Kings 10.21.

106. The house that Solomon built for the Lord is reported to have been 60 x 20 x 30 cubits, and to have taken seven years to build; whereas his own house is said to have been 100 x 50 x 30 cubits, and to have taken thirteen years to build (1 Kings 6.2, 7.1–2). Compare this with God's complaint concerning the perversity of the priesthood in the days of Eli and his sons: "Why do you … honor your sons above me, making yourselves fat with the best of all the offerings of Israel, my people?" (1 Samuel 2.29).

107. For example, 1 Kings 7.8.

108. 1 Kings 6.27–30, 9.15–22. As Wildavsky points out, there is a point at which impressment and taxation begin to look like slavery, and kingship like the idolatry of Egypt. See Aaron Wildavsky, *Moses as Political Leader*, pp. 257–258. See also Diana Lipton, *Longing for Egypt* (Sheffield: Sheffield Phoenix Press, 2008), p. 24.

109. 1 Kings 11.28.

110. 1 Kings 12.3–4.

111. 1 Kings 12.10–11.

112. 1 Kings 12.13–17.

113. 1 Kings 12.1 8.

114. But notice that this story has its roots much further back in the History. Already in the time of Avshalom's rebellion against David, we hear a Benjaminite cry

out the same words just quoted: "What portion do we have in David? We have no inheritance in the son of Jesse" (2 Samuel 20.1). This bitterness is to be understood as stemming from David's having deposed the line of Saul, who was a Benjaminite. But when the deceased Saul's captain, Avner, brings the Benjaminites and the rest of Israel to an agreement to make David king, it is David's own cut-throat general who murders him (2 Samuel 3.12–35). The implication is that if David had been able to make this alliance with Avner, the disdain of the northern tribes might have been averted for good.

115. See 1 Kings 14.30, 15.6, 7, 16; 2 Kings 13.12, 14.8–14, 16.5–9; Isaiah 7.1–9, 9.19–20.
116. Jeremiah 3.18, 30.21; Ezekiel 34.23, 37.15–24; Hoshea 2.2. Also Isaiah 11.13–14.
117. 1 Samuel 8.5, 20.

6. Jeremiah and the Problem of Knowing

1. See my discussion in Chapter 1, Section I.
2. Plato, *Republic* 509d–520a.
3. By this I mean that for Jeremiah, the world of our experience is all there is. There is, to be sure, a heaven above, and Sheol below. But these seem to be a part of our physical world. If you had a tower high enough, you could get there. Many thinkers introduce a second metaphysical realm that is not physically contiguous with ours in this way, and that you can access, if at all, only by mental or mystical or magical means. One such scheme is Plato's, which introduces a realm of "true being" in addition to the realm of illusion in which we live every day. See *Republic* 514a–520a. There is no way physically to travel to this place, which can only be reached by philosophical or mystical ascent. Similarly, in the Gospel of John, Jesus tells the people of Jerusalem, "I know where I come from and where I am going.... You judge by worldly standards.... [W]here I am going, you cannot come.... You belong to this world below, I to the world above. That is why I told you that you would die in your sins" (John 8.14, 22–24). Here, too, we are discussing a second metaphysical realm besides our own. There is no way physically to travel to the world Jesus is talking about. One gets there, if at all, by faith – just as one gets to Plato's realm of true being by way of certain philosophical techniques. Jeremiah is not, in this sense, a dualist, since he knows of no second realm that is metaphysically distinct from ours. A similar view is proposed by Claude Tresmontant, *A Study of Hebrew Thought*, Michael Francis Gibson, trans. (New York: Desclee, 1960 [1956]).
4. These chapter divisions are of later origin, and do not necessarily reflect the original divisions internal to the text.
5. Egypt, Philestia, Moav, Ammon, Edom, Damascus, Kedar, Persia, and Babylonia.
6. The inclusion of the last passages of the History of Israel here a second time works to splice the narrative of the destruction of Jerusalem in Jeremiah into its proper place in the History, as if to indicate that the details included in Jeremiah are to be read as an integral part of the same narrative that appears in the History. One possibility is that the historical narrative in Jeremiah was at one point intended to be the concluding section of the History.

7. On *emuna* and *sheker*, see Chapter 7.

8. Compare Ezekiel 22.30; also 9.4–6.

9. The explicit comparison of Jerusalem to Sodom is made not only at Jeremiah 23.14, but also at Deuteronomy 29.21–23, Isaiah 1.10, Ezekiel 16.46, 56, and Hoshea 11.8.

10. Jeremiah 18. 26, 32.

11. On prophetic metaphor, see Chapter 3, Section II; as well as Chapter 9.

12. See Jeremiah 5.4–5.

13. For the function of the watchman and of the *shofar*, see Ezekiel 33.1–6; also 3.17–21 and Isaiah 62.6.

14. Compare, for example, Proverbs 21.1–2: "Wisdom cries aloud outside, she gives her voice in the squares. She cries in the chief place of the concourse, at the entrances to the gates of the city she speaks what she has to say."

15. Compare Jeremiah 17.10: "I, the Lord ... give each according to his ways, the fruit of his deeds." This image follows Isaiah 2.10.

16. It is particularly instructive in this context also to consider that which does *not* appear in the book of Jeremiah. There are no exhortations to read more Scripture, for the people read plenty of Scripture. Nor does Jeremiah tell the people to conduct more religious services, because there is a surfeit of these. Nor does he tell them that they should be doing more listening to the orations of the prophets, because they do a great deal of that as well. See Jeremiah 5:31, 7:4, 8:8, 23.25–32, among others. Compare Ezekiel 22.23–28.

17. Compare to Jeremiah's first experience of prophecy, in which God asks Jeremiah, "What do you see?" Having heard Jeremiah's answer, God tells the young man that he has "excelled in seeing." See Jeremiah 1.11–14; also Isaiah 5.20–21.

18. See Joshua Berman, *The Temple* (Northvale, N.J.: Jason Aronson, 1995), pp. 116–126.

19. Genesis 19.29. Also 19.21, 25. Modern Hebrew speakers use this word when they speak of *revolution*.

20. Jeremiah 2.8.

21. See also Ezekiel 7.25, 13.10, 17.

22. See also Deuteronomy 29.18; Jeremiah 9.13, 11.8, 16.12, 18.2. 23.25–32.

23. Compare, for example, "But the Lord has not given you a mind [*lev*] to understand, and eyes to see, and ears to hear, until this very day" (Deuteronomy 29.3). Similarly, when Jeremiah says that the people are foolish, it is because they do not have a *lev*, as in Jeremiah 5.21. For discussion, see Michael Carasik, *Theologies of the Mind in Biblical Israel* (New York: Peter Lang, 2006), pp. 104–124.

24. Jeremiah Unterman, *From Repentance to Redemption: Jeremiah's Thought in Transition* (Sheffield: Sheffield Academic Press, 1987), p. 113.

25. The word *shrir* means muscle, and *shrirut* is literally muscularity. The mind is thus seen to be strong, as in "head-strong," or stubborn. See Willem A. VanGemeren, ed., *New International Dictionary of Old Testament Theology and Exegesis* (Grand Rapids, Mich.: Zondervan, 1997), vol. IV, pp. 253–254.

26. This expression appears at 3.17, 7.24, 9.13, 11.8, 13.10, 16.12, 18.12, and 23.17. The only other appearances of this term appear to be in Deuteronomy 29.18 and Psalms 81.13. Ezekiel, who does not use this expression, provides an

alternative, speaking instead of the people setting up idols in their own minds. See Ezekiel 14.1–8.

27. Jeremiah 8.7.
28. Jeremiah 3.17.
29. Another famous metaphor of Jeremiah is the "uncircumcised ear" of the people, who cannot understand the meanings of the words they hear. See Jeremiah 6.10.
30. Jeremiah 2.8.
31. Jeremiah 23.16.
32. On the natural law teaching in the orations of the prophets of Israel, see John Barton, *Understanding Old Testament Ethics* (Louisville, Ky.: Westminister John Knox Press, 2003).
33. On God's role in establishing the laws of the harvest, see also Isaiah 28.24–29.
34. In Psalms, we are also told that God's law governs the heavens and the establishment of the earth. See Psalms 119.89–91. Compare also to Isaiah 1.3.
35. See, for example, Jeremiah 7.23: "But this thing did I command them [your fathers], saying: Heed my voice so that I will be your God and you will be my people. And walk in all the way that I command you that it may go well for you." Much the same language appears in Deuteronomy 5.30, 6.3, 10.13.
36. Jean Bottéro, *Mesopotamia: Writing, Reasoning and the Gods*, Zainab Bahrani and Marc van de Mieroop, trans. (Chicago: University of Chicago Press, 1992 [1987]), pp. 113–137.
37. Jeremiah 3.17.
38. Compare Jeremiah 3.17: "In that time, they shall call Jerusalem 'Throne of the Lord,' and all the nations will assemble there in the name of the Lord, in Jerusalem, and will no longer go after the arbitrariness of their evil minds."
39. For discussion of the laws of Moses as a law for mankind, see Chapter 8, Section V, especially note 73.
40. 1 Samuel 12.21; Jeremiah 2.8, 11, 7.8, 12.13, 16.19, 23.32; Isaiah 30.5, 6, 44.9, 10, 47.12, 48.17, 57.12; Havakuk 2.18.
41. Francis Brown, S. R. Driver, and Charles A. Briggs, eds., *A Hebrew and English Lexicon of the Old Testament* (Peabody, Mass.: Hendrickson, 2005 [1906]), p. 418. But compare VanGemeren, ed., *New International Dictionary of Old Testament Theology* vol. II, pp. 487–488, which locates no known root for this word.
42. See my discussion of the distinction between the metaphors of God as a king and as a father in Chapter 3, Section III.
43. For many readers today, it is difficult to understand the sense in which this term *ho'il* is intended in such passages. Surely, Isaiah and Jeremiah cannot be speaking of that which is of *material* or *political* benefit? Are not these prophets of Israel thinking about the people's eternal souls? But the answer is that they just aren't. The reading of biblical texts such as the one just quoted (using terms such as "we are saved" – *nitzalnu*; or "salvation of Israel," *tshu'at israel*, as in Jeremiah 3.23) as referring to anything beyond the present world is the product of later religious developments that have no basis in Jeremiah's thought. What is at stake in all these passages is precisely the question of what is to be done to secure material and political benefit: the peace, justice, and material

well-being of the kingdom of Judah, and of the people of Judah, and of their posterity. Consider, for instance, Jeremiah 3.22–24, where the prophet is talking to the Jews about the effort they have wasted on pandering to foreign gods: "Return, backsliding children,... [saying] 'Truly in vain [we awaited help] from the hills, from the multitude of mountains [where we worshiped].... And the shameful thing has consumed the toil of our fathers since our youth, their flocks and their cattle, their sons and their daughters.'" Thus when the people come to their senses and understand that their idolatry has been a fraud, Jeremiah expects them to have two criticisms of it: first, that it brought them no material assistance in war or business as they had expected that it would ("in vain we awaited help"); and second, that the material costs associated with the idolatry have been great ("consuming the toil of their fathers"). Thus the futility of the idols is not some theological abstraction, but a very literal salvation from a time when men could barely scrape a living from the land in this life, and were not secure enough yet to be concerning themselves with any other life. Jeremiah's issue with the false gods is therefore primarily that they constitute false philosophies which lead to the bad life, and not the good.

44. See also Jeremiah 10.3, 8: "For the laws of the peoples are worthless [*hevel*] ... a worthless teaching [*musar havalim*], for wood it is."

45. This common biblical use of *hevel* to refer to what is transient and worthless seems to be related to the concept of false words, which have nothing to them. Words that have nothing more to them than the breath on which they ride are those which are false, which cannot stand. Jeremiah deploys this term with particular aggressiveness. For example, in the verses immediately preceding Jeremiah's metaphor of the broken cisterns, just quoted, he argues that if you rely on what is transient and without power, then you yourself will quickly achieve this very transience and powerlessness as a consequence: "So says the Lord: What wrong did your fathers find in me, that they distanced themselves from me and went after futility [*hevel*] and became futile themselves [*vayehebalu*]?" (Jeremiah 2.5; see also also 2 Kings 17.15). Jeremiah here makes a reflexive verb out of *hevel*, a noun meaning something transient and worthless, and says that generations of Israelites insisted on relying upon that which was transient and worthless. Now, as a result, they themselves have become transient and worthless, and will have to leave the land.

46. Notice that the argument here is not about whether these gods *exist*, since they obviously exist in the form of carved idols, at least. The issue is whether these gods affect or govern the world in any way, so that to appease them can bring about that which is of benefit to men. For discussion see Chapter 8, Section VI.

47. See Rashi on Jeremiah 17.13; John Bright, *Jeremiah* (Garden City, N.Y.: Doubleday, 1965), p. 118.

48. Compare Jeremiah 2.25: "Keep your feet from going barefoot and your throat from thirst. But you said, 'There is no hope. No, I have loved strangers and after them I will go.'"

49. Water spilled on the ground cannot be gathered up again – and thus represents death. See 1 Samuel 14.14.

50. Compare Isaiah 33.20, 38.12.

51. As David, on his deathbed, tells his son Solomon: "[B]e strong and become a man. And keep the watch of the Lord your God, to walk in his ways, to keep his laws, his commandments, his judgments and his declarations, as it is written in the teaching of Moses, that you should be wise [*taskil*] in all that you do, and in all to which you turn" (1 Kings 2.2–3). Similarly, Isaiah tells Israel, "[F]or it is a people without understanding, therefore no mercy will there be from him who made them, no grace from him who created them" (Isaiah 27.11). On this view, one must understand what is to be done and do it if one wishes to receive even God's mercy and grace. See also Isaiah 29.11–12, 18.

52. See also Isaiah 59.9–10.

53. In a parallel passage, Jeremiah speaks of the misconceptions being circulated by erring priests and prophets as taking them into slippery places in the darkness: "For both prophet and priest are flatterers [telling the people what they want to hear].... Therefore their way will become, for them, as slippery places in the dark. There they will be driven and there they will fall" (Jeremiah 23.11–12). The punishment for telling people what they want to hear is that one ceases to be able to distinguish that which is real from that which is not. One distances oneself from that which is real, and the result is that "for them," darkness descends. Compare Jeremiah 17.6: "He will be like a lone tree on the plain, and will not see when good comes." Not only the prophets and priests are responsible for the false conceptions that plague the people. Jeremiah also recognizes that the people have been blinded by the instruction of their parents. See, for example, Jeremiah 9.13. Related to this is a chilling turn of phrase found in Isaiah, who speaks of things "for which there is no dawn." See Isaiah 8.20.

54. See also Jeremiah 14.16: "And I will pour upon them their own evil."

55. Compare Psalms 119.67, 71: "Before I was afflicted I went astray, but now I observe as you have said.... It is good for me that I have been afflicted, so that I might learn your laws." Similarly, Deuteronomy 8.5; Proverbs 3.11–13.

56. Also Isaiah 1.5–6.

57. Compare Isaiah 50.7 and Ezekiel 3.8, where it is the face of the *prophet* that is turned to stone. Related passages in Jeremiah include this one, in which Jeremiah is likened to a fortress city: "And you will gird your loins, and arise and speak to them all that I command you. Be not dismayed by them lest I dismay you before them. And see that today I have given you to be a fortress city and an iron pillar and walls of brass to the entire land, to the kings of Judah, to its princes, to its priests, and to the people of the land. And they will war with you but they will not prevail over you. For I am with you, says the Lord, to save you" (Jeremiah 1.17–19).

58. See Jeremiah 17.15 and Rashi on this verse. See also John Bright, *Jeremiah*, p. 116.

59. See also Ezekiel 13.1–17, and the prophet's reference to the "conspiracy of her prophets within her" at Ezekiel 22.25.

60. At this point, Jeremiah's educational mission takes on a rather different coloration from the gentle hectoring that is characteristic of Socrates' "midwifery." Jeremiah's mission is explicitly related to the uprooting of the conceptions in the minds of his people. This mission is described in the account of Jeremiah's

first prophecy: "And the Lord stretched out his hand and touched my mouth, and the Lord said to me, see how I have placed my words in your mouth. See how I have appointed you today over the nations and over the states, to uproot and to tear down, to destroy and to demolish, to build and to plant" (Jeremiah 1.9–10). Similarly: "See how I put my words in your mouth for fire, and this people is wood, and it will consume them" (Jeremiah 5.14). And also: "A tower I have given you among my people, a fortress, and you will know and test their way" (Jeremiah 6.27).

61. Isaiah 19.13–14, 51.17; Ezekiel 23.33.

62. See, for example, Jeremiah 11.15: "What is there for my beloved in my house? The many do villainy to her.... [It is done] for your evil, then you rejoice." Similarly: "An appalling and horrible thing has appeared in the land. The prophets have prophesied in falsehood, and the priests have fallen in their hands, and my people love to have it so" (Jeremiah 5.31).

63. Enforced drinking is evidently a phenomenon known from the behavior of Near Eastern kings. See Esther 1.7–8.

64. Compare: "For so said the Lord, see how I sling the inhabitants of the land out this time, and I will bring them troubles in such a way that they may find them" (Jeremiah 10.18).

65. See also Jeremiah 48.47, 49.39.

66. Jeremiah 5.31.

67. Jeremiah 29.11. See also 31.15–16, where the end is compared to the wage that one receives for one's labors. It is often used, just as in modern English, to mean "in the end" – as when Moses tells the people that God left the Jews in the desert "to afflict you and to try you that it may be good for you in the end [*be'aharitecha*]" (Deuteronomy 8.16). Compare Genesis 4.3, where a similar expression which literally means "end of days" [*miketz yamim*] refers only to the fulfillment of the promise of the harvest: Cain plants and in the "end of days" he reaps and sacrifices to God. On the mistranslation of such expressions as "the end of days," see my discussion in Chapter 3, Section II.

68. It is interesting that knowing the ends of things – simply, what will happen and how things turn out – is in the Hebrew Scriptures the most characteristic power of a god: It isn't working miracles that is of greatest interest, and the object of greatest shame because the false gods cannot do it. It is the fact that they can say nothing about what will happen.

69. Deuteronomy 18.21–22.

70. 2 Kings 23.33–34.

71. Jeremiah distinguishes prophets of peace from prophets of war, despising prophets of peace for telling the people that there is no need for them to mend their ways. See Jeremiah 28.7–8. See also Ezekiel 33.33.

72. Judging from the content of Jeremiah's orations of this period, it would appear that the refrain that all would soon be well was to be heard on all sides, and that many did believe it. See, for example, Jeremiah 27.9.

73. The claim that they were sated with bread when they worshiped idols in Jerusalem is a reference to the words of the liberated slaves in Sinai, who refer to the slavery in Egypt as a time of "when we sat by the fleshpots, and at bread until we were sated" (Exodus 16.3).

74. Jeremiah sees the departure from the land of Jews who had not been forcibly exiled by the Babylonians as deepening the national catastrophe. The narrative portion of the book of Jeremiah tells us that Jeremiah himself was brought down to Egypt by the Jewish survivors against his will. See Jeremiah 42.1–43.7.

75. Recalling Jeremiah's first prophetic metaphor of the almond stick, at Jeremiah 1.11–12.

76. Many examples of words that "stand" in this way, in the face of adversity and in the face of other words, appear throughout the Hebrew Bible. Among many other examples, see Deuteronomy 19:15; Isaiah 8.10, 40.8; Jeremiah 28.6; Esther 3.4; Psalms 33.10–11; Ecclesiastes 2:8–9; 1 Chronicles 17.23; 2 Chronicles 30.5. Note that the word that is translated here as "word" (Hebrew, *davar*) is the same word used for "thing." For a more detailed discussion of what it means for words (or things) to stand in Scripture and the relationship between this and truth, see Chapter 7, especially Sections V–VII.

77. Compare Jeremiah 12.13: "They sowed wheat and reaped thorns, they suffered what is to no avail [*lo yo'ilu*]. Be ashamed, then, of your produce, and of the anger of the Lord." See also 14.19.

78. What of Jeremiah himself? Is prophetic knowledge also related to experience, or is it an alternate path to knowledge? For a preliminary look at this subject, see my discussion in Chapter 9.

79. Moreover, because Jeremiah sees the laws that sustain the world as having been imposed, it would seem that they cannot be seen as being truly eternal. The present natural law reflects the order resulting from God's having constrained the chaos that once reigned. This chaos can, perhaps, return.

80. Thinkers that may be seen as being comparable, in different ways, include John Selden, Giambattista Vico, J. G. Herder, C. S. Pierce, William James, Henri Bergson, Karl Mannheim, and Thomas Kuhn.

81. See Thomas Kuhn, *The Structure of Scientific Revolutions* (Chicago: University of Chicago Press, 1970 [1962]). For a comparison of Jeremiah's standpoint to that of Mannheim and Kuhn, see Yoram Hazony, 'The Political Philosophy of Jeremiah' (Ph.D. dissertation, Rutgers University, 1993).

7. Truth and Being in the Hebrew Bible

1. As presented in two books by the Bible scholar and theologian James Barr, the argument is that there is little purpose in studying the meanings of biblical terms in search of the standpoint of the biblical authors, since anything distinctive about the biblical teaching is presented "at the level of sentences" and not in distinctive meanings attached to the words used by the biblical authors. See James Barr, *The Semantics of Biblical Language* (New York: Oxford University Press, 1961), pp. 263–296; James Barr, *Biblical Words for Time* (London: SCM Press, 1962), pp. 153–162. In my view, this argument simply assumes that which it sets out to prove. If one does not engage in careful clarification of meanings of Hebrew biblical terms, then these terms will, as a matter of course, appear to mean more or less whatever the reader brings to them in the form of his or her own cultural prejudices. Barr's theory is advanced in the context of his famous attack on the "biblical theology" movement, best represented by

Thorleif Boman, *Hebrew Thought Compared With Greek*, Jules L. Moreau, trans. (New York: SCM Press, 1960 [1954]). Although Barr was right on a number of important points, on the whole I think the quality of his argument against Boman has been greatly overrated.

2. In many cases, the terms that are used to render biblical Hebrew into English are not even translations of Hebrew terms, but rather of Greek terms used in the Septuagint, which were themselves translated from Hebrew. Even in the best modern translations, difficulties stemming from the continued influence of the Septuagint persist. On the problematic nature of the terms used in the Septuagint translations, see Louis H. Feldman, *Judaism and Hellenism Reconsidered* (Leiden: Brill, 2006), pp. 57–64.

3. See Chapter 6, Section II.

4. So far as I know, no one expects translations of Plato's *Republic* or Aristotle's *Metaphysics* to be able to render the texts with better than a certain degree of precision. Even today, with superb English editions available, it is still the case that a reader interested in pinning down the text's precise standpoint will have to consult the original Greek, since words in classical Greek often have a very different range of meaning from their closest modern English equivalents. Moreover, even if this were not the case, an author may depart from the common usage of a word to forge the language he needs to express his thoughts. This means that while you can get a rough idea of what is going on by relying on rough English translations such as *form* (for the Greek *idea*), or *spirit* (for *thymos*), or *virtue* (for *arete*), or *opinion* (for *doxa*), this kind of substitution is never going to offer better than a vague understanding of what Plato is really saying. If you want the text to mean something very clear, and to hang together in such a way as to constitute a consistent whole, then you won't have much choice but to take a look under the hood of the translation and begin familiarizing yourself with the Greek terms, the different instances of their usage, and the way that related terms, whether in Greek or in other languages, are used. Indeed, some scholars go so far as to suggest that translations should really just leave the most important terms in the original Greek. J. L. Ackrill estimates that there are thirty or forty basic terms in Greek that are best left without any translation at all. See J. L. Ackrill, "Introduction," *A New Aristotle Reader* (Princeton: Princeton University Press, 1987), p. xii. None of this is any less true with respect to the Hebrew of the Bible.

5. Aristotle, *Metaphysics* 1011b25–30.

6. I take note of the view that what is in fact "truth-bearing" is not a given sentence in the speech or thought of an individual, but a proposition independent of such sentences. For my purposes here, I will assume that since such propositions are always couched in the form of sentences, they can be treated as if they were sentences. The difference between the biblical conception of truth and all sentence- or proposition-based theories of truth is, I think, sufficiently great to permit this simplification without prejudicing the course of the argument.

7. Since such a correspondence theory of truth requires a comparison between what is real and what is said about what is real, all such theories depend on what I will call a *dualist* metaphysics – that is, one in which reality is cleanly divided between a "realm" of speech and a world that is independent of this realm of

speech. Such a dualism can be called the *dualism of word and object*, to distinguish it from other ways in which the term *dualism* tends to be used in modern philosophy. On this view, both Aristotle and Descartes, for example, subscribe to a dualism of word and object. For a discussion of other forms of dualism discussed by philosophers, see Howard Robinson, "Dualism," in Edward N. Zalta, ed., *The Stanford Encyclopedia of Philosophy* (Fall 2009), http://plato.stanford. edu/archives/fall2009/entries/dualism/.

8. Plato, *Sophist* 263e.

9. For an overview, see A. N. Prior, "Correspondence Theory of Truth," in Paul Edwards, ed., *Encyclopedia of Philosophy* (New York: Collier Macmillan, 1967), vol. II, pp. 223–232.

10. See Hilary Putnam, "Two Philosophical Perspectives," in *Reason, History, and Truth* (Cambridge: Cambridge University Press, 1981), pp. 49–74, at p. 56. Similar suggestions are advanced by F. H. Bradley, "On Truth and Copying," in *Essays on Truth and Reality* (London: Oxford University Press, 1914 [1907]), pp. 107–126, at p. 107; Richard Schantz, "Introduction," in *What is Truth?* (New York: Walter de Gruyter, 2002), p. 1.

11. I am here following both the Greek and the biblical traditions, which understood thought to be nothing other than a kind of speech, namely, "silent speech." On this subject, see note 46. The insistence that truth cannot be a quality of individual words, but only of sentences, appears in Plato, *Sophist* 262; Aristotle, *On Interpretation* 16a10–18. This position is usefully amended by Quine, who argues that individual words may also be sentences for this purpose. See W. V. O. Quine, *Word and Object* (Cambridge: Massachusetts Institute of Technology Press, 1960), p. 9.

12. Plato, *Sophist* 263b; Aristotle, *Categories* 4a22–4b12, 14b15–20; Aristotle, *On the Soul* 429a15–17. Note especially the distinction between statements and "actual things," which turns on the supposition that an actual thing can change, while a statement is thought to remain "completely unchangeable in every way" (*Categories* 4a35). Compare Descartes: "[Lord Cherbury] examines what truth is; for my part I have never had any doubts about truth, because it seems a notion so transcendentally clear that nobody can be ignorant of it.... [T]he word 'truth,' in the strict sense, denotes the conformity of thought with its object" (René Descartes, letter to Mersenne, 16 October 1639, in *The Philosophical Writings of Descartes*, John Cottingham et al., ed. and trans. [Cambridge: Cambridge University Press, 1991], p. 139).

13. These challenges are themselves quite diverse, but together they lead to the conclusion that the correspondence theory cannot so easily be maintained. See Harold H. Joachim, *The Nature of Truth* (New York: Greenwood, 1969 [1906]); F. H. Bradley, "On Truth and Copying," pp. 107–109; Brand Blanchard, *The Nature of Thought* (Norwich: Jarrold & Sons, 1964), pp. 225–237; Peter Strawson, "Truth," in *Logico-Linguistic Papers* (Ashgate: Burlington, Vermont, 2002 [1971]), pp. 147–164; Richard Rorty, *Philosophy and the Mirror of Nature* (Princeton: Princeton University Press, 1979); Hilary Putnam, "Two Philosophical Perspectives," pp. 72–74; Hilary Putnam, "The Question of Realism," in James Conant, ed., *Words and Life* (Cambridge, Mass.: Harvard University Press, 1994), pp. 295–312, at pp. 297–300; Donald Davidson, "A

Coherence Theory of Truth and Knowledge," in *Subjective, Intersubjective, Objective* (Oxford: Oxford University Press, 2001 [1983]), pp. 137–153, at pp. 143–144; Donald Davidson, "Epistemology and Truth," in *Subjective, Intersubjective, Objective*, pp. 177–192, at pp. 183–185.

14. An alternative view, called the "coherence theory of truth," proposes that the proposition is true if it coheres with the mass of an individual's prior beliefs. As such it seems to imply a thoroughgoing relativism, which is a rather strange quality for a philosophical theory of truth.

15. For our purposes here, it is simplest to understand the term "object" as referring to any conceptually discrete object of the understanding, including, for example, a particular war, the sky, or a mirror image. See Hilary Putnam, "Sense, Nonsense, and the Senses: An Inquiry into the Powers of the Human Mind," *The Journal of Philosophy* (September 1994), pp. 445–517, at pp. 449–450. Compare Donald Davidson, "The Individuation of Events," in *Essays on Action and Events* (New York: Oxford University Press, 2001[1969]), pp. 163–180, at pp. 164–165.

16. For further discussion of the word *emet* and its cognates, see Francis Brown, S. R. Driver, and Charles A. Briggs, eds., *A Hebrew and English Lexicon of the Old Testament* (Peabody, Mass.: Hendrickson, 2005 [1906]), pp. 52–54; G. Botterweck and Helmer Ringgren, eds., *Theological Dictionary of the Old Testament*, John Willis, trans. (Grand Rapids, Mich.: Eerdman's Publishing Company, 1991 [1970]), vol. I, pp. 292–323; E. Jenni and Claus Westermann, eds., *Theological Lexicon of the Old Testament*, Mark Briddle, trans. (Peabody, Massachusetts: Hendrickson Publishers, 1997 [1971]), vol. I, pp. 134–157; Willem A. VanGemeren, ed., *New International Dictionary of Old Testament Theology and Exegesis* (Grand Rapids, Mich.: Zondervan, 1997), vol. I, pp. 427–433; Ludwig Koehler and Walter Baumgartner, *The Hebrew and Aramaic Lexicon of the Old Testament*, R. E. J. Richardson, trans. (Boston: Brill, 2001), pp. 63–64, 68–69.

17. Genesis 24.48. Compare Psalms 119.30.

18. Exodus 18.21.

19. Jeremiah 2.21. Following Isaiah 5.1–7.

20. Psalms 33.17.

21. Proverbs 31.30.

22. For a succinct discussion of the role of the Hebrew root-stem in the biblical language, see Bruce K. Waltke and M. O'Connor, *An Introduction to Biblical Hebrew Syntax* (Winona Lake, Ind.: Eisenbrauns, 1990), pp. 83–87.

23. Isaiah 22.23–25.

24. Isaiah 1.21.

25. But note that this is the same term typically rendered as *truth* in translations of Jeremiah's proposal that Jerusalem could be forgiven if a man could be found in her "who does justice and seeks truth" (Jeremiah 5.1). See Chapter 6, Section I.

26. Exodus 17.11–13.

27. Joshua 2.12–21. Compare 6.17, 22–23, 25.

28. "The wicked man does false work [*pe'ulat sheker*], but he that sows righteousness has a true wage [*secher emet*]" (Proverbs 11.18).

29. Psalms 33.17.

30. Proverbs 20.17.
31. Proverbs 31.30.
32. Genesis 24.37–38, 49.
33. Additional examples appear at Genesis 32.11, 47.29; Joshua 2.14; 2 Samuel 2.6; Ezekiel 18.8; Nehemia 9.33.
34. Thus David is said "to walk before you [God] *in truth*," by which is meant that he walks before God in a way that is steadfast or faithful (1 Kings 3.6). And Jeremiah, speaking of the Jews as the end of their state approaches, says that God will one day "plant them in this land *in truth*," meaning that they will one day be planted reliably, so that their remaining planted can be relied upon. See Jeremiah 32.41; also Joshua 24.14; Judges 9.15, 16, 19; 1 Kings 2.4; Isaiah 61.7–8.
35. One can, of course, say that a love is true even in the enthusiasm of its first days. But such a claim is a prediction, the expression of hope. We do not in fact know whether a love is true until after it has stood the test of time.
36. Were we to consider only cases in which *emet* refers to objects, persons, and actions, we would have to conclude that the biblical concept of truth is simply unrelated to that which is dominant in the tradition of Western philosophy, according to which truth is a quality of speech. Then we could say that *emet* and truth are simply two different things. What prevents us from reaching this conclusion is not only the traditional translation of *emet* as truth (in the King James Bible, as well as in all subsequent translations, which of course could be a mistranslation); it is also the fact that *emet* is the only term available to describe the truth of speech in the Bible. Thus if we were to dispense with the term *emet* as referring to the truth of speech, we would be left without any way in which biblical Hebrew could express the idea that something that someone said or thought was true! Examples of cases in which the truth of that which is spoken is described as *emet* include Genesis 42.16; Deuteronomy 13.13–16, 17.4, 22.20–21; 1 Kings 10.4–7; Isaiah 43.9; Daniel 11.2.
37. Deuteronomy 17.2–6.
38. 1 Kings 10.1–2, 6–7.
39. Jeremiah 8.10–11.
40. For discussion of the word *davar*, see Francis Brown, S. R. Driver, and Charles A. Briggs, eds., *A Hebrew and English Lexicon of the Old Testament*, pp. 180–184; E. Jenni and Claus Westermann, eds., *Theological Lexicon of the Old Testament*, vol. I, pp. 325–332; Willem A. VanGemeren, ed., *New International Dictionary of Old Testament Theology*, vol. I, pp. 912–915; Ludwig Koehler and Walter Baumgartner, *The Hebrew and Aramaic Lexicon of the Old Testament*, pp. 210–212.
41. Exodus 4.10.
42. Joshua 6.10.
43. Deuteronomy 30.11, 14.
44. Deuteronomy 15.9.
45. Joshua 14.7. Here, the spies traveled together and saw the same things, and yet Calev returns with one *davar* in his mind, saying that the peoples of the land can be beaten ("We are certainly able to overcome them" [Numbers 13.30]); and the other spies with another, saying that they are too strong to be fought. The

report (*davar*) that Calev brings back is neither an unarguable fact nor an arbitrary sentiment, but a conception or an understanding of the land as it appeared to him.

46. In the Bible as in Greek philosophy, thought is considered to be silent speech. See for example Psalms 15.1–2: "Who will dwell in my holy mountain? He that walks uprightly, and acts justly and speaks truth [*dover emet*] in his mind." See also Genesis 24.45; Deuteronomy 6.6, 15.9, 30.14, 32.46–47; Joshua 14.7; 1 Samuel 1.13, 21.13; 2 Samuel 13.33; Isaiah 59.13; Ezekiel 38.10; Jonah 4.2; Psalms 12.3, 35.20; Proverbs 23.33; Ecclesiastes 1.16, 2.15, 5.1. *Amar belibo* can also be found in numerous places.

47. Numbers 31.22–23.

48. Deuteronomy 23.20.

49. Genesis 19.22.

50. 1 Samuel 3.11–12.

51. Leviticus 4.13–14.

52. Nehemia 11.24.

53. Other words for thing, such as *hefetz*, are relatively infrequent and restricted in their usage. Even-Shoshan lists fewer than 130 uses of this term in all its variations in the Bible, as opposed to roughly 2,700 for *davar*. See Abraham Even-Shoshan, *New Concordance of the Bible* (Tel Aviv: The New Dictionary, 2000), pp. 389–390, 247–257.

54. See, for example, James Barr, *The Semantics of Biblical Language*, pp. 129–140. As far as I am able to see, Barr seems to do little more than to assert that the term *davar* must have two very different meanings (i.e., *word* and *thing*) that can almost always be readily distinguished from their context. He does admit that there are ambiguous cases, but he tells us that "in most cases the sense is clear" (p. 133). In fact, this is very far from being straightforwardly true. Oddly, Barr also admits that the term *davar* may be similar to English-language terms such as *message* and *story*, which are frequently ambiguous as to whether they are used to refer to the content of what is said or to the saying itself (see p. 135). This analogy would seem to undercut Barr's position, suggesting that the term *davar* is in fact used in a manner that often does not permit us to recognize it as definitely referring either to a word or to a thing.

55. The Hebrew terms *davar* and *hefetz*, for example, could have been opposed and brought to express such an opposition.

56. Genesis 21.10–11.

57. Deuteronomy 1.9, 12–14.

58. 2 Samuel 13.30–33. Similarly, 2 Samuel 11.18–21.

59. This characteristic of the biblical metaphysics is described by André Neher, *The Exile of the Word*, David Maisel, trans. (Philadelphia: Jewish Publication Society, 1981 [1970]), pp. 91–92. A broader and better treatment along similar lines is Claude Tresmontant, *A Study of Hebrew Thought*, Michael Francis Gibson, trans. (New York: Desclee, 1960 [1956]).

60. A related thesis, that "the name is the being" in Mesopotamian metaphysics, is discussed by Edward Greenstein, "Some Developments in the Study of Language and Some Implications for Interpreting Ancient Texts and Cultures," in Shlomo Izre'el, ed., *Semitic Linguistics: The State of the Art at the Turn*

of the Twenty-First Century, Israel Oriental Studies 20 (Winona Lake, Ind.: Eisenbrauns, 2002), pp. 441–479, at pp. 450–451. Compare Bottéro's claim that the pictographic script of the Babylonians "was not a script of words ... but a script of things" in Jean Bottéro, *Mesopotamia: Writing, Reasoning and the Gods*, Zainab Bahrani and Marc van de Mieroop, trans. (Chicago: University of Chicago Press, 1992 [1987]), p. 99. I don't know enough to judge how significant these observations are for the present discussion.

61. Joshua 14.7; Ezekiel 38.10–11.

62. Deuteronomy 17.2–6.

63. See note 7.

64. In this example, we face the awkward question of what an object such as idolatry "ought to be." This is to be read not in any moral sense, for it is evident that in the eyes of the biblical authors idolatry ought not to be at all. Rather, the question of whether something is "true idolatry" (or whether someone is, say, a true thief, or truly an adulterer) turns on whether it can be relied upon to be what something ought to be if it is to be idolatry.

65. 1 Kings 10.1–2, 6–7.

66. Jeremiah 44.27–28.

67. Deuteronomy 19.15.

68. Compare the prayer that God's *davar* should *ye'amen*, or come to be established, also using a cognate of *emet* to suggest that a *davar* can stand firm, or grow to be firm. See Genesis 42.20; 1 Kings 8.26; 1 Chronicles 17.23; 2 Chronicles 1.9, 6.17. So can a name, in 1 Chronicles 17.24.

69. The conception of truth found in expressions such as *true love* and *true friend*, semantically close to the meaning of words such as trust, trustworthy, and troth, is reported by the *Oxford English Dictionary* as a principal meaning of the word *true* in the Middle Ages. See *The Oxford English Dictionary* (New York: Oxford University Press, 1989), vol. XVIII, pp. 606–607.

70. Aristotle, for example, says that "things are false which produce a false appearance." See *Metaphysics* 1024b15–1025a15. A related conception is the view mentioned by Thomas Aquinas, according to which "a house is said to be true that expresses the likeness of the form in the architect's mind.... In the same way, natural things are said to be true in so far as they express the likeness of the species that are in the divine mind. For a stone is called true that possesses the nature proper to a stone." This passage appears in Thomas Aquinas, *Summa Theologica* (Allen, Tex.: Christian Classics, 1981), part 1, question 16. Among modern thinkers, Hegel alone seems to have reached a coherent understanding of truth that resembles that which is here under discussion. As he writes: "Truth in the deeper sense consists of the identity between objectivity and the notion. It is in this deeper sense of truth that we speak of a true state, or of a true work of art. These objects are true if they are as they ought to be, i.e., if their reality corresponds to their notion.... [Similarly,] we speak of a true friend, by which we mean a friend whose manner of conduct accords with the notion of friendship" (G. F. W. Hegel, *Logic*, William Wallace, trans. [New York: Oxford University Press, 1975], section 213, p. 276; section 24, p. 41; also section 172, p. 237). On this view, an object can be true or false if it approaches or does not approach the ideal conception of what it "ought to be." All of these views have a certain

affinity, whether greater or lesser, to the biblical conception. They seem to differ from that which prevails in the biblical texts, however, in that they apparently refer to a static reality in which an object is what it ought to be within the framework of the given moment. I have found no indication in any of these attempts to describe the truth of objects that truth is explicitly associated with reliability in time. For a brief discussion of the history of the idea that an object can be true, see Wolfgang Kunne, *Conceptions of Truth* (New York: Oxford University Press, 2003), pp. 104–107.

71. See note 13 for references.

72. André Neher, *The Exile of the Word*, pp. 91–92.

73. Deuteronomy 18.18, 21–22.

8. Jerusalem and Carthage: Reason and Faith in Hebrew Scripture

1. The revival of the Athens and Jerusalem trope has been largely due to Leo Strauss, whose own dichotomy between Jerusalem and Athens builds on Tertullian's view of the Bible as standing in irreconcilable conflict with philosophy. See Leo Strauss, "Reason and Revelation," in Heinrich Meier, ed., *Leo Strauss and the Theologico-Political Problem* (Cambridge: Cambridge University Press, 2006 [1948]), pp. 141–167; Leo Strauss, *Natural Right and History* (Chicago: University of Chicago Press, 1953), pp. 74–85; Leo Strauss, "On the Interpretation of Genesis" and "Jerusalem and Athens," in Kenneth Hart Green, ed., *Jewish Philosophy and the Crisis of Modernity: Essays and Lectures in Modern Jewish Thought* (Albany: SUNY Press, 1997 [1957]), pp. 359–403; Mark Lilla, *The Stillborn God: Religion, Politics and the Modern West* (New York: Knopf, 2007). An earlier version of this chapter appeared as Yoram Hazony, "Jerusalem and Carthage," *Hebraic Political Studies* (Summer 2008), pp. 260–288.

2. Tertullian, *Prescription Against Heretics* 7.15–22. Translations of Tertullian's texts are based on the work of Rev. Peter Holmes, available online at *www.tertullian.org*. I have edited them slightly for clarity.

3. This view has been challenged by David Rankin, *Tertullian and the Church* (Cambridge: Cambridge University Press, 1995).

4. Tertullian, *Prescription Against Heretics* 13.1–15.

5. Tertullian, *Prescription Against Heretics* 21.13–14. Brackets in the original.

6. Tertullian, *Prescription Against Heretics* 38.12. Brackets mine.

7. Tertullian, *Prescription Against Heretics* 13.15. Emphasis mine.

8. Matthew 7.7; Luke 11.9.

9. Tertullian, *Prescription Against Heretics* 9.34–10.1, 10.6–10. First brackets mine; second in the original.

10. Tertullian, *Prescription Against Heretics* 7.21–25.

11. Tertullian, *Prescription Against Heretics* 12.10–12. Brackets mine. Compare *Prescription Against Heretics* 3.10–11: "No one is wise, no one is faithful, no one excels in dignity but the Christian."

12. Tertullian, *Prescription Against Heretics* 14.4, 9. Brackets mine.

13. Tertullian, *The Soul's Testimony* 1.4.

14. 1 Colossians 2.8. Compare 1 Timothy 1.4; 2 Timothy 2.17.

15. Tertullian, *Prescription Against Heretics* 7.15–22. Here and elsewhere, Tertullian accuses philosophy of being incapable of learning the truth about anything because its methods lead to the tearing down of all things rather than building up true positions. Compare: "So then, where is there any likeness between the Christian and the philosopher? Between the discipline of Greece and of heaven? ... Between the talker and the doer? Between the man who builds up and the man who pulls down?" See Tertullian, *Apology*, ch. 46.

16. For a more charitable interpretation of Tertullian's relation to philosophy, see R. E. Roberts, *The Theology of Tertullian* (London: Epworth Press, 1924), pp. 63–78.

17. 1 Corinthians 1.4. This text concerning "the folly of the Gospel" gives Tertullian the crucial toehold he needs in the writings of Paul: "[Christ sent me] to proclaim the Gospel; and to do it without relying on the language of worldly wisdom, so that the fact of Christ on his cross might have its full weight. The doctrine of the cross is sheer folly to those on their way to ruin, but to us, who are on the way to salvation, it is the power of God.... The world failed to find him by its wisdom, and he chose to save those who have faith by the folly of the Gospel.... My brothers, think what sort of people you are, whom God has called. Few of you are men of wisdom, by any human standard.... Yet to shame the wise, God has chosen what the world counts folly.... He has chosen things low and contemptible, mere nothings, to overthrow the existing order.... Make no mistake about this: If there is anyone among you who fancies himself wise – wise, I mean by the standards of this passing age – he must become a fool to gain true wisdom. For the wisdom of the world is folly in God's sight.... We are fools for Christ's sake" (1 Corinthians 1.17–18, 21–22, 26–28, 3.18–19, 4.10). Similarly, "Of course we all 'have knowledge,' as you say. This 'knowledge' breeds conceit; it is love that builds. If anyone fancies that he knows, he knows nothing yet, in the true sense of knowing. But if a man loves, he is acknowledged by God" (1 Corinthians 8.1–3).

18. Tertullian, *The Flesh of Christ* 4.5–6, 5.1, 4.

19. Søren Kierkegaard, *Concluding Unscientific Postscript to "Philosophical Fragments"* (Princeton: Princeton University Press, 1992), pp. 210–213. A subtle exploration of Kierkegaard's relation to philosophy can be found in Jacob Howland, *Kierkegaard and Socrates: A Study in Philosophy and Faith* (Cambridge: Cambridge University Press, 2006).

20. C. S. Lewis, *Mere Christianity* (New York: Simon & Schuster, 1996), pp. 55–56.

21. For example: "[T]he improbable character of biblical belief is admitted and even proclaimed by the biblical faith itself.... [T]he improbability of the truth of the Bible is a contention of the Bible" (Leo Strauss, "Interpretation of Genesis," pp. 360–361).

22. A rabbinic adage suggests that "From Tyre to Carthage, they know Israel and their Father in Heaven" (Talmud *Menachot* 110a). And indeed, Tertullian did write a *Response to the Jews*, which presents itself as a debate with a pagan convert to Judaism. But neither this text nor the other sources available to us indicate that Tertullian's view of things Jewish was more than superficial. See Claudia Setzer, "The Jews in Carthage and Western North Africa, 66–235 CE,"

in Steven Katz, ed., *The Cambridge History of Judaism* (Cambridge: Cambridge University Press, 2006), vol. IV, pp. 68–75, at pp. 72–73.

23. We may assume that Tertullian exaggerates in saying that human beings should remain in ignorance of all other things.

24. 1 Corinthians 15.1–7.

25. Consider, for example, Deuteronomy 10.12–13, in which Moses says: "And now Israel, what does the Lord your God require of you, but [i] to fear the Lord your God, [ii] to walk in all his ways, and [iii] to love him, and to serve the Lord your God with all your heart and all your soul, [iv] to keep the commandments of the Lord and his statutes which I command you this day for your good?" But this is precisely the opposite of a catechism such as that offered by Tertullian. Instead of a finite list of concrete things that are to be believed, there is a series of four different principles, each of which opens upon an entire world of effort, belief, and action. Brackets mine.

26. Deuteronomy 6:4–9, 11:13–21; Numbers 15:37–41.

27. Some suggest that Deuteronomy 5 or passages from the first chapters of Proverbs may have served as catechism among Jews. I have to say that reading these passages leaves me unconvinced. But even if this were the case, it would hardly change the force of the argument, which is that the Hebrew Bible was purposely assembled in such a way as to make catechizing efforts seem alien and implausible.

28. See my discussion in Chapter 1, Section I.

29. See my discussion in Chapter 1, Section II.

30. For a compelling presentation of this view, see James Kugel, *The God of Old* (New York: Free Press, 2003), pp. 5–36.

31. See Section VI of this chapter. But even with such severe limitations, Moses is said to understand God clearly in comparison with other prophets. Compare Numbers 11.6–8.

32. 1 Kings 19.8–15; Isaiah 6.1–8. See also the prophet's assertion that the God of Israel is a god that hides himself at Isaiah 45.15. Of interest, too, is Ezekiel's assertion at 43.2 that the voice of God is like that of water.

33. Exodus 20.16–18, 32.1–6.

34. Isaiah attributes their failures not to deceit, but to the reading of the Scriptures line by line, without knowledge of the spirit of the law. See Isaiah 28.7–13.

35. See my discussion of this subject in Chapters 6–7.

36. A number of readers have suggested to me that my use of the expression "search for truth" is problematic because what the biblical authors are seeking is the good, rather than the true. This objection raises crucial issues that I cannot fully resolve here. But a few points should be emphasized by way of beginning this discussion. First, I agree that the use of the term *truth* in this context may be slightly misleading, since the biblical *emet* and its cognates refer to something different from truth as it is understood in Greek philosophy. In the Bible, the true is that which is reliable, steadfast, and sure, as in the English *true heart* or *true friend*. (For discussion, see Chapter 7.) This understanding of truth is in fact closely related to the biblical conception of the good because the principal epistemological concern of the prophets is distinguishing that which can be relied upon to bring mankind well-being from that which appears reliable but

is not. The search for truth in the Bible is therefore, roughly, the search for that which can be relied upon, or *trusted*, to bring about the good in this world. Thus my understanding of what is being sought in the Bible is not, I think, so different from that of my readers. However, we may disagree on the degree to which the Bible is in this respect removed from the concerns of Greek philosophy.

37. Here's Robert Alter's description of the epistemic jungle, as depicted in the Jacob and Joseph narratives of the Hebrew Bible: "Human reality ... is a labyrinth of antagonisms, reversals, deceptions, shady deals, outright lies, disguises, misleading appearances, and ambiguous portents.... [T]he characters generally have only broken threads to grasp as they seek their way" (Robert Alter, *The Art of Biblical Narrative* [New York: Basic Books, 1981], p. 158).

38. Exodus 1.15–21. In this specific case, we are told that the midwives "feared God," but in biblical parlance this does not mean that God spoke to them; only that they feared to do wrong. For discussion, see Yoram Hazony, *The Dawn: Political Teachings of the Book of Esther* (Jerusalem: Shalem Press, 2000 [1995]), pp. 98–100.

39. Exodus 2.1–10.

40. Exodus 2.11–15. See also the story of Tzipora's circumcision of their son, also at her own initiative, at Exodus 4.24–26.

41. See my discussion in Yoram Hazony, "The Jewish Origins of the Western Disobedience Tradition," *Azure* (Summer 1998), pp. 17–74.

42. Jeremiah 5.1. See Chapter 6, Section I.

43. Jeremiah 6.16.

44. Proverbs 1.20–24.

45. Proverbs 23.31–35.

46. Proverbs 6.24–35.

47. The passage quoted is from Isaiah 44.18–20. But Isaiah's argument is actually longer, beginning at 44.9, and includes important details that I have not quoted.

48. Consider, for example, the report of the book of Kings to the effect that the downfall of Solomon's kingdom begins with Rehavam's decision to ignore the voice of experience, represented by the "old men" of his father's court, and to heed instead the advice of his young friends (1 Kings 12.3–17). That the fool is he who ignores experience is stated, for example, in Proverbs 1.22, 32.

49. Jeremiah 9.10–11.

50. This in accordance with the common convention of biblical poetry, in which that which is stated in one clause is then stated slightly differently, with a somewhat modified but nonetheless parallel meaning, in a subsequent clause. See Robert Alter, *The Art of Biblical Poetry* (New York: Basic Books, 1985), pp. 3–26; James Kugel, *The Idea of Biblical Poetry* (Baltimore: Johns Hopkins, 1998 [1981]), pp. 1–58. Another possible option is to read the two clauses ("so wise that he can understand this" and "to whom the mouth of the Lord has spoken") as referring to two different things, so that Jeremiah is understood to be saying that answers to difficult questions of historical causation can only come to those who have in any case attained great wisdom; and to whom, *in addition*, "the mouth of the Lord has spoken." Such a reading leads us to understand God's word as coming only to those whose mental faculties and exertions

make them fit for it, as suggested by Maimonides. See Maimonides, *Guide for the Perplexed*, 2.36–38. I believe the first reading is correct, but for present purposes the upshot is the same: On Maimonides' reading, as well, God speaks only to those who have first acquired wisdom.

51. Isaiah 11.2–3. There are other such examples in Isaiah. The wisdom of the farmer, too, in growing his crops is attributed by Isaiah to God's wise counsels, but the prophet sees no need to explain whether these counsels came from the inventiveness of men or from God speaking to them – as this seems to be immaterial (Isaiah 28.24–29). And later in the book of Isaiah, the prophet declares that God has given him "the tongue of the learned" and that God "awakens my ear to understand as the learned" (Isaiah 50.4). Compare these passages to Exodus 28.3, where God tells Moses: "And you will speak to all who have a wise mind, whom I have filled with the spirit of wisdom." The wisdom in question in this passage is the ability to perform crafts needed in constructing the tabernacle, but the identity between those who "have a wise mind" and those whom God has "filled with a spirit of wisdom" is telling. Similar phrasings appear three more times at Exodus 31.6, 36.1–2. Much the same issue arises with respect to the wisdom of King Solomon, described at 1 Kings 3.16–28, 5.9–14, and 10.1–7. In this account, we are told that after hearing of the cases the young king had judged, "all Israel ... saw that the wisdom of God was in him to do justice" (3.28); and that men and women "came from all the peoples to hear Solomon's wisdom, from all the kings of the earth, who had heard of his wisdom" (5.14). The reader, of course, knows that Solomon has asked God for wisdom, and that in the dream God tells Solomon that he has granted this request. But there is no indication that Solomon tells Israel and the nations about this dream. On the contrary, they are depicted as recognizing that Solomon has the "wisdom of God" solely on the basis of the fact that he is exceptionally wise in matters of law and judgment, as well as in natural science (5.12–13). Here, too, there seems to be no boundary at all between that knowledge which is native to individuals and that which is granted by God. In any case, as Samuel tells the people in a somewhat different context, "It is the Lord who made Moses and Aaron" so that the question of whether their wisdom and other abilities are God-granted seems to be an empty question. See 1 Samuel 12.6.

52. Exodus 3.1–4.

53. Compare the story of Gideon, whom God approaches because he sees that Gideon resists the rule of Midian over Israel. See Judges 6.11–12.

54. Isaiah 6.1–9. The full passage is in fact even more evocative. The *saraf* moves to attend to Isaiah only after Isaiah speaks out loud, expressing his fear that he is impure.

55. Similarly, later on in the book of Isaiah, the prophet has God challenge: "Why, when I came, was there no man? When I called, was there no answer?" (Isaiah 50.2). In Havakuk as well, the prophet begins by challenging God: "O Lord, how long shall I cry and you will not hear?" Only thereafter is he met with a response. See Havakuk 1.1f. God responds only in 2.2.

56. Jeremiah 1.11–14.

57. Compare Zecharia 2.1–6, 4.2–6.

58. Genesis 11.31–32.

59. Jeremiah 33.1, 3. Compare Zecharia 1.3: "Turn to me, says the Lord of Hosts, and I will turn to you."
60. Genesis 18:17–33; Exodus 32:9–14; Numbers 14:11–20, 16.19–23; Judges 6.13; 2 Samuel 6.8–12; Isaiah 40.6–8; Jeremiah 2.9, 29, 4.10, 12:1–4; Ezekiel 9.8; Jonah 3:10–4:3; Havakuk 1:1–4, 1:12–2:1; Job 13:13–16.
61. Genesis 32.25–30. Emphasis mine.
62. Job 13.13–16. Brackets mine.
63. This is the spirit of Moses' words to the effect that "This commandment which I command you this day is not hidden from you, neither is it far off. It is not in heaven that you should say, 'Who shall go up for us to heaven and bring it to us'" (Deuteronomy 30.11–12). There is obviously a significant tension between Moses' optimism that word of God is within reach and the observation of Isaiah and Jeremiah that it is not. The later prophets do look forward to a time when mankind will come to the truth, so they do not disagree with Moses in principle. But for their own generation, they often speak as if the die has already been cast due to the decisions of previous generations.
64. Deuteronomy 4.6–8. A similar equation of justice generally with God's teaching is Isaiah 51.7: "Hear me, you who know justice, a people with my [i.e., God's] teaching [*tora*] in their minds." But note that despite the scorn the prophets of Israel generally heap upon the ways of the nations, they are not always averse to learning from them. For example, when Jeremiah asks whether the nations have ever turned their back on their god, he is in fact praising the piety of the neighboring peoples in comparison with Israel. See Jeremiah 18.13.
65. Similarly, when God gives Solomon wisdom, kings the world over can discern it. See 1 Kings 5.9–15.
66. Deuteronomy 30.15. See also Deuteronomy 10.13; Jeremiah 7.25.
67. Numbers 24:3. The meaning of the expression *shtum ha'a'in* is unknown, but it would seems to be parallel with *glui eina'im* in 24:4, which means that Bilam's eyes are open to see.
68. Numbers 23.8–10, 20–21, 24.5–6.
69. See Numbers 31.16; Joshua 13.22.
70. Jeremiah 16.19.
71. Jeremiah 12.16.
72. Isaiah 2.2–3. See also Micha 4.1–5.
73. Isaiah 51.4. Regarding teaching the nations, as a light and banner for the peoples, see also Isaiah 11.9–10, 12, 42.1–4, 6–7, 49.6, 51.4, 60.3; and Jeremiah 3.17, 4.1–2. A number of neglected passages speak of the Mosaic law as being no less relevant to the nations than they are to Israel. Consider Deuteronomy 33.2–3: "The Lord came from Sinai, and rose up from Se'ir to them. He shone forth from Mount Paran, and came from holy multitudes. From his right hand went a fiery law for them. Truly he loves the peoples." Similarly, Ezekiel speaks of what he calls "the laws of life," in which a man must walk, at Ezekiel 33.15. As he writes: "And I gave them my laws, and I informed them of my statutes, by which a man, if he do them, will live by them" (Ezekiel 20.11). Similar phrasing appears in 20.13, 21; and the reverse, concerning laws by which one cannot live, at 20.25. And Isaiah 56.1–8: "Happy is the man [*enosh*] that does this, and the son of Adam [*ben-adam*] who holds fast to it, who keeps the Sabbath and does

not profane it, and stays his hand from evil.... And the sons of the stranger who join themselves to the Lord, to do his work and to love the name of the Lord becoming his servants, every one who keeps the Sabbath and does not profane it, and all who fast to my covenant – I will bring them to my holy mountain and give them joy in my house of prayer. Their burnt offerings and their sacrifices will be accepted on my altar, for my house will be known as a house of prayer for all the nations." Notice also Isaiah 66.23. It is these passages the rabbis had in mind when they suggested that the reason the Mosaic law was given in the wilderness of Sinai, and not in any settled land, was so that all nations could accept it as their own: "The Tora was given on uninhabited land owned by no one. Had it been given in the promised land, Israel might have said that the nations had no share in it. It was therefore given in the wilderness, so that whoever wished to accept it could do so" (*Mechilta* 19.2). Similarly: "Why was the Tora not given in the land of Israel? So as not to give the nations of the world the chance to say that they only reject the Tora because it was not offered to them on their land.... Three things are associated with the giving of the Tora [at Sinai]: Desert, fire, and water. We learn that just as these are available freely to all mankind, so too is the Tora a gift to all mankind" (*Mechilta* 20.2). For further discussion of this issue, see Maimonides, *Guide for the Perplexed* 3.31, pp. 321–322.

74. See also Isaiah 43.8–12, 44.8–10, in which Israel is called to dispute with the nations, who are said to be able to distinguish truth just as Israel can.

75. Chapter 6, Section IV.

76. Psalms 19.8.

77. Psalms 119.144.

78. Psalms 119.97–104. See also 1 Kings 2.3; Psalms 19.8.

79. Genesis 15.1, 5–6.

80. Exodus 14.30–31. In a related passage, God tells Moses that he will speak before the people at Sinai so that they may believe in Moses as their leader (Exodus 19.9). The signs God teaches Moses at the burning bush are likewise so that the people may believe in Moses (Exodus 4.4–9).

81. So far as I aware, there are no passages in Hebrew Scripture that deal with God's existence as distinct from the question of whether he can be relied upon – that is, whether in practice he will reward men for their just deeds. As Isaiah has it, "And it will be said on that day, behold, this is our God, we hoped for him and he will save us.... O Lord, we have hoped for you.... My soul has longed for you in the night, and the spirit within me seeks you, for when your judgments are on the earth, the inhabitants of the world will learn justice" (Isaiah 25.9, 26.8–9). Similarly: "I will make myself known among them [Israel] when I have judged you [Edom]" (Ezekiel 35.11). I suspect that for many of the prophets and scholars who composed the Bible, if not for all of them, the possibility that God's existence could be distinguished from the empirical question of whether his action can be discerned in the world would have seemed meaningless. Some of the relevant texts are Jeremiah 2.11, 5.7, 16.20; Isaiah 37.19, 41.24; Hoshea 8.6; 2 Kings 19.18; 2 Chronicles 13.9.

82. This is not because the word *belief* cannot be used to describe propositional belief in biblical Hebrew. It can, as in the following passage: "And the people

believed [*veya'amen*] and understood that the Lord had visited the descendants of Israel and that he had seen their suffering and they bowed and prostrated themselves" (Exodus 4.31). There can be propositional belief in biblical Hebrew, but there are, as far as I know, no commandments concerning such belief, nor is it ever counted as a virtue in biblical narrative. For a version of this argument, see Martin Buber, *Two Types of Faith*, Norman P. Goldhawk, trans. (Syracuse: Syracuse University Press, 2003 [1951]), p. 7 and *passim*.

83. Because philosophers often use the term *belief* to refer to the assent to propositions, it may be that this term is misplaced here. When you trust someone, this is not precisely the same thing as assenting to the proposition that "He can be counted on," although sometimes these go together. At times, there is only a feeling or a sense that the individual in question is "solid" and "will be there." When I use the term *belief* with respect to trust in God in this chapter, I use this term in this broader sense.

84. Numbers 14.11; Deuteronomy 1.32, 9.23. Compare Psalms 78.22.

85. Numbers 20.12.

86. 2 Kings 17.13.

87. Deuteronomy 7.9–11. Other expressions seek to express the concept of "the reliable God," including *el emuna* at Deuteronomy 32.4, *elohei amen* at Isaiah 65.16, and *el emet* at Psalms 31.6. In addition, God's commandments are reliable or trustworthy as well: "All your commandments are reliable [*emuna*]." See Psalms 119. 86; also Psalms 19.9, 93.5, 119.66, 138.

88. This same term, *ne'eman*, is used to describe Abraham and what God saw in him, for example, at Nehemia 9.8.

89. Solomon repeats this understanding in his prayer of dedication for the newly built Temple in Jerusalem: "Lord, God of Israel, there is none like you in heaven above or on earth below, *a God who keeps covenant and grace with your servants* who walk before you" (1 Kings 8.23). Emphasis added. Here, too, the supposition is that only the God of Israel has issued promises that can be relied upon. Of course, the fact that the God of Israel is supposed to be the one god who can be relied upon to keep his promises means that, at least in principle, the truth of God's word can be tested – which is as Moses has it in Deuteronomy 18.21–22. The law of Moses also expressly forbids the use of miracles as a proof that one or another moral or legal claim is true. See Deuteronomy 13.2–4.

90. Jeremiah 17.7. See also Psalms 40.5, 84.13. The Hebrew word for faith here is *batah*, which means *trust*, and is a cognate of noun-forms meaning *security*, *safety*, and *confidence*. See Francis Brown, S. R. Driver, and Charles A. Briggs, eds., *A Hebrew and English Lexicon of the Old Testament* (Peabody, Mass.: Hendrickson, 2005 [1906]), p. 105. Although this word is not used in the History for faith in God, it appears frequently in other biblical works. In Psalms and Proverbs, for example, this term is the one usually used for faith in God.

91. Psalms 28.7. See also 26.1, 29.25, 125.1.

92. 2 Chronicles 20.20. A similar message appears in 1 Chronicles 5.20.

93. Isaiah 26.4.

94. Isaiah 7.9, 26.4, 43.10, 50.11; Psalms 4.6, 37.3, 5, 62.9, 115.9–11; Proverbs 3.5. This is not the only respect in which Isaiah's views tend farther in the direction

of piety than those of the History of Israel or of Jeremiah. I have already quoted
Isaiah's call to "Trust in the Lord always" (26.4) – a call that is on its face problematic given that God himself is known, even to Isaiah, to change his mind.
The book of Isaiah also includes a passage that begins "Woe to him who strives
with his maker!" and continues to argue against challenges to God of precisely
the sort that play such an important role in the ethics of the History. See Isaiah
44.9–10.

95. 2 Kings 17.7–23. In addition, the Israelites in the desert were actually punished
for their lack of trust in God. But their lack of faith is depicted as something
outrageous and even uncanny, given that they were literally seeing God working miracles to save their lives every day – so that what happens to them hardly
stands as conclusive evidence that other generations are to be punished specifically for not trusting sufficiently in God.

96. The destruction is blamed on "the sins of Menasheh, according to all his deeds,
and also for the innocent blood that he shed, for he filled Jerusalem with innocent blood, which the Lord would not pardon." See 2 Kings 24.3–4. The sins of
Menasheh are described in 2 Kings 21.1–16.

97. This is about as close as we're likely to get to pinning down the faith of the
Hebrew Scriptures in a proposition.

98. Maimonides does include something similar as the eleventh principle of his
Thirteen Articles of Faith, which appears in his commentary on the Mishna,
Sanhedrin 10. See Menachem Kellner, *Dogma in Medieval Jewish Thought*
(Portland, Oreg.: Littman Library, 2000).

99. Exodus 33.11.

100. Exodus 32.9–14.

101. Genesis 25.23.

102. Genesis 32.25–30.

103. We are told that Jacob gets his name because he is born holding Esau's heel,
at Genesis 25.26. Esau says explicitly at Genesis 27.36 that Jacob has cheated
or tricked him out of his inheritance and his father's blessing, using the verb
vaya'ekveni, again based on the word *ekev* (heel) to mean "he has cheated me"
or "he has tricked me."

104. Exodus 3.13–14. God continues: "So will you say to the children of Israel, The
Lord, God of their fathers, the God of Abraham, the God of Isaac, and the God
of Jacob, sent me to you. That is my name forever, and the way I will be called
for all generations."

105. The subject does not even come up. See Exodus 4.29–31. Nachmanides on 3:13
emphasizes that the simple reporting of some name to the Israelites would have
meant little to them. What they would have wanted to know is that God would
in fact be with them to save them – or, in other words, that he could be relied
upon.

106. Exodus 33.17, 19.

107. In Cassuto's paraphrase: "[T]he exercise of these qualities depends entirely on
my will.... I shall be gracious and compassionate if it pleases me, when it pleases
me, and for the reasons that please me" (Umberto Cassuto, *A Commentary on
the Book of Exodus* [Jerusalem: Magnes, 1997 [1951]], p. 436). But compare
Isaiah 27.11, which refers precisely to the question of God's grace and mercy

being discussed here, and suggests that God's grace and mercy are bound to fail where the people do not have the understanding needed to do what is right.

108. Exodus 34.5–7. Note that parts of this formulation, including the extension of reward and punishment over multiple generations, appear in the Ten Commandments. See Exodus 20.5–6, as well as Exodus 34.7, Numbers 14.18, and Deuteronomy 5.9. Jeremiah also invokes this way of looking at things at 32.18, as does Hoshea, who writes: "[B]ecause you forgot the teachings of your God, I, as well, will spurn your children" (Hoshea 4.6). A famous dissent from this view of God's nature is Ezekiel 18.1–24.

109. This peeling back of the layers before God's nature can in any degree become visible is the reason that Isaiah calls the God of Israel "a hiding God [*el mistater*]" (Isaiah 45.15). Nevertheless, Isaiah immediately corrects the possible misimpression by adding that "I have not spoken in secret, in some dark land. I have not told the seed of Jacob, look for me in the chaos. I, the Lord, speak justice, and say things that are straight [*magid meisharim*]" (Isaiah 45.19).

110. This is in line with the opinion of the rabbis, to the effect that when Moses asks God to show him his glory, he is asking him to show him the rewards of the just and explain to him why the wicked prosper. See *Exodus Raba* 45.5.

111. My reading follows Seforno's comment on Exodus 34.7, according to which God accumulates the results of justice and of sin for generations before making them known. Similarly, see *Exodus Raba* 45.6, where God is depicted as keeping storehouses for this purpose. It is because God stores up the results of evildoing that, once several generations have gone astray, the possibility of a truly effective repentance is lost, as suggested by Talmud *Sota* 9. See also Cassuto, *Commentary on Exodus*, p. 440. I think this reading fits the plain meaning of the text more easily than others that have been suggested. But consider also in this context Jeremiah's argument that the wrongdoers are being punished, but that the punishments are invisible to them. On this point, see Chapter 6, Section V.

112. In this context it is worth contemplating Donald Harman Akenson's comment in response to those who say that the God of Israel is not portrayed as a very likeable character in the History. As he writes: "[N]ot liking Yahweh is irrelevant. The reason the God of the ancient Israelites is so convincing is that ... he is the perfect embodiment of what is: Of reality. Whatever controls the lives of human beings, it is not consistently nice, benevolent, predictable, or understandable. Yahweh personifies the ultimate reality exactly" (Donald Harman Akenson, *Surpassing Wonder: The Invention of the Bible and the Talmuds* [New York: Harcourt Brace, 1998], p. 98).

113. Exodus 33.20–23.

114. That what Moses saw on Sinai was a fragment or a glimpse is emphasized by Maimonides, *Guide for the Perplexed* 1.21, p. 30; and by Seforno in his comments on Exodus 33.19 and 33.20. For just this reason, I think Maimonides goes too far in saying that "God has no essential attribute in any form or in any sense whatever." See Maimonides, *Guide for the Perplexed* 1.50. What Moses sees on Sinai is partial and uncertain, a fragment and a glimpse. But it is a fragment and a glimpse of *something*, an expression of God's essential attributes. Compare the story of Moses in the cleft in the rock to the allegory of the cave

in Plato, *Republic* 514a–520a, which touches on similar themes, albeit with crucial differences.

115. Exodus 32.31–33.

116. For example, at Deuteronomy 6.13, 24, 8.6, 10.12, 20, 13.5. See also related passages at 4.10, 5.26, 6.2, 14.23, 17.19, 31.13.

117. Psalms 111.10.

118. Deuteronomy 6.5, 10.12, 11.1, 13.

119. The equivalence between those who love God and those who keep his commandments appears, for example in the parallelism at Deuteronomy 7.9, Daniel 9.4, and Nehemia 1.5. But I think it is also straightforward enough in the juxtaposition of the command to love God with the exhortation to keep his law that occurs, as far as I am aware, in every appearance of the commandment to love God.

120. 1 Kings 15.3.

121. 2 Kings 23.25.

122. 2 Chronicles 24.3 tells us that Josiah was sixteen years old when, as king, he "began to seek the God of David, his father," and that when he was twenty he began to destroy the foreign cults in Jerusalem.

123. 2 Kings 22.19. The translation of Josiah's *lev rach* as though he had a "soft heart" hardly does justice to this aggressive king who dealt so harshly with his enemies. Rather, the meaning is that he had an "open mind," and was able to change the course of the kingdom when he realized that his actions had been mistaken.

124. Numbers 20.12.

125. John 3.16.

126. Romans 1.16.

127. As Maimonides emphasizes, the entire purpose of law is that "we do not do every one as he pleases, desires, and is able to do," but rather that which permits everyone to contribute to the common welfare (Maimonides, *Guide for the Perplexed* 3.27, p. 312). But if the law is directed to the common welfare, and to that which is beneficial in general, it will necessarily be harmful to certain individuals whose circumstances are exceptional. As he writes, "[W]hatever the law teaches ... is founded on that which is the rule and not on that which is the exception; it ignores the injury that might be caused to a single person through a certain maxim or a certain divine precept.... It is impossible [that it] be otherwise" (Maimoides, *Guide for the Perplexed* 3.34, p. 328).

128. Plato, *Crito* 43a–54e.

129. Note that such a conclusion of reason "needs no sacrifice of mind, no leap into the void." The leap of faith associated with the embrace of the absurd is not present in a reasoned decision to commit oneself to a person as whole, flaws and all, as happens in a marriage; or to a system of laws. See Jonathan Sacks, *Radical Then, Radical Now* (New York: Continuum, 2000), p. 86.

130. Deuteronomy 30.19.

131. I refer to the fact that no one has to obey the commandments in the law of Moses. There are also laws of nature that man does have to obey – not only physical laws but psychological laws. It is these psychological laws that we see in operation in biblical passages in which God forces man to do something, as

when he tells the kings of Judah "You will certainly drink" from the cup of fury in Jeremiah 25.28.

132. As the medieval commentator Abravanel argued, the law is set before us so that we may know how to live, while the narratives in which it is embedded give us the basis to strive to reach the truth. See his commentary on Exodus 19.1–3, section 3. See also my discussion in Chapter 3, Section III.

133. On the relationship between the Mosaic law and the narratives in which it is embedded, see Diana Lipton, *Longing for Egypt* (Sheffield: Sheffield Phoenix Press, 2008), pp. 174–176; Ze'ev Maghen, "Dancing in Chains: The Baffling Coexistence of Legalism and Exuberance in Judaic and Islamic Tradition," in Jonathan Jacobs, ed., *Judaic Sources and Western Thought* (New York: Oxford, 2011), pp. 217–237.

9. God's Speech After Reason and Revelation

1. For a brief further discussion, see the Appendix after this chapter.

2. Ronald de Sousa, *The Rationality of Emotions* (Cambridge, Mass.: Massachusetts Institute of Technology Press, 1987); R. H. Frank, *Passions Within Reason: The Strategic Role of the Emotions* (New York: Norton, 1988); Alan Gibbard, *Wise Choices, Apt Feelings: A Theory of Normative Judgment* (Cambridge, Mass.: Harvard University Press, 1990); Robert Solomon, *The Passions: Emotions and the Meaning of Life* (Indianapolis: Hackett, 1993); Nico Frijda, "The Place of Appraisal in Emotion," *Cognition and Emotion* 3–4 (1993), pp. 357–387; Antonio Damasio, *Descartes' Error: Emotion, Reason and the Human Brain* (New York: Penguin, 1994); Paul Thagard, "The Passionate Scientist: Emotion in Scientific Cognition," in Peter Carruthers, Stephen Stich, and Michael Siegal, eds., *The Cognitive Basis of Science* (Cambridge: Cambridge University Press, 2002), pp. 235–250; Christopher Hookway, "Emotions and Epistemic Evaluations," in Peter Carruthers, et al., eds., *The Cognitive Basis of Science*, pp. 251–262; Mick Power and Tim Dalgleish, *Cognition and Emotion: From Order to Disorder* (Hove: Psychology Press, 2008), p. 16.

3. Suzanne K. Langer, *Philosophy in a New Key: A Study in the Symbolism of Reason, Rite and Art* (Cambridge, Mass.: Harvard University Press, 1942); Suzanne K. Langer, *Feeling and Form* (New York: Scribner, 1953); Mary B. Hesse, *Models and Analogies in Science* (Notre Dame, Ind.: Notre Dame University Press, 1966); George Lakoff and Mark Johnson, *Metaphors We Live By* (Chicago: University of Chicago Press, 1980); George Lakoff, *Women, Fire, and Dangerous Things* (Chicago: University of Chicago Press, 1987); G. M. Douglas and D. Hull, *How Classification Works* (Edinburgh: Edinburgh University Press, 1993); Mary Douglas, *Leviticus as Literature* (New York: Oxford University Press, 1999), pp. 13–40; Keith J. Holyoak and Paul Thagard, *Mental Leaps: Analogy in Creative Thought* (Cambridge, Mass.: Massachusetts Institute of Technology Press, 1995).

4. See, for example, the essays collected in Robert J. Sternberg and Janet E. Davidson, eds., *The Nature of Insight* (Cambridge, Mass.: Massachusetts Institute of Technology Press, 1995); and Michael R. DePaul and William Ramsey, *Rethinking Intuition: The Psychology of Intuition and its Role in Philosophical Inquiry* (New York: Rowman Littlefield, 1998).

5. For a survey of modern thought on this kind of monism, understood as being "neutral" between mind and world, see Leopold Stubenberg, "Neutral Monism," in Edward N. Zalta, ed., *Stanford Encyclopedia of Philosophy* (Winter 2003 Edition), http://plato.stanford.edu/ entries/neutral-monism/. The most important treatment of the monism of the Hebrew Bible to date is Claude Tresmontant, *A Study of Hebrew Thought*, Michael Francis Gibson, trans. (New York: Desclee, 1960 [1956]).

6. Jeremiah 1.4–10.

7. The doubling of the vision, using two metaphors to describe something rather than one, is a pattern that is familiar from other biblical texts. Recall, for example, Joseph's dreams in Genesis 37.5–9; and Pharaoh's dreams in Genesis 41.17–23.

8. See Rashi on Jeremiah 1.11. Compare Numbers 17.16–26, where the almond stick is associated with Aaron the high priest, from whom Jeremiah is descended.

9. For Jerusalem as a seething pot, see also Ezekiel 11.3, 7, 11, 24.3–12.

10. In the History of Israel, we are told that prophets had, in Samuel's time, been called simply "seers." See 1 Samuel 9.9.

11. Another clue that prophecy is dependent on the circumstances of the prophet is Jeremiah 42.5–7 and Ezekiel 3.15–16, where the prophet must strive for a week or more before receiving an answer to the question that is troubling him.

12. A similar description of prophecy appears in the book of the prophet Zecharia, who desribes an angel "who waked me, as a man that is wakened out of sleep" in order to ask him "What do you see?" Zecharia, too, responds with what he has seen before hearing God's explanation. See Zecharia 4.1–7.

13. See Chapter 3, Section II.

14. This suggests that prophetic metaphor may be considerably more important than has often been supposed. I have in mind, for example, Abravanel's unsympathetic treatment of prophetic metaphor as being channeled through the "imaginative faculty," as opposed to the prophecies of Moses, which were channeled through his reason (hence the absence of metaphor in Moses' teachings). See Abravanel's commentary on Exodus 19.1–3, section 2.7–8. A not unrelated reevaluation is perhaps due in philosophy as well, where the capacity for seeing one thing as another – "seeing as" – has become well known due to its treatment by Wittgenstein. See Ludwig Wittgenstein, *Philosophical Investigations*, G. E. M. Anscombe, trans. (New York: Macmillan, 1958), part II, section 11. But so far as I am aware, Wittgenstein does not raise the question of how "seeing as" advances us toward truth.

Appendix: What Is "Reason"? Some Preliminary Remarks

1. But see Eleonore Stump, *Aquinas* (New York: Routledge, 2003), pp. 217–243, which challenges this view.

2. For an accessible and compelling discussion, see Morris Kline, *Mathematics: The Loss of Certainty* (New York: Oxford University Press, 1980).

3. Nicholas Wolterstorff, *Justice: Rights and Wrongs* (Princeton: Princeton University Press, 2008), p. xi. See also pp. 360–361.

4. Alvin Plantinga, "Reason and Belief in God," in Alvin Plantinga and Nicholas Wolterstorff, eds., *Faith and Rationality: Reason and Belief in God* (Notre Dame,

Ind.: Notre Dame University Press, 1983), pp. 16–93, at pp. 78–82. For a more detailed and updated version of this argument, see Alvin Plantinga, *Warranted Christian Belief* (New York: Oxford University Press, 2000), pp. 67–198.

5. Wolterstorff says that the entire argument of his book *Justice* is merely "hypothetical." See p. 360.

6. Alvin Plantinga, "Reason and Belief in God," pp. 82–87.

7. Isaac Newton, *The Principia: Mathematical Principles of Natural Philosophy*, I. Bernard Cohen and Anne Whitman, trans. (Berkeley: University of California Press, 1999 [1687]), pp. 381–382.

8. Newton's crucial supposition that arguments "may be looked upon as so much the stronger, by how the induction is the more general" appears in Isaac Newton, *Opticks* (Amherst: Prometheus, 2003 [1730]), p. 404.

9. Ernan McMullin, "The Significance of Newton's *Principia* for Empiricism," in Margaret J. Osler and Paul Lawrence Farber, eds., *Religion, Science, and Worldview: Essays in Honor of Richard S. Westfall* (Cambridge: Cambridge University Press, 1985), pp. 33–59.

10. Ernan McMullin, "The Significance of Newton's *Principia*," pp. 56–58; George E. Smith, "The Methodology of the 'Principia'," in I. Bernard Cohen and George E. Smith, eds., *The Cambridge Companion to Newton* (Cambridge: Cambridge University Press, 2002), pp. 138–174, at p. 161. Smith proposes *abductive* and McMullin *retroductive* inference, each of them relying on Pierce. See also Gilbert Harman, "Inference to the Best Explanation," *Philosophical Review* (1965), pp. 88–95; Peter Lipton, *Inference to the Best Explanation* (New York: Routledge, 1991).

11. Isaac Newton, *Opticks*, pp. 404–405. Newton's conception of a *cause* is very different from that to which we are accustomed. By a "general cause" he means something abstracted from a combination of concrete causes. The result, which is a cause of a category of effects rather than of any particular effect, bears a resemblance to an Aristotelian "formal cause," rather than to an "efficient cause."

12. On the meaning of the terms *mass* and *force*, see Ernan McMullin, "The Significance of Newton's *Principia*," pp. 41–44, 57.

13. Suzanne K. Langer, *Philosophy in a New Key: A Study in the Symbolism of Reason, Rite and Art* (Cambridge, Mass.: Harvard University Press, 1942); George Lakoff and Mark Johnson, *Metaphors We Live By* (Chicago: University of Chicago Press, 1980); George Lakoff, *Women, Fire, and Dangerous Things* (Chicago: University of Chicago Press, 1987); Mary Douglas, *Leviticus as Literature* (New York: Oxford University Press, 1999), pp. 13–40.

14. Mary B. Hesse, *Models and Analogies in Science* (Notre Dame, Ind.: Notre Dame University Press, 1966); Keith J. Holyoak and Paul Thagard, *Mental Leaps: Analogy in Creative Thought* (Cambridge, Mass.: Massachusetts Institute of Technology Press, 1995). See also Ernan McMullin, "Structural Explanation," *American Philosophical Quarterly* 15 (1978), pp. 139–147; Stuart S. Glennan, "Mechanisms and the Nature of Causation," *Erkenntnis* 44 (1996), pp. 49–71; Stuart S. Glennan, "Rethinking Mechanistic Explanation," *Philosophy of Science* 69 (2002), Supp. pp. 342–353.

15. Eleonore Stump, *Wandering in Darkness: Narrative and the Problem of Suffering* (New York: Oxford University Press, 2010), pp. 40–63.

16. As discussed in note 11, the Newtonian term "general cause" may be misleading, and it may be easier for some readers to substitute the term "nature" for what it is that Newton is getting at. If I observe that human beings, having been enslaved, can be relied upon to seek a strong leader or tyrant to return to them the security of their years in servitude, I am describing an aspect of human nature. And if I observe that the state can be relied upon to expand indefinitely until it exhausts its available resources, I am describing, in part, the nature of the political state. In the same way, the *Principia* deploys terms *force* and *mass* to refer to natures that Newton has devised or discovered, and the definitions and axioms in which these terms appear constitute his descriptions of these natures.

17. Thus it is Newton's introduction of mathematical propositions into his description of the natures of *force* and *mass* that permits him to advance from highly abstract statements to a system of extremely precise deductions and predictions. And the same will be true in other cases, even where mathematics is not introduced, so long as the deductive inferences are made to follow rigorously from the premises.

Index of Names

Index of Scriptural References

3. Other Rabbinic Sources

II. Christian Bible

On the cover, the Spanish Baha'i painter Fernando Roca Bon (1940–2009) approaches the city of Jerusalem through the lens of geometry, which he sees as representing the universal underlying reality, "the foundation of civilization, the beginning of everything." For more on the art of Roca Bon, go to http://www.rocabon.com.